Vancouver

7860 miles

San Francisc

Los Angeles

C

I

F

I

C

HAWAIIAN
ISLANDS
Honolulu
Hawaii

7450 miles

E

A

C

EQUATOR

LINE
ISLANDS

WITHDRAWN

N   N

COOK
ISLANDS
Tahiti

Pitcairn I.

Easter I.

Controller of H.M. Stationery Office

THE RISE AND FALL OF THE JAPANESE EMPIRE

THE RISE AND FALL
OF THE
JAPANESE EMPIRE

BY
DAVID H. JAMES

LONDON
GEORGE ALLEN & UNWIN LTD
RUSKIN HOUSE MUSEUM STREET

PRINTED IN GREAT BRITAIN
IN 11-PT BASKERVILLE TYPE
BY WILLMER BROTHERS AND CO. LTD.
BIRKENHEAD

PREFACE

I have written this account of *The Rise and Fall of the Japanese Empire* to meet the needs of the general reader who wishes to obtain an outline of Japanese history in addition to the major factors contributing to the debacle of 1945.

To-day, Japan is stripped of her armaments and her overseas possessions. She is no longer a menace to the peace of the Orient but—as a puppet state—is a vassal of the United States of America during her period of instruction in democracy. The tenure of this tutelage is to be governed by conditions outside the control of the nominal government of Japan—the Peace Treaty is postponed because the Communists have gained control of China and might gain control of Japan if the armed forces of America were withdrawn from the country.

The Japanese Government are in full agreement with their American overlords, that the country is 'thoroughly democratic', and that the metamorphosis is genuine, and not a thin outer coating of sophism to harmonize the wishful thinking of their mentors, and that the ethics of the Shinto State are as dead as the dodo. But there are many 'observers' in Japan who hold to the opinion that the engrafting process has only scratched the surface of the real problem—democratic rule under the ægis of the divine traditions.

Putting these and other topics aside there is the over-riding problem of the ideological aggression of the U.S.S.R. Few questions—since the conclusion of World War II—have excited more anxiety than the 'cold war' in Europe and the dramatic extension of Communism in China and the Far East. In her present revolutionary epoch, China has broken adrift from the purely traditional 'civil war' of her long political history. Buddhism, Confucianism, Mohammedanism and Christianity in its Nestorian, Roman Catholic and Protestant forms are being abolished in the name of Communism inspired by the U.S.S.R. Social stability is to be restored by totalitarianism not only in

China but in Burma, Siam, Indo-China, Tibet, Korea, Malaya, Indonesia, India and so on. So to meet this various attack, Japan—occupied by American troops—is regarded as an excellent base of operations for the 'cold war' in the Far East. It is not a question of building up Japan as a democracy but using Japan as a buffer state in the event of the cold war developing into World War III.

However, if there is any truth in these suggestions—regarding the 'value' of Japan as a pawn in the new ideological war—would it not be better to discard the histrionic for the realistic doctrine of self-preservation in our future dealings with Japan?

In my opinion it is playing with fire to expect any Japanese Government to agree to play the role of Simple Simon for an indefinite period as a 'demilitarized democracy' when she is surrounded by militant Communists. Surely, to meet attack on so large a scale in the Far East an equally various defence is needed? If an Atlantic Pact is necessary so is a Pacific Pact, and—under the prevailing conditions—Japan would be justified in re-arming to the same degree as Chinese Communists or any of the satellite states of the U.S.S.R. in Europe.

Sooner or later the army of occupation, and the numerous proprætors in the prefectures, must leave Japan to her own devices to work out her own salvation according to the 'new democracy', or according to a revised version of *sai-sei-itchi* (unity of state religion and government administration). But it is to be hoped that the present confusion in China will not prevent the United States of America, and the British Empire, from concluding a Peace Treaty with Japan, with—or without—the blessing or veto of the U.S.S.R. now that she has taken over the role of Nazi Germany as the enemy of civilization in theory if not in fact.

As one small contribution to stability in the Far East, the British Government sent reinforcements to Hong Kong, but this token force is of purely local importance—it will exert no influence on the spread of Communism inside or outside the 'iron curtain' in Europe or in China. Not Christianity only but all spiritual values are challenged by Communism, so it is folly to burke the issue and shelter behind the flimsy 'security' of the fiats of the United Nations organization. Religion may be superstition and morality a mere convention, but, even so, it is better for the future of the human race than 'intellectual liberty' inside a concentration camp controlled by an Ogpu.

In this book I have dealt fully with Japan's aggression and all the vileness of her actions in Peace and in War. She was severely punished. The mass of the population—if not the real culprits—were taught a bitter lesson by the armed forces of the United States of America and the British Empire. She accepted defeat with dignity, but it would be asking too much to expect an indefinite period of complaisance, and obedience to orders, if the army of occupation remained until the sight of their uniforms became associated chiefly with 'women, wine and song' and not with the martial arts which brought them to the country.

August, 1949   D.H.J.

CONTENTS

APPENDICES

xii

CHAPTER I

THE JAPANESE

When Townsend Harris negotiated the Japanese-American Treaty of Amity and Commerce at Yedo, on 19th August, 1858, a long period of national isolation was brought to an abrupt end. The weak asiatic nation, Japan, was compelled to accept friendship and trade with the United States of America and the rest of the world.

Then, through an industrial revolution, Japan made rapid progress from feudalism to a modern capitalist state, and from a modern capitalist state to Imperialism. Japan travelled fast, under a military dictatorship, on the road to ruin, and her bid for an Empire in Greater East Asia failed on August 19th, 1945, when General MacArthur signed the Armistice Agreement at Manila which terminated her aggression against the United Nations.

From Townsend Harris to MacArthur, from Yedo to Manila —from Amity and Commerce to Unconditional Surrender— bridges an interlude in history of less than ninety years. The rise and fall of the Japanese Empire, in so short a time, may not be of major importance in the age of the atomic-bomb and guided missiles, and it may not be as important an event as the defeat of the Saracens at Poictiers in A.D. 732, barely one hundred years after the death of Mohammed, the founder of the Moslem Empire, but the cause of the debacle is just as interesting.*

The victory of Prince Karl Martel rescued Christendom from Islam—in the struggle between the Crescent and the Cross—but the fight between Japan and the United Nations had little or nothing to do with Christianity or religion. It had nothing to do with the New or the Old Testament, or the Koran—nothing to

* See Appendix XIII.

do with the faith of the Christians, the Jews or the Arabs—or the Chinese. It was concerned with domination over Greater East Asia and was the logical outcome of monopolist capitalism directed by military dictatorship.

*In 1937, Japan had decided to enlarge her Empire. She had special advantages, of military preponderance, coupled with proximity to China and the Orient. And—to quote Lenin on the subject of capitalism—'Imperialism is capitalism at that stage of its development when the domination of monopolies and finance capital has reached its zenith, when the export of capital has become of major importance, when all the territory of the earth has been finally divided between the most capitalist countries, and international trusts or cartels have begun to divide its resources between themselves.' Japan was ruled by the GUMBATSU (militarists) and the ZAIBATSU (plutocrats) and the masses were bemused by veneration of TENNO HEIKA, the god of the Shinto state.

I hold no brief for the Japanese, who by their chicanery built up a national cult of militarism, based on mythology, and then sheltered behind the 'divinity' of the human pretender to the throne to sanctify their vile projects of aggression at home and abroad, and I have nothing but contempt for the creatures who destroyed Japan and humiliated their 'sacred Emperor'. At the same time I am not so prejudiced as to ignore the history of the country and the abject conditions under which the masses were governed for centuries by a minority of sub-men. Sub-men who were steeped in a vile ideology; degenerates who were spawned by neoplatonism, posing before the world as direct descendents of a KAMI (god) exclusive to the Japanese nation, a nation which for many generations had been inhabited by Ainu, Mongols, Malays, Koreans and Chinese of normal miscegnation.

Many and curious ideas have prevailed regarding the subjects of Tenno Heika. They have been described as a magnificent race, the true leaders of the Orient, progressive people with splendid patriotism and magnificent loyalty to the Emperor. Brave in war, tolerant in peace, proud and sensitive—fond of flowers and of children. Simple in their habits, lovers of nature, efficient in trade and commerce—progressive in every way. Then again they have been referred to as people devoid of all

* See Appendix XI and XIII

morals, destitute of finer feelings or religion—pagans who cut their bellies at the slightest provocation, fanatics, militarists, aggressors, petty imitators without imagination, liars in diplomacy, tricksters in trade—in short, the scum of Asia.

Between the extremes of adulation and contempt there is ample room for a middle course without destroying the basic truth which lays behind the various assertions.

Subsistence

One subject is uppermost in the minds of most Japanese—the pressure of living, the cost of rice. They are always most willing to discuss SEIKATSU—existence, livelihood, to keep one's pot boiling. And perhaps the problem of Japan, past and future, can best be expressed in terms of Rice, Population, Geography, Military Rule and a State Controlled Cult and Education.

The History of Japan affords ample evidence of the repression of the majority by a minority of soldiers and priests. The two-handed-sword of despotism, which ruled by conveniently preserved Tennos, cloaked the real purpose of Shogun, Daimyo and hired Samurai. And, unfortunately, the proletariat produced no leaders: they shirked civil war against the Shoguns and left the fighting to be done by rival bands of Samurai. This left them slaves and they were absorbed by the system in their struggle for existence even after the Restoration in 1868 when the intrusion of the western Powers indicated to them an alternative to feudalism and the law of the Samurai.

The physical and mental stagnation of the masses was due to centuries of under-nourishment and sub-normal living conditions: most of the time they existed near the border-line between malnutrition and health. And when the rice harvest failed they were reduced to geophagy—living on root crops.

The food problems were not improved by the practice of destroying its vitamins when most of it was so low in nutritive value. Furthermore it was the habit in rural Japan to pay taxes, rents and wages in rice or other agricultural products: the ill-fed farmer had to feed the nation in addition to his own family and hired labourers as well as cater to the needs of the lazy priests.

A few facts and figures will present the real problem of rice and population. For instance: in 1868 the population of Japan proper was 32 million, and the area under rice cultivation was 6 million acres with a total yield of 125 million bushels. The average consumption per head of poulation, per annum, was just below 4 bushels, so there was enough rice to feed the nation.

By 1940 the population had risen to 73 million, the cultivated area to 8 million acres and the total yield to 325 million bushels of rice. Average consumption was 5¼ bushels so there was a rice shortage of 65 million bushels in 1940.

This deficiency would have been much greater had there not been improved methods and extensive use of imported fertilizers: the yield per acre in 1868 was 20 bushels—in 1940 it had been raised to 40 bushels per acre.

The population in 1949 was well over 80 million but the area under rice cultivation was not much more than in 1940. The natural increase, in population, in Japan is over one million per annum so at this rate it will be close on 85 million in 1952 confined to itspresent area of 142,700 square miles (Potsdam Declaration). If we compare this area and population with that of the United Kingdom's 47 million spread over 94,200 square miles, we may arrive at a pretty clear picture of the dismal outlook of the Japanese.

The production of rice, the staple diet, will not be increased beyond its present level, by any new methods I can think of, to take care of the increasing population. It cannot be increased by the magic of a new constitution anymore than control over Japan's industrial economy will provide the necessary employment for the adult population necessary to raise the present subnormal standard of living. Indeed, hunger and discontent are more likely to produce conditions in Japan like those in China than to advance the United Nations conception of Democracy.

The acute agrarian problem has always been exploited by the KAIS (secret societies) and the GUMBATSU, for half the adult population of Japan are farmers and most of the men were passed through the military-educational machine into the army, the spear-head of aggression, after the Restoration. Indeed the expansionist policy of Japan was in the melting-pot in the first half of the nineteenth century which bred the patriotic schools— the militarists.

One of these super-patriots was YOSHIDA SHOIN of the CHOSHU clan. He wrote an interesting book, dealing with policies and purposes, for the edification of the Samurai. Yoshida Shoin advocated the Restoration (Meiji) as a prerequisite to continental expansion at the expense of Korea and China with a reorganised army based on Western arms and munitions. Among his principle disciples were ITO, INOUYE and YAMAGATA the architects of modern Japan—the men who laid the foundation of the Shinto State.

Yoshida Shoin came to an untimely end in 1859 but his policy outlived him and dominated the SATSUMA-CHOSHU regime (Navy and Army 'clan' government) during the Meiji era which isolated the throne and instituted the GENRO (Elder Statesmen) control of the Diet.

ITO the administrator did not always agree with YAMAGATA the soldier on the subject of Japan's Policies and Purposes but they had the same definite purpose in mind which was Imperial Expansion, military and economic: the idea of Imperial domains politically and in culture part and parcel of the mainland.

However, to revert to the subject of rice and poulation. The policy of the military governors of Japan was control of Korea and Manchuria which in time would give them access to millions of bushels of rice, barley, maize, wheat and soya bean: expansion in China would take care of the food problem, and the increase of population. That was the policy of Ito and Yamagata: that was the policy of General ARAKI (War Minister 1931-1934) who said that 'Japan should not submit to the limitations of her position but go to meet them and pursue her destiny regardless of perils in her way,' The invasion of Manchuria, the purchase, transfer or exploitation of Chinese owned land was Araki's policy for the—'External expansion of arable land'—solution of the food problem.

It was the policy pursued in Korea where the production of rice rose from 45 million bushels in 1912 to over 90 million bushels in 1933. Thus the military control of extra-territorial supplies, necessary for national economy, fitted in to the over-all plan of Japan's imperialists.

More than one Japanese military economist informed me that if Japan, after the Restoration of 1868, had remained a passivist state and not become an aggressive state she would have become a colony of U.S.A., Russia, France, Germany or just part of the British Empire—eating crumbs from the white man's table. To

The high cheek bones betray the Mongol strain, and—according to legend—the first inhabitants of 'Japan' were cave dwellers who were given the name of Koro-poku-guru by the Ainus who supplanted them. At a later date the so called 'Yamato tribe' crossed over from Korea and settled in Kyushu, and 'about 660 B.C.' the Yamato tribes—under Jimmu Tenno, the first human Emperor of Japan, went from Awaji, near Kobe, to Shikoku before going on to make the first settlement on Honshu.

These Yamato-jins referred to the Ainu as Yebisu, barbarians, and waged war on them but did not subjugate them for centuries. The newcomers, under Jimmu Tenno, claimed to be the immediate successors of AMATERASU, the Sun Goddess of mythology. The original universal religion of the Yamato tribes was a cult of ancestors and heroes, similar to other primitive people: the sun, the moon, the elements and the powers of nature were worshipped, also the souls of dead people of merit were worshipped under the name of KAMI or invisible spirits.

Chinese history does not support the fiction of the Yamato-jins. According to their records, there lived in 1300 B.C., a primeval race of men known to them by the name of TUNG-HU who roamed the country between Peking and the Arctic Circle. These Tungus tribes—Su-Shen, Mieh-ho, Fu-yu and Kao-li—gave the northern Chinese some trouble before dispersing to the East. One of these tribes, the KAO-LI continued to acknowledge a Chinese monarch—Chi Tzu—and in 1100 B.C. there was a kingdom of Kao-li established in the valley of the Yalu River.

The Kao-li Tungus crossed the river and wandered down the peninsula which became known as Kao-li-ya, or Korea. One branch of the Kao-lis are reputed to have gone across the Behring Straits to Alaska, another branch to have crossed Tsushima Straits and landed in Kyushu. The religion of these people was Shamanism—a primitive paganism.

At a later date, the SHANS—sometimes referred to as the aborigines of China—came to Southern Kyushu and they were followed by the HANS and other Chinese from the mainland. After the Hans came people from South Asia—mostly Malays—who settled in Honshu and helped the Yamato-jin deal with the Ainu. Africans, Arabs and Egyptians found their way to Japan, just a few to mix their blood with the Mongols, Chinese and Malays.

Even to this day the high cheek bones, well knit stocky frame and the delicate moulding of the small hands and feet betray the Mongol-Malay strain. But the Ainu were brought into complete subjugation in A.D. 805, by the expeditionary force of Kammu Tenno, and the strain has not survived in the modern Japanese.

Geography

Japan is essentially a land of mountains—it consists of a long cluster of islands from Hokkaido to Kyushu. From its physical features Japan proper—Hokkaido, Honshu, Shikoku and Kyushu—may be divided into three parts, southwestern, central and northeastern. The southwestern part, Kyushu, Shikoku and the western part of Honshu—is not characterized by lofty mountains, but the central part is marked by numerous towering mountains, including Fuji and the Japanese Alps. And Japan is also conspicious for its epochs of volanic and seismic activity.

The principal volcanic chains are (a) Daiton, from west of Formosa to Kyushu, (b) Kirishima and Aso in Kyushu, (c) Hakusan northwest Kyushu, (d) Norikura and Fuji in central Honshu, (e) Nasu in Northeast Honshu and in the Hokkaido Nasu and Chishima.

Festivals, tidal waves and earthquakes: matsuri, tsunami and jishin: are all part of the daily life in Japan and they have helped to form the character of the people just as much as Buddhism and Shintoism. The sudden appearance of new islands is often mentioned in Japanese history, and there are many references to the raining down of 'blood' and of 'snow blood'—volcanic ash mixed with rain water—which destroyed the crops. But, like many other things in Japan, these calamities are dismissed with a shrug of the shoulder and the inevitable 'shikata-ga-nai'—it can not be helped.

Mountains figure prominently in the mythology of many lands as the abode of gods and goddesses and this is particularly true of Japan where many legends are associated with Fuji, the volcano in the Fuji chain. This sacred mountain, rising 12,000 feet, is reputed to have made its appearance over-night in the who 'saw a white heron taking a bath and thereby discovered the hot-spring of Takeo in Kyushu.'

The ancient Floral Festival in Japan owes its origin to a tradition concerning the birth of Siddhartha Guatama, called the Buddha, born in 550 B.C. When Buddha (in Japanese BUTSU) was born 'two streams of water fell from the sky, one cold and the other hot, wherewith was performed the washing of Bodhisattva and his mother.' And on 8th April each year all Buddhist temples in Japan place images of Butsu within reach of worshippers who buy sweet tea and pour it over the object of their devotions. In Tokyo there used to be a special religious parade in Hibiya Park when a small shrine, in which reposed a bronze image of the infant Butsu, was placed at the centre of the Flower Temple (Hana-mido) and the ceremony commenced when a curtain of gold brocade was rolled up revealing a small bronze image of Butsu standing with his hand pointing to heaven, in the act of saying: 'I am the chief being in the world, I am the best in the world, I am the first in the world.' Flowers were laid at the altar, incense burned and the entire company sang the national anthem.

The Japanese, by adopting Buddhism and Shintoism placed in the path of political development many stumbling-blocks but it is interesting in retrospect to consider how history itself might have proceeded in Europe and the Middle East if the Christians had deleted Jehovah out of their religion and been content with the New Testament. The Jewish account of creation, bound up with the Christian theory of Redemption, certainly excluded an open mind regarding geology, zoology and even anthropology.

Reverting to Buddhism and the Floral Festival. It is not without interest to compare the Sino-Japanese version of the birth of Guatama with the more poetic version given by Sir Edwin Arnold in 'The Light of Asia'. Here it is:—

'Thus came he to be born again for men.

That night the wife of King Suddhodhana,
Maya the Queen, asleep beside her Lord,
Dreamed a strange dream; dreamed that a star from heaven—
Splendid, six-rayed, in colour rosy-pearl;
Whereof the token was an Elephant
Six-tusked, and white as milk of Kamadhuk—
Shot through the void; and, shining into her,

Entered her womb upon the right. Awakened,
Bliss beyond mortal mother's filled her breast,
And over half the earth a lovely light
Forwent the moon. The strong hills shook; the waves
Sank lulled; all flowers that blow by day came forth
As 'twere high noon; down to the farthest hells
Passed the Queen's joy, as when warm sunshine thrills
Wood-glooms to gold, and into all the deeps
A tender whisper pierced. 'Oh ye' it said,
'The dead that are to live, the live who die,
Uprise, and hear, and hope! Buddha is come!'

In this wise was the holy Buddha born.

Queen Maya stood at noon, her days fulfilled,
Under a Palsa in the Palace-grounds,
A stately trunk, straight as a temple-shaft,
With crown of glossy leaves and fragrant blooms;
And, knowing the time come—for all things knew—
The conscious tree bent down its bows to make
A bower about Queen Maya's majesty;
And Earth put forth a thousand sudden flowers
To spread a couch; while, ready for the bath,
The rock hard by gave out a limpid stream
Of crystal flow. So brought she forth her child
Pangless—he having on his perfect form
The marks, thirty and two, of blessed birth;
Of which the great news to the Palace came!'

The belief in India, in 550 B.C., was that at great intervals of
time WISDOM came to earth and was incarnate in a chosen
person who was known as BUDDHA. Guatama's followers declared that he was Buddha even as Jesus was proclaimed the
Messiah. But the teaching of Guatama was simple: his was a
doctrine of suffering and he asserted that all men were equal
and that suffering came out of selfishness: he preached the spirit
of charity to all men, of parental respect, love of children and
care for the old, the sick and the needy. It was left to one of his
later followers, King Asoka, to send out missionaries into India,
Ceylon and Burma in 225 B.C., and it was not until the birth of
Jesus that Buddhism was introduced into China where it was
adopted as the State religion in the fourth century A.D. And it
was not until 1000 years after Guatama that it came to Japan.
By that time it had lost most of its original character and become
the plaything of Priests with its idols and temples. It travelled

magic sword, 'The God of War'. It is an interesting story, from the point of view of the Samurai and his sword, and here it is.

The Scythians, a nomadic tribe of northern Asia, worshipped as their god a bare sword. In Attila's time that sword-god was supposed to have disappeared from earth. One day a herdsman, who was tracking in the desert a wounded animal by the drops of blood, found a mysterious sword standing fixed in the ground, as if it had 'darted from heaven'. The herdsman carried it to Attila who thenceforth was believed by the Huns to wield the Spirit of Death in battle.

It was Amaterasu who gave Ninigi a sword when she sent him to reign over Japan and no one will deny the fact that the Samurai, and the modern Japanese, worshipped their swords and were as brutal as the Huns of Attila in using them. But of the religious propaganda of the Nestorians or the Mohammedans, or of the teaching of the Old or the New Testament, there is little trace in the Nihon-shoki.

The difference between the belief in Jesus Christ and the cult of Shintoism—the Japanese theosophy based on special individual relationship with kami, or spirits and their own cosmogony, to the exclusion of the rest of mankind—is the fundamental difference between a religion and a biological absurdity. It is all the difference there is between a theocratic religion— where divinity stands higher than man and nature— and a theanthropic faith which sees divinity in man and nature.

Shrine-Shinto, the religion of the Shinto State, was built up— step by step— and the dual foundation of theanthrophy needs mass repudiation by the Japanese in favour of monism (an outlook on life based entirely on science and excluding theology, mysticism, and metaphysics) as applied to the theory and practice of government if the nation is to rid itself of domination by Tenno and Gumbatsu. This does not imply repudiation of religion but the adoption of creative thought, creative intelligence and objective thinking: a new orientation of life, resting on the harmony between Japanese and the rest of the world, is urgently required.

Unfortunately, 'the rest of the world' has little in the way of 'religious machinery for creating permanent peace' to offer as a substitute for Shintoism—except the complicated mechanism of the atom-bomb. Christendom itself is a hotch-potch of conten-

ding religions—Catholic, Protestant, Jewish and Pagan democrats erecting mental and physical barriers to agnostic Communists who exercise a veto on the normal functions of the
idealists in the assembly of the United Nations. The actual
requirements of ordinary human-beings is something transcending twentieth century religion: something which will dispose
of the fiction that there are chosen people, white, yellow or
black.

But the self appointed missionaries seek to uproot beliefs that
conflict with their ideology without excluding from it the
atrocities, persecution and aggression which went with the early
Christian Church. All they offer is a vicious repetition of
historical religion under the name of Totalitarianism. And they
would have us all believe that our intricately organized universe
originated in a lifeless cloud of gas uninfluenced by any supreme
Cause. Even Darwin wrote—'The grand sequence of events the
mind refuses to accept as the result of blind chance. The
understanding revolts from such a conclusion'.

The Christian Church condemned Democracy, at the time of
the French Revolution, just as it condemned Socialism and now
warns us against Communism and the dangers of a Third World
War and yet it was only as recently as January 16th 1920 when
57 nations joined the League of Nations the Council of the
Federation of Christ in America announced: 'The League of
Nations is the political expression of the Kingdom of God on
earth.' But we do not want a politically expressed Christianity
nor a regimentation of mankind under a totalitarian form of
government which holds men in bondage— nor do we require
Anglo-American imperialism as the bulwark of Protestantism.

Within two years of the foundation of the League of Nations
we had Fascism followed, eleven years later, by the rise of Hitler
the prophet of the Nazis who suppressed the Jews and in 1939
total war broke out between the ideologies of Christendom: the
details of that conflict require no immediate comment and
Japan's participation in it will be commented on in another
part of this book.

World War II, the total war, ended when the Fascist Powers,
Germany, Italy and Japan (minus Soviet Russia, the Communist
partner of the original alliance of aggressors, who contracted out
when attacked by Hitler) accepted unconditional surrender but

of Man' or the 'AGE OF REASON' and knew nothing about trials for high treason or the dictum: 'All hereditary government is in its nature tyranny.' And they were a spent force when Darwin's Origin of Species and the Descent of Man were published to proclaim the 'dangerous thought' that man descended from an ape and had not been created by God in his own image.

Language

Tokugawa Iyemitsu's decrees had the effect of blockading Japan against the infiltration of the dangerous thoughts of western civilization. The puzzled subjects of the cloistered Tenno Heika were despoiled of the opportunity of exchanging goods with foreigners or learning another language which might have enabled them to clear their minds of some of the cobwebs of the theoretical philosophy diffused for so many centuries by Sino-Japanese Buddhists, sword-swinging Samurai and autocratic Shogun.

The masses had been taught to rely on images, temples and shrines for their thinking—to accept 'creation' as Amaterasu and themselves as kami. Their primitive language was based on myths and fables—like other savages—and they personified gods and forces of nature and named them as best they could. Then the Chinese-Buddhists arrived with a ready made language which they had to learn to speak, write and to translate into 'Japanese'.

Chinese is a difficult language to master. It is monosyllabic with few vocables and the written language has developed a non-alphabetical system combining types of writing devised outside of the great Chinese Empire. The prototype was probably Azilian—10,000 B.C.—the symbolic rock scratching of vertical and horizontal lines—like Chinese characters for man, above, below, earth, river, great, heaven, etc.—or more likely Sumerian, the early Egyptian writing when pictures were used to indicate what a thing suggested, about 6500 B.C.

The Chinese written language is supposed to have originated during the reign of the Emperor FU SHI (2963-2848 B.C.) when TSANG CHIEH was said to have been born with the knowledge of writing and lived to perfect the art. The so called 'Eight Diagrams' are said to have been revealed in 2852 B.C., and this is the date usually given in Chinese records to the time when marks were devised to indicate spoken sounds but it never reached the alphabetical stage like Sumerian.

This written language of the Chinese is divided into classes: simple indicative three horizontal stroke characters (numerals, etc.) pictograms, true ideograms, and phonograms which comprise ninety per cent of the language. The characters consist of a section which indicates the sense and a section which indicates the pronunciation: the radical and the phonetic. In many cases the two parts are the result of combinations of characters and to attempt to transliterate such a system leads to great confusion because of the scarcity of sounds. In conversation it is necessary to overcome the difficulty by using compounds to indicate which of the several meanings a sound possesses is to be understood in a particular case. Because of this and other difficulties it is almost impossible to transliterate foreign words—as it is done in Europe—and the alternative is to coin a new word and give it a character or characters.

Although the various spoken languages of China have something in common there are so many dialects that in extreme cases they have diverged to such an extent that it is not easy to reconcile them with the official language Kwan-hwa(Mandarin) regarded as the lingua franca of the Empire,.

I have experienced the difficulty since 1902 when I began to study Chinese at Ichang in Central China and it persisted to 1942 when I was interrogating Hakkas, Cantonese, and various other Chinese in Malaya. And—between those dates—I tried to make myself understood in North China and Manchuria (up-country and in treaty ports) on the Rand Gold Mines in 1905, with the Chinese Labour Corps in France in 1917—not to mention the odds and ends of Chinese in Borneo I had dealings with between 1922 and 1941. My twentieth century difficulty was simple compared with that of the Japanese when they commenced to adapt Chinese to literature and their every day requirements.

Chinese dialects is a large subject of limited interest but I would like to interpose a few remarks to illustrate the movement of Chinese tribes within the vast Empire. Take the Hakkas, for example. Their home was Shantung but these aborigines were driven out of Shantung in 250 B.C., and scattered over Anhui, Honan and Kiangsi. Pressure from the northern tribes com-

pelled then to move into the mountains of southeast Kiangsi in
A.D. 400, where they remained until A.D. 600 when they were
forced into the Fukien ranges. The final trek came in 1360 when
they settled in Kwangsi and southwest Kwantung: but, ever
since 250 B.C., the Hakkas have been on the move inside the
country or overseas.

I have previously mentioned that in A.D. 286,—long before
Buddhism came to Japan—Koreans arrived, bringing with
them the Confucian Analects and the 'One Thousand Selected
Characters'. Japanese sounds were given to the Chinese ideo-
graphs and writing was first attempted by a few of the ruling
class and it was under the inspiration of Chinese and Koreans
that the early history of Japan was put on paper in Chinese
characters. But although the Japanese wrote 'kanji' (Chinese
characters) in exactly the same way as Koreans or Chinese the
pronunciation was entirely different.

The Chinese reading of their characters was also influenced
by the part of China (or Korea) from which they came. The
first of these influences came from a province named Go and the
next from KAN (the ideographic script was commonly called
KAN-JI, or kan letter). The sound of the character was called
ON as it was pronounced by Chinese and KUN as it was pronounced by Japanese, so there arose two renderings of each
character.

To complicate matters still further there was the GO-ON and
the KAN-ON which had to be turned into the Japanese Kun,
when they imitated their language masters.

It was not until A.D.805, that the Buddhist priest, KOBO
DAISHI (founder of the Shingon sect) returned to Japan from a
visit to China with an additional aid to the study of Chinese—
the two syllabaries, KATAKANA and HIRAGANA, commonly
known as KANA from which the GO-JU-ON (fifty sounds) or
I-Ro-Ha became part of the Japanese language.

Although all Japanese, Chinese or Foreign words can be
written with kana it only plays a minor role and has not at all
supplanted kanji. At present Japanese partly consists of kanji
and partly of kana—the former is identical in meaning, but
not in pronunciation, with the Chinese character, the kana
always indicates a single idea and each sign signifies only one
syllable: there may be 40,000 characters, there are only 73

syllables in kana. To help the ordinary Japanese man in the street, kana is written alongside a character to indicate the pronunciation which gives a clue to the Japanese meaning, and the sense of the sentence.

In 1885 a Roman system of writing, for the Japanese and Chinese script, was invented by Japanese and Foreigners but it has only added the word ROMAN-JI (Roman letters) or rather, Roma-ji as it is called, to the rest of the Chinese language. Now there are a mass of Sino-Japanese syllables, pure Chinese and composite Chino-Japanese words of four or more syllables to keep pace with the growth of Japanese civilization and western science.

And, in addition to this, there are three kinds of writing, KAISHO, for printing, three kinds of SOSHO for script and handwriting, five kinds of TENSHO for fancy writing, inscriptions etc., three of GYOSHO, round and semi-cursive as well as Reisho for ceremonial purposes.

As word-formation is the key to the human mind, and the understanding of a civilization, the Japanese can not be said to have made it easy for a foreigner to unlock the door of their modern language, literature or history and gain an insight into their civilization. And they have made it difficult for Japanese to study the evolution of the human mind outside their country, or to obtain clear and distinct ideas of the progress of the rest of the world.

The effect of Tokugawa Iyemitsu's decrees of 1634 was to reduce the period of contact between Japanese and foreigners from 315 years to 90 years only. Massacre of Christians and enforced isolation was brought about by the Shogunate to maintain its control over Tenno Heika and the lesser kami, over government and the people. But it may be an over-simplification of the problem, of Japan in her relation to western civilization, to suppose that 315 years of contact with it would have prevented her twentieth-century aggression. World History of the nineteenth and the twentieth century is a record of material progress punctuated by increasingly brutal and scientific slaughter. Hitler had nothing to learn from the Tokugawa Shoguns, Araki or Tojo.

In 1945 a couple of atom bombs intensified the terror and havoc already created by B 29's. But it was not the atom bomb which compelled obedience on Japanese and the acceptance of unconditional surrender. Japan was still a united family in defeat and the edict of Tenno Heika was the decisive factor.

To destroy masses of Japanese, men, women and children by fire-raids, high-explosives and atom-bombs, was one way of exterminating a race of aggressors but it cannot be advanced that it was based on the teaching of Jesus Christ. On the contrary it was the triumph of western super-science over an inefficient eastern pupil: it was in no sense a victory of Christianity over Jinja-Shinto.

From the point of view of culture and democracy what was required was not the destruction of people but the obliteration of basic anachronism by example and precept. But is western civilization not dangerously poised on the very pinnacle of blatant materialism and 'Thanks God' in an aside that the U.S.A. produced the atom-bomb ahead of her co-belligerents? Indeed there are many who say that our belief in an Almighty God is quite secondary to our blind faith in the scientist to whom we turn in the hour of danger and to whom we give praise and thanks for our preservation, past, present and future. In any case it may be well worth pondering over before we leap to conclusions, regarding the best way to convert the heathen to the democracy of present day western civilization, and destroy the temples and shrines of the wicked Shinto State of Japan.

Shinto

It is claimed by Japanese, particularly by many of their eminent professors of ethology, that the characteristic spirit of the nation may be summed up in one word—Shinto. By 'Shinto' they mean 'kokumin dotoku' the modern national morality which is based on 'Sai-sei-itchi'—the fusion of a *state religion* with an *undemocratic government:* in short, the compulsory worship of a Divine Ruler and the compulsory obedience to an autocracy of military dictators. By 'Shinto' they mean *Jinja-Shinto*–Shrine Shinto—based on the twelve groups of shrines: Kampei-Sha, the Government Shrines, and all the Kokuhei-Sha, National Shrines, in Kensha (Prefecture), Gosha (District), Sonsha, (Village) and the 70,000 un-graded (Mukaku-sha) shrines, and the tens of thousand little shrines on hilltop and by the side of the road and on the kami-dana, the family god-shelf.

And, above all, they mean the Ise Dai Jingu—and Amaterasu-o-mikami, the Sun Goddess.

However, the autochthons of Japan had a nameless religion until 6th Century A.D. when Chinese scholars (Buddhists and Confucianists) arrived in the country with the art of writing, and with the art of naming things. They were well versed in matters of cults and religions, for rulers and for people of the soil, and they soon had a name for 'the way of the gods' the religion of the natives.

Using three Chinese characters for 'follow', 'God' and 'way' they produced the combination meaning 'follow the will of the gods without question'. And, in due course, this became 'Kannagara-no-michi', or—'Kami-no-michi'. Then, by using only the last two of the three characters, it was pronounced Shin-to.

According to Dr. Genji Kato, an authority on the subject— 'Shinto is indeed a *religion* peculiar to and inherent in the Japanese mind, so that it cannot be displaced or eradicated by any conflicting religious power from without.' And this is carried a stage further by the statement: 'Shinto is a thorough-going *national religion* throughout each and every phase of its long development, from the stage of nature religion to that of culture religion, with the Jinno or DIVINE RULER of the nation at the centre of worship, keeping pace with the progress of Japanese civilization in general, so that in the mental texture of the people their religious faith and national consciousness have been so closely interwoven as now to be incapable of separation.'

That was Kato's opinion in 1935 but it is mentioned in the Nippon Shoki (A.D. 720)—in connection with Kotoku Tenno (645-654)—that: 'We have commanded our son to rule according to the will of the kami and hereby the land has been ruled by a Tenno since the beginning of Heaven and Earth.'

The phrase . . . 'to rule according to the will of the kami' . . . (kamu-nagara mo) was translated in 1912 by T. Iida, in his Shinyaku Nihon Shoki, to mean *to follow Shinto and of oneself to possess Shinto*.

No doubt the compilers of the Nippon Shoki had in mind the events up to A.D. 720 for there is very little confirmation, in Japanese History, of the sanctity of the Tenno as 'Divine Ruler of the nation at the centre of worship' in the attitude, or methods, of the majority of the Clans, Regents or Shoguns who in fact ruled the nation and controlled the religions.

However, even before A.D. 720 the precarious existence of the Jinno was made quite clear. For instance: Yuryaku Tenno (457) is credited with the murder of the father of Kenso Tenno (485)—Sujun Tenno (588) was poisoned by the clan leader, Soga Umako who had married his own daughter to Kimmei Tenno (539), and when this was done to his satisfaction he replaced him with the Empress Suiko (593) who was the consort of Bidatsu Tenno (572). The next ruler, Jomei (629) was placed on the throne by Soga Emishi—and so it went on. After the Soga clan, the Fujiwara clan took over the role of supplying the Tenno with their consorts. A daughter of Shomu Tenno (724) (who had married a daughter of Fujiwara Fubito) came to the throne as Koken in 749, her son—Junnin—succeeded her in 759 but she decided to remove him in 764, and when he had been strangled she re-occupied the throne as Shotoku in 765, abdicating in 770 in favour of Konin Tenno.

As head of his clan the Tenno, from Jimmu 660 B.C. to Suinin 29 B.C. ruled for longer periods than the following hundred or so who were on the throne to 1847. The first eleven rulers average 60 years but the next twenty-two averaged a bare 24 years and this average (for the next fifty) dropped to 12 years only an average higher than the following twenty. But then, it must be added, in explanation of these 'averages' that some of the earlier Tenno were giants who had many wives. For example: Keiko Tenno (A.D. 71-130) stood 10 feet 2 inches in his bare feet and fathered a tribe of eighty children to ensure the continuity of the Divine Emperors and Empresses.

As time went on, various clans mingled their blood with the Clan of divine descent and this, in turn, produced a plethora of branch and off-shoot lines which provided most of the material for the numerous civil wars. By the end of the 15th Century these internecine struggles had destroyed most of the oldest of the Imperial branch lines and the Emperors of the period (1465-1491) — Go-Tsuchimikado, Go-Kashiwabara, Go-Nara and Ogimachi—were reduced to penury and the Throne had lost all its pomp, ceremony and status in the wild struggle for power of the Samurai and the Daimyo of Imperial descent.

Certainly there was little or nothing left of kamu-nagara,

kannagara-no-michi or Shinto; nothing at all of sai-sei-itchi the so called religious practices of the nation and the government administration inseparably united 'and completely identified in one entire whole.'

However—reverting to Shinto as a religion. In 1875, after the Meiji Restoration, the new government decided to manufacture a State religion. The first step was to issue instructions for the definite separation of Shinto from Buddhism. Then, in 1900, regulations were passed which separated Shinto shrines from religious matters and the Shrines became part and parcel of the affairs of the Home Office. It was maintained, by the Government, that worship at Shinto shrines had a national and not a religious importance and that Japanese-Buddhists (for instance) were Shintoist because they were Japanese.

In 1941, Shinto was clearly divided into *Sectarian Shinto*, consisting of thirteen sects, and the *National Shinto Faith* of the entire Japanese people. The latter, which is called Jinja Shinto, consists of Emperor and Shrine worship and 'kokumin dotoku' which was taught in all schools.

Sectarian SHINTO, or Shuha-Shinto, is religious Shinto and is divided into five sections: *Pure Shinto, Confucian, Mountain, Purification* and *Faith-healing*. Each of the thirteen sects, although founded earlier, were not fully established (*i.e.*, not recognized by the Government) until after the Restoration in 1868.

The churches, of Shinto sects, are called *Kyokai*, the temples of Buddhists are Tera, and the Shrines are called Jinja. In 1937 the Department of Education gave the total number of adherents of the thirteen sects as 17,372,519, although some of the sects claim much higher figures than those given by the authorities. For instance, Tenri-kyo claims over 6,000,000 followers with a working staff of 62,000, for their 10,000 churches, and a teaching staff of 75,000 men and 30,000 women.

The following summary will make clear the relative numerical strength of the various sects in 1936.

PURE SHINTO	Government Recognition	Adherents	
Shinto Honkyoku	1872	1,268,430	Main Bureau of Shinto
Shinri Kyo	1894	1,503,076	Divine Reason Teaching
Taisha Kyo	1882	3,365,955	Great Shrine—of Izumo
		6,137,461	

Shinto Honkyoku teaches reverence, patriotism, humanity, the worship of early Shinto pantheon and of kamu-nagara, with special emphasis on Emperor worship.

Shinri teaches that the whole world is one family and makes a special point of the relationship between Tenno and people.

Taisha is concerned with the largest, oldest and most influential of all shrines (except Ise)—The Great Shrine of Izumo, in Kitsuki, Shimane prefecture, on shore of Inland Sea. Teaches its followers to serve the Imperial family in the spirit of kamu-nagara. The Shrine was erected to glorify the spirit of Okuni-Nushi-no-kami who as ruler of IzUMO retired in favour of the Kyushu-Yamato clans who set up the dynasty of the Sun Goddess.

CONFUCIAN	Government Recognition	Adherents
Shusei Ha	1876	408,683
Taisei Kyo	1882	727,918
		1,136,601

Shusei teach the moral law through worship of Amaterasu and they believe that Confucianism had its origin in Japan and not in China. They believe that the Divine spirit of creation has but one source, and that serving man is to serve the gods.

Taisei was founded by a Samurai (Hirayama) who served under the last of the Tokugawas. Seeks to preserve the spirit of kamu-nagara and preaches Confucian ethics.

MOUNTAIN	Government Recognition	Adherents	
Jikko Kyo	1885	407,839	Founded by Hasegawa 16th Century
Fuso Kyo	1882	551,111	Worship of Mount Fuji
Mitake Kyo	1882	2,051,546	Worship of Mt. Ontake
		3,010,496	

Jikko have their shrines on the hill tops and believe that mountains are the dwelling places of gods rather than of humans.

Hasegawa, the founder, born in 1541 came to Fuji during his wanderings and regarded the 'sacred mountain' as the home of

'the Great Spirit of the Universe'—he died, aged 106, in a cave
on Mount Fuji. His followers believe that in the government of
the Jinno are to be found the 'outward manifestations of the
hidden things of kami: Jinno is a god revealed in human form
and the place of adoration is the Palace of Awe—in the Imperial
Palace at Tokyo. They also believe that Fuji is the seishin
(soul) of the earth and they pray for the 'eternity of the unbroken line of Jinno'.

Fuso is an off-shoot of Jikko, Fuso being the poetic name of
Nippon and of Fuji. The teaching is that of Hasegawa, and his
disciples, with a tendency to polytheism.

Mitake stress the worship of the Jinno, and kamu-nagara, but
are also polytheistic. They worship Mount Ontake, a ten-
thousand feet peak in the Japanese Alps, and have three main
shrines, *Omiya* (great), *Wakamiya* (young) and *Yamamiya* (mountain) and their principal kami is Kuni-toko-Tachi-no-mikoto—
the first of the kami mentioned in the Nihonji.

The followers of Mitake Kyo believe that universal peace
will follow the acceptance throughout the world of the Jinno-
centred Jinja-Shinto of Japan. They are firm believers in the
'unity of Shinto worship and of government' (sai-sei-itchi) the
aim of which is 'the universal peace of mankind'.

PURIFICATION	Government Recognition	Adherents	
Shinshu Kyo	1880	777,117	Divine learning
Misogi Kyo	1894	343,008	
		1,120,125	

Shinshu: stress the 'Sacred Way of old Shinto'—the kamu-
nagara-no-michi—and were founded by the Meiji Restoration
Loyalists. They have several purification ceremonies: *Chinka-
shiki* (fire walking), *Kugatachi-shiki* (hot-water ritual) *Misogi-ho*
(cold-water), *Batsujo-ho* (Expurgation of evil), *Monoimi-ho* (food
and drink taboos) and *Shinji-ho,* the admission of divine spirit
to prevent stagnation of the human spirit.

Misogi was founded by a Shinto priest to perpetuate and
extend the doctrines regarding purification through rites, and
they have three purification agencies, *sword, jewel* and the
mirror. Like the Shinshu Kyo they follow the 'Sacred Way of
old Shinto'.

	Government Recognition	Adherents	
FAITH-HEALING			
Kurozumi Kyo	1882	563,407	Church of modern Shinto
Konko Kyo	1885	1,092,046	Like Christianity
Tenri Kyo	1888	4,312,383	Claim over 6 million adherents

5,967,836

Kurozumi Kyo was founded by M. Kurozumi whose father was chief of the Amaterasu Shrine at Kami Nakano. He claimed Temmei jikiju' (direct receipt of heavenly command) and a Shrine was erected to him on Kagura Hill, Kyoto, in 1862: this was honoured by worship on behalf of the Tenno. All the teaching is based on Amaterasu and the Jinno.

Konko Kyo was founded by Kawate Bunji who died in 1883. Konko is not bound by any of the traditional ceremonies or superstitions—it repudiates entirely all magic and official rituals —relies on the genuine worship of One True God who loves those who trust in him as a child loves a parent—the God is 'Tenchi-kane-no-kami': the God who gives unity to heaven and earth.

Tenri Kyo is one of the most active of the Shinto sects. It is a curious religious movement founded upon divine revelation with the emphasis on the salvation of mankind. Its objects are more concerned with holding the balance between ultra-socialism and individualism than with kamu-nagara. Followers of Tenrikyo say that Tenrio-no-mikoto ('God the Parent') descended from heaven into the person of the foundress, Miki Nakayama, on 26th October 1838, and from that moment she became Divine.

According to Tenri, Jiba (about 20 miles from Nara)— where the feet of Miki Nakayama stuck fast to the ground—is the centre of the universe. There is a four-foot square, in the dead centre of the main Sanctuary at Jiba (completed in 1934). Above this spot there is a small opening in the roof and on the square an altar has been in construction for many years. This altar may not be completed to an eighty-two inch six-sided tower of stone until the teaching of Tenri has gone round the world. On the altar has been placed a shallow saucer filled with barley flour and into this saucer 'God' sends down from above a life giving nectar (kanro).

The altar is known as the KANRO DAI and the final stage of the erection is to take place when the reformation of men's mind and of the world is accomplished. This *kanro-dai* (sweet-dew altar) is mentioned in the Nihon Shoki and the Tenri Kyo was made a sub-section of Shinto Honkyoku (Main Bureau of Shinto) in 1888.

Like the Buddhists, all the adherents of the thirteen Shinto sects are part and parcel of the national Shinto State, based on the Jinno and Jinja-Shinto, from which there was no escape for a Japanese.

CHAPTER II

SYNOPSIS OF
JAPANESE HISTORY
Jimmu Tenno to Meiji Restoration

i. Kami-no-michi (The Way of the Gods)

A red disc in the centre of a field of white is the National Flag of Japan: it signifies the Rising Sun and it is known as 'Hino Maru'—the sun flag. The sun is the representation of the mythological ancestress, *Amaterasu*, of the Imperial Japanese Dynasty, and even as the sun is the centre of the universe so is the Imperial Dynasty the centre of Japanese race life.

According to the Nippon Shoki, Amaterasu was the source of creation, and the energy of growth. It is in this explanation of creation that the tradition of divine ancestry, as well as the relationship between Tenno, Land and People (their common origin) originated. The same authority states that Japanese were bound together from the beginning of time into one household—*Hakko-ichi-u*. This theory was promulgated by Jimmu Tenno in his first edict (issued from the site of the Imperial Palace at Kashihara, in Yamato, in 660 B.C.) which runs in part as follows :

> 'Thereafter the Capital may be extended so as to embrace the whole land and under the heaven as far as the Tenno's rule extends may be formed so as to compose a single household.'

Hakko-ichi-u — under heaven a single household. Born out of legend, this cult was developed by Tenno, Priest, Samurai and Shogun, to become the driving force of Japanese national progress—to bind the nation to face centuries of tribulation : feudalism, dictatorship and—in the end—bitter humiliation.

Even if we ignore the Nippon Shoki the cult of Amaterasu is old, but the 'Hino Maru' is a modern idea. It was merely an item in the nationalistic propaganda associated with the restoration of the quiescent 'divine rights' of the Tenno and was adopted as the 'national flag' in 1868 after the Meiji Restoration. It revived *Shinto*—the original faith of Japanese—which was the worship of all 'kami' centred in the veneration of the Sun Goddess, Amaterasu.

The Nippon Shoki is a Chinese type of History *except* for the special emphasis on the Amaterasu-origin of Japan as set down by Prince Toneri and the Fujiwara Shogun, Fubito, in A.D. 720, and this tendency—to underline the *divinity* of the Tenno—is the outstanding feature of all Japanese history books including histories of Japanese-Buddhism, art and literature.

Jimmu Tenno's date, in Japanese history, is based on the details in the Nippon Shoki, although some other historians place it in the first century B.C. and not in the seventh century.

The archaeologists, uninfluenced by Kami-no-michi signposts, state that the Stone Age in Western Japan extended to the third century B.C., and in Eastern Japan to a few centuries longer, and that the Aenolithic Age (co-existence of metal and stone) extended from the end of the second century B.C., until third century A.D., when authentic history—based on documentary evidence—begins.

What scanty unwritten evidence there is, of early Japanese culture, is to be found in the burial mounds of the people and their rulers, such as those of SUI-NIN TENNO (29 B.C.–A.D. 70) in Yamato Province; OJIN TENNO, buried A.D. 310 in Kawachi Province; and KIMMEI TENNO, buried A.D. 571.

These burial mounds came into existence betweeen third century B.C. and third century A.D., the period in which the natives used stone implements together with bronze spear-heads and daggers. Many of the mounds are surrounded by moats and have hundreds (sometimes thousands) of terra-cotta cylinders and figures called HANIWA.

The origin of HANIWA—figures of men and animals—and the placing of haniwa on the burial mounds—is mentioned in the Nippon Shoki as dating from the burial of Prince Yamato-hiko in Sui-nin Tenno's reign (29 B.C.–A.D. 70). When the Prince was buried his servants were buried alive with him. The moaning and groaning of the human sacrifices excited the pity of the mourners to such an extent that it caused Sui-Nin Tenno to ban the custom and when his consort, HIHASU-HIME, died he ordered 100 potters from Izumo to make figures of men and animals to set up on and around the burial mound. Another version is given in the KOJIKI which merely states that a 'man-fence' was put up on Prince Yamato-hiko's grave and that the potters (hani-shibe) bureau—to make figures and utensils—was established when the Empress Hihasu-hime died. The custom, borrowed from China, of burying people alive did exist because it was prohibited in the Taika Reform Edict of A.D.645.

Another authority mentions the burials of Emperors Kogen, (158 B.C.), Sujin (30 B.C.) and Suinin (A.D. 70), under burial regulations which included stone coffins and haniwa.

There were four types of burial mounds: round, square-fronted with round back, square, and round-top on square base.

The square-front and round-back type is said to be purely Japanese in origin and was used for OJIN-TENNO (A.D. 310) and NINTOKU TENNO (A.D. 399). Part of the burial mound of Nintoku's resting-place fell to pieces in 1872 and exposed a stone coffin, suit of armour and other items of antiquarian interest. Today a special department of the Imperial Household is in charge of the Tenno's burial mounds and has "marked out and provided protection for the tombs of each of the 123 Tenno."*

The square type of burial mound was similar to that used by Chinese Emperors in the HAN DYNASTY—209 B.C. to A.D. 220 —and was first introduced to Izumo Province (regulations regarding the construction and ceremony are included in the Taika edict of 645 A.D.), and was used for Yomei Tenno (587) and for Empress Suiko in 628.

There are very few of the round-top on square base type—the best known is that of JOMEI TENNO (671) and of a Prince buried in Kawachi Province.

Some of the burial mounds are quite imposing: Nintoku's was 1600 feet long with a round back of 800 feet in diameter: Ojin's 1350 feet and 800 feet: Richu's in A.D. 405 was over 1200 feet long and 654 feet diameter for the round back—the last of this type was that of Bidatsu Tenno who died in A.D. 585. On

* See Appendix I to VIII.

Nintoku's mound there were nearly 6500 haniwa with another 4800 outside the moat.

A much higher culture existed in Keishu, south-eastern Korea, the ancestral home of the Yamato tribes who settled in Kyushu shortly before 660 B.C.—the date given for the accession of Jimmu Tenno.

In Keishu and in Heijo (Pingyang in north Korea)—the ancient site of the Chinese colony of Lo-lang which existed from 108 B.C. to A.D.313— many tombs have been excavated and some of the lacquer cups unearthed bear dates which correspond roughly with 86 B.C. to 8 B.C. and from A.D. 3 to A.D. 69, and on some are the names of the government factory responsible for them. Bronze weapons of 225 B.C. and 41 B.C. have been recovered from Lo-Lang tombs.

However, to revert to the Nippon Shoki and Jimmu Tenno. The authors of Nippon Shoki would have in mind the birth of Guatama and of Confucius (sixth century B.C.) and perhaps the birth of Muhammad (A.D. 570) and even of the Shu-king and the Shi-king. They would ponder over spirits and heaven and decide that the Sovereign alone should worship Shang-ti—the Supreme one. But it is just as well to remember—before we leave this point—that the worship of AMATERASU was confined to the Imperial House until 97 B.C., and it was not until 29 B.C. that the Goddess became the centre of the faith of the entire nation, and ceased to be only the uji-gami (clan deity) of Tenno Heika. So the purely Japanese idea of SHINTO—The Way of the Gods—prevailed even if the actual name of the faith did not come into existence until the Buddhists arrived in Japan in A.D. 552.

Let me illustrate this by mentioning a minor matter of personal experience. In 1883 I went out to Kobe. The early name of Kobe was KAMBE which means the Door of the Gods. But I was soon to learn that there were many KAMBE in Japan, because from about 97 B.C., each local shrine had its village to care for it—that which was nearest to IKUTA SHRINE (close to where we lived at the time) was made the Kambe of Ikuta. Certainly, Kobe in those days—before the visitation of B 29's— had many temples and shrines and TORII, the Shinto gateway to the shrine.

Now although the sacred mirror of Amaterasu was enshrined

in the Ko-dai-jingu—on the banks of the Isuzu River in Ise—in 29 B.C., it was not until 1890 (some time after the Meiji Restoration) that Jimmu Tenno was enshrined in the Kashihara Jingu at the foot of Mount Unebi in Nara prefecture. And it was only on 11th February 1873 that the beginning of Jimmu Tenno's reign was established as the accepted commencement of the Japanese era. Ever since then, Kigensetsu—11th February—has been Empire Foundation Day and observed as the most important national holiday.

The Japanese Government set its seal on the authenticity of Nippon Shoki, Jimmu Tenno, and the foundation of theEmpire, in 1937 with the announcement that: 'Japan International Exposition for the Commemoration of the Twenty-Six Hundreth Anniversary of the Foundation of the Empire': would be held at Tokyo in 1940.

We may therefore accept this assertion with the same kind of credulity which was given to the pronouncement of Bishop Ussher in England in the seventeenth century: 'It is calculated that man was created by the Trinity on October 23rd 4004 B.C., at 9 o'clock in the morning.' And if something more recent is required, what could be more dogmatic than the 1948 statement in the Watch Tower Bible and Tract Society of Brooklyn, New York, U.S.A.'s book—'The Truth Shall Make You Free'—that: —'From Adam's creation to the end of 1943 A.D., is 5971 years: each creative day is 7000 years and a period of 42,000 years only has passed since God said toward the earth 'Let there be light'.

To forbid the propagation of beliefs, sacred or secular, would be considered harmful to the freedom of thought: to propagate the opinion that the end of the world can be calculated in precise years, days and hours may be equally harmful so nothing is gained by expert calculations on the exact year, day and hour that Jimmu Tenno founded the Japanese Empire.

Before Jimmu Tenno was enthroned, on the first day of the first month, his tribesmen had seen several years of active service against hostile barbarians in Yamato and elsewhere. At the end of his expedition he gives thanks to Amaterasu for his victory but admits that there are 'wicked men' on the frontiers of his limited domain. These wicked men, with crude and primitive minds, live in caves but he promises his divine ancestress that he will follow the way of his ancestor Ninigi-no-mikoto when he descended from Takama-gahara to rule the land, destroy the savages, ensure the livelihood, prosperity and happiness of the people, and observe KODO, the WAY of the TENNO.

The Nippon Shoki sheds very little light on the incidents in the life and rule of the next eight Tenno. We have the names and the relative date of their reigns but nothing further until the tenth Tenno SU-JIN (97 B.C.). Then there is reiteration and amplification of the duties of Tenno, Land and People. Su-jin Tenno realised that the prosperity of the Empire depended on the encouragement of agriculture, and the imposition of taxes. He sent members of his family to different parts of his domain, to extend his authority and collect tribute in kind.

For a period of 560 years (?)—660 B.C. to 100 B.C.— the Consort came from the clans (UJI) outside the 'Imperial Clans'. This was done in order to widen the influence of the Tenno, but with the enthronement of Su-jin Tenno the branch lines of the Tenno's family supplied the Consort in order to build up the tradition of the divinity, and unbroken descent of Tenno Heika. His successor, SUININ TENNO (29 B.C.), came to the throne when peaceful conditions prevailed but the next ruler, KEIKO TENNO (A.D. 71), was less fortunate and had to deal with unruly rival tribes who menaced his enlarged patrimony. (*)

Tenno succeeded Tenno on much the same basis of authority and there is little of interest to record from the time of Keiko Tenno (A.D. 71: A.D. 131) to that of SEIMU TENNO who followed in his footsteps. By this time the population of Japan had been increased from overseas and the cultural development of the nation was stimulated by the influx of Chinese and Koreans in the second century A.D. They introduced various arts and crafts in which they were much more advanced than the natives.

These alien immigrants were named KIKA-JIN (naturalised subjects) and it is to them that Japan owes her real intellectual development. It is recorded that when the first Kika-jins made their presence felt in the Tenno's domain it coincided with pestilence and confusion in China which disorganised the elaborate political system in that spread-eagled Empire.

Although registered under a separate category of 'Imperial subjects', the KIKA-JIN were soon assimilated by the indigenous stock and racially became Japanese: by the ninth century they

* See Appendix I and II.

MOMMU, and it was then that the principle of primogeniture for the Imperial Family of Japan was established by decree.

MOMMU TENNO married a daughter of Fujiwara Kamatari's son, Fubito, and this was the beginning of a system of Fujiwara inter-marriage with the Imperial Family which continued to 1868. In 708 the *mother* of Mommu Tenno came to the throne as GEMMYO TENNO and, in 715, she was followed by her *daughter* as *Gensho* until she abdicated in favour of the Crown Prince who became SHOMU TENNO in 724.

SHOMU TENNO married another daughter of Fujiwara Fubito (by a different wife) but because the Fujiwaras were *Shinbetsu* and not *Kobetsu* they were not regarded by the Imperial Court as Empress when married to the Tenno. Fujiwara Fubito's chief opponent, on this matter, was the Imperial Prince Nagaya so he took steps to dispose of him and then his daughter, Asuka, was proclaimed Empress.

In 748, SHOMU abdicated and was succeeded by his daughter as Empress KOKEN but she vacated the throne in favour of her son in 753 and he commenced his rule in 759 as JUNNIN TENNO.

Empress Koken was a strong supporter of the Buddhist priests in Nara and in 752 she presided at the inauguration ceremony of the DAI BUTSU which had been under construction since 743 on the orders of Shomu Tenno and his consort the Empress Komyo. In 753 the abdicated Empress Koken became a nun and formed an intimate friendship with the great Buddhist priest DOKYO, resident in Nara. As a direct result of this intimacy, Empress Koken, in 765, removed Junnin Tenno from the throne and reoccupied it herself, as EMPRESS SHOTOKU.

DOKYO and Empress KOKEN (or Shotoku) continued their intimacy and there was a plot to make Dokyo the Emperor but this was brought to nothing and one of the 'advisers' of the movement, Fujiwara-no-Nakamaro, grandson of Fujiwara Kamatari, lost his head for his trouble and in 770, Empress Shotoku was replaced by KONIN TENNO.

* I have inserted these few remarks, regarding the electing or removing the occupants of the throne, to illustrate the methods of the various clans from SOGA to TOKUGAWA—from 539 to 1868. And if I refrain from similar details, in subsequent chapters, it is only because it would be repeating these episodes

* See Appendix I, II and III.

under so many different names of Emperors, Shoguns, Regents, Daimyos and mere Samurais who made and unmade the nominal rulers to suit the needs of their particular family in its relationship to the 'divine' Tenno.

ii. Nationalism based on Imperial traditions

It was the Regent, Prince Shotoku (572-621) who initiated the Taika Reforms. In 607, Shotoku Taishi dispatched the first official mission to the Chinese Court. This mission was entirely composed of priests and students of kika-jin descent. When the members of the mission returned to Japan they realised that the existing conditions were a serious obstacle to reform, and it is to these kika-jins that the Taika Reforms owed its inspirational framework.

In A.D. 607, despite the various hakko-ichi-u edicts there was very little evidence of a family system in the country. Clans now owned large tracts of land and attached to the land was a working class of vassals. Under the guidance of Shotoku Taishi, and the kika-jins, the ancient form of ancestor worship, and reverence for nature, was blended with the philosphic metaphysics of Indo-Chinese Buddhism. This mingling of religions became known as RYO-BU SHINTO and prevailed until 1868 when Shintoism—the creed of Tenno and Kami— was resuscitated as the national cult.

The Taika Reforms were put into operation in 646, during the second year of the reign of the 36th Tenno, KOTOKU—65 years before Nara became the Imperial Capital. The intention of the reformers was to completely change the social, economic and political structure of the country. The entire social organization had to be redefined and re-established so that the State could be adjusted to the requirements of the times and to ensure the continuation and expansion of its power and influence.

There was strong opposition to this establishment of a centralized State around the throne. The chief opponents were the powerful SOGA clan so it was decided to destroy them. This was accomplished by the Imperial Prince Naka-no-Oye with the help of Nakatomi Kamatari—better known by the name of FUJIWARA. But there were also other clans who refused to co-operate. They were securely established in their respective districts outside the influence of the Tenno, and his supporters, who had established their capital at Naniwa (Osaka) which was a convenient political centre with good land and water connections.

Clans, at this period of Japanese history, varied greatly in size and power: they owned tracts of land corresponding to the extent of their wealth and influence with the Court and the land was worked for them by serfs under the supervision of hereditary craftsmen called KAKIBE. Powerful clans, like the Soga, became ambitious and threatened the existence of the system of government based on Tenno (divine Emperors) and it was one of the objects of the Taika Reforms to bring all land in the realm under state ownership. Clans were to be dissolved, all the people were to become citizens under a central government and to effect this change the support of the land-owning clans was absolutely necessary.

It was an ambitious programme. Persuasive, and then more convincing methods were used to deprive the clans of their vested interests. Under this militant socialism clansmen were appointed officials of the state and permitted to exercise their former rights over the serfs. Part of their income, derived from land ownership, was retained by them as emolument while the balance was handed over as a contribution to taxation. They were given court rank which corresponded to the acreage of their former estates.

This system conformed to that existing in China where the central government levied taxes through the provincial governors and these Mandarins squeezed the peasants dry.

The whole country was divided into three sections. The Imperial Capital where the superintendents (KEISHI) resided: the Provinces, surrounding the Keishi, were termed Home Provinces (KINAI) and the rest of the country was designated Outer Provinces or CHI-HO.

Kinai and Chiho were subdivided into KUNI (próvince), GUN (district) and RI (township). The basic unit of the new social and political structure was Five Households (Go-Ho) known under the Tokugawa era as Gonin-gumi.

Households were the base of a rigid hierarchial system which supported the respective administrators of townships, districts and provinces. Governors were appointed from among the court officials and the district supervisors were nominees of these provincial magnates who were favourably inclined to the new regime. In this way was the local administration retained by the Clans, subject to the control exercised by court officials, to carry out the policy of the Tenno.

The Reform aimed at a distribution of public land, giving to the people a proportion of the whole, subject to a re-allotment every six years. It also created the basis for taxation and population registry.

There were three main taxes: Rice, Labour and Household: but it was such a complicated system of taxation that it required frequent amendment before the social, economic and political structure was organized to suit the Court Officials. From 661 to 700 there were three other similar Reforms—Tenchi, Taiho and Mommu—for it was found necessary, as an inducement to the numerous officials, to reward them with grants of land according to their court rank. This was a definite reversal of policy. But, as the 'reforms' progressed, the gap between theory and practice widened and a new set of landlords came into being.

For his services in destroying the Soga Clan, Nakatomi Kamatari received large grants of land and became the strongest political power in the country under his new name of FUJIWARA. But the net result of the various reforms was to destroy particular clans only to create others of greater power in their place: the transfer of power was in the interest of the Tenno and the Court and did little to improve the lot of the farmers.

During this period the Capital had been located at Naniwa, Atsuka, Otsu, Attsuka (second time) Fujiwara (702) and then to NARA in 710 when the new State came into existence under FUJIWARA FUBITO.

By this time the FUJIWARAs had weakened or destroyed most of the opposing clans and during the time that Nara remained the Capital the family continued to consolidate tremendous political power and influence in the country.

The foundations of the Throne were firmly established when the 45th sovereign, SHOMU TENNO, came to the throne in 724. Shomu Tenno had married Fujiwara's daughter and the Fujiwara family were raised to the highest court rank. Around the new aristocracy, of officials, priests and monks—with their splendid temples and monasteries—the Imperial Court of Japan flourished.

Fujiwara Fubito busied himself with the compilation of the Nippon Shoki—the collection of myths and legends against a mythological background—which was aimed to clarify the political principles of the state: rule by Sovereigns of divine ancestry: and that the people formed a single household under Tenno Heika.

The Nippon Shoki brought the History of Japan down to the year A.D. 697, and the history books which followed underlined the Tenno's divinity. In each period of Japanese History, from A.D. 700 to 900, the actual rulers, FUJIWARAS, left behind them the histories centred around the Tenno and their own family, although in theory only a portion of ruling authority was relegated to the Shoguns.

There are six National Histories of Japan compiled by one or other of the Fujiwara Shoguns. *Nippon Shoki*, by Fubito: *Shoku Nippongi* (40 volumes) by Tsuginawa, 797: *Nippon Koki* (40 volumes) by Fuyutsugu, 840: *Shoku Nippon Koki* by Yoshifusa, 869: *Montoku Tenno Jitsuroku*, (10 volumes) by Mototsune, 879: and the *Sandai Jitsuroku* of fifty volumes by Tokihara. With the Sandai Jitsuroku the official chronicles ended but from 900 to 1900 there were numerous other histories, which will be referred to later in this book, which express the scholars' conception of what Japanese History should be; idealism handed down from generation to generation. These historians selected material according to their own fancy, adjusting the factual with the traditional and never leaving out the over-riding need to stress the divinity of the Tenno.

Buddhism was the guiding principle of the new nationalism of Nara under Shomu Tenno. Buddha was the personification of the native Kami, and the culture of Nara was further influenced by intercourse with China, then under the greatness of the T'ANG Dynasty—Chinese traders came to Japan in increasing numbers and with them the civilization of India and Persia. Under these new conditions of stability the Temples, Monasteries and Officials serving the Fujiwaras prospered. They owned vast tracts of land and lived grandly on their independent economic foundation. On the other hand, many minor officials left Nara in order to free themselves from the throttling influence of Fujiwara domination: these were the people who a few centuries later became known as the SAMURAI.

However, the spread of Buddhism scattered ideas which became a political doctrine running contrary to the native tradition by challenging the omnipotence of the Tenno. What had at first served to strengthen the Imperial principle now gave rise to doctrines which challenged it. Men like DOKYO were inspired by political ambition to place themselves on the Throne. In view of these facts those who wished to preserve the Imperial tradition started a counter movement to rid the Capital of evil doctrines, and it was decided to move the seat of government to Nagaoka and then to HEIAN-KYO—Kyoto. Nara was left to the Buddhist priests and the city of the Great Buddha, the Temples and the Monasteries steadily declined in status to one of the famous sights in Japan.

One of the sights of Nara is the DAIBUTSU, the 53 feet high bronze statue of Vairocana which was completed in A.D. 749. It is housed in the TODAIJI temple, in the Daibutsu-den reputed to be the largest wooden building under one roof in the world and probably the oldest one of its kind in existence. The Todaiji temple was established by Shomu Tenno and in 752 there was an 'eye-opening ceremony' performed for the inauguration of the Buddhist image.

The ceremony was attended by 10,000 priests from India and China and other countries. In 756 the abdicant Shomu Tenno died. He may have been like the Yomei Tenno (540-587) who 'believed in the Law of Buddha and reverenced Shinto or the Way of the Gods' or like Kokotu Tenno (596-654) who 'honoured the religion of Buddha and despised the Way of the Gods.' But on the forty-ninth day of his death, when a Buddhist ceremony was performed, his consort the Empress Dowager Komyo dedicated to the Vairocana Buddha most of his personal treasures which were placed in the temple warehouse—shoso. The Shoso-in of Nara became the treasure-house of the Nation. and its contents will be referred to in a subsequent chapter.

The Tenno's treasures were dedicated to the Great Buddha whose image Shomu caused to be made. The dedication by the Empress was accompanied by a memorandum of dedication— Kenmotsucho—a fifty feet long scroll ten and a half inches wide. It opens with a prayer by the Empress which denotes the firm hold which Buddhism exerted over the Imperial Family. The following passage will illustrate this better than any comment of mine.

' . . . I donate to the Todaiji as a votive offering to the Vairocana Buddha, various other Buddhas, Bodhisattvas, and all the saints. May these gifts, I humbly pray, help his spirit on the Wheels of Sacred Laws to speed on its way to the temple of the Lotus World. There may he always enjoy heavenly music, and may he finally be admitted to the sacred hall of the Buddha of Light, and assuredly enjoy the company of Fugen Bosatsu (Visvabhadra) and together with Monju Bosatsu (Manjusri) spread the divine influence. Thus may his benevolence extend to the ten milliards and his virtue disseminate over a billion worlds . . . . '

And far from the splendour of Nara the *heimin* (common people) clapped their hands and worshipped Buddha saying aloud: 'Namu Tensho-Kodaijingu-sama' for Buddha in the Todaiji was no other than Amaterasu enshrined in Ise.

iii. The FUJIWARA Era (800–1192)*

It was to free government and politics from priestly interference that NARA was abandoned in 784 and the Capital ultimately established in 794 at HEIAN KYO (Peace and Tranquillity Capital) better known as KYOTO. KYOTO remained the Capital for 1075 years, until the Restoration in 1868, although the seat of the Government was not always in Kyoto—under the rule of the Shoguns and Samurais.

During the first four hundred years of the Heian period there was a rapid growth in the size and number of tax-free estates and it was this development which led to the breakdown of the Fujiwara-Heian (Shogun and Tenno) system and the ascendancy of the warrior class the SAMURAI.

Although the Fujiwaras were on intimate terms with the family of the Tenno, with whom they were related by ties of blood—by maintaining the maternal side for generations—they did not attempt to usurp the throne for their Clan. But from 790 to 890 the Nara priests remained powerful and were always interfering in politics and challenging the position of the Tenno and the Fujiwaras.

In 864 there was created an office of the highest order known as SESSHO-KWAMPAKU or Regent. The holder of the rank was a Sessho during the minority of the Tenno and a Kwampaku when the sovereign took over the reins of Government.

Fujiwara Yoshifusa, six generations removed from the founder

* See Appendix IV and V.

of the Clan, was the first one to hold this office. Then for a thousand years, with the sole exception of Toyotomi Hideyoshi in 1585, it was filled by a Fujiwara.

As I have mentioned in a previous chapter, the Chinese language was the medium of expression in the literary world of Japan until the beginning of the tenth century when the Buddhist priest, Kobo Daishi, invented the I-ro-ha syllabary, and kana was added to kanji. But this merely helped the historians and the limited circle of Japanese to read the Chinese classics, the Nippon Shoki and similar Sino-Japanese books—it left the masses without mental stimulation, without the ability to read or write, without years of study of thousands of complicated characters.

But there was plenty of work for the kika-jins, the naturalized subjects, and the autochthons who preceded them if not for the Ainu who had been subjugated by Kammu Tenno in 805 and driven away from the centre of Japanese culture under the Fujiwaras.

The kika-jins were helping to build temples and shrines while the serfs were tilling the soil. By A.D. 900, there were no less than 3132 Shrines for the devotees of Shintoism and thousands of Temples for the followers of Buddha.

The original doctrine of Buddha knew only one way for people to redeem themselves—by their own strength, with no mediator between god and mortals but in the 3rd Century B.C. images became a permanent institution of the Buddhist church. It was Shomu Tenno who proclaimed his intention to erect a Kokubunji Temple (National Temple) in each province of the Empire to promote the prosperity of the people. His proclamation makes interesting reading, here it is:—

'It is said in a sutra (Konkomyokyo) that if a monarch causes this sutra to be circulated throughout his realm by revering it, reading it, and lecturing on it himself, the four guardian gods will always stay in the land to protect it from all disasters and epidemics, and will also fulfil all the desires of the monarch to his complete satisfaction. Believing these words, we command the governor of each province to raise a seven-storied pagoda and to put in it ten sets each of the Konkomyokyo and the Hokekyo. For ourselves, we will write in letters of gold a set of the Konkomyokyo for each pagoda. Our only wish in launching this project is to bring about the prosperity of the country and the welfare of the people through the spread of the Holy Teaching.'

E

In comformity with this proclamation the Kokubunjis were built all over the country—the TODAIJI of Nara is the mother-temple of them all. But the erection of the Todaiji, and the hundreds of other Kokubunjis, almost exhausted the wealth of the country.

There was an accumulation of the wealth by the temples in the years that followed and the Buddhists claimed that the four guardian gods protected the country from natural calamities and social disasters. And it was not until 1281, when the Mongols of Kublai Khan attacked Kyushu, that the abdicant Kameyama Tenno prayed at the Hachiman Shrine of Iwa shimizu and sent his proxy to the Ise Shrine of AMATERASU to petition her for divine help which came (?) in the shape of KAMI-KAZE the divine wind.

Between 572 and 621 forty-eight large Buddhist temples were constructed but it was not until Kobo Daishi (Kukai) and Saicho returned from China in the ninth century that the movement for combining Shintoism (reverence and worship of ancestors) and Buddhism (faith in a future state of happiness) became an accomplished fact. And although the origin of the sacred dance is based on Amaterasu and her refusal to leave the cave it was MIMASHI—a kika-jin—who introduced a musical dance from South China (690) which became part of the religious ceremonies of Buddhism under the name of Gigaku and was developed into Bugaku about A.D. 850.

In addition to the kokubunji and kokubun-iji (monasteries and nunneries, or temples) the Daigaku (university) had been established in Nara, and the Kokugaku (national schools) in many provinces for the education of government officials. These schools, temples and monasteries taught Buddhist philosophy of the Hosso, Sanron, Kegon, Kusha, Jojitsu and Ritsu sects which did no good to the Fujiwara conception of government But with the transfer of the Capital to Kyoto the aristocratic society produced a native style of literature, the 31-syllable poem called Waka made possible by Kobo Daishi's introduction of the i-ro-ha syllabary. And between 905 and 922 the collection of small poems, Kokinshu, were compiled under the auspices of the Tenno.

As time went on the aristocrats of Heian-kyo extended their power under the divine-umbrella of Tenno Heika. The masses who were harnessed to the system of hakko-ichi-u tilled the soil: the economic wealth of the country, vested in the chosen few, increased by leaps and bounds. Court officials owned the land but the control of it was in the hands of their local representatives.

Soon, the Estates (Sho-En) began to bear the names of the landlord (Myo-Shu) who developed them: Myo-Shu controlling large estates were called Dai-Myo (great landlord) and the lesser agents became Sho-Myo (small landlord). Thus there came into existence an over-lord who had direct control of estates, closer contact with the serfs, and a measure of economical and political influence.

Myoshu shared the revenue from the sho-en with the aristocrats (kizoku) and there came into force dual and even triple ownership under the shoen system. To safeguard their estates the Myoshu organized and maintained their own military establishments in addition to commanding the military guards sent to them from the Heian headquarters of the kizoku. And it was due to this arrangement, of home-guards and regular forces, that the Feudal Baron—Buke, commonly known as Samurai—attained authority in due course.

Under such a system, life was pleasant and easy for the aristocrats if miserably hard for the peasant. Even so, there was a drift away from the public-land to the tax-free estates. As this public-land was abandoned it was absorbed by the sho-en. Times were hard when the kami failed to regulate rain-fall to the needs of the rice crop. Then the Government issued seed-rice, from their ample stocks, to relieve the burden of the agrarian population but this was a mixed blessing for it had to be returned in kind, after the harvest, and returned with interest on the loaned capital, so it stimulated the abandonment of public-lands. Widespread unrest followed in the wake of crop failure: the unemployed became vagrants and thieves. To guard the Capital a Police Commission (Keibi-shi-cho) was established but even it was unable to cope with social unrest which had attained alarming proportions.

Governors were appointed to control all state-owned land and some of them found it an excellent opportunity of remaining in the provinces and taking over the national property for their own use. They had a good reason for this action. The Fujiwaras were so dominant in Heian that it was hopeless for lesser clansmen to compete with them for a share of the Tenno's patrimony.

It was from these land-grabbing provincial off-shoots of the Fujiwaras that the powerful clans of TAIRA (Heiki) in the west and MINAMOTO (Genji) in the east arose. These clans, several generations earlier, sprang from branch lines of the Tenno's family and they became prominent in a later period of Heian history.

The entire country was now broken up into numerous tax-free estates and the Fujiwara family absorbed many of them in order to extend their wealth and power until they grew into an auto-cracy at the expense of the State and the Tenno. In addition to the rapacity of the Fujiwaras there was another element working against the peaceful progress of the Imperial Rule. The Bud-dhist clergy: under the cloak of religion they had built up a mental ascendancy over the masses and now turned it into the channels of political strife. At first they had served the State by disseminating the correct principles of 'Imperial Rule' through certain of the Buddhist scriptures. For this service they had been generously rewarded by grants of tax-free land so—for the first hundred years of Heian period—they were to maintain a mode of life equal, if not better, than that enjoyed by the most prosperous of the aristocratic bureaucracy. But now, with the changed conditions, the Temples and Monasteries ceased to be purely religious centres as the Monks and Priests took their stand as part and parcel of the rising power of feudalism.

The Buddhist movement started in 805-6 when the two famous priests, Dengyo Daishi and Kobo Daishi, broke away from the NARA tradition to found the Tendai and Shingon sects. Now the academic pursuit of Buddhism was switched over to the promotion of national welfare through religion. The priests became allies of the Heian clique and were not concerned with the living conditions of the farmers or the fisherman. The labourers, on land and sea, had to slave from early dawn to late at night in order that priest and bureaucrat should prosper. They were serfs in the RYO-BU-STATE—serfs who were taught that their only consolation was in offering prayers to their UJI-GAMI (tutelary deities) in the hope that when their miserable lives were ended they might find a haven of rest with their kami in the land of lotus flowers.

However, the fact remains that Buddhism was the chief source of inspiration in the arts. Under the influence of the Tendai and Shingon sects the images, in sculpture and painting departing from symbolism reflecting divine grace to the characteristics of the human form. Architecture began to blend with natural surroundings: dwellings of the aristocracy became magnificent palaces and grand castles surrounded by moats and kept up by well fed and well clothed retainers.

Domestic industries were established and the need for money arose as the tillers of the soil left the land to manufacture the luxuries and the necessities of his kami—his superiors. Cloth and gold dust were used at first to facilitate trade. Then coins were imported from China and a token of common value was established to take the place of barter in the exchange of commodities.

Literature was not neglected. In addition to the Fujiwara 'National Histories' which concluded with the Sandai Jitsuroku in 901, there followed in 1000 the EIGA MONOGATARI and the O-KAGAMI—both concerned with the family history of the Fujiwara. Details of court life were recorded in diaries like Mido Kwanpaku-ki, Sho-yu-ki, Chu-yu-ki and Tai-ki. But perhaps the best known piece of Heian literature is the Genji Monogatari, written in 1023 by Murasaki Shikibu (Lady Murasaki) and the Makura-no-Soshi (Pillow Book) written by Sei Shonagon—another court lady of the same time.

I have previously commented on the fact that during the first four hundred years of the Heian period the small-holdings were transferred into extensive tax-free estate with the consequent decrease in public-owned land. In 1068, the expansion of Fujiwara power was checked when Go-SANJO Tenno decided to attend in person to the affairs of State. He decreed the confiscation of all SHO-EN formed since 1045 and of all other estates of earlier creation which could not produce valid charters. This edict served to curb Fujiwara aggrandisement but was without much effect on the DAIMYO themselves.

Foiled in this attempt to rule his dominions outside the Capital the Tenno, SHIRAKAWA, in 1073, established an administration known as INSEI (cloistered government). Shirakawa—

who had abdicated—maintained a separate Palace and was assisted by his own officers. The INSEI lasted for fifty years and helped to restore some political authority to the Throne. This cloistered government was followed by the KAMAKURA regime in 1168 which came into existence as a result of Imperial recognition of the SAMURAI and resulted in Japan being dominated by a combination of Samurai, Fujiwaras and Buddhist priests.

In the twelfth century, among the prominent Samurai class in the provinces were the TAIRA and MINAMOTO clans who had attained great influence in their respective domains in western and in eastern Japan. As descendants of Imperial branch lines they were held in great respect by other Samurais. In 1156 and in 1160 these two clans were involved in incidents, arising out of an internal strife (inside the Fujiwara family circle) regarding the Imperial succession. After four years of fighting against each other the TAIRA were victors under KIYOMORI their leader and he was appointed to the office of Prime Minister by the Tenno, in 1165.

The TAIRA clan established their headquarters in Heian and thoroughly enjoyed the luxurious atmosphere of the Capital. They lived on the fat of the land, became soft and lost a lot of their fighting quality whereas the MINAMOTO clan, smarting under their defeat, reorganized their forces and (after a few years of preparation) reopened hostilities. There was heavy and bitter fighting, in eastern and western Japan, but in 1185—at the sea battle of Dan-no-ura, near Shimonoseki—the Minamotos under their leader YORITOMO gained the victory and ended the war against the Taira clan.

Yoritomo established his headquarters at KAMAKURA, the home of his ancestors.

iv. The Samurai Regimes. (KAMAKURA: 1192–1334)*

Minamoto Yoritomo was appointed 'General of the Imperial Guard' following his victory at Dan-no-ura, and in 1192 received the title of Sei-i-tai-Shogun, with instructions to maintain order in the country. He was given permission to appoint, from among his own vassals, supervisors of the SHO-EN with authority to collect taxes from all manors at the rate of one-fifth of the rice yield.

* See Appendix V.

When he was appointed Shogun (1192), Yoritomo obtained a national as well as an official position for his Samurai regime, and—warned by the fate of the Taira clan—he remained at Kamakura, to be clear of the demoralizing influence of Heian and the court clique. His followers developed the martial side of their newly founded regime free from the frivolities of the aristocrats and the priests.

Yoritomo was succeeded by his eldest son, YORIIYE, who was followed by his son SANETOMO both of whom became Shogun by Imperial appointment. But strife followed the death of Yoritomo. The Minamoto Regime had been established with the support of the most powerful of the eastern clans—the HOJO. With the passing of Yoritomo the defacto authority at Kamakura went to the Hojo clan, and while dispossesed Samurai were being organized against the Hojo they themselves clashed with Heian court officials and the result was the Shokyu War of 1221.

To the Heian bureaucracy the rise of the KAMAKURA SAMURAI was deemed contradictory to the traditional principles of government centred in the Imperial throne. The HOJO REGENT, Yoshitoki, declared that his Samurai were hostile only to the court officials. If the cloistered TENNO should command an army against him he would immediately halt his troops. However, a battle was fought between the contending factions, and as a result of it—the three former Emperors, GO-TOBA, JUN-TOKU and TSUCHIMIKADO were exiled to Oki, Sado and Tosa together with the court officials responsible for the anti-Kamakura movement.

The Hojo Regent made no attempt to usurp the throne for himself. In 1222 another Tenno—Go-Horikawa—was raised to the doubtful dignity of 'divine ruler' under the patronage of the Samurai. But the regency of the Hojo differed from that of the Fujiwara: Fujiwara was appointed Sessho-Kwampaku by the Tenno to *assist in the administration of the government,* the HOJO Regent—or 'Shikken'—was self-appointed to assist the SHOGUN Tokugawa.

The banished Tenno, Go-Toba, was fond of flowers—especially the Chrysanthemum. He had the design of a double, sixteen-petal, Chrysanthemum placed on his robes and personal belongings. Other Tenno also used the design and it became the MONSHO or Imperial Crest.

In olden days the people compared this flower to the Sun and called it 'The Spirit of the Sun', and in later years the 'Supreme Order of the Chrysanthemum' became the highest Japanese decoration followed by the 'Rising Sun', 'Precious Crown', 'Sacred Treasure' and the Military Order of the 'Golden Kite'. But it was typical of the times that it was a banished Tenno who originated the Imperial Crest during the Samurai Regime of Kamakura.

The growth and expansion of the Kamakura Regime led to a general collapse of the old Heian social and economic order. It caused a mental and spiritual shake-up of the old order among those whose entire lives had been founded on the pleasant arrangements of Heian. Some of the aristocracy advocated co-operation with the Kamakura Samurai as the best solution of their troubles but the majority decided to continue in the best Heian traditions.

In the thirteenth century the basis of livelihood, of all classes was rice and rice yields. With the advent of money-tokens price fluctuation raised its ugly head despite numerous government regulations and methods of price fixing and trade regulations. As this price movement was also linked to the contemporary development of 'industry and commerce' the price control method was ineffective.

The land-tax itself eventually came to be collected in cash instead of rice. But land values also fluctuated. Economic uncertainty resulted and this enabled the money-lenders to increase their importance in society, by holding land in security and loaning cash. Business thrived for a time. Money-lenders made fortunes and they were appointed magistrates with direct political control over the land which came into their possession all over the country.

The foremost characteristics of Kamakura history are to be found in the intrigues among the priests, two-sworded Samurai, aristocratic parasites, and the rise to the top of the money-lenders.

Social conditions deteriorated, unrest increased. The masses turned more and more to the inspiration of Buddhism. Religious movements battened on misery and discontent; and the aristocrats and literators continued to produce books for their own pleasure and edification—the mass of the people were illiterate and remained so until after the Restoration in 1868.

In 1223, Fujiwara Kanezane's GUKANSHO was completed, and—at about the same time——the AZUMA KAGAMI, dealing with the Kamakura Regime, appeared. This was followed by the first of many books dealing with Shinto—the 'Shinto-gobu-no-sho'. It expounded Shinto by means of the logic of Buddhism, Confucianism and Taoism, and it is popularly described as the 'Shinto Pentateuch' although considered by modern Japanese to be too foreign to the real conception of Shinto. However, it was not Shinto—as a cult or as a religion—but Chinese—Buddhism which had revolutionized philosophical and religious thought in Japan.

With the manufacture of paper, and wood-block printing, great advances in 'civilization' had been made when Minamoto Yoritomo, 'General of the Imperial Guard', was appointed Shogun in 1192. The rise of the Samurai, under Minamoto Yoritomo, coincided with the renewed activities of the Mongols under Temujin—better known as Jengis Khan, 'Emperor of All Men', who was born in 1159 in the Gobi Desert.

The T'ang Dynasty passed away in the tenth century. Now there were three 'Empires' in China proper: in the north there was the Tungus KIN Dynasty with a capital at Yen-king, near the modern Peking: in the south there was the native (Chinese) SUNG Dynasty having its seat of government in Nanking, and—in addition—the 'middle-kingdom' of HSIA.

The KIN, or 'Golden Dynasty', were a branch of the Khitan (Cathay) tribe of Mongols who founded the Liao Dynasty, in the Liao-tung area of Manchuria, in 936. The Khitans were but one of the numerous nomad tribes—Mongols, Tartars, Niu-chi, Karaits, Naimans, Kirghiz—roaming the country north of the Great Wall of China to Siberia.

The MONGOLS were of Ural-Altaian or Turanian stock. Their native religion was Shamanism, a mixture of spirit and ancestor worship not unlike the 'religion' of the earliest inhabitants of Japan, but they were not hostile to Buddhism, Confucianism, Taoism or Christianity. One of the tribes, the Keraits (or Karaits), who ranged the steppes to the south-east of Lake Baikal, were converted to Christianity in the eleventh century by Nestorian traders and missionaries driven out of China proper by hostile Emperors.

One of the lesser Mongol tribes was led by Yesukai the father of TEMUJIN who became famous as Jengis Kha Khan in 1206 after his horde defeated the Keraits and occupied their 'city' of KARAKORUM in the Gobi Desert. Jengis (or Genghis) Khan had united under his rule the tribes to the north of the Gobi Desert and among his followers were the Tatars (or Tartars) and other wandering Turks.

Jengis Khan had two objectives—the conquest of China and the conquest of the West. In 1214, Jengis Khan as leader of the Mongol confederates defeated the forces of WAI WANG, Emperor of the 'Golden Dynasty', and captured Yen-king and the country in the vicinity of the Great Wall of China.

In 1210, when Jengis Khan was still a 'subject of the Golden Emperor', and expected to pay tribute to the over-lord, he had been given the title of 'Commander Against Rebels'. Now, as the master, he appointed the Mongol general Muhuli as ruler of all Cathay with instructions to conquer the Sung Empire in the south.

Jengis Khan returned to Karakorum to prepare for his second objective—the conquest of the West. But it was not until the spring of 1219, when the Regent Hojo Yoshitoki had disposed of the Yoritomo leaders and beheaded the Shogun Sanetomo, that he marched out of the Gobi Desert with 250,000 men for Persia—a mere 2,000 miles away from his base of operations.

The 'objective' was the domain of Mohammed Shah of Kharesm which extended from India to Baghdad and from the sea of Aral to the Persian Gulf. The struggle was between the Mongol horde and the Turks—between Mohammedan and unbeliever. But although Jengis Khan was known as the 'Scourge of God' all 'religions' were protected within the Mongol frontiers.

From 1219 to 1227—when Jengis died—the Mongol hordes carried their 'banners' through Turkestan, Armenia, Kiev, the Crimea and into India as far as Lahore. Two years of mourning followed the death of the 'Scourge of God', then—in 1235—the second stage of the Mongol conquest was set in motion by OGOTAI KHAN from his base in the Gobi Desert. In the interval, the Mongols had consolidated their position in the Middle East under the generals Chatagai, Tuli, Batu and Subotai. From 1238 to 1241 the Mongol hordes overran the Russian cities and the steppes of the Black Sea—stormed Kiev and raided Ruthenia in Poland.

Subotai was the master-mind of the well disciplined, well armed and well mounted Mongol army. In 1241 he was opposed by a mixed force of Poles, Bavarians, Teutonic Knights and Templars out of France, Bohemians, Austrians and Magyars from Hungary. On 18 March 1241, the Poles were defeated at Cracov, and on 9 April the Germans and Poles were exterminated at Leignitz. Then the horde ravaged Silesia and Moravia and defeated the Magyars, Croats and Germans at Mohi. This victory was followed by the storming of Pesth and the outskirts of Gran. In less than two months the Mongols overran Europe from the Elbe to the sea and defeated three 'western armies' and saddled the 'Tartar Yoke' on the Russians.

Batu and Subotai went on as far as the gates of Vienna and the Adriatic but withdrew in 1242 when the news of the death of the Kha Khan Ogotai reached them. The leaders returned to Karakorum, to elect another Kha Khan, but the Mongol horde settled down in Persia and in the territory of Hungvar the seat of Attila's Empire which was founded at Buda on the Danube in A.D. 445.

The death of Ogotai (1241) was followed by an interregnum of several years during which period Ogotai's widow acted as Regent for her eldest son—Kuyuk—who was serving in Hungary.

Kuyuk was elected Kha Khan in 1246. He died in 1248 and his death was followed by a feud, between the houses of Gengis Khan's sons, Chatagai and Ogotai, which lasted until 1251 when (according to Mongol custom) the general assembly of princes, members of the ruling family and high officials, decided in favour of Mangu and Kublai, sons of Tuli who was the youngest son of Jengis Khan by his consort Bourtai.

It was about this time (1246) that the Regent Hojo Tokiyori decreed that all future Regents of Japan should be chosen from the Fujiwara houses of Ichijo, Nijo, Kujo, Konoe and Takatsukasa and not—as previously—from Kujo and Konoe only and that the Fujiwaras were to continue to supply Empresses for the Tenno and consorts for the Shoguns.

In 1251, Mangu Kha Khan despatched Hulagu Khan (brother of Kublai) with a large army to destroy the Ismailis and the Caliphate.

The third Mongol conquest lasted from 1251 to 1281 but these Mongol operations in the west were subsidiary to those against China. Hulagu, co-operating with a son of the great Mongol general Subotai, invaded Mesopotamia and captured Baghdad in 1258 after the conquest of Persia and Syria. After the destruction of Baghdad, Damascus was occupied, and Cairo was the remaining great centre of Islam. The Mongols were ruthless in their methods of warfare: they massacred the population of Baghdad and reduced Mesopotamia into a wilderness, and they had the most amazing success against European armies.

Antioch became subject to the Mongol horde who penetrated into Asia Minor as far as Smyrna—a short distance from the city of Constantinople. However, the Egyptian army of Turks and Circassians—known as the Mameluk—under their general Baybars defeated the Mongols at Ain-Jalut on 3rd September, 1260. The Mongols were checked: Hulagu returned to Karakorum following the death of Mangu Kha Khan in 1260, and the Empire of the Khan—in the Middle East—was broken up into enclaves, the fierce nomads from the Gobi Desert embraced Buddhism or the religion of the Moslims.

Mangu Khan's mother, Suirkukit, was a member of the Christian Kerait tribe and Mangu's creed is said to have been: 'We Mongols believe that there is only one God by whom we live and by whom we die, and for whom we have an upright heart. But as God gives us the different fingers of the hand, so he gives to men divers ways. God gave you (the Christians) the Scriptures, and you do not keep them; he gave us diviners, we do what they tell us, and we live in peace.'

Kublai Kha Khan

After the subjugation of the Sung Empire, 1250, Kublai was made Governor of 'China' (1251) and, after the death of Mangu in 1260, elected Great Khan of the Mongols. Kublai was the first of the Mongol Emperors to rule inside the Great Wall of China—he moved his capital from Karakorum to Khan-baliq 'City of the Khan'—or Cambulac, the Mongol name for modern Peking.

Soon after his accession to the rank of Kha Khan, Kublai adopted the Chinese name of 'Yuan' as the title of his Empire in Europe and Asia. His Mongol hordes extended his frontiers down to the Malay States and beyond Tibet into Bengal. By the year 1279 he had completed the conquest of 'China' which included Korea, Indo-China and Burma, but when he died—in 1292—there were independent Khans in Mongolia, Persia and Russia and the great Mongol Empire was breaking up again.

The whole interior of Asia was under the rule of the Mongols and there was safety for travellers. To Cambulac came envoys from the Pope, Buddhist Priests, Parisian and Italian artificers, Persian and Indian astronomers and mathematicians. Among the earliest visitors were Nicolo and Maffeo Polo—jewellers from Venice. They created a good impression and were sent back to Europe with a message from the Kha Khan to the Pope. They left Cambulac in 1266 and reached Acre in 1269 by the overland route but it was not until 1273 that Nicolo Polo and his son Marco arrived at the court of Kublai Khan, with the reply of the Pope.

The Polos remained in China for seventeen years. Marco was a particular favourite of the Mongol Emperor and he sent him on many missions to different parts of his domain—South China, Tibet and Burma—and for three years Marco ruled as Governor of Yang-chou—but he did not go to Korea or to Japan. After accumulating a large fortune the Polos left China by the sea-route in 1292 with a fleet of fourteen ships provided by the Kha Khan. They travelled by the way of Malaya, Ceylon, the Persian Gulf and thence overland to Constantinople and Venice which was reached in 1295.

I have indulged in this digression, regarding the Mongols, in order to remind the reader that the warriors of Japan, in 1941-45, had most of the traits of their ancestors the Mongols: they had the same type of brutal military efficiency, discipline, and grandiose conceptions of Empire. And also to set the scene for the abortive 'invasion' of Japan by the Mongols in 1274 and 1281.

It was Marco Polo who fired Kublai Khan's imagination regarding the Japanese barbarians and the amount of gold in the country.

Supported by the Koreans, the Mongols made the first attempt—in 1274—to conquer Japan but the invaders were repulsed with heavy casualties. An envoy was sent by Kublai Khan to the Hojo Regent Tokimune to demand tribute but he answered by decapitating them. In answer to this insult to his

'over-lordship' the Kha Khan ordered another expedition in 1281.
Four thousand ships, manned by 150,000 (?) Mongols and
Koreans attacked Kyushu. But this armada suffered the same
fate. The Mongol horsemen were accustomed to swift movements on land and not versed in the arts of amphibious-
warfare—like the Japanese of the twentieth century.

Forewarned of the intentions of the Mongols the Japanese set
aside their religious and secular problems and prepared to
defend the sacred soil of the Yamato-jin. The Samurai were put
to the supreme test and fought with the courage of desperation
for they were under no illusions regarding the issues involved—
the unarmed masses flocked to the temples and shrines to pray
for help from their kami. The abdicant Tenno—Kameyama—
prostrated himself, before the Hachiman Shrine of Iwashimizu
near Kyoto, and sent a messenger to the Ko-dai-jingu at Ise to
pray to Amaterasu O-mikami for divine assistance.

During both invasions the elements helped the defenders—
storms came to the rescue of the Samurai and scattered the
Mongol fleet, and the few who landed were cut to the ground by
the two-handed swords of the natives. At the time of the second
invasion the issue was in doubt for fifty-three days. Then the
Mongol fleet was wiped out by a Tai-Feng (Typhoon—'Great
Wind') which raged near the 'Islands of Five Dragons'. But—
according to the Japanese—a miracle had been performed by
Amaterasu O-Mikami and Kami had fought on Japan's side in
the shape of wind. From that time the word 'KAMI-KAZE'—
Divine Wind—has symbolized the faith of the Japanese in the
belief that 'Providence' is constantly with them in times of national
adversity, and like the sacred Mount Fuji became part and parcel
of the Shinto traditions of the nation in peace and during war.

Although the Yuan Dynasty—founded by Kublai Kha Khan
—lasted until 1368 no other attempt was made by the Mongols
to subjugate the Japanese. The revolt of the Chinese against
their Mongol rulers (1368) resulted in the rise of the Ming
Dynasty under Chu Yuan-chang but it was not until 1555 that
the Mongols lost the last of their strongholds in Russia to Ivan
the Terrible.

Commerce and industry made rapid strides after the failure of
Kublai Kha Khan to gain a footing in Japan and explore the

gold mines of the country. Merchants and craftsmen organized themselves into guilds for mutual benefit. Trade with South China, which was hostile to the Mongolians, became increasingly active and profitable to both sides. But there was 'a fly in the ointment': the Samurai who had played the active part in defeating the Mongols—by aid of the 'divine Wind'—demanded more agricultural land as gratuities for their services with the sword and, by this time, the Kamakura Regime had lost most of its political power and had no spare rice-fields to bestow on Samurais in Kyushu or elsewhere in the country. Indeed, Kamakura's economic prestige had been on the decline since 1264 because of the national unrest which has already been mentioned in this chapter.

And now the priests and monks, the moneylenders, nouveau riche (narikins), the Hojo, Fujiwara and other sycophants were acting together under the banner of 'Back to Traditional Government centred in Tenno Heika' in an intrigue to pacify the people of the soil and undermine the power of the Samurai.

It was this insincere 'patriotic movement' which inspired the exiled Tenno, Go Daigo, to assert his 'rights' in 1334. Go Daigo had occupied the throne since 1319 but had angered the Regent Takatoki by setting up his son as Crown Prince in defiance of the ruling of the Regent that the throne should be held alternatively by Go Fukakusa's line and that of Kameyama. This revolt of the 'sacred Emperor' was quelled and Go Daigo exiled to Oki, to join Go Toba Tenno and the others, but his followers continued the insurrection. The Regent's party ordered the Ashikaga general Takauji to destroy them but the Ashikaga clans joined the Imperialists and captured Kyoto. At the same time, a Minamoto clan (Yoshiie) attacked and destroyed Kamakura, routed the Hojo army and ended the rule of the Hojos. This was the end of Kamakura as the military capital of Japan.

Ashikaga Takuji was appointed Shogun and he made an attempt to recover Kamakura for the Hojo family but this brought about war between the Ashikagas and the Imperial Family. The Imperialists were defeated at Minatogawa, near Kobe: Go Daigo surrendered and was imprisoned but escaped to Yoshino where he set up a rival Court when Komyo Tenno was placed on the throne by Takuji in 1338.

Between the years 1156 and 1319 there were twenty Emperors of Japan all nominated by Regent or Clan. Their reigns averaged a bare eight years so their importance, and the precarious nature of their authority—under the aegis of Shogun, Regent or Samurai—may be estimated at its true value in the Shinto State of those days.

Conditions generally, if we exclude the numerous Tenno, were similar to those which existed in England under Norman Rule: land was divided into feuds held on condition that the tenants supported their warlords. Tenants owed allegiance to the most powerful of the Daimyo, to the Shogun or to the Regent and his clique, and with the decline of the Kamakura faction another Samurai regime stepped in to perpetuate the methods of administration instituted by Minamoto Yoritomo in 1192.†

v. ASHIKAGA: *Samurai Regime (1340–1570)* *

The next 250 years of recorded Japanese history is a recitation of disorder, turmoil and instability at home coupled with a rapid expansion of overseas trade. The evolution of Japan, in this particular period, was (to a limited extent) the counterpart of the historical evolution of England in the later Middle Ages *plus* the Hundred Years' War, War of the Roses and the Tudor Period *without* the focus on the divinity of the Sovereign in relation to Mythology—and, of course, without a Parliament.

(This synopsis of Japanese history is not intended to appeal to serious students of 'dates and facts' arranged in precise chronology. There are many excellent books on Japanese History, written by Japanese or European experts to which the student may turn at his leisure. The information which I am presenting has been culled from the bulk of evidence contained in books written by modern Japanese historians, or foreign commentators. My very limited objective is to shed light on Bushido, Shinto, Buddhism, Hakko-ichi-u and Samurai lore, and on the inaccurate claims about loyalty to the Tenno existing in all ages, under all conditions from the Nara period to the Tokyo period of 1941-45. Any inaccuracy—regarding facts—is due to the historians' who placed it on paper in the first instance and not to any bias on my part. My comment is based on an intimate knowledge of Japan and the Japanese from 1883

* — † See Appendix V.

—including first hand experience of the Russo-Japanese War and the recent episode in the Far East.)

Samurai Regimes were the logical outcome of Fujiwara conception of government: a Divine Ruler controlled by force and manipulated by religious propaganda to dupe illiterate subjects into an acceptance of despotism by a minority of opportunists. Twelve-hundred years of Fujiwara, Kamakura, Ashikaga and Tokugawa dictatorship (the medley of Shogun, Daimyo, Monk and Samurai followed by the Shinto-Military subjugation of body and soul of the common people from 1868 to 1945) may have penetrated the national character too deeply to permit of an emotional change within the next generation unless the physical and mental domination of the victors in World War II is tempered by a wise understanding of the problem to be solved before Japan becomes a Christian Democracy in the best sense of the meaning of the words.

The Restoration of Go Daigo Tenno (Kemmu—1334) was aimed at refusing recognition of the Kamakura but it was merely a means to an end. The development of commerce and spread of money-economy made the simple ownership of land insufficient for the luxury of priests and layman cluttering the Heian capital—the 'restoration' was a simple way for plundering and exploiting the commoner. First of all it was decided to reorganize the system of land tenure so that land would be re-distributed to the partial exclusion of certain Samurai and their cohorts. This was a failure—the Samurai were well armed, they fought for their 'rights' and this brought about the Yoshino period of fifty years of conflict.

When Go Daigo was banished to Yoshino the Ashikaga Samurai made their headquarters at MUROMACHI, in Kyoto. Go-Komatsu Tenno was enthroned in Heian in 1393 but from 1332 to 1393 there had been another line of Tennos, the Koku-cho or Northern Dynasty. Go Komatsu was the sixth Tenno, in this group, and had been on the 'throne' since 1384. But now he was enthroned in the *direct* line of succession to the exclusion of Go Daigo's branch of the Imperial Family.*

The ASHIKAGAS, blood descendants of MINAMOTO YORITOMO, took over the Kamakura system of political administration

* See Appendix V—Ashikaga Shoguns.

F

which had been established two hundred years earlier but they ruled in HEIAN and not in KAMAKURA. That was their undoing. The environment was too much for them—they became easy victims of the lascivious plutocracy which lacinated their morals and undermined their physique, with the result that the administration of the country 'went to the dogs'. Because they were nothing more than Daimyo landlords (on a grand scale) the Ashikagas were unable to maintain political control over the 'land-and-rice' economics when trade was increasing by leaps and bounds. Realising this they joined forces with the merchants and by contact with 'trade' their physical control of the nation lost much of its virile samurai characteristics. But it was not the 'profit motive' but internal strife over another succession dispute which destroyed the Ashikaga Regime and caused the ten year War of Onin with the attendant sword-swinging and land grabbing by the rival factions.

This breakdown of the clan-system and the birth of the family-system was not confined to the Ashikagas. Other Daimyo joined in, taking sides in the dispute to correspond to their territorial requirements and safety. Territorial groups were engaged in ceaseless fighting to expand their power and authority, now—as never before—the code of the Samurai—the law of the two-handed swordsmen—and the 'spirit of Bushido' had ample scope for expression in an orgy of blood-letting. No code of morals was involved in the War of Onin—the internecine tribal rivalry had as its incentive the sordid scramble for a share in trade. Priests, moneylenders and Samurai had their money-spinning ventures to protect and to expand.

Japan was trading on a vast scale (for a small industrial nation) with the Ryukyu Islands, Formosa, Korea, China, Siam, Java, Sumatra and India. The Ming Dynasty placed restrictions on foreign trade but Japanese traders found little difficulty in overcoming Chinese laws. They sailed up the Yangtze to Chekiang and Nanking—their armed junks made trips to Hainan, Canton, Fukien, Shantung and Liaotung although this 'trading' was tantamount to piracy. Profit—from this overseas trade—added to harsh internal taxation, enriched the Ashikagas and the warring Daimyo but it forced those Samurai who were excluded from the 'rackets' to combine their forces with discontented farmers and the serfs.

The malcontents were not too well armed so they staged riots and resisted the profiteers by refusing to work for them. It was an age of scramble: traders, merchants, pawnbrokers, daimyos, samurais, priests and monks all feathering their nests and there was not a vestige of the earlier conception of 'one household under the heavens' in the attitude of the rulers to Tenno, People or the Sun Goddess enshrined at Ise; all that had gone in fact if not in the fiction handed down in the histories. Early in the fourteenth century the Japanese had lost touch with Shinto but, about 1350, Kitabatake Chikafusa wrote the JINNO-SHOTOKI (True Successions of the Divine Emperors) for the edification of Go MURAKAMI Tenno, and this loyalist expounded the kamu-nagara theosophy that Japan 'is a country of the gods'.

According to Professor Komazo Mizoguchi, an authority on Shintoism, writing in 1935, the reasoning of Kitabatake Chika-fusa's JINNO SHOTOKI is that . . . ' our Great Japan has been founded by the Goddess, ancestor of all the Emperors, and has been governed by her divine descendants from generation to generation according to her principles. This is characteristically peculiar to Japan, and therefore, he concludes, Japan is a divine country. This reasoning is more advanced than that of the Shinto-gobu-no-sho.'

The reasoning may be different but it does not square with the historic facts. This persistent explanation of the thearchy of Japan under Shogun, Samurai and abdicant Tenno is in keeping with the 'National Shinto Faith' of the twentieth century, under the Gumbatsu, and is typical of the theanthropic mind of Japanese.

A few years later (according to the same authority on Shintoism) Urabe Kanetomo, a scholar of the Ashikaga period, wrote the Yuiitsu-Shinto-Myobo-Yoshu (Catechism of Genuine Unitary Shinto) in which he declared . . . ' that the way of the Japanese Gods was only one; that although there were numerous gods, yet the way of the Holiest Deity, Amaterasu Omikami, the ancestress of the Emperors, was the only way, and was free from all the influences of Confucianism, Buddhism or Taoism, as it had been cultivated purely on Japanese soil. This theory went a long way to purify Shintoism and restore it to the indigenous Japanese spirit.'

But the Japanese were by no means free from the influence of Buddhism. In 1237, the Kamakura BUDDHA AMIDA was erected, a 35 feet high image of one of the five meditative Buddhas, of the Mahayana doctrine, Amitabha. The Amitabha dogma, based on the personification of endless light, came into existence in Kashmir during the second century A.D., and was probably introduced into Japan in the Nara period. This Buddhist saint 'thrones on a lotus flower in the Paradise of the West where everyone is free from suffering, surrounded by wonderful scenery, beautiful trees, ponds and lotus flowers, and pavilions made out of precious stones' and no doubt appealed to the imagination of the Japanese just as much as Amaterasu, because the KAMAKURA period was one of intense human suffering and want. The priests, Honen, Shinran and Ippen assured them that they would attain happiness if they had absolute faith in Buddha.

It was during this period of unrest that NICHIREN appeared: he based his teaching on the Lotus Scriptures, seeking to bring peace and security to the people by stabilizing the State around the Throne. But perhaps the greatest influence was exerted by the ZEN temples of Enkakuji and Kenchoji in Kamakura.

BODAI DARUMA (Bodhidharma) was the founder of the ZEN sect of Buddhism. Son of a South-Indian King he settled in China about A.D. 520, and is reputed to have remained motion-less in a temple—absorbed in meditation—for nine years until his arms and legs rotted from his body. He died (?) on October 5th A.D. 535, and his mission was left in charge of two disciples —Eka and Do-iku Zenshi.

In the year A.D. 613, DARUMA rose from the grave: standing on reed leaves he sailed for Japan. One day (so the story pro-ceeds)—in A.D. 613—Prince Shotoku found a man dying by the roadside and had him buried. His attendants were surprised at this action of their Prince but he informed them that the man was an old friend of his in a former life, a saint—Daruma, the High Priest of Southern Heaven who had come to pay him a visit and that he had now returned to his heavenly abode.

The attendants went to the grave and found it undisturbed— they opened up the grave. The coffin was intact. The body had disappeared leaving only the garment which had been placed around the man by the Prince. Shotoku wore the garment ever afterwards, carved an image of the Saint and had a Shrine built over his tomb.

The spirit of ZEN has influenced Japanese thought and art more than most other Buddhist sects. Zen temples had halls of discipline where the priests composed their thoughts. Regular members of the sect were assigned a tatami (straw mat 6 feet by 3 feet) on which to sit in meditation, or to sleep on during the night. Each priest's problem was written for him on a wooden tablet: sitting cross-legged, hands placed one on top of the other in front of him to give ease and body balance, necessary for mental equilibrium, he breathed gently through the nostrils until he reached the simple and unbiassed mental state of a child. Then he concentrated his soul upon the problem on the tablet of wood before him.

Day after day he sat and meditated until he had reached a solution. Then he went from the hall of discipline to the temple, sounded the gong and waited to receive a hearing from the high priest. When the high priest was ready he rang a bell: the noviciate entered the high priest's room and recited the solution of his problem. If the solution was correct he was given a fresh problem to work out—if not he returned with the old one and started all over again.

There were 2700 problems to be solved before a priest could consider himself enlightened sufficiently to answer with a simple Yes or No to the problems of his followers.

Although esoteric Buddhism was the religion favoured by the Court and the Shogunate during the Ashikaga period, the cult of ZENSHU—teaching meditation, reflection and self-absorption and not the study of holy writings, words or deeds—spread among the middle classes and made its influence felt in literature, manners and customs, and in art and architecture. Its aim was to transmit truth from one mind to another without the medium of words.

The design of Japanese gardens express the ideals of Zenshu and Zen priests were mainly responsible for the writing of NOH drama in its early days when complete self-annihilation in death was considered necessary in order to reach Nirvanah.

NOH plays are often concerned with spirits of people detained on earth by their memories, unfulfilled passions or jealousies: only by giving up self completely might they reach eternal peace: thought was creative—a person could be what he 'thought himself to be', and Zenshu catered to the military mind, was the inspiration of Bushido, in the seventeenth century, and of Cha-no-yu the tea ceremony.

It was Kobo Daishi who brought back from China some tea seed in A.D. 806 but tea drinking did not become a habit until 1191: ZEN demanded concentrated thinking so bowls of tea were given to the priests to keep their minds alert during contemplation, but it was also a substitute for sake—rice wine.

In 1214 when Shogun Sanetomo was suffering from excessive use of sake, the priest Eisai administered a bowl of tea. Its beneficial effect was so marked that the Shogun encouraged the use of tea among his sake drinking vassals. But it was not until two-hundred years later (Ashikaga period) that Noami, a henchman of the Shogun Yoshimasa, originated cha-no-yu—tea served in a special room with the aid of a stand.

The Ginkakuji Temple (Silver Pavilion) in Kyoto is the birth place of ikebana (flower arrangement) and cha-no-yu (tea ceremony) originated in a small 4½-tatami room dedicated to the memory of Buddha. This temple was built by the eighth Ashikaga Shogun—Yoshimasa—when he abdicated in favour of his son Yoshihisa and he also built a small villa, which was set in a beautiful garden, and a three-storied temple the ceiling of which was plated with silver.

This was in 1487 and the ex-Shogun Yoshimasa, attended by cha-bozu (tea-priests), superintended cha-no-yu and ikebana as a devotee of Zenshu. Cha-no-yu was founded upon the adoration of beauty as we find it in the daily routine of life, and the grandmaster of cha-no-yu—Yoshimasa—lived like Amitabha 'in the Paradise of the West, surrounded by wonderful scenery, beautiful trees, ponds and lotus flowers, and pavilions made out of precious stones.' But all this had to do with the Zen sect of Buddhism and not with Shinto, Amaterasu, hakko-ichi-u or the divine Tenno.

The best room in almost every Japanese house, however humble, had an alcove of tatami size (6 feet by 3 feet)—like a Buddhist praying mat—called the *Tokonoma*. Here was placed, on this family altar, an image of Buddha, an offering of flowers and a pot of burning incense, before which—morning and evening—the whole family gathered together to worship. But the *tokonoma* was devised for the purpose of venerating Buddha and not for invoking Amaterasu.

However, the involution of Buddhism and Shinto kept pace with the times. In the Nara period there were six sects of Buddhism—Jojitsu, Sanron, Kusha, Hosso, Kegon, and Ritsu—to which were added (in the earlier Heian period) Tendai and Shingon. Then, in the Kamakura era, Jodo, Zen, Shin and Nichiren sects appeared on the scene. The building of temples, and of shrines, became a major occupation for the priests and their vassals while the Daimyo continued to erect their secular strongholds in all parts of the country in order to supervise their slaves.

The fortified homes of the Clans began to appear in the pre-Nara period of Japanese History and from primitive earthworks developed into magnificent Castles modified to suit the changing conditions of tribal warfare, but it was the introduction in 1543 by the Portuguese of the first matchlock which had the greatest effect on the construction of the strongholds of the major and the minor Daimyo and Shogun.

The massive and solid type of Japanese Castle owes its inspiration to the military requirements of Oda Nobunaga and Toyotomi Hideyoshi in the Momoyama period of 1573 to 1602. Most of the important castles were built in central Japan, from Nagoya to Hiroshima, and their location indicates the zone of operations of the earlier rule of the Shogunate. Among the most prominent, which still exist—with the date of erection—are: Nijo in Kyoto, (1603)—Osaka (1586)—Nagoya (1610)—Himeji (1550)—Wakayama (1585)—Okayama (1573)—Fukuyama (1619)—Hiroshima (1593)—Hikone (1604)—Inuyama (1440) —Matsumoto (1504)—Ogaki (1596)—Matsue (1611)—Kumamoto (1601)—Oita (1597)—Takamatsu (1550)—Matsuyama (1610)—Kochi (1350)—Sendai (1500)—Hirosaki (1601)—Yedo (1457 reconstructed by Tokugawa Ieyasu in 1590). Hirosaki is in N.W. Japan: Takamatsu, Kochi and Matsuyama on Shikoku, Kumamoto and Oita on Kyushu.

vi. The MOMOYAMA period (1573–1602)

Oda Nobunaga and Toyotomi Hideyoshi are famous names in Japanese History. They destroyed the power of the Ashikagas, and their Japanese-Buddhist allies, and restored something of the dignity—if not the actual importance—of the Tenno in the administration of the country. *

* See Appendix V—restoration of Sai-sei-itchi.

Oda Nobunaga, son of the Daimyo of Owari, began his military career by destroying the local influence of Imagawa Yoshimoto at the battle of Okehazama. Then he turned his attention to the subjugation of the Daimyo Uesugi (in the north) Takeda (in the east) and Mori—in the west. These Daimyo had superior military power at their disposal but they lacked Oda Nobunaga's organising genius. Oda trained the peasants who had lost their land, he raised foot soldiers and instituted a system of promotion which created loyal commanders: he made short work of the Buddhist clergy because their teaching had incited uprisings, among the converts, and was in opposition to his over-all plan of national unification based on Shinto and the Tenno.

In 1576, Oda Nobunaga built the castle of Azuchi on a piece of land jutting into Lake Biwa—the lake made famous for its association with the 'over-night appearance of Fujiyama'. Azuchi was only thirty miles from Kyoto so it was convenient to the Imperial Court in addition to being well sited to deal with his remaining adversaries.

During the interval between his success at Okehazama—1560 —and the building of Azuchi Castle, 1576, Oda Nobunaga directed some of his energy towards the rehabilitation of 'divine traditions' by the restoration of Ise Shrine and the observance of kamu-nagara.

He rebuilt the Ko-dai-jingu, re-established the rule of sai-sei-ichi and refurbished the Tenno's Palace in Kyoto. Then he abolished trade barriers, erected by the rival Daimyo, but— although he liberated trade—he compelled thousands of artisans and merchants to settle around Azuchi Castle in order to build up the economics of his regime.

The Jesuit Mission, under Francis Xavier, had arrived at Satsuma in 1549. Two years later, Xavier went to Kyoto to explain his religion to Go-Nara Tenno, and the Ashikaga Shogun Yoshiteru, and when Oda Nobunaga came to power in 1560 he made use of the new religion in his campaign against the Buddhist priests. In 1568, Oda Nobunaga met Father Aloysius Froez and encouraged him, and his mission, to compete against the Buddhists in order to create friction and sap the feudalistic power of his bitter opponents.

Oda Nobunaga, like many other dictators, combined ability

to administer with extreme brutality and—in the end—the protagonist of national unification met his death at the hands of Akechi Mitsuhide one of his own followers in 1582.

The campaign in west Japan, against Mori, had been entrusted to Hashiba Hideyoshi a peasant soldier who joined the ranks in 1555, at the age of nineteen, and been promoted by Oda Nobunaga in 1574 to command an army. Akechi Mitsuhide, another commander, was detailed by Oda Nobunaga to lead a force against Takamatsu while he returned to Kyoto. However, instead of obeying orders, Akechi Mitsuhide arranged to waylay the Vice-Shogun Oda Nobunaga in his lodgings—in the Honnoji Temple—and disposed of him in correct Samurai style.

But the new dictator of Japan did not live long to enjoy his blood-letting in the Temple. Hashiba Hideyoshi made peace with Mori and then marched his army to Yamazaki, near Kyoto, where he defeated Akechi Mitsuhide and avenged his master. And, after that victory, Hashiba Hideyoshi proceeded to deal with various other Daimyo—Shibata, Ikeda and Niwa—and in eight years he became the dominating military force in Japan.

In 1585—three years after his rise to power—Hashiba Hideyoshi was appointed Kwampaku by Ogimachi Tenno to succeed *Fujiwara Akizane*. This was a break with tradition for the hereditary holder of the office of Kwampaku (regent) since its inception by the Tenno in 864 had been a Fujiwara. But the dictator, of humble origin was ambitious and the Tenno was exceedingly grateful and pliant—in 1586, Hashiba Hideyoshi was granted the family name of TOYOTOMI, and—as Toyotomi Hideyoshi—he took over Oda Nobunaga's role of leader of national unification.

Toyotomi Hideyoshi's first military headquarters were established at Osaka. He lost no time in building the Osaka Castle on a far grander scale than that of Oda Nobunaga's Azuchi Castle on Lake Biwa. At Osaka the tower keep was eight stories high and roofed with gilded tiles. Upon the ridge of the topmost roof were placed a pair of golden dolphins and the walls, of the upper stories, were decorated with pictures of cranes and tigers—the crane being the symbol for longevity and the tiger for prowess.

The next step, taken by Toyotomi Hideyoshi, was to compel merchants and artisans to establish themselves at Osaka and to conduct themselves in accordance with his instructions. From

his base at Osaka the new ruler sent out prospectors and sur-
veyors and ordered a national census of property and households—in order to bring under his direct control the areas
having the highest yields in rice and precious metals. Then,
gold and silver were called in for minting into coins—*o-ban* and
ko-ban—to take the place of the copper coins in circulation.

At the same time, as he was accumulating capital for his
personal and national enterprises, the ambitious Kwampaku
brought the trading ports of Hakata, Nagasaki, Hyogo and Otsu
(on Lake Biwa) under his military control.

However, not content with the Osaka symbol of authority,
Toyotomi Hideyoshi built for himself the Jurakutei at Kyoto so
that he could supervise the Imperial Court and regulate its procedure to conform to his political and economic requirements.
The Jurakutei was a fortified mansion erected within a fortified
area—in addition to the Palace numerous other buildings were
erected, inside the 'prohibited area' at a prodigious cost in
labour and materials.

In 1588, when national unification was more or less established in central Japan, Toyotomi Hideyoshi sent instructions to
those Daimyo who accepted his overlordship to gather in Kyoto.
When they had obeyed his orders he received a visit of Go-yozei
Tenno at the Jurakutei. Then the Daimyo were assembled, in
the presence of the Tenno; the Kwampaku ordered them to
swear an oath of loyalty to the divine ruler of Japan, and the
personal supervision of the 'loyalty of the daimyo' was accomplished in accordance with the 'Imperial traditions'—handed
down from generation to generation.

Even so, Toyotomi Hideyoshi was not too certain himself
about the loyalty of the Daimyo—he always had, at the back of
his mind, the fate of Oda Nobunaga who had promoted him
from the ranks to an army commander at the age of thirty-
eight. So, to be on the safe side, he took the precaution—in
1591—to ring the city of Kyoto with a 35 feet high earth-wall,
seventeen miles in length, protected by a 65 feet wide moat.
Three years later, as an additional precaution, Fushimi Castle
was built on a hill to the southwest of Kyoto.

No doubt Hideyoshi's defensive arrangements at Kyoto, in
1591, were made necessary because of the active hostility of

Buddhist priests who were backed up by numerous Daimyo who by no means accepted the peasant soldier as Kwampaku (Regent) instead of a hereditary holder of the office—a Fujiwara. But it was Oda Nobunaga not Hideyoshi who had stirred up the religious hornets nest.

Not content with inciting Japanese—Christians to compete with the Buddhists for converts, Oda Nobunaga waged war on them in brutal fashion. In 1570 he defeated the monks—and their 'army'—near Lake Biwa, destroying temples left and right. Then he turned his attention to the Honganji-monks at Tennoji, and—at Nakashima—gave vent to his fury by destroying their stronghold and wiping out twenty-thousand monks in addition to crucifying two-hundred women. Indeed, it was said of Oda Nobunaga, that 'he slaughtered every son of Buddha that lived on the holy mount Hiye.'

Mount Hiye—outside Kyoto—was at that time the head-quarters of the Monto-shu (Ikko sect of Buddhism) who were followers of Saint Shinran, and it was Dengyo Daishi (founder of Tendai sect in 805) who built the Enryakuji monastery, on the flank of Mount Hiye, which exerted such a powerful feudal influence and which Oda Nobunaga raised to the ground.

Some of the Japanese-Christians, inspired (?) by Nobunaga took a hand in destroying temples but this religious activity did not gain Hideyoshi's approval and—in the end—it was the Japanese Christians who were persecuted. In 1597 the Spanish ship San Felipe ran ashore at Tosa (Shikoku): twenty-three Franciscan and three Jesuit priests were captured and paraded through the streets of Kyoto, Osaka and Sakai before being taken to Nagasaki and crucified.

Years later—1616—fifteen *foreign* priests were put to death, and in 1624 the torture of Japanese-Christians began—the Christians were hung up, head downwards, in a pit till they were dead or had recanted. And this method was used by Japanese against British Indian troops at Kuala Belait (North Borneo) in April 1945.

In 1630 when the Christians in Kyushu revolted they were killed to a man, and when the Portuguese sent an embassy to protest in 1635 the four envoys and fifty-seven members of the crew were beheaded.

The Buddhist monks were not pacifists for they carried

swords, under their cloaks, and used them as readily as the most aggressive of the Samurai. But it would not be correct to say that the Buddhists in Japan—like the Christian church—began a cruel policy of persecution when it had the power to do so, nor did it fight separate wars for each phase of the persecution. And if we contrast the behaviour of the Nazis with that of the Japanese (against the Christians) we shall arrive at a correct estimation of persecution and atrocities in the West and in the East in the relative periods of civilization.

However, in other matters, Hideyoshi was thorough in his methods. When the Daimyo were brought to heel he denationalized his army: the peasants had served his purpose, now he compelled them to devote their attention to cultivation. He confiscated all weapons in their possession and the functions of farming and of fighting were separated again. The peasant soldier, raised by Oda Nobunaga, was demobilized and a special warrior class created anew to replace it for the personal use of the Kwampaku.

Pushing on with the economics of his dictatorship, more or less secure from attack in his Kyoto stronghold, Hideyoshi began by curtailing the circulation of Chinese copper cash and substituting his own metallic currency based on silver and gold which were diverted from gilding temples and castles to a more prosaic use.

This policy succeeded. Many ports were opened to foreign trade and considerable profit gravitated into the paws of the new rulers in Kyoto. But Hideyoshi, like General Araki, had his eyes on China and as the first step in that direction sent an expedition across Tsushima straits to deal with the King of Korea in 1592 but his troops were halted at Heijo. A second invasion of Korea, in 1597, was a greater success but before the Koreans could be defeated Hideyoshi died a natural death in Japan.

Behind the expeditions to Korea was the ambition of Hideyoshi to become a Ming Emperor but the Chinese offered to make him the Emperor of Japan under the suzerainty of China.*

Perhaps, at the back of Hideyoshi's mind was the idea that— in time—he might (as a Ming Emperor) follow in the footsteps

* See Appendix VI and VII.

of the Mongol adventurers of the 14th Century and carry his
Samurai sword into Western Turkestan as the great Timerlane,
a descendant of Jengis Khan, had done in 1369 with 'inhuman
atrocities and cold-blooded massacres of thousands of prisoners
and non-combatants': but that role was reserved for the
Japanese generals of World War II.

Those are but idle thoughts. The first expedition to Korea
returned with many captive artists and artizans with suggestions which stimulated the work of the kikajins. And because
Christianity cut across the worship of the Tenno and the rule of
the Kwampaku the Jesuits were expelled in 1594. But despite
the prohibitions of 1587, and the persecutions, the converts to
Christianity had risen to 200,000. However, with the death of
TOYOTOMI HIDEYOSHI the new doctrine of the non-hereditary
Kwampaku was ended and the new-imperialism checked until
1894 when Korea was once more the battlefield on the
continent of Asia.

vii. The TOKUGAWA Regime (1600–1868)

Oda Nobunaga and Toyotomi Hideyoshi were responsible for
the political bridge between the Ashikaga Samurai rule of instability and the renascency of 'Imperial Traditions' or sai-sei-
itchi. The TOKUGAWA REGIME was an absolute dictatorship
which functioned behind the bamboo-curtain of national
isolation.*

Tokugawa Iyeyasu, the founder of the dictatorship, claimed
descent from Minamoto Yoritomo founder of the Kamakura-
Samurai Regime. The Minamoto Clan were a branch of the
Imperial Clan so he could claim blood relationship with the
Tenno. His domain was in the province of Mikawa and he had
been associated with Nobunaga and Hideyoshi in the national-
unification campaigns so he considered himself by birth and
prestige as the natural successor to the great Hideyoshi, the
commoner. Other Daimyo with ambitions in the same direction were quick to contest his claim to the overlordship of Japan.

The usual civil war followed. Iyeyasu rallied to his cause the
Daimyo in the north-eastern part of central Japan where the
opposition against him was strongest. Tokugawa forces met the
army of the Toyotomi clan in a battle at Sekigahara and

* See Appendix VI and VII.

defeated them decisively. The commander of the Tokugawa force, Ishida Mitsunari, used OGAKI Castle (north of Nagoya) as his battle headquarters when the battle at Sekigahara was fought in 1600.

Ogaki Castle was one of the 'castle-on-plain', as opposed to the 'mountain castles' type of stronghold used by the Samurai. The tower-keep consisted of four stories only which made it unique in Japan where the number 'four'—*shi*—is pronounced the same way as *shi* for death and the similarity was objected to by ancient soldiers.

After his first victory over the enemy, Tokugawa Iyeyasu was elevated by Go-Yosei Tenno to the dignity of Sei-i-tai SHOGUN (Barbarian-subduing Great General) in 1603. In this honour he followed in the footsteps of Minamoto Yoritomo who was given the title of Sei-i-tai Shogun in 1192—after his bloody victory at Dan-no-ura, near Shimonoseki. But Tokugawa was not appointed Kwampaku (Regent) in succession to Hideyoshi.

Tokugawa did not proceed to the conquest of Korea but made his headquarters in the north at Yedo where he rebuilt the Castle of Ota Dokan on a magnificent scale. The Tenno remained inside the Kyoto enclosure, constructed by Hide-yoshi, from 1600 to 1868 a passive divinity in the Shinto State.

By Tokugawa's directions all feudal lords of the country had to bear the cost of extending the castle from 1603 to 1636 when it was completed. In the meantime the Toyotomi malcontents raised the banner of Hideyoshi's son, Hideyori, who was living in the family castle at Osaka. Osaka Castle was stormed in 1615 and Hideyori, and his supporters, disposed of with samurai two-sworded thoroughness. Then the SHOGUN turned his attention to the discipline of the Daimyo. The Fudai-Daimyo (feudal lords) who contributed to the Sekigahara victory were suitably rewarded with tax-free sho-en, those in hereditary vassalage to the Tokugawa (and other blood rela-tions) were placed in control of sho-en at strategical points up and down the country. Other Daimyo—not in hereditary vassalage—he banished to remote sho-en where they could fend for themselves.

To complete the discipline, Tokugawa promulgated the Buke Hatto (Samurai Law) which was framed to restrict the activities of Daimyo and Samurai and bring them under his direct supervision.

Tokugawa Iyeyasu died in 1616 and was succeeded by his son, HIDETADA who had been acting for him for a year or two before his death. Go-Mizuno-o Tenno granted him the posthumous name of Tosho-Dai-Gongen and he was ultimately buried at Nikko where a magnificent shrine was erected to perpetuate his memory. All the Daimyo were called on to contribute in money or material to the erection of this monument which was started by Hidetada and continued by his successor Iyemitsu.

The YOMEI-MON, a gateway of remarkable splendour is a tribute to those who constructed it and a never ending source of admiration for Japanese and foreign sightseers. It is a splendid piece of craftsmanship but it had nothing to do with Shintoism or the divine Tenno, it was set up for the glorification of the Tokugawas.

The events which brought about national isolation have been mentioned in the previous chapter. In short: the Christians, and the foreign traders, were banished from Japan in 1634: Japanese were prohibited from leaving the country, the Portuguese, Spanish, Dutch and English traders banned from entry: in 1614, Hidetada issued the edict that every household must display a Buddhist idol in the tokonoma and pray before it night and day, and (in 1638) the Japanese Christians were massacred at Shimabara. The scene was set for a true Japanese civilization free from foreign contamination.

Respect for traditions, and the pursuit of national ideals, is alleged to be expressed in the veneration of the Tenno by the Japanese from the earliest days to the year 1945. But the truth is that there is more of feudalism than idealism recorded in Japanese History. The TOKUGAWA SHOGUNATE of 268 years is a perfect example of the working of the system—co-ordination of Shogun, Daimyo and Samurai for the exploitation of the Do-MIN, the people of the soil.

All the TOKUGAWAS (good, bad and indifferent despots) were cradled in the 'spirit of ancient traditions' but they acted as if they had been ordained by birth and ordered by Amaterasu to rule with a rod of iron. The immediate successors of Iyeyasu made it clear from the outset that control of the Tenno's part in the affairs of government was their exclusive and perpetual monoply. The rest of the Samurai-Aristocracy were prohibited from direct contact with the divine Tenno who was to be venerated as Kami. Kyoto was the heaven of the human Emperor of Japan—Nikko the mecca of the Samurai—Yedo was the Capital of the country. And from Yedo, where the administration functioned, a network of edicts, laws and ordinances was cast over the land to ensure the supremacy of the Tokugawas.*

Tokugawa finance was based on their proceeds of their share of the total rice crop of twenty million koku—roughly one hundred million bushels. One fifth of the agricultural land was owned by the Tokugawa family or by the Daimyo in hereditary vassalage to them. The land was cultivated by seventy-five per cent. of the population so the basis of economic stability was assured.

To make certain of this revenue, the Tokugawas brought under their direct control certain areas each producing about twenty-million bushels of rice—the rest of the area producing rice was parcelled out to other Daimyo. Taxation was paid in rice and in most areas was based on fifty per cent. of the crop. In addition to rice, the farmers raised barley, wheat, vegetables and mulberry leaves for silkworms, and the fishermen plied their calling for the benefit of themselves and the overlords.

Other sources of revenue, for the Tokugawa administration sprang from the manufacturing industries which were now fairly well established to produce necessities and luxuries. But even so, Yedo alone soon had a population of nearly three-quarters of a million non-producers—civil servants, soldiers and parasites—who consumed large quantities of rice out of the granary of the Shogun. Each Daimyo had to maintain his establishment in Yedo and spend part of the year there (with retainers) to make sure that his allegiance was one-hundred per cent. to Tokugawa and not one-per cent. of it to the cloistered Tenno in Kyoto. Every Daimyo, according to his rice income, had to contribute to the coffers of the Shogunate, so it was necessary for the peasant to eat little and work long to keep the system running smoothly in hakko-ichi-u.

* See Appendix VII.

Oda Nobunaga had encouraged the propaganda of the Jesuits in order to curb the activities of the Buddhist priests. Now it was the turn of the Buddhist priests to purge former Christians and bring them back to the fold. After the Shimabara uprising had been quelled, the Priests were instructed to supervise those who had reconverted to Buddhism and to make certain that the recantation was genuine and not based on a desire to escape death or persecution. They were also detailed to compile a census of peasants, for the use of the tax-collectors, and authorised by law to prohibit the do-min—people of the soil—from moving from parish to parish, to marry or even bury their dead without permission of the area supervising priest.

The JISHA-BUGYO (Magistrate of Temples and Shrines) was established to supervise the agrarian classes. Tokugawa decrees of the third SHOGUN, Iyemitsu, increased the discipline over the peasants. They were to rise early and work in the fields until dusk and then make ropes and sacks: they were not to drink saké or tea: they must be content with plain food: husband and wife must work as a team—if the wife was lazy, or drank tea, she must be divorced: peasants should not smoke—tobacco was no substitute for food, had no medicinal value and was often the cause of fire.

Yes—life was hard for the peasants. But, after all, the Japanese refer to cha-no-yu and ikebana as 'furyu no asobi'— or elegant amusement—and (in the old days) 'furyu' was 'to lose oneself in the joys of peace and to shun all strife'. But that was for the 'kami' not for the 'domin'. Indeed when Yoshimasa lived at the Ginkakuji (1478) as a Buddhist monk his 'furyu' was 'to arrange flowers in a vase, to drink tea, or to breathe the perfume of incense'. And his companions, the *chabozu* No-ami, Gei-ami and So-ami (three generations of experts) wandered with him in the 'fairyland of beautiful trees, ponds and lotus flowers': so much for the ethos of furyu and the ethics of Buddhism when the 'kami' banned the use of tea—by the peasants.

As for tobacco—the Portuguese brought it to Japan in 1570 but it became so popular (among the peasants) that Tokugawa Iyeyasu banned its use and prohibited its cultivation in 1612. But the bad habit persisted and one of the most profitable enterprises of early Meiji days was the Japanese Tobacco

G

Monoply. And, in the sixteenth century, one of the artistic gems was the 'Netsuke' which were used to attach the leather pouch, the leather pipe cases and the *sagemono*—hanging object. Still later, Netsuke were in common use by most classes of Japanese to attach their smoking utensils.

Among art objects, exclusively Japanese in creation and development, Netsuke are supreme and in the absolute perfection of detail the art of the Netsuke is considered to rank superior to the achievements of all other people.

Another of Iyemitsu's decrees placed merchants and artisans in an inferior position to farmers. They were prohibited from changing their class or their occupation and compelled to remain in whatever trade they were engaged in at the time of the decree. They were not permitted to have a family name or to carry a sword which was a right reserved for Samurai. However, despite the decrees, the merchants and artisans (cho-nin) managed to make a living out of the ruling classes in Yedo and the numerous 'castle-towns'.

In order to meet the rising cost of 'peace'—and idleness— the Samurai (employed by Daimyo) increased the taxes levied on the already hard pressed farmers. And the Tenno, relieved of all his authority, devoted himself to the regular performance of court rituals—venerating Amaterasu—or to study of the classics which detailed the life of his ancestors, hakko-ichi-u and kamunagara.

The Fujiwara custom of maintaining maternal relations with the Imperial line was taken over by Tokugawa Hidetada who gave his daughter to Go-Mizuno Tenno. A daughter, born of this union, succeeded to the title of sovereign under the name of Myosho Tenno and it was during her reign that Tokugawa Iyemitsu completed the super-magnificent To-sho-gu Shrine at Nikko. And when Myosho abdicated, in 1643, she was succeeded by a *son* of Go-Mizuno Tenno by a different wife. None of the other 'rulers of Japan'—stationed in Kyoto— were related to the Tokugawas while they held the Shogunate. But the Tokugawas were responsible for the erection of many castles between 1600 and 1868.

Nijo Castle in Kyoto was built for Tokugawa Iyeyasu, in 1603, to vie with the Juraku Palace of Toyotomi Hideyoshi, and it became the Kyoto headquarters of the Shogunate. NAGOYA

Castle, one of the finest built in Japan, was erected for Iyeyasu in 1610: he compelled twenty-two of his feudal lords to share in the cost of the undertaking. The roof of the first floor is shingled with tiles but the upper ones are copper plated—the ridge of the topmost is ornamented with a pair of dolphins nine feet high plated with gold. When the castle was completed it was occupied by Iyeyasu's ninth son, Yoshinao, and remained in the family until the Meiji Restoration. FUKUYAMA Castle was built in 1619 by Lord Mizuno (by order of Iyeyasu) and HIKONI Castle in 1604 by Lord Li for Iyeyasu's military purposes.

The building of temples and castles produced excellent architects, craftsmen and skilled labour. The kika-jins had been absorbed by the natives, the country was closed to the outside world, nothing new was coming in but what was in the country was developed to the fullest extent. The prohibition of job-changing resulted in the establishment of group specialists in various areas with great advantage to the production of utilities by successive generations of family experts.

Iyeyasu brought to an end the 'five hundred year war' but warring-spirit of the Samurai remained. The develpment of art, by the Tokugawas, did much to divert the spirit from the use of the sword to the more peaceful requirements of the times.

But the artists were not inspired by the profit motive, they were—for the most part—part of the family of a Prince, Daimyo or wealthy Samurai who clothed, housed and fed them. The art creations—painting, carving in wood, ivory and bamboo; the lacquer and potter articles, metal work, silk weaving and so on—were produced at leisure without regard for the buyers or the sellers market. It was true art, for art's sake, and the examples of it are highly praised by western connoisseurs.

The distribution of Daimyo, with their attendant Samurai, artisans, artists—skilled and unskilled workers—developed centres of local government. In these towns and cities the local scavengers were a class apart. Named ETA they were the outcasts of society—the unclean people. It was left to the Eta to bury animals and human beings for in early Shinto even the graves for the dead were considered a polution: on the sacred Shinto Island of Miyajima there is not a single grave. In the days of the Tokugawas there were several million Eta, and most villages had a few to cater to their needs.

*There were fifteen Tokugawa Shoguns but I shall not burden these pages with their names and their exploits in detail. During the period 1688 to 1704 the living conditions of the bannermen in Yedo deteriorated while the plebians made steady progress under the changing conditions. Some of the Daimyo went into the wholesale trade, opening rice markets in the largest cities and selling to the highest bidder, others who were hard up mortgaged their future prospects and lived on the proceeds while the rice crop was ungarnered. And very soon the hard-hit Samurai were bowing to the chonin (townspeople) instead of being bowed to in accordance with tradition. And some of the highly interbred samurai found it of financial advantage to marry into the family of the common merchant.

And the people of the soil were the ones who paid the price of living in the artistic age of plunderers. They could not rise in the social scale by intermarriage with the tax-collector, it was left to them to keep the brothels supplied with unwanted daughters—young girls who were not profitable enough to feed and clothe. And as the misery of the farmer increased so the sale of children grew until almost all the cities had their little cages of prostitutes in gay kimono. And if their face and body were fair to look upon they were raised in the profession and became entertainers or geishas.

Geisha (singing girls) entertained in restaurants and tea houses in the vicinity of the brothels. The instrument which they used, to accompany their songs, was the samisen a three-stringed, rectangular banjo which was introduced into Japan from the Loo Choo Islands in 1650. The samisen is the musical instrument of the lower classes, the koto (dulcimer) the instrument used in gakaku, the music of the court. It is an oblong, hollow wooden instrument with thirteen silken strings and is played with the right hand, with plectra on the fingers. In later years the koto and samisen were used together, but at first it was used only for 'sacred music' not ribald songs.

But the only music of the people of the soil was the croaking of the toads in the pond near the cesspool, or the tread of the ox

*See Appendix VII.

in the rice mill: not for them the pleasures of the tea house, and the samisen. Sometimes they would drink too much saké but it was easy enough to sober up by chewing a few red beans and then clap their hands before the shrine of their Ujigami, or wander up to the Inari shrine on the Day of the Horse to leave bean-curd for the hungry foxes. For the Inari deity was said to dispense clothing, food and dwelling and no one engaged in agriculture could hope for good fortune unless they paid their devotions to Inari. And what more could a peasant want of the gods?

The farmers were producing enough rice for the entire population, more than enough on the basis of consumption in 1868, but the allocation of it was determined by the Shogun and the Daimyo and the producers were the last to be considered. Still their lot was better than the negro slaves from the West Coast of Africa who were shipped to Virginia in 1620 to work for tobacco planters; and that traffic went on until 1833— almost as long as the Tokugawa Shogunate lasted in Japan.

Comparisons may be odious to the Anglo-Saxons and the people of Europe but nothing is gained by damning the Tokugawas if we are too cowardly to admit our own short-comings during the period 1600 to 1868, or between 1868 and 1949 if we want to bring international morality on to the praying-mat of our own advanced but definitely materialistic age. True, we had Magna Charta in 1215 when the Hojo Clan took over in Kamakura and exiled three Emperors, and we had our Simon de Montfort heading a rebellion, taking over the government of England, and laying the foundation of Parliament which came into being in 1295—a Parliament which included representatives of church, nobles and judges. True, we had no Buddhist priests in Parliament and no divine rulers— but we had some autocrats, also Peasants' Revolts headed by Wat Tyler owing to 'discontent caused by low wages, high taxation, and oppression'. That was in 1381 when the Ashikagas ruled the roost in Japan: and we had Kings who lived on the fat of the land and who were deposed; and the sons of Kings who were murdered, in the same fifteenth century of our Lord. And we also had our Defender of the Faith followed by The Pilgrimage of Grace in 1536—another insurrection because the monastries were dissolved—only seven years before the first matchlock was introduced into Japan by the roving Portuguese.

Then there was Queen Elizabeth, who came to the throne of England in 1558. She established Protestantism and by law became 'Supreme Governor of the English Church' and this was a few years before the rise of ODA NOBUNAGA who rehabilitated the divine tradition and restored the ISE SHRINE. And—to continue this comparative record of historical events—it was Mary, Queen of Scots who begat James I (1603-25) who 'firmly believed in the divine rights of Kings': so did TOKUGAWA IYEYASU in 1603 when he was elevated to the dignity of SHOGUN by GO-YOSEI TENNO.

But, at this point in history, Japan did not produce an Oliver Cromwell because there was no Parliament in the country—just the Capital of the Shogun and the castles of his Daimyo. And in 1685, (approximately) the English were laying the foundation of the Colonial Empire while the Japanese were shut up in their islands and sealed off against the world. But two-hundred years later they began to build up naval and military power on the British scale in order to found a Japanese Colonial Empire.*

These few remarks merely scratch the surface of the subject and take no account of the progress of religion and democratic government in other parts of the world. Still, at the risk of mere reiteration and because it is germain to the rise and fall of the Japanese Empire, I must interpose this analogy: in 1620 the Pilgrim Fathers emigrated to North America; in 1783 the independence of America was fully established; in 1837 (fifty-four years later) the United States of America sent the ship *Morrison* to Yedo Bay to open up trade with the Tokugawa Shogunate. The new Republic was open to immigration from people of the old world—Japan was closed to it for 268 years, and retained her own language and customs. The literature of the western world was a closed book to her people—they knew nothing about Decartes, Locke, Leibnitz or Rousseau or those other thinkers who followed in their footsteps.

But to return to our muttons—the Tokugawa Shogunate, in the Genroku era (1688-1704), when Reigen Tenno appointed (?) TSUNAYOSHI the fifth Tokugawa Shogun.

* See Appendix XIII.

Tsunayoshi was an extremist. Born in the year of the Dog he decreed the extreme penality for anyone killing that animal: he was quite sane at first but lost his reason later on and his lack of common sense only added to the worsening of conditions in the country. The Daimyo encouraged industry and increased taxation and the Samurai became more and more like the 1949 'spivs' of England under the austerity of Socialism. It was in this period that the ZAIBATSU (big business, or plutocrats) became prominent in Yedo and Osaka, headed by MITSUI Hachirozaemon.

The MITSUI family were the principal moneylenders. To facilitate business they opened Exchange Bureaux in Yedo, Kyoto and Osaka and had their own money-order system. There was no foreign trade but there was plenty of business to be financed inside the ring which manipulated the rice market. Feudalism was now being buttressed by Capitalism and the pleasures of the Samurai were taken care of in the splendid (?) brothels of YOSHIWARA in Yedo, SHIMABARA in Kyoto and SHIN-MACHI in Osaka.

It was the age of the 'spivs' and the 'touts'—the contact men between Samurai and Chonin—and the Samurai were more interested in women, wine and song than in preserving the divine right of the Tenno, with their sacred-swords. The debauchery took such a firm hold of the Daimyo and the Hatamoto (attendants on Daimyo) that the Tokugawa headquarters issued orders banning them from the brothels.

It may be agreed that there is nothing in this brief survey of conditions, under the TOKUGAWAS, to support the contention of many Japanese historians that the ideal toward which they were striving was to make the nation a single household of contented people under the auspices of the Tenno. On the contrary, the hakko-ichi-u oneness of the Japanese national family (unity of Sovereign, State and People) was merely a phraseogram passed on from generation to generation by a succession of common tyrants (Shoguns, Daimyo and Samurai) to a nation of un-tutored bondsmen.

The policy of rigid isolation was enforced to maintain a fixed feudal order without the slightest consideration of the welfare of three-quarters of the population. This policy failed through the defects in its structure even before the display of force by the

United States of America ended the period of isolation. Reforms were instituted from time to time, first by the 8th Shogun
Yoshimune in 1716, then by his successors—Iyeshige, Iyenari
and Iyeyoshi—but the reforms were only devices to maintain
Samurai domination, and when they debased currency (to
reduce the wealth of the Chonin) it added another item to the
general social unrest: another load of metal for the backs of
the people of the soil.

Confucianism and Bushido under the Tokugawas

I have already mentioned Urabe Kanetomo's book,
Catechism of Genuine Unitary Shinto, written in the Ashikaga
period, which was purported to purify Shinto and restore it to
its 'indigenous spirit'.

This book held the field until the early days of the Tokugawa
Shogunate when it was criticised by Hayashi Razan in his
Honcho-Jinjako (Studies in the Japanese Shinto Shrine). He was
a Confucian of the Chu-Tzu school (Doctrine of the Mean) and
in his opinion the Shintoism, so far advocated, was muddled
with Buddhist philosophy which should be rooted out. But his
own philosophy was based on Confucianism and this reduced
the value of his opinions in the eyes of other Japanese authorities on the subject.

Still later, early in the eighteenth century, four Japanese
scholars endeavoured to justify Shintoism without the aid of
any Chinese philosophy, they were Yamazaki Anzai, Kada-no-
Azumamaro, Kamo-no-Mabuchi and Hirata Atsutane.

Yamazaki Anzai, a super-patriot, declared that 'the Japanese
should respect the Emperor as the central force of their national
life. This,' he said, 'was the very soul of Shintoism'. The other
three agreed—emphasising the importance of loyalty to the
Tenno—but kept clear of religion.

It was the works of these Shintoists which influence the more
famous writer, MOTOORI NORINAGA, to his conclusions that the
Japanese should base their faith in the SHINTO of the Kojiki and
not in the SHINTO of Chinese philosophers or Buddhist priests.
And out of this literature came FUKKO SHINTO—Restoration
Shinto—the Shinto behind the Meiji Restoration.

However, the Tokugawas, of the eighteenth century, turned
to the social theories of Confucius for inspiration and for

material for their so-called reforms. The hirelings of the totter-ing SHOGUN attempted to popularise the doctrines of Confucius by promulgating it up and down the country. In this propa-ganda the importance of peasantry was stressed anew. They were reminded that they still ranked next to the Samurai in national importance.

Under the high-sounding name of SHIN-GAKU (Heart Learning) this new code of morals, intended for the people of the soil, was adopted by the Samurai and on it they founded certain 'rules of conduct' which they called BUSHIDO or the Way of the Samurai in order not to confuse it (?) with KAMI-NO-MICHI or the Way of the Gods.

In an earlier period of Japanese history—about 1650—BUSHIDO had been founded by Yamaga Soko. BUSHI-DO was 'the ways which fighting nobles should observe in their daily lives: the Precepts of Knighthood, the *noblesse oblige* of the warrior'. The BU-SHI were SAMURAI or Fighting Knights a privileged body of men, well horsed and clad in armour, who made fighting their sole occupation in life. They were pro-fessional soldiers, employed by Daimyo, so they required a 'gentleman's agreement' covering a common standard of behaviour when they went about their business of fighting or tax collecting.

Yamaga Soko's BUSHI-DO had nothing to do with Con-fucianism or Heart Learning: Buddhism was the original in-spiration of Bushido, and what was lacking in Buddhism was found (?) in Shintoism's 'loyalty to the Tenno, reverence for ancestral memory and filial pity' which were added to make it into the 'Soul of Japan'.

It was during the siege of Port Arthur by the Japanese, at the time of the Russo-Japanese War, that I became interested in Bushido.

Baron General Nogi was commanding the III Japanese Army and he had his battle-headquarters near the dugout in which I was living at the time. We became friends. One day, while he was sipping tea outside my dugout, we were discussing the progress of the siege—and the hard fighting of September, 1904—when he asked me if I understood the meaning of Bushido. I had to confess that I had only a passing knowledge of the subject so he sent to Japan for a copy of Inazo Nitobe's

Bushido which he presented to me on 11th October. I found it
more convincing then than I do today.

Nogi was born on November 11th, 1849—roughly twenty
years before the Meiji Restoration. His clan was subject to
Lord Mori, Daimyo of Choshu, and when the *Tokugawa Shogun*
sent troops to subdue the Choshu Daimyo in 1866, he fought
against them and was wounded. After the Restoration he
joined the new army and was a Major at twenty-three. Fifteen
years later he went to Europe, for two years, but retired from
the army in 1893. At the outbreak of the Sino-Japanese War
he rejoined as a Brigadier and captured Port Arthur in 1894.
After a spell as the *First Governor* of Formosa (the first of the
Japanese Colonies) he retired again, only to return once more
in 1904 to command the 3rd Japanese Army in Manchuria. At the end of the Russo-Japanese War he retired and
became Principal of the Peer's College in Tokyo: in 1911, he
went to England for the Coronation of King George V.

I met him frequently; during the siege of Port Arthur and
in Tokyo in later years. In my opinion he was all that the
writers on Bushido could have desired—he was a living example
of the way 'fighting nobles should observe in their daily lives'
but he was very bitter about the conduct of the younger generation of Japanese officers.

Nogi carried his loyalty to the Tenno to the grave. On 30th
July, 1912, Meiji Tenno died: his funeral was on 13th September. On the night of 12/13th September, Nogi and his wife
spent the time beside the coffin. Next day, when his servants
had gone to see the procession, the soldier and his wife went to
an eight-mat room in the house.

In that room, kneeling before a portrait of Meiji Tenno, they
committed junshi (self-immolation of an attendant on the death
of his lord) and took leave of a world now empty of all meaning
to them.

For them, time stood still—they cared nothing for the origin
of Haniwa, eighteen centuries before they were born—they
lived in the past and died in the present.

But there was another side of Nogi's character which interested
me—his ruthlessness in action and his introspection as the
casualties mounted. And it was not until both his sons had been
killed during the campaign that he could reconcile his con-

science with his duty to the Tenno. He explained his reactions to me after the death of his remaining son on 203-Metre Hill, in this way: he was now heirless, and his bereavement answered the clamouring souls of the departed men he had, by unhappy duty, sent to their death. And when the Siege was over a Shrine was erected, between the Russian fortifications and the Japanese line of investment, and before the altar he addressed the departed spirits:—

'On the 14th of January, in the 38th year of Meiji, I, Nogi Masaki, Commander-in-Chief of the Third Japanese Army, have caused this fete to be celebrated with saké and many offerings, in honour of the officers and men who have fallen.

For over 210 days and nights you bravely battled, facing death by fire, sword and disease—and you were killed; but your efforts were not in vain, for the fleet of the enemy was destroyed and the fortress forced to surrender. This was but the reward of your sacrifice.

But I and others swore death or victory, and I surviving have received the Imperial thanks, and now unworthily monopolise this glory; and I beseech you who are gone to the hereafter, share with me this glory.

Fate ordaining, sadly places me in command of these hills, streams and forts, all so stained with your life's blood; here, before this altar raised on consecrated ground, I invoke your spirits to partake of our humble offerings.'

After the officers of his command followed Nogi, and paid homage to the dead, I saluted the cenotaph. But, mingled with my thoughts was Major-General Nakamura's order of the day to the men of the 2nd Brigade, before the Third General Attack on Port Arthur—over the ground I was standing on. It was curt and brutal:—

'The object of our detachment is to cut the Port Arthur fortress into two. No man must hope to return. Should I fall, Colonel Watanabe will take my place, and should a similar fate befall him, Lieutenant-Colonel Okuno will take charge. Every officer of whatever rank shall appoint his successor. The attack shall be chiefly effected with the bayonet. However severe the enemy's fire, our men must not return a single shot until we have established a footing. *The officers are authorized to kill those men, who without proper reason straggle behind or separate themselves from the ranks, or retreat.*'

That was the Nogi fighting spirit, the spirit which sacrificed so many lives at Port Arthur. Nakamura and Okuno were killed and one-thousand men of the Brigade were placed hors-de-combat. On another occasion a unit of the 9th Division did turn tail: most of the officers were killed. The survivors were taken out of the line and quartered near my dugout. All day they were drilled and lectured. Just before sunset they paraded before a Shinto shrine to listen to a recitation of their cowardice, how the entire unit had refused to face certain destruction even after the Major in command had been killed setting an example of Bushido.

This went on until the Siege was over. Even then, when the Third Army were ordered to Liaoyang, Nogi refused their colonel's request to re-join the Army with his regiment, or to commit seppuku (suicide by disembowelment), but he was allowed to follow the army *on foot* when they entrained for the north.

Nogi had the moral realism of Confucius. His idea of military discipline was—'if you cannot serve men how can you serve spirits?', to adapt one of the Sage's remarks on the unseen world. And the maxim of kill or be killed by your own side was followed in 1941 as closely as in 1904.

I have related these personal incidents because it was to Lord Mori's CHOSHU CLAN and Lord Shimazu's SATSUMA CLAN that Meiji Tenno addressed his appeal for their help in destroying the Tokugawa regime, in 1867. And it is fairly accurate to say that if there had been no foreign intervention, to unite the nation, there would have been civil war between the Tokugawa faction and the Daimyo's of Choshu, Satsuma, Hizen and Tosa.

Bushido was a code of conduct to suit the times. It was refurbished under the Tokugawas to tighten the discipline of the Samurai and to strengthen the structure of the Shogunate. Its rules, according to Nitobe and other authorities on the subject, may be summarised as . . . 'to be contented with one's position in life, to accept the natal irreversible earthly status and to cultivate oneself within that allotted station, to be loyal to the master of the family, to value one's ancestors, to train oneself in the military arts by cultivation and discipline of one's mind and body' . . . 'Death involving a question of honour was accepted in Bushido as the key to the solution of many complex problems, so that to an ambitious samurai a natural departure from life seemed a rather tame affair'.

But the sword was the real *soul* of the samurai. The two swords—katana and wakizashi—the long and the short sword, the constant companions of the 'warrior.' These were the symbols of loyalty and honour, worshipped and handed down from generation to generation.

The end of Isolation

Output of literature increased toward the close of the Tokugawa Shogunate. In 1715, a new History of Japan was completed. Like many other similar efforts it was a contribution to the records by one of the Shoguns. Tokugawa Mitsukuni began the compilation of *Dai Nippon Shi* in 1657 and its central theme was the old one of the relationship between the Shogun and the Tenno. But, after his death in 1700 the completion of the work was undertaken by other members of the Mito Clan to which he belonged. This gave rise to what have been called the *Mito Studies* and is said to have encouraged those Daimyo who were opposed to the autocratic rule of the Tokugawas.

Although there was a ban on trade, and the entry of foreigners, a section of the bamboo-curtain had been raised in Kyushu where the Dutch had been allowed to maintain a trading post at Deshima, near Nagasaki. It was through this portal that knowledge of the western civilization entered again in 1700, at the time of Shogun Yoshimune, and stirred up Kyushu opposition to the feudalism of the Tokugawas. The teaching of the Dutch was called RAN-GAKU to distinguish it from KOKU-GAKU or National Studies.

Rangaku was stimulated by the arrival of the Germans, Engelbert Kaempfer and (at a later date) Philipp Franz von Siebold, both of whom were professors of western science. It was Siebold, who came in 1823, who established a school of science at Nagasaki and it is to this famous German surgeon that Japan owes her primary knowledge of medicine and pharmacy. Scholars from all over the country found their way to Deshima and it was not long before Japanese professors were teaching medicine and writing books on the subject. And it was due to the influence of the Dutch East Indies Company that the embargo on *non-religious books* was lifted in 1720.

But although the science and civilization of the West was now impinging on Chinese philosophy and stimulating a critical study of Tokugawa ideology, based on national isolation, the people of the soil continued to worship the clay images on the Kamidana—god shelf—and toiled on in complete ignorance of languages, ancient or modern, native or foreign. A minority ruled them and it was a minority of another kind who studied rangaku and kokugaku and ate the rice they produced in the plains and up the side of the hills—terrace on terrace, plot by plot wherever soil could be found to take a seed.

Holland was the principal trading nation in the Far East, at the commencement of the nineteenth century, closely followed by England whose spearhead of commerce (after the conquest of India) had nailed Hong Kong to the framework of Empire. Hong Kong (Victoria Island) was added to the crown in 1841 and then England turned her attention to Japan, as others had done before her.

In 1837 the United States of America sent the s.s. *Morrison* on a peaceful trading mission to Uraga—in Yedo Bay—but the Shogunate proved definitely hostile. Then she went to Kagoshima, in Kyushu, to try and gain admittance through the back door but was received with round-shot by the defenders of isolation. Then, in 1845, the English sent their warship *Samarang*, to try and do better. She failed in her mission so the U.S.A., sent two warships (*Columbus* and *Vincennes*) under Commodore Biddle in 1846. This task-force anchored in Uraga Bay: the Commodore presented the local authority with copies of the latest treaties concluded by England, France and the U.S.A., with China. But it was no good. This auto-suggestion elicited no favourable response from Yedo—it was July and very hot in the Capital. Still, the English were persevering. They sent another warship—the *Mariner*—in 1848 only to draw one more blank refusal in Chinese characters.

It was not yet the days of self-determination of nations, or the four freedoms, so the United States of America ignoring the war with the English, or the Declaration of Independence, decided to make the Japanese 'talk turkey'.

Commodore Perry, commanding the warships, *Sasquehanna*, *Saratoga*, *Plymouth* and *Mississipi* entered Uraga Bay in July 1853.

He had with him a letter from President Fillmore to the Sovereign of Japan. But the Tenno, who retained (?) the right to negotiate with foreign powers, was in seclusion in Kyoto and the Shogun refused Commodore Perry's request for treaty negotiations.

Perry answered this refusal by bringing his fleet to Kanagawa (Yokohama) in Yedo Bay and demanded an audience with the Shogun. Confronted with this display of force, so close to Yedo Castle, the Shogun modified his attitude by sending a representative of the *government* to meet the Commodore at Kurigahama close to Uraga.

President Fillmore's letter was handed over with the intimation that an answer would be called for the following Spring.

On the way to Japan, Commodore Perry stopped at Ogasawara, in the Bonins, and at Naha on Okinawa in the Ryukyu Islands. The names of Iojima (Ogasawara) and Okinawa made headline news in 1945: both islands were the battleground of U.S. Marines and Japanese soldiers in some of the bitterest fighting in history—American courage was matched against Japanese bushido, and they fought it out until there were few if any Japanese left to tell the tale.

Later on, in 1945, both Iojima and Okinawa were used as bomber and fighter bases for the final stage of the subjugation of Japan by the American Air Force.

In March, 1854, Commodore Perry returned. This time he was in command of seven warships and there was no difficulty in making the Japanese conclude the 'Japanese-American Treaty of Amity and Friendship' which was signed and sealed before the month was out.

The treaty, composed of twelve articles, provided for the opening of Shimoda and Hakodate to trade. In order to see that this was done, Commodore Perry visited Shimoda and Hakodate and prolonged his stay on the coast for four and a half months. With the signing of the Treaty a new chapter in the uneasy life of the mass of Japanese was added to the Dai Nippon Shi of the Tokugawas.

But the Anglo-Saxons were not the first imperialists to disturb Japan's isolation. As early as the close of the seventeenth century, Russian ships were on the move toward north Japan from the Amur River territory and the coast of south Kamchatka. They already had a Russian Embassy in Peking, dating from 1567, and a treaty with China in 1689 which permitted the extension of the Russian Empire to the northern boundary of Manchuria. And after they had looked over the possibilities of trade in the Kuriles the Russians came to the Chiba Prefecture (near Tokyo) in 1739 but could obtain no concessions from the Shogunate.

Russia returned to the attack in 1778, 1792 and 1804 but made no progress, and it was not until after Perry's first visit in 1853 that Admiral Putiatin visited Nagasaki harbour with three warships. This was as fruitless as the previous attempts, and when a second visit was made the following year the result was no different.

England was watching Russia. In August ,1854, Sir James Stirling, with four warships reached Nagasaki: England and France were at war with Russia and Sir James had been busily engaged chasing Putiatin's fleet out of Japanese waters. As a direct result of this visit to Nagasaki, the 'Anglo-Japanese Treaty' was signed on 14th October, 1854—its terms being similar to those of Commodore Perry's Treaty earlier in the same year.

On 7th February, 1855, Admiral Putiatin managed to conclude a 'Russo-Japanese Treaty' at Shimoda which was now an open port under Perry's Treaty with the Shogunate. In the following January, Holland was granted similar trading rights and the bamboo-curtain had been raised considerably.

These preliminary trading-pacts were superseded by more exacting documents based on the Japanese-American Treaty of Amity and Commerce negotiated by Townsend Harris on August 19th, 1858. By this treaty the ports of Kanagawa (Yokohama), Nagasaki, Niigata, Hyogo (Kobe), Yedo (Tokyo), and Osaka were thrown open to foreign trade. Furthermore, provisions were made in the treaty for regulating customs duty and consular jurisdiction.

Agreements (?) on the same lines were concluded with Holland, Russia, France and England.

These treaties certainly expressed in definite terms the Imperialistic nature of the foreign powers—it was 'guns or butter' and the Japanese decided on butter until they had guns themselves.

And it came about that in 1945 in each of those 'treaty-ports' the Japanese established camps for Prisoners of War, and in those camps were American, British from all parts of the Empire, Dutch and other Europeans captured during Japan's bid for an Empire in Greater East Asia. And, unfortunately for those of us who were guests (?) in those camps, they were now and again bombed by accident by the British and the American exceedingly efficient Air Forces.

From 1853 to 1858, Shogun Iyesada ruled in Yedo but the 'rights' of the Tenno had been infringed when he negotiated agreements with foreign powers—agreements which established exterritoriality, and control over custom duties, in the six 'treaty ports'. The unfortunate (?) Iyesada was followed by Iyemochi who had to face up to the difficulties as best he could.

An anti-foreign movement was added to the hostility of the four principal Daimyo in the west—Satsuma, Choshu, Hizen and Tosa—who were bent on restoring the Tenno to his rightful position. Inflamed by the agitation some of the retainers of the Daimyo Shimazu of Satsuma assassinated an Englishman, named Richardson, not far from Yokohama, on 14th September, 1862. This act of folly was punished by the action of the British fleet when it bombarded Kagoshima, the capital of the Satsuma Clan, in 1863.

The next attack was made by men of the Choshu Clan in June, 1863. Their victims were American sailors from the *Pembroke* who were fired on when the vessel was at anchor in Shimonoseki harbour.

Other foreign ships were fired at and this affront was answered in kind when British, French, Dutch and American warships bombarded Shimonoseki in September, 1864.

Komei Tenno was on the throne but he was unable to check the growing wave of unrest. The chief desires of the foreigners was for tea, raw silk and works of art: the sudden demand outran the limited supply, prices soared and profiteering created more discontent among the Samurai who had nothing much to sell—except themselves and their swords.

Shogun Iyemochi was succeeded by Shogun Keiki in 1866 and the next year Komei Tenno died. Conditions were ripe for the change-over from Tokugawa-feudalism to the Restoration of the Divine Rights of the Tenno under the banner of 'Respect for the Throne'.

H

The first act of the new ruler, MEIJI TENNO, a young man of fifteen, was to appeal to the Satsuma and Choshu Clans for their assistance in getting rid of Shogun Keiki. But before they could act, Keiki solved their problem by abdicating and dissolving his regime in 1868.*

* See Appendix VII.

CHAPTER III

MEIJI RESTORATION

i. Raising the bamboo-curtain

On 30th March, 1854, Commodore Perry negotiated the
'Japanese-American Treaty of Amity and Friendship'. Shimoda, in Izu province, and Hakodate in Hokkaido, were
opened to trade. That was the first turn of the wheel of Japan's
progress to a 'first-class' military power.

There is a granite tablet in the compound of the Gyokusenji
Temple in Shimoda. On it is carved these memorable words,
taken from Townsend Harris's own diary:—

'Thursday, September 4, 1856. Slept very little from mosquitoes
—the latter enormous in size. At seven, a.m. men came on shore
to put up my flag-staff. Heavy job. Slow work. Spar falls; breaks
cross-trees, fortunately no one hurt. At last get a reinforcement
from the ship. Flag-staff erected, men form a ring around it, and,
at two and a half p.m. of this day, I hoist the first consulate flag
ever seen in this empire. Grim reflections—ominous of change—
undoubted beginning of the end. Query—if for the real good of
Japan?'

Who can tell? On Sunday, September 2nd, 1945, at 10-45
hours, on board the U.S. battleship *Missouri*, General Mac-
Arthur signed the instrument of surrender as *Supreme Commander
for the Allies.*

I was in Tokyo Bay, aboard H.M.S. *Speaker*—not far from the
battleship *Missouri*—and I could not help thinking (as I raised
my glass in the ward-room) that it was only eighty-nine years
since Harris raised the Stars and Stripes at Shimoda. I mentioned this to Lieutenant Donald Perry (of the U.S. *San Juan*)
who was our guest that day. Perry was commanding the
detachment of G.I. who released us from Omori P.O.W. Camp:
Perry was from New Hampshire—maybe he belonged to the

clan Perry—the Perry who brought the 'blackships' to Shimoda in 1854—certainly he was in the service of 'Shogun' MacArthur, supreme commander of the greatest collection of warships ever assembled together by the Anglo-Saxons.

Townsend Harris, the first American consul on the sacred soil of Japan, lived in the Gyokusenji temple for a year. His companion, in the temple consulate, was Huesken—the Dutch interpreter. It was a lonely existence for Harris if not for Huesken who had many an affair with the local beauties. Still, there is the 'romance' of Harris and O-Kichi-san left on the records.

Poor O-kichi! She nursed Harris—the hairy barbarian— and looked after him for less than six-months. But that was enough to turn Shimoda against her: she took to saké and ended her life by jumping into a pond. There is a shrine to O-Kichi in Shimoda—pilgrims may still offer up prayers and burn incense to comfort her soul. But a more important shrine is that of YOSHIDA SHOIN—the great patriot who advocated the Restoration and the conquest of Korea and China.

Yoshida Shoin went to Shimoda, when the Black Ships were there. He wanted to go abroad but it was still a capital offence for a Japanese to leave the country. One night, he and a friend rowed out in a sampan to one of Perry's ironclads. He pleaded in vain to be taken abroad: the Shogun heard of it and he was put in prison and executed in 1859 the year that Townsend Harris opened the first American Legation at the Zempukuji Temple in Tokyo.

The first American treaty with Japan had been signed in the Ryosenji Temple at Shimoda, the first American flag hoisted in the compound of the Gyokusenji Temple at Shimoda, the first Legation opened in the Zempukuji Temple: 'undoubted beginning of the end'. Yoshida Shoin was dead but his policy remained.

In 1867, when Imperial and Shogunate causes were still in the melting-pot, the leader of the Reform—Saigo Takamori— was approached by Ernest Satow (then official interpreter of the British Legation in Tokyo) and offered British help for the Tenno because France was offering to aid the Shogun, but Saigo declined the offer. Nothing came of this 'balance of power politics' because Tokugawa Keiki would not accept war-ships and munitions of war from the French Minister, Leon Roches.

The Shogunate made it clear to the French that they had no intention of taking up arms against the Tenno. There was no civil war. Keiki retired to his ancestral fief in Mito. Yedo Castle, the feudal headquarters since 1603, was presented to Meiji Tenno who had been living a sheltered existence in his father's palace in Kyoto.

The Restoration was popular with the masses and supported by nearly all the Daimyo and Samurai. But the reformers, and the Tenno's advisers, were handicapped by the restrictions imposed by the Powers on self-government. The restrictions which had been agreed to by the Shogunate—provisions regarding tariffs, extra-territorial rights granted to foreigners in the treaty-ports—kept the anti-foreign spirit very much alive.

In theory, 'all authority was restored to and concentrated in the Throne', but in fact it was the authority of the Tokugawas which had been transferred to the Satsuma and Choshu Daimyo and their immediate supporters: even as Taira and Minamoto rule had been followed by Samurai rule, and the Ashikaga by the Tokugawa so were they displaced by the Sat-Cho (Satsuma-Choshu) combination. It was a change in name, not a change in method of rule.

Of course, the usual edicts followed—in the name of the new Tenno. In December, 1867, Meiji Tenno's edict referred to the foundation of the Empire by Jimmu Tenno and that, 'the State must share together all joys and sorrows . . . people must discard antiquated customs and advance with unswerving loyalty to the Throne', but the great majority of the people hardly knew what it was all about.

If we are to credit native records, Japan's population of thirty-two million in 1868 must have contained an illiterate mass of sub-human creatures whose mentation could be directed, or misdirected, with ease by an autocratic minority. Writers, like Dr. Okabe and Professor Ikeda, even refer to the custom of killing every other child, irrespective of sex, as one method of keeping down the birth rate increase and aid the struggle for existence. It would seem that 'during famine they gathered round the body the moment the person was dead and ate the flesh on the spot'.

Of course, infanticide was not confined to Japan. As late as 1902, I saw heaps of bleached bones at the bottom of circular stone-walled pits near Ichang, in Central China. Japanese, in the Tokugawa period preceeding the Restoration, were no doubt only following a Chinese custom of throwing unwanted girls into communal pits—to overcome the shortage of rice after the annual floods.

Still, it is unfortunate that the Sat-Cho dictators selected for the people of the soil a 'patriotic education' centred in the theory of divine origin, with its concomitant worship of the dead in general and ancestors in particular. It suited the purpose of Buddhism and Shintoism but it was wicked to dupe them that they were something apart from other men on earth— 'kami' in their own right.

On April 6th, 1868, Meiji Tenno held his first court. Before the Daimyo and the aristocracy he took an oath of fidelity. The five articles of this oath, made standing before the Shrine of his Imperial Ancestors, were:—

All measures of national policy shall be determined by public discussion in a popular assembly to be duly established.

All people, both governing and governed, shall unite in promoting the welfare of the nation.

Public offices, civil and military, shall be open to all—lower ranks shall be encouraged to achieve their aims without creating causes for popular discontent.

Civil life shall be governed by justice and righteousness and absurd usages of old shall be got rid of.

Knowledge shall be sought for wherever it exists for the building up of the foundations of the Empire.

It is doubtful if the oath of fidelity was inspired in any way by Meiji Tenno's personal knowledge of government of the people by the people. But it served the purpose of the Lord Sanjo, head of the new government, and the Tenno's representative, Prince Arisugawa, and looked well on paper.

Tearing up the roots of the old regime was the next step in the reformation of feudalism. In 1869, all the Daimyo—two hundred and seventy-three—returned their feudatories to the Tenno. Territory until then held by Feudal Lords passed into the Tenno's possession, and when title deeds were transferred the Daimyo became HAN-CHIJI (Clan Governors) with authority to administer their former lands as officials of the government. The Han-Chiji continued to collect taxes but were allowed to retain only one-tenth of the revenue as personal income, the balance was transferred to Government Officials in the capital, which had been renamed TOKYO on 17th July, 1868.

In 1870, the first daily newspaper was published in Yokohama but very few people outside the towns and cities could read it; the first section of the national railway in Japan, the line between Yokohama and Tokyo, was opened with foreign engine-drivers and firemen on the footplate. By 1871, the old feudal clan system was a dead letter—in theory at any rate. A new prefectural system came into existence: Feudal Lords were deprived of their power to govern and two-million Samurai were granted pensions—pensions so small that they had to work to pay for their upkeep, like the rest of the former 'idlerich' retainers of the Daimyo.

Tokugawa administrative and military strongholds of Yedo, Kyoto and Osaka were re-named Urban Prefectures or FU, the other forty-three strategic areas became simple Prefectures or KEN under governors appointed by Tokyo. The Shogunate class-distinctions of Samurai, Peasant and Merchant-Artisan, were abolished: the ETA were confirmed as 'untouchables' to continue their offal and sanitary duties with their own residential quarters or—'eta-ghetto'—in each district—Fu or Ken.

The aristocracy were regraded. Daimyo and Court Nobles became KAZOKU (Peers): Samurai became SHIZOKU (Gentry): the rest of the population were just HEIMIN (Commoners) and —in 1884—the peerage ranks of Prince, Marquis, Count, Viscount and Baron were created.

But the most important reform, from the point of view of the Sat-Cho allies, was the alteration of the 'military system' in January, 1873. New regulations were introduced to modernize the 'army'. The profession of arms, previously the privilege of Samurai, was extended to heimin (commoners). All males, on reaching the age of twenty were made liable to compulsory military service and the 'national defence force' modernized on the European system. French and German methods were chosen for the army by the Choshu clans, and British methods for the navy by the Satsuma clans who directed the conscription of Samurai and heimin.

Primary education was made compulsory for all over the age of six: the new 'Ministry of Education' aimed at one primary school for each six-hundred of the population. The country was divided into eight 'educational districts' in each of which there were to be thirty-two secondary schools and one university. Of course it took some time to complete this ambitious scheme but in 1940 there were 46,000 schools of all types and grades with a total enrolment of fourteen million—at that time one-fifth of the entire population.

Left to educationalists the system would have produced intelligent citizens. Unfortunately, the gumbatsu (militarists) linked education with conscription for the army and navy by making full use of the educational facilities for inculcating imperialism and fostering state-shintoism as the mental bridge between school and universal service in the armed forces. Conscription was established in 1873, but many years elapsed before it was found necessary to impose state-shintoism in the schools.

Industrial and educational contact with western science and learning led to an assimilation of new ideas and 'dangerous thoughts' and it was then that the Ministry of Justice, the Home Office and the Navy and Army Ministry combined to control education.

This unholy combination had already perverted Shintoism from a religious doctrine, or cult, to an instrument of nationalistic propaganda. It degraded education by a rigid 'control of thought': it used the Tenno as an image and compelled young and old to bow down and worship TENNO HEIKA as the godhead of the armed forces and the one and only arbiter of their lives: and it also controlled the Diet (Parliament), Police, Industrialists, Authors, Journalists, and Bankers—socialist, democrats, communists, left-wing or right-wing aristocrats, politicians, and simple people of the soil—by the weapons of intimidation and assassination carried out by thugs, kais (secret societies) or the super-military-police, the Kempei.

The cabinet system was established in 1885. On 11th February, 1889 the Constitution was promulgated by Meiji Tenno, twenty-one years after the Restoration and sixteen years after the introduction of a modern system of conscription. The restoration of 'divine rights' did not confer the franchise on the people but it did confirm Shogunate rule in another form, although there were elections in July, 1890, for the First Session of the Diet.

Direct access to the Throne was not altered by the grant of a Constitution to the people. The Army and the Navy were placed outside parliamentary control. Clans still functioned. Choshu and Satsuma had replaced Tokugawa and they alone continued to be responsible to the Tenno and not to the Heimin. *

In order to remove the slightest grounds for misunderstanding of the position between themselves and the Diet, as it concerned the Tenno, regulations were passed in January, 1894 (after the suspension of the fifth session of the Diet, in December, 1893) *restricting* the cabinet portfolios for the Army and Navy to the ranks of *serving* Naval and Military officers *nominated* by the General Staff.

This *regulation* was made specific in 1911 and it placed every subsequent administration at the mercy of the GUMBATSU (military clique) because no cabinet could be formed without contribution from the services for the two important ministries.

The method adopted, to make a farce of the franchise by direct control of the Diet, was for the General Staff to refuse to nominate officers, and refuse permission to serving officers to accept office in the cabinet. This veto was *in addition* to the right of direct access to the Throne *vested in* the Chief of the General Staff.

Another relic of feudalism was the GENRO (Elder Statesmen) created by the Choshu leader, Prince Yamagata, 1902: for more than twenty-years the Genro was the hub of the military dictatorship: they made or un-made treaties, determined peace or war, dictated home or foreign affairs, and generally prevented the *elected* members of the government from functioning except as a subordinate tax-collecting bureau.

And all this—and more—to carry out the 'guiding principle of education' so clearly expressed (in the so often quoted) IMPERIAL RESCRIPT on Education, of Meiji Tenno on 30th October, 1890 :—

'. . . . Our Imperial Ancestors have founded our Empire on a basis broad and everlasting and have deeply and firmly implanted

* See Appendix X.

virtue; Our subjects ever united in loyalty and filial piety have from generation to generation illustrated the beauty thereof. This is the glory of the fundamental character of Our Empire, and herein also lies the source of our education. Ye, Our subjects, be filial to your parents, affectionate to your brothers and sisters; as husbands and wives be harmonious, as friends true; bear yourselves in modesty and moderation; extend your benevolence to all; pursue learning and cultivate arts; and thereby develop intellectual faculties and perfect moral powers; furthermore advance public good and promote common interests; *always respect the Constitution* and observe the laws; should emergency arise, offer yourselves courageously to the State; and thus guard and maintain the prosperity of Our Imperial Throne coeval with heaven and earth. So shall ye not only be Our good and faithful subjects, but render illustrious the best traditions of your forefathers.

The WAY here set forth is indeed the teaching bequeathed by Our Imperial Ancestors, to be observed, alike by Their Descendants and the subjects, infallible for all ages and true in all places. It is our wish to lay it to heart in all reverence, in common with you, Our subjects, that we may all thus attain the same virtue.'

The Imperial Rescript, of Meiji Tenno, on Education was the set piece for every Japanese child—to be learned by heart, to be recited reverently, bowing before the portrait of Tenno Heika in the classroom. In time this alphabet of the divine traditions, the a.b.c., of hakko-ichi-u, was to become the x.y.z., of State-Shintoism the cult of Nippon Banzai—the shout which greeted the promulgation of the Constitution in February 1889.

Nippon Banzai! Tenno Heika Banzai! Hail Japan, long live the divine Emperor! I was in Kobe, in February, 1889, watching the lantern processions outside the Settlement. Tenno Heika Banzai—the brand new national cheer raised in Toyko for the first time the previous day—it sounded fine and went well with the paper lanterns and the cheering crowd. I was young—it was very exciting.

I heard it on a grander scale in 1904, when the Russians at Port Arthur surrendered to General Nogi: I understood much better, their patriotic emotion in the hour of victory over the white man who threatened their Empire. But in February, 1942, at Fort Canning in Singapore, I listened to that same national shout of encouragement with entirely different feelings. This time it was the British—under General Percival—who had *surrendered unconditionally* to the Japanese Army under General Yamashita.

I learned by bitter experience all there was still to know about Nippon Banzai, Bushido, Shintoism and the spirit of the Samurai during three and a half years, one of their prisoners of war.

Their true nature bubbled to the surface as they threw off the mask of pseudo civilization: they were Huns who lost no time in inflicting death, torture and humiliation on their foreign captives. But it was but the waving of their 'school certificate' for they had matriculated in sadism the guiding principle of the Imperial Rescript on Education scrambled into Kodo by the Gumbatsu.

ii. Dangerous thoughts

In 1868, the population was thirty-two million. At least twenty million were uneducated and those who were above 'school-age' were never educated at all if they were living outside the towns. In any case, in those days, there were few books and no newspapers so even if they knew enough Chinese characters—say 3,000—there was nothing much to read except the classics.

Even in 1949, I doubt if more than 8,000 kanji out of the 15,000 in a modern Japanese dictionary are ever used in a newspaper or in books and kana has to be used to identify them. And Japanese journalese is in a class by itself not easy to read and understand without much practice.

The young men over school-age, without education, who went into the Army were taught discipline and how to use modern arms and after their first period of service with the colours went back to work, on the farms or in the factory, until called up again to service in one of the numerous reserves. Because of the grouping of artisans, which I have already mentioned, there was in 1868, the nucleus of craftsmen exceedingly efficient and readily absorbed by industry but the mass of the population were still engaged in agriculture and remained, more or less, illiterate.

Even so, in the first election for the Diet in July, 1890, only a little over *one per cent.* of the total population voted by virtue of the franchise—a mere 400,000 out of 40 million. In 1918, under the 'Three Yen tax qualification' the percentage was only five per cent. higher and barely 3½ million out of 60 million had the right to vote. Quite apart from the fact that the vote was valueless to hold the militarists in check at any time between 1868 and 1945. Under these conditions it was almost impossible for real public opinion to show its head above ground.

But the writers were busy. When the ban was lifted, many thousands of Japanese went abroad—to Europe and America—to learn about military matters and to study western civilization.

The first few years, after the Restoration, there was an intensive study of European History and in 1877, Dr. Ukichi Taguchi commenced his *History of Japanese Civilization* in the light of his knowledge of European History. This was followed by Government sponsored institutions of research into Finance, Justice, Foreign Affairs, Agriculture and Commerce and so on. But the information was not passed on to the public. Then followed the Bureau of Historiography to collect material for the *Comprehensive History of Japan* from the Sandai Jitsuroku period of A.D.900 to the Yedo period. Divided into sixteen sections, each under a chief editor and numerous assistants, no less than 130 volumes had been published by 1937.

The output of 'History' was terrific and would take many hundred pages of this book to mention and comment on. But only a tiny fraction of it was ever read by the people of the soil or the people of the factories. None of it helped to build up any public opinion worth mentioning, but the emphasis on political history—in unrelated fragments—permeated primary, middle and high schools and overloaded education with the dead wood of the dark ages. Monthly and quarterly magazines added their quota to thought of the times. Japanese socialists began to 'study Japanese History' in order to build up their own political doctrines—they picked on the material most suited to their theories but were soon checked by the Home Office and sent about their business which was working according to their masters and thinking according to the Nippon Shoki.

Other scholars wrote more and more books on Shintoism—the Fukko-Shinto, the pure, logical Shinto of Motoori Norinaga and Hirata Atsutane. And there were others, like Dr. Genji Kato who expounded Shintoism in its relation to foreign religions and made it superior, in spirit and science, to all other religions ancient or modern.

But, Shintoism did not have the field to itself. The study of Buddhism kept pace with it in the Imperial Universities, the Denominational Colleges and Academies, and in the Temples. The Denominational Colleges pursued two courses: study of the tenets peculiar to one sect and study of Buddhist tenets in general. The Academies were maintained by various sects (Chizan, Bukkyo, Seizan, Kyoto, Rinzai, Shinshu, Hiyezan, Sozan and Chuo Academies) and followed the same course of study—Shujo (sectarian tenets) and Yojo (Buddhist tenets in general). But in none of the Universities was shujo dealt with because they did not belong to any particular sect and only dealt with research into yojo.

There were twelve main Buddhist sects and fifty-six branches in the country, and the output of books on Buddhism: Indian Buddhism, Chinese Buddhism and Japanese Buddhism exceeded the flood of literature devoted to Japanese History mentioned above. And the difference in meaning of 'The History of Buddhism' as used by the authors in Japan began to interest the sinologists and the pundits.

A history of Japanese Buddhism was not the history of Buddhism in Japan, or a history of Japan with special reference to Buddhism: and from that as a talking point numerous books were issued. Then there was the linguistic study of Buddhism—comparing the Pali (language used in canonical books on Buddhism) original of scripture called agamas with the Chinese version, and trying to decide if Pali scriptures (preserved in Ceylon) do in fact represent the teachings of the founder of Buddhism and if Pali was the language he used. And between the Pali and the Sanskrit, and the Chinese and the Sino-Japanese texts there was plenty of confusion and plenty of reconciliation necessary.

Then there was TENRIKYO—a religious movement which originated not far from Nara in the early part of the nineteenth century, as one of the Shinto sects, and in 1940 had a following which exceeded six-million. The followers of Tenrikyo believe that 'God the Parent' (Tenrio-no-mikoto) descended from heaven into the person of the foundress, MIKI NAKAYAMA, who became Divine at the moment appointed by God, 26 October, 1838. It is a religion founded upon *divine revelation* and its fundamental principles are the salvation of mankind.

Miki Nakayama, according to Tenrikyo, was at once divine and human, and she came to establish a new order in Japan. The headquarters of Tenrikyo are in the city of Jiba, about twenty miles south of Nara. The specific instructions of the religion are to be found in the Mikagura-uta (Holy Psalms) and the Ofudesaki (Sacred Text) and the main Sanctuary at Jiba was completed in 1934.

In Tenrikyo there are three divinely ordained concepts: the 'Soul of the Foundress'—JIBA, or the 'Residence'—and the 'Important Moment', three in one, so ordained by God the Parent manifesting Himself in the person of Miki Nakayama.

The *Residence* was the centre where God the Parent created the universe: Jiba the home of mankind, the cradle of salvation where the Kanrodai is to be erected when the reformation both of men's minds and of the world is accomplished: The Important Moment was the 26th day of the tenth month of the ninth year of Tempo—1838.

Tenrikyo combated the two extremes of ultra-socialism and of individualism and hoped by steering a middle course to bring about a spiritual and moral reform. Perhaps there is nothing about the religion of Tenrikyo, which is not found in Christianity, to convert the materialist so we had better leave it at that.

But the Buddhists were not impressed. On 20th October, 1936 a gigantic statue of Kwannon Buddha (Avalokitesvara)—goddess of mercy and charity—built of reinforced concrete, was dedicated at Takahashi City. It stands 133 feet above the ground and is divided into twelve stories each of which can hold five-hundred people—twenty people could sit on one hand of the statue.

The worship of Kwannon commenced in Japan in A.D.610—Tenrikyo began in A.D. 1838. The Dai Butsu at Nara is only 53 feet in height, cast in metal: the Jiba Sanctuary is made of the hinoki wood gathered from all parts of Japan: the statue of the 'Goddess of Liberty' (New York, U.S.A.) is a mere 89 feet high and represents democracy at the time of its erection before Perry set out for Japan?—maybe, I do not remember, but these are dangerous thoughts on ideology better left to the imagination.

CHAPTER IV

THE MEIJI ERA
(1868-1912)

i. *The Industrial Revolution*

The skill with which Japanese utilized western knowledge and picked the brains of foreign experts, to build a first-class military and industrial power on the bare foundations of feudalism amazed the world. The motive force was the Daimyo and the urge behind it all was a desire to make up for lost time under the Tokugawas, and to save the country from the aggression of foreign capitalists and militarists.

Out of the Restoration came Japanese militarism which owed its modern success to the generous financial and material assistance provided by European and American capitalists, their respective governments, their respective arsenals and their respective dockyards.

One and all, in the blind rush for trade to keep their own industrial machine working at full pressure, contributed to the rapid rise of Japan to the final menace she became to all their vested interests in the Far East.

When I arrived in Japan, in 1883, Japanese industry was on its first legs. Kobe was still known as Hyogo. There was a small cotton-mill, near Ikuta Shrine, run by Hunter who started an ironworks in Osaka. But a start had been made in all the treaty-ports which were humming with trade. Great Britain, with her experience in industry and Empire-building, took full advantage of the profit to be made on contracts for machinery, cotton-goods, munitions and plant for steelworks and arsenals, merchant vessels and warships.

Skilled mechanics, in British yards, built gunboats, then cruisers and battleships for the Japanese navy, and tramps and liners for the Mercantile Marine. British engineers produced machine-tools for Tokyo and Osaka military arsenals and for Yokosuka, Kure, Sasebo and Maizuru naval yards. And—at a later date—helped to bring into existence the great steelworks at Yawata and at Muroran.

British, French and American banks floated loans or financed the import of the raw material required for the expansion of industry and the manufacture of armaments. Australia and Canada extracted profit from the sale of wool, fats and lead. Malaya contributed tin and rubber; Scandinavia wood-pulp; India and the U.S.A., cotton and scrap iron—in fact the markets of the world all benefited by the rapid industrialization of Japan.

However, the most valuable contribution to the economy of Japan was the supply of enormous quantities of fertilizers for agriculture, and drugs and chemicals for pharmacy and industry.

Perhaps the United States of America had the better balanced trade at first. She purchased eighty per cent. of Japan's raw-silk and sold in return most of the cotton Japan required for her ever growing textile industry.

Before the Russo-Japanese War, Japan's exports of raw silk, tea, matting and the output of her light industries was sufficient in volume to create the required exchange to cover the cost of her imports of raw materials. But it was not long before the mass production of her cotton industry placed her as the most formidable of Britain's competitors in the Far East in the lower grade qualities. Japan had 500 looms in 1903, 25,000 in 1913 and 500,000 in 1940.

Heavy industries made similar progress and the manufacture of iron, steel and machine tools kept pace with the requirements of dockyards, railways, building and general purposes. Chemical works, cement works, paper mills and so on sprang up all over the country and the development of electric power generation (domestic and industrial) was rapid and widespread: in 1903, 80,000 kilowatts were produced for industrial purposes (hydro-electric and thermal), this was raised to 6,000,000 kilowatts before 1935.

As Japan's revenue increased so did the Gumbatsu's—the Sat-cho militarists—share of the increase. From whatever total was available (including foreign loans) fifty per cent. of it was

taken for the expansion of the Army and Navy: the extent
of the industrial expansion was the accurate index for the scale
of progress being made by militarism in Japan.

The Army established arsenals at Osaka and Tokyo, the
Navy built dockyards and arsenals at Tokyo, Yokosuka, Kure,
Maizuru and Sasebo. The main steelworks were erected at
Wakamatsu (Yawata) in Kyushu convenient to the coal fields
of that island : commercial interests, linked with the services,
proceeded with the building of shipyards in Yokohama, Kobe,
Osaka and Nagasaki.

Capitalism had transformed Japan from an agricultural to
an industrial economy but the Daimyo never lost control. In
the first place (after the Restoration) the capital of the feudal
lords—concentrated in selected banks—was used to finance the
industrialization programme under the name of Furoku Kyohei
(Wealthy country, strong in arms) and there came into existence
at once the new plutocracy—the ZAI-BATSU.

At first, the heavy industries, primarily in the field of armaments, were kept under the direct control and management of
the Sat-cho government while the light industries were handed
over to the private enterprise of the old aristocracy. In this way
there grew up—year by year—a close connection between
Gumbatsu and Zaibatsu, a profitable co-operation between
government and big-business interests which was carried into
the political arena at a later date, when the Satsuma and
Choshu factions disagreed about the distribution ratio for Army
and Navy out of the fifty per cent. of the total revenue they
compelled the Diet to vote them.

The steady increase in population, plus a higher standard of
living of the urban manufacturing districts, placed additional
strain on the farmers. But by the wide use of fertilizers they
managed to double the yield of the rice crop acreage and the
shortage was made up by imports of rice from Indo-China and
Burma.

ii. Sino-Japanese War (1894)

Directly Japan had completed her basic reforms in finance,
education, currency, taxation and justice, the Gumbatsu
decided that the national structure could be tested by using the
military machine against China as a means of expanding an

I

overseas market and to see how it compared with the military efficiency of the Western Powers.

Korea was the natural gateway through which Chinese culture reached Japan—Korea offered the best excuse for attacking China because she was 'close to Japan' and China had robbed her of her independence and 'threatened Japan'. Rather far fetched—but quite sufficient to justify (?) Japan's first act of aggression under Meiji Tenno.

Sino-Japanese War was of short duration. But it did serve to demonstrate the fact that China's out-of-date Army and Navy was no sort of match for the westernized forces of Japan: the Japanese were delighted—it was Banzai! Nippon Banzai! all the way. But their triumph was short lived: there were other imperialists interested in the disintegration of China if not in the independence of Korea.

Japan had not taken into account the 'China policy' of her European tutors in Imperialism. Her leaders had yet to learn the meaning of diplomatic action based on force.

China had been defeated. At the Shimonoseki Peace Conference, China agreed to surrender the Liaotung Peninsula—South Manchuria—Formosa and the Pescadores, to pay an indemnity and to recognize the 'complete independence of Korea'. This treaty was signed on 17th April, 1895, but it did not suit the plans of Russia, Germany or France in China and they had the naval force on the spot to back up their objections.

A strongly worded diplomatic note was sent to Japan to the effect that the possession of the ceded territory, by the Emperor of Japan, would be detrimental to the lasting peace of the Orient. Japan was not then in a position to answer force by force so she reluctantly agreed to cancel that part of the treaty to which objection had been raised.

On 30th November, 1895, in accordance with this decision, Japan—having destroyed the defences of Port Arthur—returned the territory which had been ceded to her in perpetuity and full sovereignty. The surrender to force was carried out with an outward show of dignity but this 'foreign interference' was deeply resented by the people and their indignation was made the most of by the Gumbatsu to fan the flames of nationalism. The children of the Restoration were now twenty-seven years old—old enough to replace their parents in thought and action.

The Sino-Japanese War was a milestone in the progress of Japanese militarism. The Restoration altered the status of Daimyo and Samurai, conscription brought an entirely new class of warriors into the war machine—the conscripts were clay in the hands of the potters and (as it turned out) with mortification they watched the conspiracy of the three foreign powers end in the occupation of Kiao-chiao by Germany and Port Arthur by Russia, in 1896—less than a year after Japan had handed back the territory to China.

From 1870 to June, 1894 Japanese statesmen were agitating for a revision of the treaties. In 1894, the British Government proposed a new treaty—to come into effect in 1899—which abolished consular jurisdiction and the tariff, but the tripartite intervention sign-posted the only (?) road to continental expansion. And Japan took that road from 1895 to 1945.

But the real, or perverted, idea of the sanctity of treaties (Peace or otherwise) in power politics was put succinctly by President Theodore Roosevelt. Writing in the *Outlook* magazine in September, 1914—referring to Korea—he wrote:—

' . . . But Korea was itself helpless to enforce the treaty (with the U.S.A.) and it was out of the question to suppose that any other nation, with no interest of its own at stake would attempt to do for the Koreans what they were utterly unable to do for themselves. Therefore when Japan thought the time had come, it calmly tore up the Treaty and took Korea . . . . '

This lucid exposition of the value of 'scraps of paper' may not have been commonly held in Europe or America but it had its following in Japan, Germany and Russia and requires no chapter and verse to be quoted by me.

Leaders in Japan, from 1868 to 1912, were few in number but powerful in office. The best known of these Meiji Era stalwarts were Saigo, Okubo, Kido, Ito, Okuma, Yamagata, Oyama, Matsukata, Fukuzawa, Shibusawa, Itagaki, Goto and Saionji. They were patriotic and ambitious men of undoubted ability, with a personal sense of loyalty to the Tenno but they were not very much different from the Tokugawa fraternity in their attitude to the people of the soil and their right to a voice in the government of the land.

iii. Russo-Japanese War: 1904-5 and Russian expansion in Asia

Before we proceed over the ground of Japan's progress as a real military power in the Far East we should glance at Russia's policy in China—and particularly in Manchuria and Korea.*

Early in the sixteenth century, Cossacks and European Russians began to cross the Urals dividing Europe from Asia. In 1567, they were sufficiently interested in China to establish an embassy in Peking, and in 1689, signed a treaty which permitted the extension of the Russian Empire to the northern boundary of Manchuria. But it was not until 1858 that the vast territory north of the Amur River was *ceded to Russia* by the Manchu politicians.

A few years earlier, as a result of the Sino-British Wars of 1839-41 and 1856, Victoria Island (Hong Kong) was ceded to the British, and—in 1857—Canton was occupied. This was followed by the occupation of Taku (North China) in 1858 by the 'allies'.

After the capture of Taku Forts, the 'allies' concluded the Tientsin Treaty but were refused permission to proceed to Peking.

This was rectified by force and the Peking Convention was signed by China, Russia, France and Britain. Foreign troops remained in Peking and this was resented by the Manchus. It was then that Russian diplomacy took its own line of action.

General Ignatief concluded a bargain with the Manchus. He offered to use Russian influence to persuade France and Britain to withdraw their troops from Peking. He succeded. China ceded to Russia the maritime province of Manchuria with six hundred miles of coast line which included the harbour of Vladivostok. This gave Russia an outlet for her new territory of Eastern Siberia and Manchuria. But the aims of Muscovite politicians were not limited to these objectives of Ignatief. They had in mind the building of an Empire to the east of the Urals.

By 1891, the Trans-Siberian Railway—linking the old with the new Russia—was on the map. In 1895, the railway had reached Chita on the Manchurian border but the terminus was to be at Vladivostok. Six-hundred miles of railway construction

* See Appendix IX.

could be saved by taking the short cut to Hailar and then across Manchuria to Vladivostok instead of building it in Russian territory north of the Amur already ceded to them by China.

The Sino-Japanese War was over. Russia approached China on the subject of the railway crossing her territory. China agreed to the proposal. A treaty was concluded and it contained a secret clause providing for a Russo-Chinese Military Alliance directed at Japan, for there was more than the construction of a railway at stake: China had already ceded to Japan all the land south of a line drawn from the mouth of the Yalu River to the port of Newchang on the Liao River. This territory, if held by Japan, was detrimental to Russian policy in North China: Port Arthur was an excellent naval base, Talien (Dairen) a warm-water port of geographical and political importance.

When the terms of the Shimonoseki Treaty were made known to Russia she acted promptly. There was no difficulty in persuading France and Germany to act with her in protecting China from the menace of Japan. Britain declined to join in the protest but it made little difference to the issue—Japan quit Manchuria, Russia marched in a few months later.

The Russian bear and Chinese dragon became playmates at the expense of the people of the Rising Sun. Having gained permission to build a 'Chinese-Eastern Railway' from Manchuli to Vladivostok, Russia prepared for the next move.

Li Hung Chang visited Moscow in 1896 and was presented with a million roubles by the Tsar's Minister of Finance, Count Witte: the agreement covering the C. E. Railway, and another military pact aimed at Japan, was signed. Russia loaned China four-hundred million francs at four per cent. interest to pay off the Japanese war indemnity.

Having made sure of one concession, Russia (the same year) secured a lease of the Liaotung Peninsula and authority to build a branch railway line from Harbin, on the C. E. Railway, to Port Arthur and Talien which they renamed Dalny—'far away'. By 1899, both the main railway across Manchuria, and the branch line to Dalny, were under Russian *military control*. There was a Russian garrison at Port Arthur, being rapidly modernized by Belgian engineers, and the fishing village of Talien was being transformed into the city of Dalny with first-class harbour facilities.

Russian expansion in China did not pass unobserved by the Gumbatsu but Japan was not yet ready to scramble again for Chinese territory. In 1871, Japan concluded her first treaty with China—in 1874 she sent an expedition to Formosa and in 1881 China recognized her sovereignty over the Liu Chu islands: in 1876 Japan had concluded a treaty with Korea.

European expansion in China kept pace, on a smaller scale, with that of Russia. France, as a result of the Franco-Chinese War secured Annam in 1884—they had annexed part of Cochin China in 1867. Germany established herself in Shantung in 1897, with a naval base at Tsingtau. Britain had occupied Burma, Hong Kong and Wei-hai-wei and added Kowloon to the far-flung Empire.

This rivalry of the powers in China created anti-foreign feeling which culminated in the Boxer-rising of 1900. It had the support of the Chinese Empress Dowager and Li Hung Chang —one of the richest men in China. The battle cry of the Boxers was simple—'Drive the foreigner into the sea'. It is difficult to say what inspired Li Hung Chang who was reputed to be worth over sixty-million pounds sterling and was the 'Prince of Squeeze' in a land where bribery was part of the system of government of the Manchus.

In 1900, Kaiser William II, issued his famous message to German troops, ordered to march on Peking and relieve the Legations:—

'Give no quarter. Take no prisoners. Fight in such a manner that for one-thousand years no Chinaman shall dare even to look as-kance upon a German.'

and, from his safe retreat in London, or in Switzerland, Lenin and his followers, issued their statements calling on the en-slaved humanity of the Far East to make a clean sweep of their enemies and establish Bolshevism.

The Chinese had the choice—Lenin or the Kaiser's blood-hounds—but the Allies quelled the rebellion, Peking was relieved and the indemnity fixed at £67,500,000 in September, 1901.

Russia had increased her army in Manchuria to 150,000 men: a protocol was signed in Peking—officials responsible for the murder of foreigners in China were to be punished, the indemnity to be shared by the powers, a fortified Legation-quarter in Peking, foreign troops to be stationed on the lines of communication between Peking and the sea.

Japan sent troops to join the expedition and was now in the selected group of powers with 'special interests to protect in China'—but England was uneasy about the dominating position of Russia not only in China but on the borders of the Indian Empire. She deemed it prudent to conclude the Anglo-Japanese Alliance in 1902—just to be on the safe side of clipping the bear's claws.

Russia, by signing the Manchurian Convention, agreed to withdraw her troops from Chinese territory *outside the leased area* on successive dates. She displayed no intention of doing so. The Tsar made this quite clear in 1903, when he created the Vice-royalty of East Asia to control the diplomatic, civil, military and commercial affairs of Russia *in her sphere of influence in China.*

When this was made known to Japan, and that Korea was also within the sphere of influence of Russia, she immediately suggested diplomatic negotiations to adjust the clash of vested interests. Russia agreed to discuss the matter but declined to pledge herself regarding the sovereignty of China, and she rejected out of hand equal treatment to all nations having commercial relations with China. Numerous restrictions were suggested, regarding Korea. Japan was asked to recognize that country as a neutral zone completely outside her sphere of influence. Furthermore, Russia declined to recognize that Japan had any interests in Manchuria, or its littoral, maintaining that she must consider the area beyond her political ambitions.

These diplomatic negotiations dragged on to an inconclusive end. Japan was ready for war. It was time to drop the mask of suppliant in favour of casque of Hachiman—the God of War. The Anglo-Japanese Alliance warned off the interventionists of 1896—the Japanese armed forces did the rest with remarkable speed and efficiency. Russia may not have been forced to accept unconditional surrender but she managed to lose every major engagement at sea and on land before the war ended in stalemate.

From 1902 to 1904, I lived in China—Central China, North China and in Manchuria and I was with the Japanese Army in Korea and Manchuria in 1904-5 during the major part of the campaign.

Between 1899 and 1902, the Japanese Government borrowed twenty-million pounds sterling in London and during the war they borrowed eighty-million more in New York and London-the war cost Japan £200,000,000 and her total investments in China in 1902 were only one-million dollars—£200,000. Britain's investments in China were £52,000,000; Russia's £50,000,000; Germany's £30,000,000; France's £18,000,000 and the U.S.A.'s only £4,000,000. So Japan spent a lot of money to protect her 'vested interests'.

During the Japanese campaign against Russia I met some of the Japanese leaders who were responsible for the Restoration and the creation of the 'new Japan' of Meiji Tenno. They were all from Samurai or Daimyo stock—Ito, Oyama, Yamamoto, Nogi, Fujii, Kuroki and Fukushima—Princes, Counts, Admirals or Generals the statesmen or fighting men responsible for putting paid to the account of the 'Colossus with the feet of clay'. And I also met the rising generation of Empire builders, Kato, Tanaka, Takarabe, Ide and others, to say nothing of unit commanders from General to 1st Class Private. I gained valuable experience of Japanese methods of warfare—their ability to handle modern weapons no less than their fighting spirit. The ZEN philosophy of spending years on the solution of problems was much more thorough than that of their rough and ready opponents in the field.

At Port Arthur, the Russians fought well. Like the Japanese they had to have the gun in their backs at times to encourage the 'fighting spirit' but as they were the first troops to be hammered with the 28-centimetre howitzers firing a 500-lb H.E. shell I do not blame them for wanting to quit their posts. And, as I wrote at the time, 'You can have but a faint idea of the hopelessness of speculating on the terrors of death when you are being shelled with eleven-inch high explosives, for hell must have less triumphs than this phase of war, and you lie still and resign yourself to fate, unless you care to run away, and it was this that the Russians would not do on the afternoon of the 15th October, 1904'.

Since then, of course, we have progressed in the art of mass slaughter but I was young—and I was impressed by it all. I must have been for when I made a visit to 203 Metre Hill on December 5th, there were two-thousand corpses of the belligerents on the hillside; they were ' mostly denuded of their clothing, scorched, deformed and defaced beyond recognition, and in the trenches there was a pulp of mutilated humanity. The sight of those trenches heaped up with arms and legs and dismembered bodies all mixed together and then frozen into compact masses, the expressions on the faces of the scattered heads of decapitated bodies, the stupendous magnitude of the concentrated horror, impressed itself indelibly into the utmost recesses of my unaccustomed brain—there to remain and ever remirror itself into my eyes, and shame me for my very callousness that I did ever look on it. What man has done, man will will do again, and human shambles will not be confined to this solitary instance, although they may never exceed its greatness'.

There were only twelve thousand five hundred casualties—eight thousand Japanese and four thousand five hundred Russians—in the battle for the hill 203-metres in height: the fight went on for eight days, first one and then the other held the hill-top. An average of one thousand 28-centimetre shells a day were driven into the trenches defending it: Russians lay on the top of dead and wounded Japanese: into friend and foe the 500-lb shells, filled with high explosives, plunged again and again and it was this that littered the hillside with fragments of frozen humanity.

Of course it was just a curtain-raiser for World War I and World War II, but maybe worth recording because it was the first time that 11-inch shells were used against infantry in trenches.

Before I went over to Korea, soon after the outbreak of the war with Russia, I was in Kure—not far from Hiroshima. The Kempei arrested me but I was released when I showed them my pass from the Imperial Household. They shipped me to Nagasaki that night and I was not allowed into Hiroshima because the Hiroshima Castle was the headquarters of Meiji Tenno. The Castle was built by Lord Mori in 1593, and taken over by Lord Fukushima when Mori was *transferred* by Tokugawa to another fief, and later on it was taken over by Lord Asano. The Castle, made famous by Meiji Tenno's residence there during seven months of the Russo-Japanese War, was carefully preserved. The first atom-bomb was dropped on Hiroshima.

iv. Communism or Imperialism and The integrity of China

The integrity of China figured largely in the pronouncements of nearly all the Powers, interested in enlarging their trade and spheres of influence in the country, from the sixteenth century, but it was left to Russia and Japan to make it the cockpit of their respective ideologies.

Bolsheviks—after the Russo-Japanese War—came to regard Asia in general, and China in particular, as the most fertile soil for sowing the seeds of Communism which would flower into the grand World Revolution. The Japanese had their own ideas of what was best for Asia and I can not better the words of a well known Japanese banker, Hirozo Mori, who had this to write on the subject in October, 1937:—

> 'Our population is increasing, and this increase can be supported only by expansion of trade and industry, for which the nearest market is China and the Asiatic mainland. Herein lies our economic future. There is no gainsaying the fact. We want the world and the Chinese people to understand and recognise it.
>
> Expansion toward the continent is the destiny of the Japanese people, Heaven decreed, which neither the world nor we the Japanese ourselves can check or alter. The Sino-Japanese War, the Russo-Japanese War, the Manchurian incident of 1931 and the armed conflict now going on, when traced to their origins, have resulted from an attempt to resist the economic expansion of the Japanese race. We do not covet our neighbour's territories. We aim only at the furtherance of peaceful trade relations and have endeavoured most sincerely to accomplish that purpose . . . .
>
> The National Government of China has concluded the Sino-Soviet non-aggression pact and the Red colour is deepening.
>
> When all China is Red, there will be no place for the capitalist Powers there. Their flags will simply disappear. Our own very existence will be in danger. Therefore this is a war of defence for us. Whether we can check this dangerous trend in time and save the Far East and humanity from the worst fate will depend solely upon our unflinching determination and steady will to stick to it to the bitter end. . . . '

What Chinese peasants thought about it did not matter very much to Tokyo or Moscow. But, from the point of view of Japanese peasants, who formed over forty per cent. of the population, and were hard-put to feed the other sixty per cent., it might have been wiser to spend less money on arms and more on subsidized fertilizers.

Let me make this point clearer by reducing it to percentages and decimal fractions of profit and loss in industry and in agriculture in 1933, as disclosed by this table:—

Corporation Profits by Businesses

	1923	1925	1929	1931	1933
Agriculture ..	loss 0.5%	profit 5.2%	loss 2.3%	loss 3.1%	loss 0.1%
Fishing	profit 2.9%	„ 7.3%	profit 5.3%	profit 1.1%	profit 6.6%
Mining	„ 3.5%	„ 3.9%	„ 4.9%	„ 0.5%	„ 6.1%
Manufacturing	„ 4.5%	„ 8.3%	„ 8.0%	„ 4.4%	„ 7.6%
Trade	„ 7.1%	„ 8.8%	„ 5.8%	„ 3.2%	„ 6.7%
Transportation	„ 2.4%	„ 4.2%	„ 3.9%	„ 2.5%	„ 2.7%

(N.B.:—1923 was the year of the Tokyo-Yokohama earthquake)

Soviet Russia's aims may have been to improve the lot of the Chinese peasant—Japan's aims have been stated quite clearly by Mr. Hirozo Mori. Japanese finances, in 1931, had been operating in the red and the heavy war expenditure involved increasing taxation which was ruthlessly imposed by the Gumbatsu and accepted by the Zaibatsu who relied on more stolen assets to swell the bank balances. And bank deposits had certainly increased from a total of £11,149,000 to £1,396,800,000 from 1893 to 1936—from the time just before the Sino-Japanese War to the China Incident.

Setting aside all questions of international morality, and altruism, this is certain: Japan improved conditions in Korea and Manchuria more in thirty years than the Chinese did in three-thousand years. And out of a total population of 30,959,164 in Manchuria in May, 1933, there were only 300,000 Japanese and 750,000 Koreans, and no less than sixty-eight per cent. were engaged in agriculture out of the entire population. Less than two per cent. of the population were soldiers, and the number of Chinese who migrated and settled in Manchuria in the ten years between 1923 and 1932 was 2,705,183.

On the other hand, Soviet Russia's contribution to the welfare of Manchuria, or China proper, consisted of propaganda and military aid in civil war—nothing more and little less than was done for the country by Japanese militarists in counter measures to dominate the people.

The first 'reform movement' in China was started by Sun Yat Sen in 1898, but he was foiled by the astuteness of the Empress

Dowager Tsu Hsi who had controlled the government of the country since 1861. The Cantonese leader was relying on the active help of Yuan-shi-kai in the elimination of Tsu Hsi but the wily Manchu, understanding that the Empress had the most beautiful collection of 'silver shoes', took cash and let the credit go: he informed his royal mistress of what was in the wind, she very promptly took the hint. The young Emperor of China was jailed in the Temple of Heaven, guarded night and day by the foreign trained soldiers of Yuan-shi-kai.

The next reform movement, Boxer Rebellion in 1900, was brought about by Empress Tsu Hsi to divert attention fron Sun-yat-senism to anti-foreignism. It cost China some territory and a lot of cash but was of no benefit to the peasants. For lack of genuine inspiration the anti-foreign movement died in its first bath of blood.

On 27th August, 1908, Empress Dowager Tsu Hsi issued an edict which assented to the 'New Constitution for China'. Japanese influence was evident in this Constitution for it was designed to vest power in the ruler, protect court officials, and sidetrack the rights of the governed. Legislative, judicial and executive power was vested in the sovereign who alone was to control the Army and Navy, to make War, declare Peace and settle the Budget.

It was a crude imitation of Ito's Constitution, granted by Meiji Tenno to the Japanese in 1889 to preserve the Dynasty by controlling the armed forces.

In October, 1908, Tsu Hsi and the imprisoned Emperor Kuang Su died within a few days of each other. Prince Chun succeeded as Regent and he promptly relieved Yuan-shi-kai of his military command because of his connivance in the imprisonment of the late Emperor. The following year the Provincial Assemblies came into existence on the mandate of less than .3% of the population!

However, in October, 1910, the National Assembly of two-hundred members came into existence. The appointees of the Emperor, Manchu, Chinese, Mongolian and Tibetian nobles numbered one-hundred; the others being nominated by Provincial Assemblies. President and Vice-President of this 'National Parliament' were to be appointed by the Emperor at the first session in 1913.

In 1911, when it appeared that the Cabinet would be made up of members of the existing boards of control, with the approval of the Emperor, there was a general outburst of indignation from the non-participating members of the National Assembly.

Yuan-shi-kai was recalled and appointed President of the National Assembly but it was too late to save China from the Revolution. The genuine reformers were led by Sun-yat-sen and Wu-ting-Fang of the Cantonese Party and they were supported by many of the Tuchuns (Governors) of the anti-Manchu Provinces—against them were the Imperial Family and the satellite Nobles.

The Revolutionary Party, at a conference in Shanghai, elected Sun-yat-sen provisional President of the Chinese Republic with its Capital at Nanking. In theory at any rate the Reformers had established a government elected by the people. Unfortunately it did not work out that way in practice and from 1912 to 1949 there has been no 'Parliament' elected by popular vote in China.

However, faced with revolt, Yuan Shi Kai opened direct negotiations with Sun-yat-sen. There was a compromise. The Emperor Pu-yi abdicated on 12th February, 1912, Sun-yat-sen resigned his provisional appointment and Yuan-shi-kai became the first President of the Republic of China. The Manchu Dynasty failed to emulate the Japanese Dynasty because it lacked the driving force of Shintoism to stimulate patriotism and worship of the Emperor. Buddhism and Confucianism were not sufficiently alive as political forces to rouse the emotion of the illiterate masses who had not been taught that they were bound to the Dynasty by ties of common descent from a Sun or a Dragon Goddess, so the Manchus lost the throne to the Revolutionists. And it was no consolation to them that Pu-yi, some years later, was enthroned as 'Emperor' of Manchoukuo with the title of Chief Executive of the 'Independent State'.

The first President of China had ambitions. He suppressed Sun-yat-sen's parliamentary rule by force—Sun fled to Japan—Yuan-shi-kai made an unsuccessful attempt to alter his status to that of Emperor, in 1915, but before he could succeed he died and was succeeded by Li-yuan-hung as President. Other attempts to restore Manchu sovereignty also failed. President Li was followed by President Feng-kuo-chang in 1917, but he was only too glad to hand on the title to Hsu-shi-chang in August, 1918, and by that time the rebel leader Sun-yat-sen had started his 'Southern Movement' from Canton.

Sun's new movement was hustled along by a 'students' anti-Japan' movement, and this, further complicated by war between General Wu-pei-fu and General Chang-tso-lin—the respective leaders of the Republic in Peking and Mukden— gave ample opportunity for Japanese militarists to create incidents in order to consolidate their position in Manchuria and North China.

The more or less empty title of President went from Hsu-shi-chang to Lihuan-hung and then to Tsao-kun in 1923. All these Presidents were in the pocket of the Japanese military clique— year after year they 'sold China' in return for loans and concessions and no amount of Southern or Student Movement could make any headway against the Sino-Japanese combination of grafters.

From 1908 to 1913, I travelled extensively in Central and North China, Manchuria, Siberia, Korea and Japan. During my travels—selling steel—I visited (more than once) all the Naval and Military Arsenals, Dockyards, Railway Workshops, Coal Mines, Steelworks and Industrial Plants of any importance from Hankow to Shanghai—Shanghai to Peking—Port Arthur to Harbin—Harbin to Vladivostok—Antung to Fusan and from Kagoshima to Hokkaido. I went to Moscow by the Trans-Siberian Railway and I travelled over the Chinese Eastern Railway more than once. Then, in 1914, I joined the Chinese Salt Gabelle, under Sir Richard Dane, to supervise the collection of Salt Tax in an area of roughly 380,000 square miles of the provinces of Manchuria. During World War I, I was on active service in France until wounded in 1916. Recovering from wounds, I helped to organize the first battalion of the Chinese Labour Corps, in France, and then returned to the Far East in the British Secret Service to observe the operations of the three-power intervention in Siberia—aimed at the formation of a second-front against the Bolsheviks.

Previously, in 1902, I had supervised the collection of junk and river taxes on the Yangtze River above Ichang for the Imperial Chinese Government: then I worked on the Tongshan

Coal Mines in North China until the outbreak of the Russo-Japanese War.

After the Russo-Japanese War I went to South Africa to work on the Rand Gold Mines as a Controller of Chinese Labour and during my stay in the Transvaal saw service with the Imperial Light Horse in the Zulu Campaign of 1906.

These experiences, added to my adventures as a gold-miner in Alaska in 1899-1901, made me observant and interested in human nature—especially in the non-European races. And it followed that I had ample opportunity of learning about Japan's industrial progress, military expansion, methods of administration and general policy in the Far East. Not only that but I got to know something about 'communism' and 'imperialism'—in the East and in the West—to say nothing of the attitude of the white to the yellow and the black races, the labour-fodder of the capitalists of the West, and the attitude of the Japanese to their own cheap labour to build up their Empire in Greater East Asia.

I have indulged in this tedious egotism merely to illustrate this small point: no matter how much you may travel about the world, or what you may do in sixty-years, the actual number of people you meet and talk to yourself represents too small a proportion of the whole to enable you to make dogmatic assertions regarding the attitude of an entire nation to any given subject.

And when the people have no say in the actual government of their country—be it China, Japan or Russia—you can find out very little about the working of their mind and if they prefer any of the ideologies dished out to them from time to time by their overlords—imperialists or communists.

China's population of five-hundred million is scattered over four million square miles of flats, hills and rivers: Japan's population of eighty millions clutters up only 142,270 square miles of flats, hills and rivers. The density of population is roughly one hundred and twenty-five to the square mile in China, 575 to the square mile in Japan—it is only four hundred and forty per square mile in Great Britain.

Whereas the density of population over the *whole of Japan* is at the rate of five hundred and seventy-five to each square mile that of the area of greatest concentration in Great Britain (one-sixth of the area) has a density of one thousand five-hundred persons per square mile, so we are not the only densely popula-ted nation by any means. Of course, from the Japanese point of view, the seven million Australians are far from being cramped in their 2,977,600 square miles of territory reserved for pure white socialists, communists or royal-blues.

In China the greatest concentration is in the lower Yangtze River area. About eighty per cent. of the entire population depends directly on agriculture but only a mere ten per cent. of the total area is arable land. In many districts, seventy-five per cent. of the land is owned by twenty per cent. of the popula-tion and taxation—land and farm produce—is often as high as sixty per cent. In these areas, governed by landlords and local militarists, communists were popular when they cancelled debts and redistributed the land among the peasants and their own followers.

Communism appealed to the landless classes more than capitalism did to the treaty-port workers in foreign or Chinese factories, but China could get along now, as she did in the past, without the aid of either. She is the world's third largest producer of cotton—the world's second largest exporter of silk—can grow all the rice, wheat and other crops she requires if she could only be allowed by foreign and native militarists to settle down to modern methods of irrigation and cultivation.

Sun-yat-sen wavered between socialism and communism but by 1920 he managed to form a military Southern Government at Canton when Tsao-kun and Wu-pei-fu (Northern Tuchuns) took Peking and drove out General Hsu-shu-tseng. On 5th May, 1921, Sun was elected President of China by the Canton Parliament: there were now three 'Governments of China' and the country was back to the eleventh century when there were the 'Empires' of *Sung*, in the *South*, Hsia in the middle and *Kin* in the North. Now it was Hsu-Shi-Chang in Peking, Wu-pei-Fu in Nanking and Sun-yat-sen in Canton, with Chang-tso-lin in control outside the Great Wall.

On October 27th, 1921, I went to Canton (with Lord Northcliffe) to see Sun-yat-sen but he was up-country with the army. We talked to Wu-ting-fang who claimed that Sun's government represented the views of one hundred and thirty million Chinese in Yunnan, Kueichow, Kuangsi, Kuangtung and Szechuan. During the conversation I suggested to Wu-ting-fang that Sun should spend the rest of his life consolidating the position in the south and not attempt to go north of the Yantze or join with the Tuchuns in any of their adventures. But Sun was pledged to the unification of China under a central government—one hundred and thirty million people was too small an Empire or Republic to stem the tide of Japanese aggression.

To my suprise, Sun decided to co-operate with Chang-tso-lin against Wu-pei-fu. This alliance with the Military Governor of Manchuria was tantamount to backing Japanese military aspirations in China through their puppet. I made my views known to Sun-yat-sen. He made known his reasons in a letter to me dated 13th April, 1922. The following extracts from that letter may be of interest to the reader.

'There are two ways of effecting this unification of the country. The method of material force, i.e., civil war; and the method of moral force, i.e., negotiation and agreement. Now, the effective military strength of the country may be roughly classified into four groups as follows:—
   (a) The Canton Group of which I am the leader;
   (b) The Chihli Group of which Wu-pei-fu is leader;
   (c) The Fengtien Group of which Chang-tso-lin is the leader;
   (d) The Tuan-chi-jui Group formerly known as the Anfu Party, of which Tuan-chi-jui is the leader.
Both Chang-tso-lin and Tuan-chi-jui have sent their delegates to me and expressed their willingness to co-operate with me in effecting the unification of the country by eliminating Hsu-shi-chang, who is admittedly Chief Executive at Peking as a result of an illegal election, and the establishment of an effective central government based on the Chinese Constitution. This has been called an unholy alliance. The reply is simple. Both Chang-tso-lin and Tuan-chi-jui are Chinese like myself. They are the leaders of forces which must be taken into account before unification can be effectively effected. They come to me and accept my terms of settlement. Am I to chase them away because, it is said, they have had a dubious past? They may or may not be sincere. Their future conduct will tell. If they turn out false, I shall face and deal with that when and if it arises. The alternative to this is to fight them in spite of their willingness to join me. My plans are not altered by Chang-tso-lin's defeat. . . .'

But I still think I was right. The Canton troops were commanded by Genral Chen-chiung-ming not by Sun-yat-sen and

K

he was also opposed to northern expeditions. Sun tried to get rid of him but it was Sun who had to flee to Shanghai. He was in 'exile' until some of the 'loyal troops' recaptured Foochow at the end of 1922, and in January, 1923, Canton was re-occupied by the pro-Sun faction and General Chen left hurriedly for that haven of refugees, Hong Kong. Sun returned to Canton—so did Chen and the summer of 1923 was spent in the local civil war which went on into 1924 in various phases of give and take.

Sun-yat-sen died in 1925. There had been no national unification during his lifetine. In 1926, Chiang-kai-shek assumed the leadership of the 'People's National Party'—the KUO-MIN-TANG —and held it until early 1949, when General MAO-TSE-TUNG began his drive on Nanking with his army of communists.

The Kuomintang, the political child of Sun's social and economic ideology, was based on the three simple principles: the people's livelihood, nationalism and equality; and was called the San-Min Chu-I. Sun fought all his life against ancestor-worship, militarism and confucianism. He was the inspirator of Chinese nationalism which in 1926 began the real assault against corrupt war lords and corrupter politicians in North China. And it was Sun-yat-sen who turned to Russia in the end for financial, military and diplomatic support for San-min Chu-i.

After Sun's death his latest policy of co-operation was carried on by Chiang-kai-shek. Soviet arms and munitions, money and the weapon of propaganda among the people of the soil carried nationalism and equality into the stronghold of the Tuchuns. The Kuomintang was reorganized on the communist pattern: Soviet political and military advisers came to Canton to spread the ideology of the Bolshevik.

But Chiang-kai-shek, after his first successes, turned sharply to the right again and double-crossed his mentors and their fellow travellers north-west of the Yangtze. Civil war went on and with it grew the aggression of the Japanese, first in Manchuria, then in Central China and lastly in all parts of the country easily getatable by their troops. The communists joined, halfheartedly, in Chiang's stubborn defence but when the war was over they would have nothing further to do with the Kuomintang.

In my opinion there are two defects in the character of the Chinese which contribute to their undoing in peace and in war: corruption and the lack of patriotism. Corruption springs from centuries of practice in the art of extracting taxes out of taxation —the tax farmer who paid for the right to collect tax from land and agriculture, the tax-collector who paid for the right to collect taxes for the Mandarin who paid for the right to keep part of the taxes for himself, and so on from village head to Emperor or President. It became a fine art—we call it bribery; they call it various names according to how it effects their own pocket. The lack of patriotism arises from the fact that there are five-hundred million Chinese without anything to be patriotic about—their chief concern is the first of the San-min-chu-I's—people's livelihood. And it does not matter very much what particular ideology they are asked to accept so long as they are allowed plenty to eat.

The moment a Chinese rises in society, in the village or in the city, he wants to become a tax-collector. Your servants, head-boy to water-carrier, are tax-collectors: your baker, butcher, tailor and tinker each must contribute something for the honour of serving you through your servants. It may only be cents or dollars but if it is not paid on demand your servants provide good reasons for changing their patronage.

I found this to be the case, in my own home, in the Customs on the Yangtze, coal mines at Tongshan, gold mines on the Rand and in Manchuria collecting Salt Tax. The labourer was bad enough but the official was shocking: in one year I raised the total Salt Tax collections in my area from two million dollars to six million dollars.

The Japanese are also past masters in the same art of 'taking a slice from the melon' so they found it an easy matter to co-operate with Chinese politicians. If communism can alter this squeeze system it should get quite enough revenue from simple taxation to finance all its plans and schemes. But I doubt if that will be in my lifetime.

The U.S.S.R. and Chinese Communism (1920–1949)

With regard to the 1949 conquest of China by communist forces, led by General MAO TSE-TUNG, it may be of some interest to set down the views of Japanese in 1937. From a mass of material, I select the following comment which appeared in a special edition of the *Osaka Mainichi* on 20th October, 1937.

. . . . 'As recorded in history, at the time of the World War, the Imperial Germany which produced Karl von Clausewitz sent back to Russia by a 'sealed train' some 300 communists including Lenin and Radek to dynamite the Czar's government. Germany succeeded in attaining her object, but not only did those communists crush the Czar's regime but they later blasted even the Kaiser's government. Furthermore, they plotted a world revolution to bolshevize the entire world.

JOSEF STALIN, 'the King of the U.S.S.R.', is now actually seeking to accomplish the ideological conquest of the world inspired by the principle of 'Red Imperialism'. He has succeeded in his attempts at ideological invasion in some cases: *if it is no mistake* to say that the ideological conquest of other nations is an act of war, it will follow that the U.S.S.R. has been long waging war with powers whose national ideas do not accord with the guiding principle of the COMINTERN.

The U.S.S.R. has actually invaded Chinese territory in the ideological sense. One will recall, in this connection, LENIN's declaration that the first signals for the opening of the world revolution drive should be raised in China and Spain. His instructions have been observed. China has been overrun by the Communist and Communist armies for the last year or more. Should the Soviet attempt to Bolshevize the whole territory of China be successful the Comintern will doubtless extend its destructive influence thence to other parts of the world, *using China as a base of the operations for the world revolution.*

The efforts of the Comintern to accomplish its aim of a world revolution may be said to be directed at the following two objectives: (1) To attack capitalistic and imperialistic countries by every means available and (2) instigating independence movements among the natives of colonies and semi-colonies.

The Comintern reasons that (1) the collapse of capitalistic and imperialistic states will lead to the independence of the natives in colonies and semi-colonies and that (2) racial movements on the part of such natives will menace the existence of capitalistic and imperialistic countries. The racial movements among the natives of colonies and semi-colonies are not always identical in point of significance. The drives aimed at world revolution, therefore, cannot always be carried on by the Comintern in the same way.

LENIN, in a speech at the committee meeting on 26th July, 1920, said that there is not the least doubt that all nationalistic movements will, without exception, turn into bourgeois-democratic drives because the majority of backward nations are agrarian states supporting the principle of bourgeois capitalism. Therefore, he declared, supposing that it is possible to organize proletarian parties among backward nations, it will be utopian to expect that these parties can apply communistic and revolutionary policies in such nations without establishing a definite relationship with the agrarians and actually assisting in their nationalistic movements. Such being the case, LENIN said, it is up to the Communists to support the nationalistic movements among the bourgeois elements of colonial peoples. Lenin added, however, that the support should be offered *subject to the conditions that* (1) . . . the movements are revolutionary in nature and that (2) their promoters do not hinder '. . . *our attempts to train and organize, in accordance with revolutionary principles, the masses which are being exploited* . . . '

Failing these conditions, Lenin declared, the communists should fight the reformist-bourgeoise directing the nationalistic movements because they will be in the same category as the leaders of the 2nd Internationale. Presenting to the committee his draft plan for the settlement of racial and colonial problems, Lenin stressed that all attempts to disguise bourgeois-democratic nationalistic movements as communistic must be decisively defeated.

It will be necessary for the Comintern temporarily to establish contact with democratic bourgeoisie, among colonial and backward peoples, Lenin pointed out, but it is by no means advisable to unite with such peoples. The Communists must always keep intact their characteristics as proletarians.'

The present position in China, Indonesia, Indo-China, Burma and in Malaya is sufficient testimony of the efficient methods of the Comintern in using CHINA as a base of the operations for the world revolution. But, to continue with the *Osaka Mainichi's* comments :—

' . . . The Chinese Communists once made common cause with the Kuomintang, but the co-operative relations between them did not last long. Parting with the Kuomintang the Communists returned to their own camp. The two again became mutually hostile.

The tables turned, however, in the early days of 1937. The Communists have since then urged the necessity of co-operation and compromise with the Kuomintang, hoisting the banner of anti-Japanism. The COMINTERN, needless to say, has assisted the efforts of the Chinese Communists to organize their party, directing their organization movement through Chief Wachinsky of the Far Eastern department of the Comintern and others.

It is noteworthy that the first manifesto issued by the Chinese Communist Party anticipated collaboration with the Kuomintang This may be interpreted as indicating the determination of the Comintern to start a vigorous fight for the cause of the proletarian revolution—a struggle against the imperialistic powers' influence in China, which is to be staged by placing the Kuomintang under Comintern control and utilizing the Kuomintang recovery movement.

The contents of the manifesto were decided, it is known, in the 2nd Congress of the Communist Party held in July, 1922. The proclamation said that the object of the party was to create a communistic society after first establishing an autocracy of the proletariat and *abolishing the system of private property by means of class strife*. It was added, however, that the Chinese Communists, in view of the present situation in the country, must, in the interest of the proletariat, *assist democratic movements and organize a common front* with workers, farmers, and 'petit bourgeois'. The Chinese Communist Party was willing to support the Kuomintang as a means of overthrowing the military cliques.

The ultimate aim of the party is to create a proletarian autocracy, first, by assisting the national bourgeois movement with a view to eliminating the military cliques and, next, by dethroning the bourgeoisie following its victory over the military group.

One of the remote causes for the breach between the Kuomintang and the Chinese Communists, after three years of collaboration was the Communist Party's disapproval of the northern drive launched by the Kuomintang. When the national revolutionary troops occupied the Wuchang-Hankow sector during their military operations, the Communist Party assisted the Kuomintang to establish a government there. The party then forced the Kuomintang to offer government posts to Michael Borodin, the right-hand man of the Comintern, Hsu Chien, Teng Yen-ta, Tang Sheng-chih and Chang Fa-kuei. Then, the Communist Party started operations to expel rightist elements from the government service—including General Chiang Kai-shek himself.

Following his successful northern drive, General Chiang Kai-shek befriended the bourgeoise in Shanghai, particularly the Chekiang financial clique. He also came to terms with various capitalistic powers. At the same time, taking advantage of the success of his military operations, he launched a vigorous offensive against the Communist Party. Thus he succeeded in establishing the Nanking government on 18th April, 1927, laying the foundation for his subsequent brilliant record. An ex-Communist he joined the bourgeoisie, which is diametrically opposed to the Communist Party. The dispute within the government established in the Wuchang-Hankow region originated from the complete difference of interests between the Kuomintang and the Communist Party.

However, the COMINTERN did not abandon hope regarding China. Recognizing the failure of its attempt to take advantage of the bourgeois-democratic revolution in China, it launched subterranean movements aimed at winning over workers and agrarians. It adopted as its fundamental policy the creation of a

Soviet Regime of the proletariat by carrying out the following three measures:

(1) An agrarian revolution to crush the landowning class,

(2) anti-imperialistic agitation to unify the country, and

(3) armed revolts to overthrow the bourgeois-democratic regime.

The Comintern paid special attention to the Chinese revolution in the course of the 45th sitting of its 6th Congress on 29th August, 1928. In a resolution entitled—'The International Situation and Duties of the Comintern'—adopted by the Congress, the Comintern said: 'The Chinese revolution is, in nature, an anti-imperialistic self-emancipation movement. Although it is nothing but a bourgeois-democratic revolution in the present stage of its development, there is a possibility that the revolution will eventually lead to a proletariat revolution. The struggle against the imperialistic influence, therefore, is inseparably related with that for the recovery of land and the strife against the anti-revolutionary bourgeois bureaucracy. This self-emancipation of China will be accomplished only by means of the struggle against the bourgeoise, the strife to recover land from landowners through an agrarian revolution, and the fight to deliver the agrarian community from the shackles of heavy taxes. The object of realizing self-salvation will not be attained without (1) establishing the autocracy of the proletariat and agrarians, (2) recovering land, and (3) nationalizing foreign enterprises in China, banking and transportation. New situations in world politics have been created by the Chinese revolution, new developments of colonial agitations, and the expected aggravation of the revolutionary situation in India. *We are now convinced that we can upset the relative stability in the capitalistic order.*'

The 7th Congress of the Comintern held in Moscow from 25th July to 20th August, 1935, attracted the attention of every class of society throughout the world. Mr. Manuisky—secretary of the executive committee of the Comintern—in his report, said that the principal purpose of the Congress was to proclaim a war which would be fought for the purpose of defeating imperialism, insuring future peace, and protecting the U.S.S.R.

A resolution adopted by the Congress with regard to the question of racial movement said: 'The Communists should extend assistance to the strife for the racial emancipation of peoples of colonies and semi-colonies, particularly in the case of the fight of the Chinese Red Army with the Kuomintang and imperialistic states, including Japan.'

Chief Secretary Georgi Dimitrov of the Comintern also said: ' . . . The Chinese Soviet alone may become the central force for organized strife against the imperialists' attempts to partition and enslave China by its enlisting of the anti-imperialistic influences in the campaign for the national emancipation of China. We offer our ardent assistance to the heroic soldiers of the Chinese Red

Army who have been trained through the experience gained in innumerable battles. We guarantee to the people of China the extension of determined assistance to the struggle, which is aimed at completely delivering the Chinese people from the hands of imperialistic plunderers and their Chinese tools.'

Attention must be given in this connection to a speech made by CHEN SHAO-YU, representative in Moscow of the Chinese Communist Party, during the course of the 7th Congress of the Comintern on the subject of '*The Revolutionary Movement in Colonies and Semi-Colonies and the Strategy of the Chinese Communist Party.*' He said, ' . . . the time to start revolutionary movements is now ripe or is ripening . . . the capitalistic world is now confronted with the increasing danger of a crisis, as a result of the aggravation of the domestic and international disputes of capitalistic states . . . colonies have proved danger zones in the camp of international capitalism . . . The Chinese Soviet must, therefore, become the central force for the organized struggle *to emancipate the entire* people of China. . . . '

The Chinese Communist Party is at present (1937) led by Chu Te, *MAO TSE-TUNG* and *CHOU EN-LAI*. Among the Chinese who hold *important posts in the headquarters of the Comintern at Moscow* are Chen Shao-yu, Li Li-sa, Tsai Hai-sen, MAO TSE Tung, Chang Kuo-shou and Chou En-lai. Li Li-sa and Tsai Hai-sen reside in Moscow, Chen Shao-yu visits Ulan Bator and Moscow to maintain contact with the Chinese Communist Party, Chang Kuo-shou and Mao Tse-tung reside usually at Fushih—Shensi province, China—Chou En-lai makes the circuit of Fushih, Nanking and Shanghai to direct Chinese revolutionary operations. Headquarters of the Chinese Communist Party are at present (1937) established at Fushih. A characteristic of the *Chinese* Communist Party, as compared with similar bodies in other countries, is the fact that *leading members* of the party *rule over a definite area* where they have established their own government independent of the central regime at Nanking. The party has its own army and is estimated to be approximately 200,000 strong. The central organ for the direction of the *Chinese* Red Army is called 'The Revolutionary Military Affairs Committee, and exercises the highest authority with regard to matters relating to military operations, supply and organization. The members of the committee include Chu Te as the chairman, Chou En-lai as the vice-chairman and Wang Chia-chiang. It is noteworthy that Foreign Commissar MAXIM LITVINOV of the U.S.S.R. sits on the committe as an adviser.

According to what Mao Tse-tung told an American leftist writer, anti-Japanese agitation carried out by the Chinese Communist Party is aimed at forcing Japan (1) to renounce her policy of 'Chinese invasion' (2) cancel the Doihara-Chin Te-chun agreement concerning the four north-eastern provinces (Manchoukuo) and northern Chahar and to abolish the present system of government in Manchoukuo and the autonomous regime in East Hopei; (3) to withdraw the Japanese garrison forces in North China; and (4) to withdraw members of the Japanese special service corps now in various parts of China. To attain those objects, Mao Tse-tung declared, the Chinese Communists were willing to come to terms with the Nanking government and the Kuomintang, disregarding the traditional enmity between them.

The Communists were in a position to profit from protracted warfare. They therefore decided to enlarge the incident (at Lukouchiao on 8th July, 1937) into a national conflict between Japan and China through the aggravation of the hostilities.

To that end they instigated the masses to start large-scale agitation against Japan, assassinated national leaders reported to be friendly toward Japan, and encouraged the young officers of the 29th Army to challenge Japanese troops to a major conflict.'

The *Osaka Mainichi* was stating the Japanese case against the Chinese Communists in 1937. Events in China, since 1945, appear to confirm the Japanese theory that the U.S.S.R. intend to use 'China as a base of the operations for the world revolution'. Mao Tse-tung and Chou En-lai are the Chinese Communists responsible for the downfall of the Kuomintang and General Chiang Kai Shek in 1949. Regarding the active participation of the U.S.S.R.—in bringing about the Sino-Japanese War of 1937–45—the *Osaka Mainichi* said:—

' . . . Major-General Lepin, military attache to the Soviet embassy in China, concluded a military accord with Feng Yu-hsiang, leader of the pro-Soviet faction, as follows:—

'The Chinese Central Army agrees to co-operate with the Soviet Communist forces in fighting an anti-Japanese War. The Nanking government gives de facto recognition to the existence in China of a RED AREA which is under the influence of the Moscow government.

The Chinese Communist forces pledge to observe general instructions which may be issued by the Nanking Government with regard to the anti-Japanese agitation. The RED AREA will not be subjected to invasion or alteration so long as the instructions are observed.

The Chinese Communist forces agree to deliver to the Central Army *part of the war materials which were supplied from the U.S.S.R.* '

On 13th July, 1937 Chou En-lai, representative of the Chinese Communist Party, visited General Chiang at Loshan and concluded this agreement: The Chinese Communist Party shall undertake the general mobilization of Japanese, Manchoukuo, and Soviet Communists to make a concerted attempt with the Soviet Communist Party to enlarge the bolshevization movement and instigate riots in Japan and Manchoukuo . . . . The National Congress shall be authorized to draft a new constitution . . . guaranteeing to the people the right to enjoy democratic freedom . . . . organize a democratic central government and unify the nation along the line of resistance against Japan. . . . Deputies shall be selected through free competitive elections among members of various political parties and factions. . . . .

Chu Te was appointed commander-in-chief and Mao Tse-tung assistant commander-in-chief of the Chinese 8th Route Army in the North China area.

Mao Tse-tung is reported as saying: 'In case the struggle against Japan proves a success, the Communist Party will next demand that the powers interested in China *voluntarily renounce their rights.* He warned that in case the Kuomintang and the Nanking Government do not recognize Communism the Communist Party will resort to action consonant with the will of the masses.' The ultimate objectives of the Chinese Communist party are, in sum, the elimination from China of the influence of all foreign powers and the bolshevization of the entire territory of China.

The recently intensified activities of the Chinese Communists, therefore, should be interpreted as a meaning that the COMINTERN has advanced another step in its attempt at world bolshevization and that the step is tantamount to a declaration of war on the leading nations of the globe.'

The reader is at liberty to dismiss all the above quotation from the special edition of the *Osaka Mainichi*, 20th October, 1937, as of no importance and without connection with the Chinese Communists rapid advance from Manchuria to the vicinity of Canton *after* the U.S.S.R. intervention in Manchuria in 1945 *after* Japan had decided to accept unconditional surrender. For my part I find it rather interesting, when we are rushing British troops to Hong Kong and hunting Chinese Communists in Malaya, to say nothing of present conditions in Europe and particularly in Greece, in 1949.

For thirty-seven years the Chinese have provided cannonfodder for civil war, or for war against the Japanese. During this period the education of the masses has stagnated until now, 1949, I doubt if even one per cent. of the population are able to read and write Chinese characters. According to the 'Nine Years' Programme of Constitutional Preparation'—formulated in 1908—it was hoped that by 1916 between *one and two per cent.* of the population of China proper would be able to read and write but events have brought to nothing the extension of primary education. And so, like the Japanese in 1868, the Chinese in 1949 are an illiterate mass of people who can be taught to worship Communism, as the Japanese worshipped Amaterasu, without a clear understanding of the motives of the self-appointed guardians of their body and their mind.*

v. Anglo-Japanese Alliances and The integrity of China and Korea: (1902–1911)

In the first Anglo-Japanese Alliance of 1902, the 'High Contracting Parties' promised to safeguard mutual interests in China and Korea: the second Anglo-Japanese Alliance was for the consolidation and maintenance of the general peace in the regions of Eastern Asia and India. It was signed on 12th August, 1905, and Articles 3 and 4 recognized Japan's political military and economic interests in Korea and Great Britain's special interest in all that concerned the security of the Indian frontier: Article 6 provided for Great Britain's neutrality— during the Russo-Japanese War—unless another Power joins Russia. But the most important part of the new treaty concerned the preservation of the common interest of all Powers in China by insuring the independence and integrity of the Chinese Empire.

The Alliance was renewed in 1911 and was a political handicap in our dealings with China, and Korea, and did a great deal to help the gumbatsu and lower our prestige in Asia. The manner in which it helped our mutual interests in Korea can be seen by this summary of events in that country: In 1876, Japan sent a military mission to Korea. Korea signed a treaty and Japan refused to recognize China's suzerainty. In 1882 there were Anti-Japanese riots in Korea which were crushed by Chinese troops—Korea paid £20,000 damages: in 1884 Japanese secret societies (kais) organized a rebellion, aimed at overthrowing Korean Government and placing a Japanese puppet on the throne. The following year Japan and China (Tientsin Treaty, 18th April, 1885) agreed to withdraw their troops from Korea. Japanese civil pressure on the Korean government culminated in the rebellions of 1893–94—China and Japan sent troops to restore order. In June, 1894, Japan presented demands to Korea and China, including an ulti-

* See Appendix IX.

matum to the Korean King which was refused: Japanese troops occupied Seoul, overthrew the Government, set up their own puppet Government which it forced to declare war on China on 1st August, 1894. Sino-Japanese War followed: the Queen of Korea was murdered by Japanese in October, 1895 and in February, 1896 the King of Korea fled to the Russian Embassy in Seoul. These events were followed by Russo-Japanese agreements (regarding Korea) in 1896 and 1898 which became scraps of paper after the Russo-Japanese War: Japan became ADVISER in 1904, CONTROLLER of Foreign Relations in 1905 and in 1907 the King abdicates in favour of his son—in 1910 Korea is annexed and in 1911 the Anglo-Japanese Alliance is renewed for ten years.

The Russo-Japanese Treaty of 30th July, 1907 contained secret clauses which fixed the demarkation of spheres of influence in Manchuria and non-interference in Japan's sphere of influence in Korea. Other treaties followed, in 1910 and 1912, which dealt more specifically with zones of influence in Manchuria and Mongolia. Still later, after Japan's twenty-one demands on China in 1915, Russia and Japan, in June, 1916, concluded a treaty which bound the countries into a close military alliance to fight any third power attempting to establish dominion over China.

These were but trifles in the dismemberment of the Chinese Empire and the Chinese Republic: Korea, Formosa, Tonkin, Burma, Tibet, Manchuria, Mongolia and Turkistan—a million square miles or so of territory—came under foreign influence, Soviet, Japanese or other predatory powers; Christian or Atheist, Democratic or Communist influence and none of it helped the peasant in Suiyang, Lanchow, Chengtu or Yunnan to grow larger and better crops of rice.

CHAPTER V

THE TAISHO ERA
(1912-1926)

Mutsuhito—MEIJI TENNO—died on 30th July, 1912 after a very remarkable reign of forty-four years during which Japan rose fron an insignificant state to a world power in trade and in armaments.

I was in Japan when Mutsuhito's death was announced. It stunned the simple people of the soil more than the knowing ones in towns and cities throughout the country. To the peasants in the interior, Meiji Tenno was the father of his people—Tenno Heika who had by his knowledge and virtue made all things possible for Japan. They loved him and they worshipped him because he was human and yet he was divine—and there was no vice in them when they flocked to the shrines to bid farewell to his soul. They required no orders from the police to hang out the Hino-maru or to be sad by proclamation from Tokyo. They were not concerned with Bushido, Shinto or Yamato-damashi—patriotism—or with their own problems of seikatsu.

But during those forty-four years the character of the Japanese people had altered. The over-rapid industrialization of the country created a new set of problems for the real rulers of Japan. It was no longer a rice economy. There was a new generation of serfs forced to work long hours at low wages in shipping, mines, factories, cotton mills, steel works, arsenals and dockyards. Low wages to cheapen goods for export—to expand trade and produce wealth for armaments. Low wages, which reduced purchasing power at home, depressed prices for necessities and added to the difficulties of farmers burdened by taxation and the high cost of fertilizers. And—added to all this

—the never ending friction between the Choshu and the Satsuma factions for their fifty per cent. share of the revenue for expansion of Navy and Army.

General Katsura—Yamagata's protege—Marquis Saionji and the Genro (Yamagata, Matsukata, Oyama and Inoue) had dominated the administration from 1901 to 1911. Shortly before the death of Mutsuhito, Katsura resigned again in favour of Saionji to try to restore 'respect' for the working of the Constitution by the Genro, Gumbatsu and Zaibatsu.

Prince Ito, the 'father of the Constitution', had been assassinated by a Korean on Harbin Station in 1909: Prince Yamagata, the main prop of the Choshu clans, was rid of his great Satsuma rival but there were rebels within the ranks of both Choshu and Satsuma who had neither respect for the Constitution, Genro or the Diet.

General Nogi was never interested in politics. He was a Samurai of the old school. After the Russo-Japanese War he became Principal of the Peer's College in Tokyo and what he saw in the Capital disgusted him with the new generation of military opportunists and grafters with their pseudo respect for the Tenno.

On 13th September, 1912, Nogi and his wife committed junshi—it impressed the nation and restored some of the lost faith in Shintoism, and in Amaterasu-o-mikami. But their method of leaving this world for the next one had its critics—Japanese and Foreign.

Two days after the incident, I wrote the under noted comment which may explain my own thoughts in 1912 on the subject of Nogi and junshi:

'The tragic suicide of Count and Countess Nogi, coincident with the Imperial funeral, is surely relieved of all spectacular barbarism by the knowledge that the great General lived up to the principles of Bushido to which he owed allegiance. . . . Just for the nonce, draw the charitable veil of forgetfulness over the mode of his end; ignore the precise rules of morality which should govern actions and consign the pros and cons of junshi, and the ethics of bushido —which you may not understand—to the tender mercy of the deontologists.

No doubt we are less peccable if our ideas synchronise with prevailing opinion, but the disturbing fact remains that the great Christian nations still prefer War to Arbitration. Such being the case, we can but count it an asset of war if the people are stirred to

intense patriotism by the last action of their hero. The stability of
a nation depends on more than the mere number of its battleships
or the number of its soldiers; the human element is a very necessary factor, and the people want tuning up occasionally by drastic
measures. All this, of course, from the military point of view. Nogi
was a soldier by profession and a professor of ethology by incli-
nation.

A precognition of Nogi's character convinced the writer that
nature had endowed the man with active and with speculative
power. He was ultra-patriotic, and this certainly made him prone
to impulsive strategy which seemed at times to almost threaten his
record as a soldier. But he had the powers of genius adequate to the
military tasks he was called on to perform; he had the potency and
character necessary to impress the troops with the potentiality of
his ideas. The lavish waste of life, during the first great assaults
on the permanent forts, was but the grim expression of his moral
supremacy. They blindly obeyed, blindly charged again and
again, and were slaughtered because the unscientific spirit of
bushido impelled Nogi to attempt the impossible, not once but
many times.

. . . But—and here's the rub—the steadily piling up heap of
dead and wounded caused him to ponder on the matter of his
responsibility, and he began to ask himself if his personal share in
the national sacrifice was adequate. . . . Nogi was no sycophant,
for he devoted his life to Japan, the wealth of his intelligence and
the blood of his two sons. To him the Emperor and Japan were
synonymous—with the death of his Liege his worldly obligations
ceased . . . . Then oblivion, for in the words of the great Persian
poet:—

'Yesterday, This Day's Madness did prepare:
To-morrow's Silence, Triumph, or Despair:
Drink! for you know not whence you came, nor why:
Drink! for you know not why you go, nor Where.'

And into this cock-pit of ethics and corruption came to the
throne of Japan, Yoshihito—TAISHO TENNO. Yoshihito, third son
of Mutsuhito, was born in 1879. He was a delicate child and at
the age of thirty-three, when his father died, was not fitted—
mentally or physically—to rule in a constitutional monarchy
let alone exert any authority over the genroism of his Shinto
State—but he was suitably protected from dangerous thoughts
and lived quietly in the Imperial Palace.

The incapacity of Taisho Tenno suited the ambitions of the
Clans and Big Business. China was a Republic in name, if not
in fact, and the Army required two new divisions for expansion
in Manchuria and internal security in Korea. Saionji refused

to co-operate so the Genro forced him to resign in favour of Katsura. Katsura, by now too big for his sword and his boots, decided to form his own political clique—the Doshikai—and free himself from Yamagata's patronage. He split the Choshu clans only to increase Satsuma influence and was succeeded by Admiral Yamamoto, in 1913.

By this time the racket in armament orders had brought to light scandal after scandal in military and naval circles, and—to mark time while the dirty-linen was being washed in public—the Genro brought in Okuma to give an air of respectability to the passing of the Naval Estimates. Then World War I broke out in Europe and there was 'full employment' in Japan for the Zaibatsu had the Far-Eastern market all to themselves.

Pressed by Yamagata (and Choshu interests), Okuma re-introduced the Army Increase Bill. It was defeated, on that occasion but passed in May, 1915. The Army were in the saddle now. On January 18th, 1915, the 'Twenty-one Demands of Japan' were presented to China and the real attempt to conquer that country became part of the Japanese national policy.

Japan participated in the war against Germany but—right to the end—she was toying with the idea that the allies would be defeated. As the price of her adherence to the terms of the Anglo-Japanese Alliance she received many Pacific Islands, north of the equator, which would have delighted the soul of Yoshida Shoin, enshrined at Shimoda.

Between 1915 and 1918, Japan by direct and indirect methods lent or gave to the leaders of China, who were opposed to Sun-yat-sen, a sum exceeding 500 million yen. And in return obtained concessions for building railways and consolidating their position in Manchuria and North China. In October, 1916, General Terauchi became head of the Tokyo administration and held office until the Expeditionary Force—to 'open the second-front in Siberia'—had established itself on the mainland. Most of the trading profits, made during the War, were squandered on this expedition (and the Russo-Japanese fighting which followed in its wake) or in loans to China.

i. The labour movement

There were Socialists in Japan at the time of the Sino-Japanese War but their influence was of little importance to the

Labour Movement until the death of Meiji Tenno. They were hounded from pillar to post and forced out of politics in 1911 as a result of 'direct action tactics' in 1908, but reappeared in 1916 as a political party. But it was the Rice Riots, of 1918, which gave them their real opportunity to contact the masses who were being ruthlessly exploited by gumbatsu and zaibatsu.

I was in Kobe during the Rice Riots. Strikes, against the rising cost of living, had been going on for some time all over the country. The price of rice went up by three-hundred per cent. between 1915 and 1918: the narikin (profiteers) manipulated the rice market by buying and holding stock for a rise. Wages had gone up, it is true, but the rise bore no relation to the rocketing of world prices for commodities and comestibles. The manipulating of the price of rice was the last straw and troops had to be called out to deal with the rioting. There was some fighting (in Kobe) but the people and the soldiers seemed, to me at any rate, to be in sympathy with each other although the policemen ran amok at times.

The Expedition to Siberia coincided with the Rice Riots. General Terauchi resigned office—the Genro decided to by-pass the Sat-Cho applicants for office in favour of Mr. Hara, leader of the Seiyukai, and he became the first civilian to be appointed Premier. As I have previously mentioned, only a bare one per cent. of the total population had the right to vote until Mr. Hara raised it by the three-yen qualification to six per cent. in 1918. This meant a mere three and a half million out of a population of sixty million and led to demands for universal suffrage during 1919 and 1920, when the Throne dissolved the Diet again.

In the May election (1920), Hara was returned to office but it was the militarists who still controlled the administration and held the labour movement in check.

ii. Secret Societies

The most vicious method of intimidation and control over the Japanese was exercised by secret societies, or KAIS. For centuries the kai formed part of the Samurai stranglehold on the people of the soil. More recently, the Black Dragon (Roku-Ryu-Kai) Society—associated with the name of Toyama

L

Mitsuri—and the Black Ocean Society (Gen-yo-sha) founded by him in 1879, were the most active.

The Gen-yo-sha was the model for the GESTAPO, of the Nazi, and the OGPU, of the Soviet police system. In early Meiji days, the Gen-yo-sha was the directing force behind the kempei. Then the population was harassed by political bullies, SOSHI, an their hirelings the GORO-TSUKI hooligans. After Meiji, the kais shared out the work in hand with the various criminals, kidnappers, assassins, blackmailers and thugs who were directly —and indirectly—employed by Gumbatsu and Zaibatsu to ensure the smooth running of the Tokyo administration.

Since the Sino-Japanese War the kais have been responsible for the assassination of four or five Prime Ministers and a round dozen Cabinet Ministers who would not come to the heel of their masters. To detail each incident would add nothing to what was made public at the time but it may still be worth while to try and explain the inability of the extensive ramifications of the Japanese press, and literature of Japan, from 1900 to 1941, to create a public opinion capable of expressing itself with realism against the Gumbatsu and their kais.

In the first place. The KEMPEI-TAI, by a special law, were responsible directly to Imperial Headquarters as *Special Police to guard the security of the State*. They had the right to hold their prisoner for one hundred and twenty-one days without a warrant or a formal charge being preferred. Acting in close co-operation with the *Home Office* and the civil police they applied most terrible methods of torture to obtain *confessions of guilt* out of innocent Japanese, Chinese, Koreans or Foreigners arrested on information supplied by any member of a kai. In the second place, Japanese journalists, educationalists and authors combined their talents to spread State-Shintoism as a necessary coefficient of expansion of Empire.

Such editors, professors or authors who held to a contrary opinion were deemed, by the kais, to be guilty of the crime of *lese-majeste* and this—in their opinion—warranted severe punishment which was inflicted without recourse to the law courts.

In the judgement of the kais they were journalistic-eta—the outcasts whose touch would defile Shintoism—socialists, communists, labour leaders, all of them harbouring dangerous thoughts.

When Toyama founded the gen-yo-sha his personal objectives were in Korea, Formosa and North China. Members
of the roku-ryu-kai were planted in these centres to operate
much as Communist-cells do outside the U.S.S.R. today. By
1894, kais were already fully recognized as a secret agency of
the government, and it was the tripartite intervention, 1895,
which brought many embittered Japanese supporters into
Toyama's movement. They were the ready tools for creating
incidents in Korea and Manchuria, incidents which were made
the most of by the gumbatsu.

I shall give one personal illustration of their methods. It
concerns the first quasi-democratic Prime Minister of Japan,
Mr. Hara, and the labour movement in 1921.

Hara's term of office—1918-1921—coincided with the rise of
labour unions in Japan. I was interested as an onlooker.
Through Count Soyejima I passed on the suggestion to Mr.
Hara that he should abolish Clause 2, para. 17, of the Police
Regulations and thereby permit labour to organize into unions
with the right to use the strike weapon when negotiating with
employers. As the matter stood, 'those who, with the object of
causing a strike, seduce or incite others, shall be sentenced to
major imprisonment of one to six months with additional
penalty of three yen to thirty yen', and this Police Regulation
was used to break up ordinary labour meetings.

Mr. Hara replied, through Count Soyejima, that he was well
aware of the repressive nature of the Regulations but he did not
intend to commit political hara-kiri by acting on the suggestion
just then.

As Prime Minister there were many other things of benefit to
the country he could accomplish before he died, or lost office.

That was in July, 1921 when we had labour trouble in Kobe
shipyards, and labour disputes in many cotton and spinning
mills in Osaka and Tokyo. I went to Borneo and South China
for a few months and returned with Lord Northcliffe on 2nd
November, 1921. Hara was already a marked man: he had not
helped the unions but he had violated the rule that Naval and
Military portfolios must be held by serving naval or military
officers. He had taken over, as a civilian, the Naval Office
when the Navy Minister—Admiral Kato—went on to the
Washington Conference.

Lord Northcliffe, at my suggestion, had arranged to meet Mr. Hara outside of Tokyo if possible, to discuss the abolition of the police regulation I have mentioned and also the non-renewal of the Anglo-Japanese Alliance which was no good to either country in their relations with China. No good that is to the spread of democratic ideas as opposed to imperialism.

But there was to be no meeting between Hara and Northcliffe. On the evening of 2nd November, just before Hara's train was due to leave Shimbashi Station, Tokyo, for Kyoto, a patriotic member of the kai stabbed him to death. Police Regulations banning the trade unions continued to function long after Hara was buried.

The assassin was canonized as a patriot who killed in order to preserve the sanctity of the Constitution. That was the fiction to cover the fact that Hara's removal was necessary in the interest of the suppression of the labour movement. The Army and Navy could have forced his resignation with ease but then he would have lived on to be a nuisance.*

When Mr. Hara was in office, Prince Yamagata—representing the Choshu clans—raised objections to the Crown Prince Hirohito's contemplated marriage with a Princess of the Satsuma clan. But this inter-clan rivalry did not lead to civil war as it did in the 'good old days'. Yamagata failed to get his own way for once and the 'very serious affair' was soon forgotten. However, in 1921, Yoshihito's 'long illness' made it necessary for Hirohito to act as Regent for his father.

Dealing with Hirohito was not the same as dealing with Yoshihito. Hirohito was the first Imperial Prince of Japan to leave his country and tour the world. He saw quite a lot of England, was the guest of King George V, and returned to Japan with western ideas of monarchy quite at variance with his 'divine rights'. This did not please Genro or Gumbatsu. Indeed his conduct, in private and in public, indicated that he was not a whole-hearted votary of jinja-shinto, kodo or the cult of the kais. The purists arranged for one attempt on his life, in December 1923, but it failed.

Hirohito was born on April 29th, 1901. He married the eldest daughter of H.I.H. Prince Kuniyoshi Kuni in 1925 and came to the Throne in 1926, on the death of Taisho Tenno.

* See Appendix VIII.

CHAPTER VI

THE SHOWA ERA
(1926-1945)

i. KODO—*the Imperial Way*

Hirohito, SHOWA TENNO, came to the throne with good intentions but the established order of things was against him. He had been Regent for four or five years and was under no illusions regarding the black-dragon clique ruling his perplexed subjects, but—from first to last—he vacillated between his sense of duty and a natural desire to live. The murder of Hara, in 1921, and the attack on his own life in 1923 warned him that the kais would stop at nothing in their determination to uphold their own traditions.

The Army had continued its Siberian Expedition until the end of 1922 at a cost to the nation of more than £70,000,000 and other millions of yen were being squandered in China. After the elimination of Mr. Hara the old Sat-Cho combination shared the spoils of office. The Diplomatic Corps and the Consular Service of Japan was the medium for explaining 'Japanese Culture' to the rest of the world. They did it politely in terms of Fujiyama, Nikko, Miyajima, Bushido, Satsuma ware, Lacquer, Tea Ceremony, Geisha and Flower Arrangements. Everything, from archaeology to anagogical interpretation of gumbatsu in heroic phrases which swathed the chivalry of the Samurai in the vestments of the Way of the Gods—Shintoism. And, all the time, the adolescent mind of Japan was being impregnated with the virus of bombastic nationalism based on Hakko-ichi-u, and Tenno Heika.

The Washington Conference had handed over to Japan the responsibility for 'Peace in the Orient'. The Naval agreements confirmed her position as the dominant sea power in the

Pacific—the Anglo-Japanese Alliance had not been renewed but the Nine Power Treaty renewed the fiction of 'respect the sovereignty, the independence, and the territorial and administrative integrity of China'.

On the other hand, Japan had to face 'American insults' to her status as a Great Power. As far back as 1894, the entrance of Japanese into U.S.A., was restricted by treaty and by 1920 there were only one hundred thousand Japanese in that country and about the same number in Hawaii. Year by year the anti-Japanese movement increased in volume which came to a head in 1924 when Japanese were precluded by law from becoming American citizens and this barred them—under the Immigration Law—from entry to the country. This was absolute exclusion and applied to other Asiatic nations and no amount of protest from Japan altered the ruling.

This racial discrimination provided propaganda for the kais. They broadcast the information and, at the same time, pointed out that U.S.A., had an area of over three million square miles and would not allow even one hundred Japanese a year to enter the country. And, also, that Canada with three and a half million square miles of territory had a population of only ten million; Australia with three million square miles of territory and six and a half million people only, whereas Japan had nearly sixty million people crammed into 142,270 square miles of territory.

Furthermore, so they argued, France had a Colonial Empire 3,848,000 square miles; the Netherlands 793,200 square miles; Britain 2,200,000 square miles; U.S.A. 700,000 square miles; Belgium 900,000 square miles Portugal 800,000 square miles and so on.

Japan was one of the great powers and she must have Colonies somewhere for her growing population to settle. If the U.S.A.—and the other Powers—did not want them to settle in their domains they had no business to interfere with Japan's expansion in Manchuria or in China. That was the argument and they made the most of it to build up the 'real Japanese spirit'.

One of the greatest of the military experts on imperial expansion was General Sadao Araki, the founder of Ko-Do (The Imperial Way) the new Shintoism for the salvation of Japan.

Araki was born in 1878, and served as a junior officer in the Russo-Japanese War and in 1926, he was the acknowledged leader of the young-officer group which forced the Imperial General Staff to quicken its paces in China. He did more than any other of the Japanese Generals to inculcate the rising generation with the need for them to die for Japan sooner than submit to an inferior status in the world. He was War Minister from 1931 to early in 1934 and directed Japan's foreign and military policy with an iron hand.

The campaign for the conquest of Manchuria was directed by Araki—he defied the League of Nations, ignored all the Pacts about China, made Henry Pu-Yi 'Emperor of the Empire of Manchukuo' by his announcement of 15th January, 1934: and he insisted that Japan leave the United Nations on March 27th 1933. His brutal North China campaigns resulted in the death of nearly half a million Chinese—soldiers and civilians. And the 1934-35 budget was Yen 2,112,000,000 out of which Yen 937,000,000 was for the Army and Navy.

Hirohito did oppose Araki's blatant China policy but did not have the moral courage to defy the kais and submit the issue to the arbitration of civil war—it would have required a superman to prevent kodoism from plunging into the abyss in 1941 because there was an almost united country behind General Araki and those who followed him at the War Office.

Araki and Hitler had much in common, apart from the fact that they were both in power in 1933. Hitler is said to have explained his state-controlled youth movement in these words: 'The Nazi Party will begin to organize you at the age of three and it will not let you go until you are in your grave'. And it took him less than ten years to put Nazi Germany on record as the greatest military power of civilization. Kodoism took a mere twelve years to complete the entire programme of Yoshida Shoin's Japanese Empire in Greater East Asia. But the state-controlled youth-movement in Japan had existed for forty years or more.

On December 20th, 1933, I was in Tokyo. In the morning I had a long conversation with Muto Sanji (founder of Kanega-fuchi Cotton Mills). Muto was an old Kobe friend. We were both interested in labour movements and in the plight of the farmers—burdened with debt and heavy taxation. In the afternoon I went to the War Office to keep an appointment with General Araki, Minister of War.

Araki was violently anti-British but was quite willing to discuss the subject uppermost in my mind—the logical outcome of Japanese policy in China, war against the British Empire. He was a patient listener but when it was his turn to speak he retorted crisply, and bluntly, that only a complete revision of British ideas on the subject of Japan's destiny in Asia would remove the danger of war. I changed the subject by suggesting that the Government might help the farmers by a National Bond issue at one or two per cent. interest which the banks and the public could take up in a patriotic spirit and thus provide cash for cheap loans to the hardest hit farmers. Araki smiled. Then he explained—the Japanese *patriotic spirit* had nothing to do with money, banks or cheap loans: the agrarian problem of Japan could not be solved by paying farmers' debts but by planting rice overseas. I did not need telling anything more about Araki's patriotic spirit, but—as I was about to leave the room—I saw on the wall a fine portrait of General Nogi riding his horse outside 'Plum Tree' Cottage where he had accepted the surrender of Port Arthur. I mentioned that I had named the cottage for Nogi. But the rest of my personal reminiscences were cut short with the remark, 'Nogi, yes, he had old fashioned military ideas'. . .

I left the War Office and paid a visit to Nogi's Shrine to see how it compared with kodoism. As a matter of fact I had a very special reason for meeting Araki. I had information that there was an intrigue against Hirohito which was said to involve Araki with the young-officer group: the plot concerned the Empress who was expecting a child that month—if it was another girl then Hirohito was to be asked to abdicate in favour of Prince Chichibu, the second son of Taisho Tenno.

On 23rd December, the Empress gave birth to a son. A few days later General Araki resigned on account of *ill health*—there was nothing at all the matter with him on 20th December. Hirohito's attitude to the China incident and the anti-British campaign in Japan made him *non persona grata* to kais and the young officer extremists and his abdication was considered necessary but the birth of a son—Heir Apparent to the Throne

—rather upset the propaganda side of their plans which they had to *postpone* for *three years*.

I never saw Muto again—I left Tokyo a few hours before they assassinated him on the night of 20th December, 1933.

Three months later I travelled as far as Ceylon with H.I.H. Prince Kaya: now he was a great admirer of General Sadao Araki.

Another incident, involving Hirohito and the kais: at the height of the China incident—December 1931—Premier INUKAI declared that Manchuria would not be occupied by Japan 'owing to the cost entailed in defending the country': on 13th May, 1932, Premier Inukai, with other cabinet ministers, discussed the matter with Emperor Hirohito. Two days later the Government announced the withdrawal of the entire Shanghai expedition. The same day, 15th May, a group of armed cadets and junior officers cornered the 77 year old Inukai in his official residence. They demanded his life for advising the Emperor to retreat from Shanghai. In the true spirit of kodo they riddled his body with bullets and added Inukai to the long list of officials murdered because of their disloyalty to the Imperial Way.

The next step, taken by the young officer group, was on 12th *August*, 1935, when they found it necessary to cleanse the War Office. The victim, this time, was Major-General Nagata— chief of the Bureau of Military Affairs. He was talking to Colonel Niimi, chief of Tokyo Kempei, in his office, when Lieutenant-Colonel Aizawa stabbed him to death. The court-martial declared it a case of murder: after this preliminary hearing Aizawa was tried in *February*, 1936 and sentenced to death on 30th *June*—the sentence being carried out on 3rd July. Aizawa defended his action by saying that it was his firm conviction that the restoration of the national spirit should be carried out through the co-operative efforts of the Army, but that the present condition of the Army is such that he felt it necessary, first of all, to reform the Army. In his opinion, Nagata was trying to check the movement for the restoration of the Japanese spirit, so he killed him.

Personally I doubt if Aizawa would have been executed in

July if the Tokyo Mutiny of 26th February, 1936, had not failed in its object—the removal of Emperor Hirohito. Let me outline the sequence of events.

The most important political and social problem in 1935 was the so-called 'Problem of the Emperor as an Organ, Theory' raised by Professor T. Minobe in his books, *Kempo-segi* and *Kempo-satsuyo*, that the *ruler is not the Emperor, but the nation*. There was an outcry from the kodoites—Minobe defended himself in the House of Peers but the Army and Navy demanded that the Government take strong action. The books were suppressed and the Government issued a long statement regarding the 'Clarification of National Characteristics', the general purport being that 'The Organ Theory is opposed to our sacred national characteristics and shows the worst possible misunderstanding of their significance. Therefore it must be eradicated absolutely'.

Now the Japanese Communist party which came into existence in 1921, under Tokuda and Nosaka, adopted a programme which included the abolition of the monarchy, privy council and the house of peers. They made little progress and in 1928 Tokuda and Shiga were arrested and jailed—they remained there until released in 1945. But, under the surface, both Socialists and Communists were stirring up the workers and forcing them to pay some attention to political matters.

A general election was held on 20th February, 1936. The result, 'indicated a remarkable advance of the Proletariat Party which threatened to overcome the other large political parties'.

After the election results were known, Premier Okada stated that the Government 'expected to establish policies in pursuance of the spirit of the constitution in the new political atmosphere created by the results of the general election.'

Emperor Hirohito's attitude to Araki's Kodo was hostile but Minobe's ideas on a constitutional monarchy did not disturb him in the slightest.

Then the kais acted. Early in the morning of 26th February, about 1,500 officers and men of the Tokyo Garrison (Guards, 1st and 3d Infantry Regiments, and 7th Field and Heavy Artillery Regiments) went into action. They seized the residences of Admiral Okada, Prime Minister; Admiral Saito

Keeper of the Privy Seal; General Watanabe, I. G. Military Education; Admiral K. Suzuki, Grand Chamberlain; Mr. K. Takahashi, Minister of Finance; Count Makino, and the offices of the newspaper *Tokyo Asahi*.

Another section took possession of the Law Courts, Police Headquarters, Diet Buildings, Navy and Army Headquarters while others surrounded the Imperial Palace.

Admiral Saito, Mr. Takahashi and General Watanabe were killed on the spot. Admiral Suzuki and others were injured. Admiral Okada escaped from death by hiding in a cupboard but his brother-in-law, Count Mitsui, mistaken for him was machine-gunned without parley.

All efforts to persuade the rebels to return to Barracks failed until the evening of 29th February, when Emperor Hirohito's edict was obeyed without more ado. There is one story which may or may not be exactly correct in detail. Here it is. After the Imperial Palace was surrounded, a young officer—detailed to deal with the Tenno—forced his way into the Palace. Suddenly he was facing his Emperor who said, 'How dare you enter my presence?' The miserable soldier was transfixed to the spot by the sound of the voice of the Divine Ruler he had been taught to bow to, morning and night. He bowed himself out of the room, rejoined his comrades to whom he told his story and then moved out of the Palace grounds before committing hara kiri.

As a result of this grave incident, kept out of the Japanese press for some time, twenty officers were cashiered. Two captains—Nonaka and Kono committed hara-kiri: eighteen other officers were confined for indefinite periods in the garrison prison; seventeen other officers found guilty were sentenced to death and executed; numerous other junior officers and non-commissioned officers also received long terms of imprisonment. Other ranks were pardoned.

For their share in the mutiny, four supreme war councillors—Generals ARAKI, HAYASHI, MASAKI and ABE—were placed on the reserve of officers list. The OKADA Cabinet resigned and the former Foreign Minister, K. Hirota, formed a new ministry. Hirota failed to 'establish policies in pursuance of the spirit of the constitution in the new political atmosphere created by the results of the general election' because the General Staff refused to nominate General Terauchi as Minister for War *until the selected personnel of the Cabinet conformed to their ideas of a national government.*

Araki's Kodoism may have received a slight check in Tokyo but General Tojo (a prominent member of Araki's kai) who was the Commander of the Japanese Army in Manchuria, welcomed with open arms some of the dupes of the mutiny when they were sent overseas for participating in the plot to depose Hirohito and place Chichibu on the throne as Regent.

The kais were delighted to have Hirota as Premier. He was a protege of Toyama and a prominent official of the Black Dragon Society: they could depend on him to clarify the idea of a true national policy.

Hirohito could do very little to break the stranglehold of kodoism and the kais. But, when the international military tribunal for the Far East pronounced its sentences, Koki Hirota was one of those sentenced to death; Araki, was condemmed to imprisonment for life but Tojo was hanged.

Araki, Tojo and Hirota helped to bring discredit on Tenno and country and were already discredited when Admiral Suzuki and Admiral Okada, who had survived the blood-bath of 26th February, 1936, were at Hirohito's side helping him to salve something of the wreckage caused by black-dragon-shintoism.

I have mentioned the fact that the rebels occupied the offices of the *Tokyo Asahi* on 26th February. In a leader, April, 1936, following the formation of Hirota's Cabinet, this is what interested me most of all:—

> . . . 'As a matter of fact the root of the trouble exists in the vital problem of providing for the increase of population, and naturally the key to the situation lies in the settlement of this problem.
>
> The chief object of a planned economy is successful competition in world markets through the complete industrialization of the country for the sole purpose of obtaining the means of supplying the nation with the necessaries of life.
>
> Japan would be satisfied as long as she could sustain her ever-increasing population without degrading her once-elevated standard of living.
>
> Japan urges on foreign nations reflection on their narrow economic bloc principles of self-supply, demands the abandonment of unnecessary measures of restriction in trade and claims the open door in every state for the free communication of men and goods.'

There was something to be said regarding 'the vital problem of providing for the increase of population' but the concluding reference to 'the open door' was extremely naive in view of the closed door in Korea and Manchutikuo (The Manchu Empire) then ruled (?) by Henry Pu Yi, ex-Emperor of China, under the title of Kang Teh.

Certainly, even during the reign of Showa Tenno from 1926 to 1936 only, the population had risen from fifty-nine million to seventy million and was increasing at the rate of one million each year. About twenty million of the working population was engaged in agriculture and fishing whereas in the United Kingdom (for instance) only five per cent. of the population—say forty-six million—were working on the land. But the United Kingdom had already established her Empire sufficiently to take care of the requirements of her planned economy, and her surplus population, and the trade unions were very sensitive about the competition of Japan's *sweated labour* in world markets. In 1949, British trade unions under a Socialist Government utterly opposed to capitalism and all its vices—real and imaginary—proposed to dictate restrictions in trade by the Japanese in order that they may work short hours at high wages, with the emphasis on increased production in order to obtain dollars with which to buy food for themselves. And not only food but all the luxuries they may require in order to maintain their high standard of living and the peace and contentment of planned economy in a socialist state. What happens to Japan is their own business and has nothing whatever to do with the moral principles of socialism—national or interntional.

However, unless the Atlantic Charter is a dead letter, the framers of a Peace Treaty with Japan—when they are formulating their pragmatic sanctions—may keep in mind the cause and the consequence of events and be guided by the declaration of 14th August, 1941, even if it was made before Japan entered World War II. And—in this connection—the following extracts from the Atlantic Charter appear to be worth repeating:

'Fourth, they will endeavour, with due respect for their existing obligations, to further the enjoyment by all States, great or small, victor or vanquished, of access, on equal terms, to the trade and to the raw materials of the world which are needed for their economic prosperity.

Fifth, they desire to bring about the fullest collaboration between all nations in the economic field with the object of securing
for all improved labour standards, economic advancement and
social security.'

ii. Japanese Culture

The control of thought by armed police flourished in Japan
from the Restoration of Meiji Tenno to the Unconditional
Surrender of Showa Tenno. But no one will deny that even the
modern Japanese are an artistic race. Art and architecture in
Japan was influenced by religion and it was Shinto which inspired the builders of Imperial Shrines and Palaces and Buddhism which inspired the builders of Temples and Castles.

In the ninth century the Tendai and Shingon Buddhist sects
changed the religious architecture: they constructed monasteries
on mountain tops and this made it necessary to alter the
arrangements of buildings, and the floor plan. About the same
time the movement to harmonize the Buddhist and Shinto
faiths brought about the introduction of the curved roof. Still
later, the Chinese and Korean ideas gave way to native innova-
tions and the Fujiwara aristocrats had magnificient dwellings
built in 'Japanese style'.

After the Fujiwaras the Samurai brought about a simplifica-
tion in constructure which was named Buke—'Samurai Style'
—and this was followed by another Chinese inspired period
before the first European influence arrived to destroy the beauty
of the landscape with blobs of reinforced concrete.

As with building, so with art. From the great Nara Buddha
to the delightful netsuke the influence of Korea and China was
evident in the skill of the Japanese workman. The earliest
examples of art treasures are still to be seen in the Shoso-In at
Nara.

In this Imperial Repository are musical instruments, swords,
bows and arrows, suits of armour, bronze mirrors, folding
screens, masks and banners, writing brushes, pewter dishes,
glass beads, curved jewels, textile fabrics and a hundred other
examples of the culture of the Japanese of twelve centuries ago.
And no one who has moved about Japan in modern times
could have failed to appreciate the pottery, bronzes, ivory
carvings, lacquer work, silks and embroideries and other fine
examples of Japanese craftsmen. And no one will deny their

ability to build aircraft, submarines, tanks or battleships with the same skill as they displayed in the carving of an image of Buddha or in the laying out of a cha-seki garden for cha-no-yu.

And when you have admitted this evidence of their skill and culture you are left completely puzzled by the vileness of their political leaders and the extreme brutality of their modern soldiers. Some say that the modern cultured Japanese were stripped of their arguments against gumbatsu and zaibatsu by the all too frequent demonstrations of the utility of force—in the spread of democracy—by the western powers. And that it was the militant spirit, translated into action, which saved Japan from becoming a dependency of one or other of the powers after the Meiji Restoration.

No doubt a blow was struck against the rise of free institutions in Japan by the flaunting of the realism of western militarism at the close of the nineteenth century, but that was a mere bagatelle compared to the control of thought and education by the gumbatsu.

The combined efforts of bully, priest and modern samurai taught the youth of Japan to believe that in Shinto they are KAMI—a culmination in material form of 'Heavenly Divine Spirit', and that the TENNO was an *ara-hito-gami* which meant that 'he is human, a person of the living present who rules over the land and its people, and—at the same time—is a god'. Thus —according to the teaching of the twentieth century—the TENNO is the basis as well as the symbol of Japanese race life.

According to the priests, SHINTO gives inspiration for *modern life:* spiritual ideas which are original in that faith, and that this spirituality means other than materiality in origin.

There is no reincarnation in Shinto: the dead do not return to life but survive in another form: the body does perish but the immaterial kami-spirit is immortal. YOMO is the land of the dead—the grave where the body rests and decays. NE-NO-KUNI is heaven—where the body undergoes change.

Shinto is not concerned with after-life: Shinto offers no kind of consolation in death. Everything which exists is Divine Spirit and the TENNO is the very symbiosis of Shintoism—the TENNO unites the people as a single national whole not only spiritually but politically, hence the dogma of unbroken ancestral line of national unification.

Shinto norito (liturgies) express thanks for nature's help to humanity and request further co-operation between nature and man—there is no praying to a theological divinity.

Confucianism and Christianity were rejected by Japanese as unsuited to their needs. In Christianity the divine spirit dwells apart from the universe—mankind may acquire an element of divinity, or reject it—and nature, materiality and animals are excluded from possessing the divine nature. In Shinto there is no difference between divine spirit and any form of material being for all is divinity.

The teaching of Confucius, like the teaching of Jesus, was plain and straightforward quite unlike Chinese-Buddhism the religion of monks and temples with grotesque and irrational observances. Jesus denounced patriotism and the ties of family loyalty. Jesus spread the gospel of universal brotherhood of mankind irrespective of colour or origin, He condemmed the economics of capitalism, private wealth and personal advantage and for that reason His teaching was rejected by Tokugawa Iyemitsu the builder of the magnificent Nikko shrine.

iii. The Atrocities of Hakko-ichi-u

The extent and nature of the criminal actions of Japanese soldiers, particularly their inhuman treatment of prisoners of war, came as an unpleasant surprise to the subjects of the United States of America and the British Empire. Not because war crimes are something new to modern civilization, or that they were considered the prerogatives of Nazism, but simply because of the documentary evidence regarding the samurai, bushido and other national characteristics of the Japanese submitted to the general public by so many native and foreign writers.

Japanese atrocities have their genesis in the hakko-ichi-u of the Nippon Shoki: the oneness of the Japanese national family —the unity of Tenno, State and People. No matter what a Japanese may do to a foreigner he acts as one of the national family. For that simple reason, one Japanese will refrain from interfering with the action of another Japanese even when he knows that it is immoral—even absolutely contrary to his own moralism.

Moral courage, to distinguish between right and wrong, is non-existent most of the time where a Japanese and a Foreigner's view point is in conflict. In the early Meiji days those of us who had recourse to the Japanese juridical system found out that the administration of justice was biased in favour of the native as against the foreign merchant. Judges seemed to lack moral courage to administer their own law fairly where a decision against one of themselves was indicated by the evidence. Of course, until the abolition of extra-territoriality, the foreigner in the treaty-ports was kami in his own right. We had our own courts and our own police and the natives were not allowed on our pavements—so I suppose we cannot complain when the table was turned on us, and we were subjected to annoyance.

Yamato-damashi and Bushido may be the spirit and the soul of Japan but the philosophical doctrines did not apply to relations between Japanese and foreigners. And if the ideals of hakko-ichi-u do underlie the political traditions of the Japanese nation—to bring the people into contact with the State, so that they may assist the throne to serve as the force behind national progress—then if that progress conflicts with vital interests of other nations no question of right or wrong arises in the Japanese mind.

Thousands of allied prisoners of war were brutally overworked and maltreated. Thousands were half-starved, tortured or bayonetted to death in cold blood. Yet, during my own three and a half years as a captive, I recall no instance when even an expression of disgust, or of mild regret, was made by a single Japanese, soldier or civilian, when an act of brutality was perpetrated in their presence.

If a Japanese private soldier killed a British prisoner of war by a blow of sword or iron bar, or killed him by slow torture, his superior officer may have asked for an explanation but would not have considered it his duty to scold or punish his subordinate.

The Imperial General Staff issued orders that prisoners of war retaken after attempts to escape were to be shot. That was Japanese military law. I made two personal appeals to General Yamashita to reconsider the death penalty imposed on the first three young English soldiers retaken after escape from Changi Prisoner of War Camp on Singapore Island. I pointed out that there had been no notification of this drastic departure from International Law and that the three young men had

M

never been informed by us, or by the Japanese, that the penalty for breaking out of camp was death.

I was informed that the matter was out of General Yamashita's hands. The men had been caught by the kempei, were tried by the kempei, and would be shot by the kempei who were responsible for guarding the security of the state. I then appealed to the Singapore commander of the Kempeitai. He read my complaint, congratulated me on a 'good point' which should be rectified by an immediate notification of Japanese Military Law to all prisoners of war.

The three soldiers were shot at sunset. They had waited outside the camp commandant's office for three hours sitting on spades and shovels to be used in digging their graves, while we tried to establish a very good point in international law.

I could fill pages with instances of similar crude and brutal mentality—I could fill pages with details of atrocities, but I refrain. My opinion, based on bitter experience, is that Japanese as a race are deficient in moral courage and proficient in killing in cold blood. I recollect no instance—during the Russo-Japanese War, Sino-Japanese Wars or in World Wars I and II —where a Japanese soldier or civilian was ever tried or punished for an act of murder or brutality committed outside of military action.

No doubt there are so-called progressive Japanese, and even sympathetic foreigners who have lived for years in Japan, who may consider my remarks as sweeping generalizations on Japan's moral code.

My critics may fall back on the delightful politeness, the valour, fortitude, bravery, fearlessness and courage of the nation and send me another copy of Bushido to revive my memories. But there were more British soldiers killed, or brutally treated, as prisoners of war than perished in fighting against the Japanese in battle during the entire campaign, and there are more Allied soldiers alive today who have suffered at the hands of the Japanese than the total number of foreigners who ever lived in Japan before 1941. They can be counted on to explain the working of Bushido better than Inazo Nitobe or his foreign admirers in England or in the United States of America.

In 1941 at any rate, the first duty of a Japanese, in or out of his uniform—soldier or civilian, kempei or gorotsuki—was blind obedience to State Shintoism. There was no divison of loyalties. At sunrise and at sunset the soldiers parade to chant the Chokuyu (Imperial Rescript). Then they turn to the east for the Reihai (homage to Tenno): their code of honour, their rules of politeness, courage and bravery, truthfulness and good faith, frugality and simplicity—all the exactness of the bowing the chokuyu and the reihai, are germane to their duty as members of the national family. Duty—in that sense—has nothing at all to do with conscience or their conduct towards foreigners.

iv. Kami-kaze: Divine Wind

When Kublai Khan attempted to conquer Japan a great storm destroyed his armada, KAMI (gods) in the shape of wind fought on Japan's side. Ever since then—1281—the divine wind, KAMI KAZE, is said to have sided with Japan when she was faced with any national adversity.

Japanese 'air-gods'—kami-kaze pilots—played a prominent part in the recent war. Their many exploits figured largely in national propaganda to uplift the morale of civilians: suicide-planes, human-torpedoes, were a real contribution to Japan's total-warfare and inflicted enormous damage on the allied fleet.

All nations, engaged in war, rely on propaganda to build up mental superiority over the enemy and they also pray to God not to desert their special cause. They all have their special kind of 'kami-kaze' but in their case it has nothing to do with the Sun Goddess of Japanese mythology.

The spiritual home of Japanese national traditions, and of kami-kaze, is the Imperial Shrine at Ise. This Shrine of Amaterasu-O-Mikami—the KO-DAI-JINGU—is rebuilt every twenty years. In it is enshrined the Sacred Mirror, one of the San-shu-no-jingi—Three Sacred Treasures—supposed to have been given by Amaterasu to Ninigi-no-mikoto her grandson when she sent him to YAMATO, with these words:—

'. . . The Luxuriant Land of Reed Plains is a country which our descendants are to inherit. Go therefore, Our Imperial Grandson and rule over it. And may our Imperial lineage continue unbroken and prosperous, coeternal with Heaven and Earth. . . . '

The other sacred treasures do not hold the same compelling power in Shinto as the Mirror. The Sword in enshrined at the Atsuta Jingu and the Jewel in the Imperial Palace. It is to the Kodaijingu at Ise that devout pilgrims wend their way to pay homage to the Sun Goddess—the fundamental inspiration of Japanese race life, and this inspiration is expressed in the National Anthem—Kimigayo—which runs:—

> 'May the dynasty endure a thousand,
>   yea, eight thousand years.
> Until the time when the grains of sand
>   changed to rocks, are clothed in moss.'

Behind that theme song there are 120,000 Shinto Shrines and 70,000 Buddhist Temples: 20,000,000 practising Shintoists, 30,000,000 practising Buddhists, and behind the shrines and the temples the *kami-dana*, the self-shrine, the family godshelf before which the devout worship morning and night. But, above all are the entire population, 80,000,000 National-Shintoists who once formed the sordid structure of the kodoists who destroyed Japan.

National Shintoism was the religion of *kodo-loyalty* to the Tenno. The TENNO HEIKA who was the united head, both political and religious, of a government patriarchal as well as quasi-constitutional. This so called unity of political government and religious cult has been known for centuries in Japan as 'Sai-sei-ichi'. Saiseiichi means 'religion of the nation and government administration which is indistinguishably and inseparably united and completely indentified in one entire whole'.

STATE-SHINTO—(Shrineor Jinja-Shinto) is based on the thirteen sects of denominational shinto and can not be separated from it without destroying the entire structure on which it is based, the Divine Emperor: divinity in man and nature of all things Japanese. Abdication of one Tenno, or even the repudiation of one Tenno of the divinity doctrine would not alter the National Shinto Faith—the theanthropic mind of Japanese—any more than a foreign directive can efface shrines or impede the way through the great Torii (sacred archway) of the Yasukuni Shrine in Tokyo. Shinto worshippers will still clap their hands, ring the bell and worship Amaterasu at Ise, and bow reverently before the family god on their kami-dana.

There are some Shinto sects, like KONKO, who worship a kami which has no connection with the Nippon Shoki. The kami of this sect is named, 'Tenchi-kane-no-kami' (Heaven-and-earth-including-deity) and transcends the boundary of a particular nation. The centre of this faith is a universal god—like the God of Christianity. The god of Jinja-shinto is Tenno Heika.

The worship of Amaterasu by Japanese is as old as the worship of Jesus Christ by Christians—Shintoism is as deep seated in Japan as Christianity may be in other countries of the world. Despite the directives of General MacArthur the fact remains that Amaterasu is enshrined at Ise, and the Ise Shrine is still the mecca of Shintoists.

Shrines, temples, monasteries, Monks and soldiers—all the feudal mixture of old and the kodoism of Araki was used to build up state-shintoism around Tenno Heika. Some of the 'divinity' of the Tenno may have been dragged through the mud of materialism by force of circumstances but it was the binding force which enabled the gumbatsu to lead a *united nation* to its humiliation.

Even as the shrines are the cenotaph of Amaterasu so was the Tenno the living expression of the faith of his people and must share the responsibility for the defeat of Japan.

Hirohito may or may not have believed in his divinity, before he commenced his rule under the protection of General MacArthur's G.I.s, but he has left on record many edicts which serve to delude the masses regarding his heavenly status, and their common divinity.

On the occasion of the two thousand six-hundredth anniversary of the ascension of Jimmu Tenno—11th February, 1940—when Japan was at the zenith of her aggression in China, his Imperial Message began:—

'At this time of emergency and celebration of the auspicious occasion of Kigensetsu all subjects should remember the initial achievements of Jimmu Tenno and think of the depth of the great Imperial Policy and the Imperial Foundation which is broad and everlasting. *In complete concert and harmony* our subjects should use their natural genius so as to overcome the difficulties and hardships Japan is now facing *to increase the national prestige.* Herewith we expect our subjects *to answer the divine spirit of the Imperial Ancestors.*'

The loyal subjects of Hirohito responded. They were to respond again, in December 1941, when the supreme effort was made to increase the national prestige in Greater East Asia. It was a failure—kami-kaze, providence, was not on Japan's side so, on August 14th, 1945, Hirohito issued another edict and it was obeyed with reverent and ready obedience. The people bowed as usual, before the sacred palace, and they chanted the chokuyu as they accepted unconditional surrender.

Behind the edict there was the spirit of Amaterasu, something transcending the voice of the Tenno Heika. There was the belated recognition that the kami-kaze of kodo was no answer to the B.29—the flying-fortress of the united nations ranged against them.

They accepted the consequences as they accept the consequences of tidal waves, floods and earthquakes—something outside their control. They did not blame jinja-shinto, kodo, gumbatsu, zaibatsu or the kais: they did not repudiate Jinno— the Divine Ruler—in the hour of defeat. They required no sacrifice of a scapegoat, no looting of the palace, to vent their spite on because their national enemies had superior killing power. Jinja-shinto had raised them from the dust to a first-class power through the virtues of Amaterasu and an industrial revolution, and it may take more than the directives of foreigners, the compulsory renunciations of Hirohito or a brand new foreign dictated constitution to destroy the 'soul and spirit of Japan'—the spirit of Japan enshrined at Ise, at Kashi-hara and on the millions of kami-danas far from the artificial democratic hot-house of Tokyo.

The Meiji Constitution was framed by Marquis Ito in 1889, to fulfil the requirements of Daimyo and Shogun: the Foreign Constitution of 1946 is designed to transform the Shinto State into a Western Democracy. Jinja-shinto is abolished, conscription is ended, Hirohito is divested of imperial prerogatives, Japan has denounced war, there are to be no more dockyards, arsenals or munition factories, no heavy industries, no army, no navy and no airforce, no colonies, no kais, no zaibatsu, no gumbatsu.

A Democratic State is to be founded on the debris of the Shinto State. Not a Communist State with an ogpu but a Democratic State with a police force. A few directives, a few elections, are to erase two thousand years of ancestor and emperor worship and to transform eighty million hungry, semi-idle Japanese men, women and children into democrats with a clear understanding of the concepts of Anglo-American ideology.

General MacArthur, and his associates, have worked wonders in a few years of patient and wonderful understanding of the great problem which has to be solved. History will record the MacArthur Shogunate as one of the most remarkable achievements of all time—a bloodless triumph of conquerors on a foreign soil. It may not gain all it set out to accomplish, its directives may be honoured more in the breach than in the observance, its critics may be right about its defects, but it is amazing to me how much of it is to be praised and how little of it to be scoffed at.

Unfortunately, Japan was not defeated by the courage and spirit of democracy but by the superior scientific knowledge and superior quantities of the munitions of war. In the spirit of jinja-shinto, Japan's army, navy and airforce did all that was asked of it by the commanders—they have no reason to seek courage or inspiration in a new ideology: Japan is by no means at the crossroads of a new morality or a new religion. Priests and Monks in Shrine and Temple do not yet complain of Christianity, agnostic or deistic competition or of empty churches—they remain quite content as guardians of an ancient pantheism in the atomic-age—they count their beads and reflect on Hiroshima.

And what of the long deferred Peace Treaty? Unconditional surrender of all the Japanese armed forces, in accordance with the Potsdam Proclamation, was accomplished with speed and without an incident worth mentioning. No doubt the Peace Treaty will be based as precisely on the other clauses of the Proclamation?

The numerous War Criminals have been tried and punished but—to quote the Proclamation—'There must be eliminated *for all time* the authority and influence of those who have deceived and misled the people of Japan into embarking on world conquest'—and if this tall order of punishment is to be carried out it would include nearly all Japanese from Hirohito to the custodian of the inner shrine at Ise. They are equally responsible for 'irresponsible militarism' whatever that may mean.

With regard to the elimination of 'authority and influence'—
the starting point would be the Nippon Shoki, and the thousands
of similar 'histories' which followed its publication, and the
finishing tape would be the Tokuhon—primary-school readers.

Clause 10, of the Proclamation, states that . . . 'We do not
intend that the Japanese shall be enslaved as a race nor destroyed as a nation . . . . . Freedom of speech, of *religion and of
thought* as well as respect for *fundamental human right* shall be established.'

I hope so. But allow me to quote Professor Genji Kato, the
author of a 'Study of Shinto, the Religion of the Japanese
Nation' published in 1935.:—

> . . . 'Shinto, characterised as faith in the Jinno or Divine Ruler of
> the nation, is not a religion *a posteriori* adopted purposely by the
> State as in the case of the State religion in a Western country, but
> the religion *a priori* of the heart and life of every Japanese subject,
> male or female, high or low, old and young, educated or illiterate.
> This is the reason why a Japanese never ceases to be a Shintoist,
> i.e., an inborn steadfast holder of the national faith, or one who
> embraces the national faith or the Way of the Gods as a group or
> folk religion, as distinguished from a personal or individual
> religion, even though he may accept the tenets of Buddhism or
> Confucianism—probably Christianity here in Japan not excepted
> —as his personal or individual religion. In effect this amounts to
> saying that abjuration by Japanese of the *National Shinto Faith*
> would mean treachery to the Empire and disloyalty to its Divine
> Ruler. . . . '

That was the accepted belief in 1935 at any rate, according to
Professor Kato. It may not be the accepted belief in 1949 now
that Emperor Hirohito himself has discarded his divinity. But
the authority and influence of Shintoism has not been destroyed
in the short period of four years although it may not be as useful
to Kodo in 1949 as it was in 1935 or 1945 before the surrender.

And now that the Kuomintang, and General Chiang-kai-shek
no longer represent China, in the comity of nations, having been
replaced by General Mao-tze-tung as head of the new Communist State of China it would be idle to speculate on the
wrangling which will ultimately take place over the future of
Japan. As Mr. Hirozo Mori predicted in 1937—all China is
Red.

CHAPTER VII

RECONCILING THE IDEOLOGIES
(1936-1941)

i. Anti-Comintern Pact

On November 25th, 1936, a few months after the mutiny in Tokyo—the German-Japan Anti-Comintern Pact was signed. It was not an alliance —just a 'defensive pact' aimed at Soviet Russia— but it brought together Hitlerism and State-Shintoism as partners in the struggle against the spread of Communism in Europe and in Asia.

The signing of the Anti-Comintern Pact puzzled Japanese. It had a very mixed reception in the press as the reader may see by glancing at this expression of opinion in the 'Tokyo Asahi' of 2nd December 1936,.

'In plain language it is too hasty we should think for Japan to decide her foreign policy without examining first whether *England is Japan's friend or enemy*.

As Chiang-kai-shek, of all people, has said that the Japan-German agreement 'is directed only against Communism and that it will not affect the Far Eastern situation' the agreement in question can by no means help Japan in pursuit of her policy towards Russia.

Why? Because it is impossible to think that Germany would lend her force to Japan in the event of any crisis between Japan and Russia. The best which Germany could do would be to supply Japan with arms and scientific instruments. Some people are lead to believe that Germany will strike European Russia in the event of any trouble happening in the Far East, but nobody can be sure of it.

Under the circumstances even if Japan took a step further and concluded a military pact with Germany she would not derive much benefit out of it. On the contrary if Japan should make an enemy out of England, which holds much latent power in the Far East, it is not difficult to imagine that England, France, America and Russia would co-operate . . . . '

Mussolini, in November, 1937, joined the Anti-Comintern Pact and it became the Berlin-Rome-Tokyo axis challenge to the Western Powers, in Europe and in the Far East. It made very little difference to Japan's policy of aggression except, perhaps, to add impudence to the curt rejection of all Anglo-American protests regarding the progress of their brutal military operations in China. And, in view of various other brutal military operations elsewhere, it should not be counted too much against Emperor Hirohito that he failed to stand up more effectively against his own unruly gang of kodoists.

The U.S.S.R., joined the League of Nations in 1934 and signed a Pact of Mutual Assistance with France to help Czechoslovakia, and then there was the Anglo-German Naval Treaty of 1935 but it did nothing to stop Mussolini's black-shirts from ravaging the 'savage state' of Abyssinia the same year, or the conclusion of the Hore-Laval Pact of December, 1935.

Europe was seeing red. In 1936 the fascist combination— Germany and Italy—tried out their military equipment and tactics in Spain. In March, 1938, Hitler—sure of his destiny— seized Austria, and followed this coup in March, 1939 by marching in and taking over Czechoslovakia—announcing grandly that his demands were completed. Britain on 31st March, 1939 hastened to guarantee Poland against attack—Mussolini hastened to seize Albania on 7th April and on the 26th of the month Hitler denounced the Anglo-German Naval Treaty.

But we still had the small piece of paper which Mr. Chamberlain had received from Hitler—the guarantee of Peace in our time. And we still had the signatures of 11,000,000 people who had signed the Peace Ballot in June ,1935: and, fortunately, we still had Mr. Winston Churchill—crying in the wilderness.

On August 11th, 1939 the Franco-British Military Mission arrived in Moscow to negotiate a treaty with the U.S.S.R., but Hitler was still one move ahead of the dilettantes of Paris and London. In Hitler's 'MEIN KAMPF'—written in 1925—he states:— 'The present rulers of Russia have no intention of concluding or keeping an alliance in an honourable manner. One must not forget that the rulers of present-day Russia are common blood-spattered criminals, that we are here concerned with a scum of humanity which, favoured by conditions at a tragic moment, overran a great State, strangled and rooted out millions of its leading intellectual classes in a wild thirst for blood, and for nearly ten years now has been carrying on the cruellest regime of tyranny of all times. And one must not forget that those in power belong to a people which combines in a rare mixture bestial cruelty with unbelievable skill in lying, and to-day more than ever believes itself called to lay its burden of bloody oppression on the whole world.'

ii. Soviet-German Non-Aggression Pact

On August 23rd, 1939, the riddle of the ideologies was made even more complex when the 'common blood-spattered criminals'—the Nazis and the Communists—concluded the pact of *non-aggression*.

Non-aggression? Then what remained of the Anti-Commintern Pact of 1936? Japanese were puzzled. The Gumbatsu were furious and forced Baron Hiranuma to resign his office of Premier because Hitler and Molotov had negotiated the pact in secret and made the Japanese look foolish.

The nature of the accord between Japan and Germany had been explained, in November, 1936, by the Japanese Foreign Office spokesman to the following effect . . . 'The agreement is for blocking the advance of the Comintern—putting up a common front against communism, and is a vivid exemplification of the Hirota cabinet's positive policy toward the U.S.S.R. . . . it is the first political agreement of the sort between Japan and an Occidental power since the abrogation of the Anglo-Japanese treaty of alliance . . . '

There was strong suspicion in Japan that the Soviet-German Pact would be followed by increasing Soviet pressure against Japan on the border of Manchuria. But when Germany invaded Poland on 1st September, 1939, and Great Britain and France declared War on Germany on 3rd September, World War II was set in motion under the blessing of the 'Non-Aggression Pact'—non-aggression between the rival ideologies.

The RED ARMY marched across the Polish Soviet frontier on 17th September: on 29th September, von Ribbentrop and Molotov signed 'The German-Soviet Treaty on Amity and the Frontier between the U.S.S.R. and Germany'. On 30th November, 1939, the RED ARMY marched into Finland—not with any aggressive intention but in self-defence and to preserve her independence which gave her the 'international right' of invasion. And, acting under the same principles, the non-aggressors had re-established the 'Curzon line' of 1920 in Poland in agreement with Articles 1., 2 and 3 of the Treaty on 'Amity and Frontiers'.

iii. The Axis Pacts

With the outbreak of World War II, Japan intensified her efforts to end hostilities in China and rearrange her troops for greater military adventures. Britain, with her hands more than full of commitments, and almost empty of military resources, made an attempt to help Sino-Japanese peace negotiations by closing the Burma Road to munitions traffic from 18th July to 19th October ,1940.

But this gesture was wasted on the Japanese. They saw an excellent opportunity, in the preoccupations of the Occidentals, to join in the pacts of non-aggression. On 27th September, 1940 they signed the Axis Pact: now the Fascist Powers—Germany, Italy and Japan—were linked with Communist Russia in a common bond of 'blood-spattered criminals'.

iv. Soviet-Japanese Neutrality Pact

The collapse of France, in June, 1940, had encouraged Japan to exploit total-war tactics in China. Irrespective of military necessity the armed and the unarmed Chinese were slaughtered to train the new conscripts in the use of machine-guns and bayonet, and the airforce targets were, more often than not, unrelated to the prosecution of the widespread campaign.

Prince Konoye, who had been replaced as Premier by Hiranuma in January, 1939, returned to office in July, 1940 and remained in power—such as it was—until *October, 1941*. The General-Staff nominated General Tojo as War Minister. They were pledged to bring the 'China incident to a close'.

In order to secure a freer hand in Manchuria, Japan signed the 'Soviet-Japanese Neutrality Pact' on 13th April, 1941.

Pact followed pact. Step by step, Stalin enlarged his support of the Fascist Powers. Soviet Russia was entirely indifferent to the Nazis destruction of Belgium, Holland, Denmark or Norway. The brotherhood of the proletarians had nothing in common

with the consanguinity of those outside the communist faith—
they were just democratic heretics.

However, by this time, perfidious Albion—of continental
derision—with the aid of the decadent British Empire (of Nazi
fiction) had accepted the role of dictator in the tragedy of
'Blood, Sweat and Tears' under the stage-management of
Winston Churchill the pugnacious epitome of civilization's fight
for freedom against tyranny, and was striking back slowly but
effectively

v. Anglo-Russian Mutual Assistance Treaty

The Battle of Britain was over. The flaming torch, carried so
gallantly by so few, brightened Britain's sky with its message of
efficient defiance to the dictators. But the struggle in the North
African desert remained clouded by drifting sands of adversity.
In vain we searched for an oasis of Victory. Then, on 22nd
June, 1941, Germany made her surprise attack on Soviet Russia:
Stalin was now forced to fight Hitler in defence of his Com-
munism.

War makes strange bed-fellows. On 12th July, 1941, the
British Empire signed the Anglo-Russian Mutual Assistance
Treaty. Now, the axis had completed the circle—now the
Communists and the Democrats had something in common. to
wage total-war on the anti-communists and the anti-democrats,
the European Fascists. But one of the Axis Powers, Japan, had
a Neutrality Pact with Soviet Russia. She was in no hurry to
denounce it. Her obligations under that Pact were definite: her
obligations under the Axis Pact were equally clear:— the three
powers concerned undertook to assist each other by all means
if one of the contracting powers was attacked by a power not
then (1940) involved in the European War or in the Sino-
Japanese conflict. In other words she could, if she so desired,
remain out of the War until the United States of America in-
tervened in Europe or in the Far East.

In September, 1941, General Tojo relieved Togo as Foreign
Minister: on 18th October, Tojo was appointed Premier, War
Minister and Home Minister with Mamoru Shigemitsu as
Foreign Minister.

With an army of 600,000 in Manchuria, Japan was in a
favourable position to deal with any Soviet movement in favour

of China. To secure her strategical position in South China she concluded an agreement, at the end of July, 1941, with Vichy France to facilitate military occupation of Indo China.

For ten years (1931-1941) the Japanese Army and Navy had been on a war footing. Officers and men had practised the art of modern warfare, over thousands of miles of Chinese territory, and gained practical experience of amphibious warfare, aerial warfare and submarine warfare. Encouraged by events in Europe, fully convinced that Germany could defeat the U.S.S.R. without her help, and that the British Empire was a spent force, Japan moved swiftly to complete her plans for the isolation of Burma from Malaya by cutting into Siam as the first step to the conquest of India and Australia.

At that time, Japan's military strength, in men and weapons, exceeded that of Britain by *fifty to one* in the Far Eastern theatre of war. She had a fully trained Army of 2,500,000 with a yearly intake of 300,000 and an enormous reserve of men fit for service apart from all the skilled and unskilled labour she required for the war effort. We had about 60,000 mixed—U.K., Australian and Indian—troops in Hongkong, Burma and Malaya, a puny airforce and a skeleton of a navy.

I left England for Malaya at the end of May, 1941, in the Intelligence Corps. On the way out I lectured to most of the 2,500 airforce personnel aboard the *Capetown Castle* regarding Japan as a military power. I am afraid that some of my remarks were regarded with polite amusement by young and inexperienced officers. The valour of ignorance is a dangerous asset —they were to learn the facts of war before the year was out. And, as a nation, we were to pay heavily in life and prestige for under-estimating the tremendous fighting power of Japan's modern Army, Navy and Airforce in 1941. No, Japan was not war-weary, she did not have a third-rate airforce or a 'paper navy'.

CHAPTER VIII

PRELUDE TO WAR
IN THE FAR EAST

i. Singapore Siesta

The realism of World War II had not disturbed the serenity of cosmopolitan Singapore when I landed from *Capetown Castle* on 3rd August, 1941. The alteration in the statistical balance, between the Occidental civilian and soldier, had been accepted by the Orientals as a stimulant to local trade and not as a spectacular contribution to the defence of Malaya in the event of War with Japan. They were not impressed. For more than ten years the Japanese had been fighting Chinese with an army of a million men—a million men well versed in the art of slaughter, so the few thousand British and Indian troops filling the streets, and the places of amusement, could do little or nothing for them if the Japanese moved south from Indo China.

The War in Europe was thousands of miles away—the War in the Far East was just around the corner. Yet the optimism of the Occidental civilians, and many of the soldiers, was as dazzling as the bright lights at night, and the foundation for it no less artificial. They were still 'living' in the days of the Boer War: the Japanese dare not risk her tired army against the power of the British Empire. Nature was on our side: the west coast of Malaya was fringed with swamp and mangrove, the east coast was laced with casuarinas, mud, swamp, jungle, mountain, forest and rivers. No—Japanese could not overcome such formidable obstacles when confronted by British troops. No— Japanese would not be so insane as to enter the war *against us* with the certainty that such action would bring the might of the United States of America against them. No—there would be no war. We had applied financial sanctions and cut off their supply of raw materials—they were at the end of their tether, let them bog their armies in China until we were ready to call their bluff.

There was an amazing underestimation of our difficulties and our slender resources in trained personnel, and material, available for the gigantic task of holding out *alone* against Germany and Italy. And there was failure to appreciate the difficulty of transporting an effective fighting force thousands of miles from its base of supplies. But the greatest mistake of all was to forget that we could not defend Malaya, or Singapore, without command of the sea and without command of the air. No amount of paper schemes, or dictates from London, could alter the fundamental military facts of the situation. We were defeated in principle before the Japanese army landed at Kota Bharu at midnight on 7th December, 1941.

Defeat was almost certain but that may not answer the question so frequently asked: did we make the best use of our limited resources? Or did we fritter those resources in an uninspired campaign which ended in tame surrender?

There is no short answer. A military commander is made, or damned, by the efficiency of his troops to fight to a finish or by their fainthearted approach to the furnace of battle. If the all-round willingness to fight is absent the Commander of any force is subordinate to the Soldier in it: when an Army is faced with every prospect of defeat the elements which compose it rise to heroic heights and achieve a pyrrhic victory—or they abandon hope and enter the stygian refuge of lost souls.

At Iojima and Okinawa, for example, the Japanese fought to a finish and were exterminated. At Singapore—after retreating for 53 days—we capitulated five days after the Japanese landed on the Island but we still had 51,000 U.K. and Australian troops and 40,000 Indian troops under Malaya Command. Unconditional Surrender was the unanimous decision of all the senior officers.

Such are the facts—now for my personal explanation, based on the *limited experience* of a *single individual* who may have wandered about the fighting front in greater discomfort than the arm-chair critic in the United Kingdom.

ii. Service in Sarawak

At the end of August, 1941, I was ordered by Malaya Command to go to Kuching, capital of Sarawak, and operate with the 2/15th Punjab Regiment. I had regularly visited North Borneo for a matter of twenty years—travelling from Japan or from the U.K.—so I knew the territory and that it was the natural supporting military base for Malaya.

A glance at the map, of the probable battle-area, in the Far East, indicated the obvious. The island-chain of the East Indies, extending for more than 3000 miles, forms a natural bridge linking Asia to Australia. Once we lost control over that gateway the Japanese would secure a base for submarine, air and surface attack against our line of communications. It would serve as the flank in the west for action against India and Australia.

All this was crystal clear to the War Office in London and Malaya Command in Singapore. But there existed (at that time) no agreed plan for military co-operation between the British Empire and the forces of Holland in Borneo, Sumatra or Java: we had one battalion of Indian troops in Sarawak and Borneo—no aircraft and no coastal defence.

What was not understood—in London or Singapore—was that Japan had the resources to attack on a grand scale, and the ability to execute their plans with thorough-going ruthlessness and fanatical zeal and that the Japanese war-machine was as perfect in its way as the German war-machine when it over-ran France.

The War Office in Tokyo knew that the Dutch were no more popular with natives in their colonies than the British in India, Burma or Malaya. Indonesians, like other subject races, chafed at foreign tutelage. These natural aspirations in Indonesia led to an abortive revolution in 1926: there were only 250,000 Dutch settlers in Indonesia which had a population of 70-million natives and 1-million Chinese so there was a fertile field for Japanese propaganda.

When I arrived at Kuching, plans were afoot to celebrate the centennial anniversary of Brooke rule in Sarawak. By a treaty, then in force, Britain assumed control of Sarawak's foreign relations and defence and it was in conformity with our obligation under the treaty that we had sent one-thousand Indian troops.

The population of Sarawak was about half a million, composed of Chinese, Indians, Malays and Dyaks. They enjoyed a contented life under a benevolent 'White Rajah' and an efficient Civil Service of Europeans and Natives. There were few roads but many wide rivers—vast tracts of jungle and the usual mangrove swamps of a muddy coast line.

The shoreline is mostly black boggy alluvial mud with thin tracks threading through dense tropical foliage: the flatlands stretch inland for a few miles to rise abruptly in mountain ranges.

This, roughly, was the territory which the Officer Commanding British Troops in Sarawak and Brunei had to protect from Japanese attack.

Kuching is 450 miles from Singapore—Brunei is 350 miles from Kuching. Communication was by water. One Company, of 2/15th Punjabis was stationed at Miri—the rest of the Battalion, was at Kuching. In addition to the regular troops there was a mixed unit of Volunteers (two-hundred enthusiasts with 50 rifles between them) and the Sarawak Rangers—a handful of Dyaks in process of formation into a scouting force.

With memories of my first week of depression trying to form the Home Guard into a 'fighting unit' to defend the inhabitants of Hinchley Wood from the threatened arrival of Hitler's paratroopers, I set about examining the Kuching-area coast line, river mouths, sea approaches and beaches. After slogging through tropical-slush to my waist-line I came to the conclusion that I should have remained in Hinchley Wood protecting the Kingston by-pass with the Home Guard, instead of playing about in the mud.

It would have required a Brigade of British troops to cover the obvious 'first objectives' of an invasion force: to deal at all realistically with the 'defence of Kuching' required a fully equipped Division as a minimum force. The token force, 2/15th., Punjab Regiment, was sent over from Singapore by Malaya Command in June, 1941. It could be sacrificed as a 'suicide squad' in defence of a small piece of ground dignified by the name of 'Kuching Landing Ground' but it was useless as an effective *defence force*, and—in any case—the landing-ground would be of little value without adequate air-cover directly the Japanese carriers arrived off the coast.

However the 'military preparations' lacked realism. It appeared that we were to rely on a few head-hunters, a few squads of volunteers without rifles, and three companies of infantry to deal with the invaders. Blow-pipes, parangs and fixed bayonets would be sufficient—on the assumption that the Japanese would land with nothing more than bow and arrow, and samurai sword and assault the beaches in sampans from a fleet of junks.

From the security point of view, Sarawak oilfields at Miri and Lutong, and Seria oilfields in Brunei, were the danger spots.

Borneo is rich in oil. There is a lot of it in the $3\frac{1}{2}$-mile strip at Miri and in the $5\frac{1}{2}$-mile coastal-strip at Seria, and in between the oilfields there is the Lutong refinery. Borneo oil is said to be of extremely high quality, so pure that it can be fed directly to Diesel engines after a relatively simple processing. There are oilfields in Dutch Borneo—and larger refining plants at Balikpapan—but the first impact of war would be felt on the northwest shore of British Borneo. To deny our oil to the enemy involved swift and certain destruction, on a large scale, of oil-tanks, pipes, wells, pumping and refining equipment.

I went to Miri, Lutong and Seria with O.C. Troops, to check up on security measures. At Lutong, in addition to two officers and 100 other-ranks of 2/15th Punjabis, we had a 2-gun detachment of 6 inch coast-defence artillery—1 officer and 50 other-ranks—and a platoon of the Loyal Regiment, besides the demolition squad of Royal Engineers, an officer and six other-ranks.

The war-task of this force was complicated and wide-spread. It had to defend beaches and a landing-strip, carry out tricky demolitions and man the two 6 inch guns. The procedure (laid down at the time of my visit) was based on a *zero-hour* synchronizing with the landing of the enemy on the beaches.

At *zero-hour*, the landing-strip was to be immobilized by raising wire-rope across a number of wooden-trestles: O.C. Miri detachment was to operate an electric-plunger, concealed under his bed, to destroy three underwater-loading pipe-lines: Royal Engineers were to scamper about touching-off explosives to blow up pumping-plant and refining equipment: Royal Artillery were to open rapid fire on the enemy task-force: rest of the force to fire oil-tanks, destroy oil-wells and fight the enemy on the beaches.

There was a similar plan for Seria, *32 miles away* across a broad unbridged river.

I returned to Kuching thoroughly depressed with the *zero-hour* military plans for Miri, Lutong and Seria. Fortunately, for the numerous suicide-squads involved in the enterprise, representations made to Malaya Command (450 miles away), resulted in the synchronization of *zero-hour* with Japan's declaration of war and not when the landing-barges were dropping their fore-ends on the miles of sandy-beach.

Security problems in Sarawak and Brunei were of a very simple nature. Japanese were not numerous. A few hundred families scattered about the country, engaged in trade or tropical agriculture. But they were well drilled by the Japanese Consul in Sandakan—British North Borneo.

Many of the Japanese lived on estates which had been selected years before for their *site value* to the Imperial Japanese Army. I was put in the picture by the Sarawak Administration and soon had a complete dossier of 'land and lease' transactions but an appeal I made, through O.C. Troops to Malaya Command, for cash to cover local and general espionage was refused.

The request for cash was refused but they called for a mass of military intelligence, local gossip and enemy under-cover activity and expected me to finance it out of my pay and allowances.

The Sarawak Government came to my rescue. They handed over to me their State Special Branch (Security) with a monthly grant of one-thousand Straits-dollars to pay my informers and office staff. So, with the assistance of Sarawak State Police, detectives and my own awkward-squad, I was able to answer all of Malaya Command's questionnaires in addition to the queeris of the Special Branch in Singapore. We took prompt avoiding-action against the most active of the 'contacts' among the Chinese, Malays and Indians at Miri, Kuching and Sibu, and dealt effectively with Indian and Malay 'cells' in Singapore.

Japanese were not arrested, for political reasons. I confined operations to telephone-tapping, mail censorship, doorstep watching and the usual non-fictional methods of obtaining reliable information. My smattering of Chinese and Japanese—language and people—helped aurally, visually and orally. But it was not until 17th October, late in the evening when I had my head-phones on that I picked up a message (between Japanese in Kuching and the Manager of the Japanese Samarahan Estate) to the effect that a messenger was to be expected. The manner in which the information was passed between the Japanese aroused my suspicion so I phoned O.C. Troops and arranged with the local P.M.G., to put the telephone line out of action.

On 19th October an aircraft appeared over Kuching. It carried out high-level recce for an hour. We agreed on the identification—Japanese Naval-recce plane—so I sent an urgent signal to Singapore Security at the same time as O.C. Troops informed Malaya Command direct. Some time later, Malaya Command acknowledged the signal and commented 'unlikely that aircraft was Japanese.'

This signal was followed, in due course, by a further comment that 'No British or Dutch aircraft had been over Kuching.' We knew that. Then a third signal came in 'No American aircraft has been in your area. Aircraft you reported must have been Japanese. In future send this type of information *immediately*.'

We kept the telephone lines out of action then raided the Samarahan Estate with a platoon of Punjabis but failed to unearth their wireless transmitter. From 20th October, after the visit of the 'messenger', the Japanese third-column principals ceased to use the Post Office for their urgent correspondence which was sent out by Chinese junk to Japanese trawlers 'fishing' off Kuching.

One of my tide-watchers reported that he had seen a small submarine surface, inshore, near the mouth of the Sarawak River, but I had no confirmation which encouraged me to start another comic exchange of greetings with Malaya Command.

But it was written in the stars that I should cross verbal swords with Malaya Command. In my dual capacity, Security Officer Sarawak and I.O. to O.C. Troops, I was ordered to attend an important conference at Kuching. This VIP Con-

ference was attended by senior Sarawak Government Officials,
O.C. Troops and Staff, Commander and Governor of Dutch
West Borneo and Dutch Military, Intelligence and Airforce
officers. The distinguished visitors were taken for a tour of inspection of Kuching defences and then we went into Conference.

O.C. Troops, Second in Command, and Sarawak officials
held long discussions on requirements and resources. For some
time I declined to inject jarring notes into the harmony of the
occasion, but at last—being pressed by the Dutch and the
British—I said my piece. First, I made it clear that (in my
opinion for what it was worth) Japan would enter the war
within a few weeks. She had raw material, food, munitions and
manpower for total-war on a grand scale. Her plans were made,
down to the latest detail. She would strike without warning. In
the second place, the initiative rested with Japan—not with the
Allies. We had been talking, for some time, about the *defence of
Borneo* as if we had time on our side which was not true.

We were still *talking* about co-operation but there was no
liaison between us in Sarawak and any Dutch airforce or airfield
—or between our respective military forces. There was still no
direct wireless or air communication between Dutch territory
and Sarawak—we had to communicate through Malaya Command, Singapore.

There existed no agreed plan for common military action:
there were no arrangements for mutual assistance or for pooling
our resources. As for Kuching landing-ground I could reach it
from water's-edge in less than an hour. It was useless for modern
aircraft operating under war conditions.

Our force in Kuching would have to fight on both sides of a
wide river crossed by one bridge: there were no pontoons. From
Kuching to the Dutch border there was no road suitable for
military traffic—there was a jungle path, that was all.

The Japanese, when they arrived, would strike hard—and
simultaneously—from several beach-heads. They would employ
one, if not two, Infantry Brigades of seasoned troops. Kuching
would be captured within 72 hours of the first landings. Our
scattered defence points could not be held any longer by eight or
nine hundred regular troops—the extensive waterways could
not be defended by Dyaks in dugouts or by Volunteers armed
with rifles.

My remarks were received with silence—no amount of polite talk could alter the facts which spoke for themselves.

The Dutch representatives promised to discuss co-operation with their own headquarters. They assured me that higher authority would rectify the position in due course and we would be informed through Malaya Command.

I replied that a state of emergency already existed. It was long past the time for proposals and counter-proposals—it was high time that we shook off our lethargy and acted. We should take the Japanese threat seriously, plan with realism within our resources, or—get out and help elsewhere before it was too late.

O.C. Troops—Colonel Peffers—went over to Singapore soon after the conference. He handed a copy of the minutes to Malaya Command. They acted with commendable speed: the signal read 'Stop circulation of minutes. Withdraw copies. Delete James' remarks. Instruct James report Singapore, immediately.'

Sarawak Government were in full agreement with my remarks as State Security Officer and they protested against my recall.

Malaya Command refused to reconsider their decision so I left for Singapore, in disgrace, on 20th November. An interview followed, at Fort Canning, at which I was informed that General Percival—G.O.C. Troops Malaya—was very angry with me. The minutes of the conference were handed to me and I was asked to read my comments, and if—on reflection—I cared to, to amend them. I agreed with the text and declined to alter one word.

I waited for the sentence. But there was to be no Court Martial so I asked for a Court of Enquiry into my conduct.

That was not considered necessary. I asked to be returned to the United Kingdom as I was already sixty years of age and objected to being treated like a naughty child. My remarks at the conference were made on request and were not volunteered out of ignorant egotism. I regretted that my conduct had displeased General Percival but I could not retract my honest opinions.

The interview ended, as it began, on a friendly note: I was thanked for my general work in Sarawak and would receive a fresh posting in due course.

The week after my return to Singapore, General Percival went over to Kuching. The mobile defence plan was scrapped —a new static defence plan was substituted based on the landing ground. The entire Punjabi force, with stores, arms and equipment were ordered to move inside a $3\frac{1}{2}$-mile perimeter and to hold the 'aerodrome' at all cost. This was a modern reversion to the laager method we adopted in 1906 when I fought Zulus who were armed with assegais and knobkerries: it went back to the days of the British infantry square when we held tight against the Mad Mullah. However—in the end—even this plan was blown sky-high.

On 23rd December, 1941, a few weeks after I left Kuching, Japanese convoys appeared off the coast. At 09.00 hours, 24th December, twenty enemy landing-craft came up the Santubong River—at 13.30 hours the Astana (Rajah's Palace) opposite Kuching Town was captured by Japanese troops wearing Sarawak State Police or Punjabi uniforms. The landing-ground was contacted by Japanese patrols at 17.00 hours 24th December: the Town was occupied about the same time. By night-fall, 25th December, the landing-ground had been blown and the remnants of 2/15th Punjabs were retiring in the direction of Dutch West Borneo: they reformed at Sanggau Ledo, (Dutch territory) on 29th December.

The Japanese used a Division in their attacks. They were in full occupation in 8 hours. 2/15th Punjabs had 120 killed in action in Sarawak and in Dutch Borneo, 261 died as prisoner of war, 70 were missing, believed killed. Out of their battle-strength of 1089 (24th December) only 638 survived their suicide-role and returned to India in 1945.

With regard to co-operation and communications: when the Japanese convoy was sighted off Kuching (23rd December) the Commander of SAFOR (Sarawak Force) signalled Malaya Command at 18.00 hours and received a reply, two hours later, instructing him to *destroy* the aerodrome and two D.F., Stations. This was done. Malaya Command were then asked for further instructions as the raison d'etre of SAFOR no longer existed: no reply to that signal—or to an earlier one sent on 25th December —was received so the Force Commander packed up and retired on Dutch Borneo.

Oilfields and refinery, at Miri, Lutong and Seria were destroyed when Japan declared War-7-8th December—and the covering troops withdrawn with minor loss. 'Aerodrome' at Kuching, and D.F. Stations, could have been demolished by Kuching P.W.D. for about £150 so it did not require 1089 regular soldiers to witness the event and then be left to fend for themselves as best they could in Dutch Borneo.

Kuching was bombed by Japanese aircraft on 19th December. The nearest aerodrome (Sinkawang II) was 80 miles away in Dutch West Borneo—20 minutes flying distance—but SAFOR had to call for support *through Malaya Command.* None was forthcoming. There was no military or air support but units of the Dutch Navy went into action on 23rd and 24th and sank a cruiser and four transports.

There had been many Allied Conferences in the Far East, before Japan entered the War. There were four plans to deal with: attack against British possessions: against N.E.I.: against American possessions: against British, Dutch, and the Americans. The initiative rested with Japan and our plans had not reached the realm of practicability when Japan attacked almost simultaneously on 7th and 8th December, 1941—but World War II had been on since 3rd September, 1939 and Britain could not get a quart out of a pint pot.

In less than three weeks after I returned from Kuching the Japanese had bombed Singapore and immobilized the American fleet in Pearl Harbour. Within three months the whole of Malaya, Sarawak, Hongkong, Borneo and Java was occupied by Japanese troops, and General Percival's British Army in Malaya were prisoners of war. The Japanese struck hard. There had been no exaggeration of their power or their intentions: my posting was unpleasant—Liaison Officer between a mass of British prisoners and a horde of exultant Japanese.

CHAPTER IX

DEFEAT OF BRITISH ARMY IN MALAYA

i. *Unpreparedness for War*

The weakness of Britain in the Far East was no secret to the Japanese in December, 1941. We were fully occupied against Germany and Italy—fighting them single-handed and sending to Soviet Russia munitions sorely needed in Malaya and Burma. Our Navy, and our Airforce was second to none but we were extended to the uttermost limit of our capacity to retain command of the Sea and gain superiority in the Air.

Our main hope, in the event of war with Japan, was prompt naval and military assistance from the United States of America. Japan knew that too. At 3.20 a.m., American time, on 8th December, 1941 105 carrier-borne bombers and torpedo planes made an attack on Pearl Harbour: eight battleships, and three cruisers were put out of action—over fifty per cent of Naval and Military aircraft were destroyed or damaged on the ground.

Japan struck without more than a few minutes warning. In April, 1942, the New York correspondent of the Nya Dagligt Allehanda (Stockholm) reported some details of this attack based on the log-book of a salvaged Japanese submarine, which had been sunk at the entrance to Pearl Harbour *one hour before* the Japanese air attack commenced. The submarine commander had been inside the harbour without being detected. He jotted down the exact position of each American warship and succeeded in leaving the harbour at 5.25 a.m. and sending a wireless message to the Japanese aircraft carriers.

According to the log-book, the submarine arrived off Pearl Harbour at 1.05 a.m., and waited until 4.30 a.m., when the submarine nets were lowered in order to let a vessel through—

the submarine followed and noted the exact position of battle-ships *Utah* and *West Virginia,* 12 destroyers, 3 gunboats and the cruiser *Trenton.*

It was necessary to the success of Japan's plans for the conquest of Greater East Asia that simultaneous attacks, without warning—diplomatic or otherwise—should be made against the British and American bases in the Pacific zone. Manila was also bombed on 8th December and the Japanese landed on Luzon the *next day:* Guam, Midway and Wake Islands were attacked by other task forces.

On the British Army front the invasion force was sighted on 6th December. It consisted of 43 large troop-carriers, mostly of 5,000-6,000 ton class, escorted by a battleship, seven cruisers and seventeen destroyers.

At midnight, 7-8th December, this task force reached the coast off Kota Bharu (N.E. Malaya) and landing parties were soon engaged with a detachment of 3/17 Dogras who were forced out of their pill-box defences. At 04.30 hours, 8th December a small formation of bombers raided Singapore, with the bright-lights still undimmed, and dropped a few bombs on the town-area before passing over Seletar and Tengah Aerodromes and the Naval Base—they were not intercepted: the anti-aircraft batteries opened up but they flew on in close formation.

Later—the same day—enemy aircraft bombed aerodromes at Alor Star, Sungei Patani, Butterworth, Penang, Kota Bharu, Gong Kedah and Machang. By nightfall we were compelled to abandon Kota Bharu aerodrome.

The strength of the British Navy at Singapore on 8th December, 1941 was: 1 Battleship: 1 Battle-cruiser: 3 'D Class' Cruisers: 7 Destroyers and 3 Gunboats.

Japan's Navy consisted of 10 Battleships: 18 Heavy Cruisers: 16 Light Cruisers: 9 Aircraft Carriers: 110 Destroyers and 64 Submarines.

Japan's *Naval* Airforce was: 500 Fighter planes: 180 Carrier-based bombers: 300 Carrier-based attack planes: 350 Land-attack planes: 340 Reconnaissance seaplanes and 15 flying-boats.

We had 141 Aircraft in all: Brewster Buffalo fighters, Sharks Swordfish, Hudsons, Blenheim IV Bombers, Glen Martins and

Torpedo-bombers: our tubby Brewster Buffalo was no match for the 'Zero' fighter of the Japanese airforce in speed or manoeuvre.

By 10th December one-third of our airforce was put out of action—lost in combat or on the ground, and most of the aerodromes were without effective ground-defence against repeated attacks.

On the night of 8th December, Admiral Phillips put to sea with *Prince of Wales* and *Repulse* and an escort-screen of four destroyers. His destination was the Gulf of Thailand. There was no other air-cover and the small fleet were sighted at dusk on 9th December, off Kuantan on the East Coast, by Japanese aircraft and submarines. At 11.15 hours, 10th December, flights of Japanese Navy 97 torpedo-bombers attacked: at 13.20 hours *Prince of Wales* and *Repulse* went down just as our fighter aircraft from Singapore arrived. Destroyers picked up 2,185 survivors— we lost 600 officers and men and our only battleship and battle-cruiser on the station.

It was fully twenty-four hours *after* the Pearl Harbour debacle when Admiral Phillips left the Naval Base to engage units of the enemy fleet covering the landings in Thai and N.E. Malaya. The formidable nature of enemy air attack on our ground installations, and their war potentiality had been amply demonstrated but this did not deter the fighting spirit of Admiral Phillips. Under all the known circumstances it may not have been wise to have proceeded up the coast without adequate air-cover. But, battles are not always won by wisdom alone and to turn tail is not one of the traditions of the British Navy.

Our fleet was now reduced to 3 cruisers, 7 destroyers, 3 small gunboats and 30 auxiliary craft. Without command of the sea and without command of the air Singapore Naval Base was reduced to the status of a Fortress incubus. The Pacific Fleet of the U.S.A. had been immobilized at Pearl Harbour—the tragic loss of our capital ships served to increase the naval superiority of the enemy. It was left to the British Army in Malaya to do the best it could under its severe handicap. What could it do? We could be held in the north and outflanked east and west—anywhere along the long coast-line and in the south it was no better for us: Singapore was no fortress, just a death trap.

We checked the enemy for fifty-three days, foiled his many attempts to outflank us. And then, alas, capitulated five days after the enemy landed on Singapore Island.

Regarding this major reverse to our arms, Mr. Churchill is reported to have told the House of Commons, in secret session on 23rd April, 1942, that we were thoroughly outnumbered by the sea, land and air forces of Japan throughout the Far Eastern theatre of War and that 'The violence, fury, skill and might of Japan has far exceeded anything we had been led to expect.'

But there should have been no secret regarding Japan's military machine, its effectiveness or of our inability to meet it on equal terms in the Far East.

ii. *The Australian Imperial Forces*

On 7th December I was ordered by Malaya Command to report for duty at 8th Australian Division Headquarters, Johore Bahru. Next morning the first wave of enemy bombers passed overhead. Two days later I went into the 'rubber'—north of Kota Tinggi—to operate with battle-headquarters of the division. After a few days, owing to alteration of orders, I returned to Johore Bahru to Divisional Headquarters.

The loss of *Prince of Wales* and *Repulse* plus the unsatisfactory news from the front-line, dominated the terse conversation of the Australians. Rightly, or wrongly, the A.I.F. thought that they should have been sent to Kota Bharu not the Indians. The 'Aussies' held the Japanese in contempt and were anxious to give them 'a taste of the bayonet'. But the 8th Division were short of a Brigade of Infantry and had no battle-practice. They were *not* short of *mechanical transport* but their officers lacked experience in modern warfare: they had very little idea of what the 11th Indian Division was up against on the Malay-Thai border and their training in 'jungle-warfare' had been on a strictly peacetime basis—uncomfortable but not productive of battle casualties.

The Japanese landed at Kota Bharu, Kelantan, and at Patani and Singora in Thai. Supported by light tanks they made rapid progress, down the Jitra-Singora road and down the railway leading to Alor Star, with a full Division. Another Division, from Patani pressed a flanking drive—across country—to Kroh on the border —aimed at cutting through to Penang on the west coast of Malaya.

A third Division—based on Kota Bharu—moved down the East Coast Railway into Kelantan with the object of securing their left flank prior to another landing at Kuantan.

By 12th December the situation in North Malaya was most disturbing. I doubt if the A.I.F.—with two Infantry Brigades—could have done better during those few days of fighting, in the Kedah and Kelantan areas, than the units of the 9th and 11th Indian Divisions. We had to face three simultaneous attacks: each attack was mounted with a full division and *an unlimited number of reserves*. Our two Brigades—22nd and 27th—would have had to face the same problems as the Surreys, Leicesters and Gurkhas in their attempt to hold the line with the Indian troops. Furthermore, the A.I.F., would not have blended with the Indian units in the same way as U.K. troops, and we were not numerically strong enough to take over the whole show.

It was not a simple question of courage, or training, but of avoiding encirclement by superior numbers. This was done, on the retreat, by disciplined troops under the command of Lt.-General Sir Lewis Heath, 3rd Indian Corps, who was not without battle experience in World War II.

The A.I.F.—in common with Indian units—had had no experience of field operations *against tanks* supported by incessant straffing from dive-bombers. Of course it was not on anything like the scale of such operations elsewhere—but the first contact with the 'novelty' of it would have had them guessing for a bit.

Another point is worth stressing. The 'Aussies' have their own idea of discipline. It is divided into two very distinct codes: the fighting code and the ragging code. In action they have a record equal to any other soldier—white or coloured—in all the military virtues that go with War: out of action they have no pedantry and are prone to peccadilloes which are by no means appreciated by onlookers.

At first I was concerned with fifth-column activity in Johore, visiting the Estates abandoned by Japanese and cutting short various activities of Malays, Indians and Chinese who were engaged in subversive practices on either side of Johore Straits. I soon discovered that the atmosphere of the Orient bemused the average 'Aussie'. The had a naive approach to the mystery of ideographics: to many of them the 'signs' were sinister secrets of the enemy. In consequence of this ideology, whenever they came across oriental scripture—Malay, Indian, Chinese or Japanese kana—on scraps of paper or on a bit of cardboard—they picked it up in the belief that it might be connected with espionage or the plans of the 'Nips'.

One day, a dispatch rider thundered into Headquarters from 22nd Brigade Hdq., with an urgent dispatch for intelligence.

A mysterious document had been found nailed to a tree on a Mersing Estate. I was instructed to deal with the matter—plus-one-priority. However, all that was written on the paper was this: 'Beware of the Tiger. Do not wander near the kongsi between sunset and sunrise. One estate labourer has been killed by the Tiger.' That was all—but it was written in Chinese.

The Tiger was not caught but —by the same active A.I.F. unit— two very mysterious natives were bagged. Searching for the Tiger (?) they hit the trail of two human beings and tracked them for a week. Then, at dawn, they rushed a native hut and arrested the suspects. They were manhandled to Brigade Hdq., where they gave endless trouble by feigning madness—jabbering a mixture of Malay and Chinese and protesting that they were not Japanese. In due course they arrived at Div. Hdq. and were passed on to me for interrogation.

They were dressed in the usual manner of Chinese estate labourers but I felt sure that they were Japanese. I dealt with them separateley: talked to them in Chinese and then in Japanese for more than an hour but could make nothing of their dialect.

I asked them their names—in every dialect I knew—and I prodded them with questions about all the things I could think of but, most of the time, they shook their heads and pretended not to understand. I repeated the questions in Japanese and they looked at me in blank astonishment.

It was rather tedious so I changed my tactics. I spoke quietly about Dai Nippon, Tenno Heika, Kodo and the sin of being captured—the disgrace it involved. Suddenly, the man I was addressing sprang to his feet and shouted: 'Nihon-jin da! Nihon-jin da! Koro-sei! Koro-sei!'

'I'm Japanese! I'm Japanese! Kill me! Kill me!' the denouement was dramatic, and emphatic.

The A.I.F. Intelligence Officer proferred the remark—'Say:
—Nihon-jin—that's the 'Nip' for Japanese!' I agreed, adding
'And he is anxious to die—take my gun, I'll feel safer with-
out it.'

I thanked him for his confession. Called on his companion to
join me at the table—handed out fags and cups of tea—and
explained that all I wanted was his name, rank and unit. As a
prisoner of war he was in no danger of sudden death—as a spy
he might be shot. Masquerading in Chinese outfit was all
wrong but I would send them on to Malaya Command for
further questioning.

During the entire campaign we captured a dozen or so Japanese prisoners—nearly all of whom were wounded. Whatever
their faults, surrender was not one of them in Malaya: they kept
in mind General Araki's words—'The Japanese soldier never
surrenders in battle; in Japanese wars there are no prisoners.
Why then should Japanese surrender to the limitations set by
nature?'

That was kodism and it was because they held such definite
ideas on the subject of 'prisoners of war' that they treated us
with contempt when we fell into their clutches in great numbers
—great numbers but small in comparison with their own abject
submission a few years later.

iii. Retreat through the jungle

After establishing themselves ashore the Japanese advanced
in three weaving prongs across the Thai border towards Alor
Star, Kroh and Grik on the Perak River—and from Kota Bharu
into Kelantan. Attacking columns converged or separated with
the change of route and terrain: the east coast contingent operating astride the railway and the west coast contingent along the
railway, highways and through the jungle.

We abandoned Penang on 19th December—leaving the
Broadcasting Station in running order for the use of Japanese
propaganda.

Penang added another base for enemy coastwise co-operation
and hastened the general retreat to avoid encirclement.

A week later, Ipoh—threatened by an enveloping movement
from Grik, and a drive down the railway from Taiping—was
hastily evacuated. In the space of sixteen days we were behind

the Perak River with our left flank resting on the coast at Telok Anson. On the east coast the enemy reached the Pahang-Trengganu frontier on 27th December and we left Kuantan on 31st to fall back —across country—to Raub, south east of Telok Anson.

Heavy fighting checked the enemy. But on 2nd January a Battalion came down the Perak River in native craft and captured Telok Anson compelling us to retire from Kampar to the Slim River area. The same day, enemy barges and landing-craft appeared off Kuala Selangor and another force was engaged coming down-coast from Telok Anson.

Casualties were heavy on both sides and this was a severe handicap to us because we had not the reserves on the spot to throw into the confused fighting that went on continuously, day and night, whereas the Japanese were ramming their front with fresh men and material.

Slim River position, covering Kuala Lumpur, was attacked in force on 7th January—infantry being preceded by small tanks. The Japanese were held up by mines and obstructions for a time but at last a breach was made by 20 tanks over-running the front lines and inflicting heavy loss on our supporting infantry on the march. The tanks penetrated our lines for 15 miles before our 4.5-inch howitzers halted them but the advance gave the Japanese control of the Slim River bridge and this led to a minor disaster for our troops.

It was dismal news for the optimists who had pinned their faith on the defensive qualities of impenetrable jungle, swift and broad rivers, numberless streams, bogs and quagmires and the so called 'natural barriers of the ambush country'. Japanese knew the difficulties. They planned for years to overcome them by the use of suitable equipment—including bicycles and small tanks.

Japan's command of the sea, never in dispute during the campaign, permitted free movement of troops and supply—free movement to keep pace with coast to coast advance, free movement to obviate any need for extended supply lines.

The attack could be switched at will—the threat to the British base at Singapore was never outside practical military considerations from the day the enemy landed in N.E. Malaya until the Johore Straits were crossed.

Our aerial support was ineffective from first to last: aero-dromes were captured, or put out of action in a few weeks but Japanese aircraft operated with impunity from the border of Siam to the Naval Base. Every major troop concentration we made was laid bare by their recce units. We had to act in the dark and counter their infantry attacks by maintaining contact on the ground as best we could. Dive-bombers and tanks provided their fresh shock-troops with any encouragement required for frontal attack on our battle-weary units.

There was vigour and unhesitant courage displayed by the enemy as they forced their way through swamp and jungle. Every means of transport was used, trucks, omnibuses, carts, horses and thousands of bicycles—bicycles which gave a silent approach, rest for the feet and transport for additional rifle ammunition and personal rations. And all this combined to facilitate the constant infiltration so damaging to our morale.

In the interior every phase of advance depended upon the command of bridges spanning a network of rivers. At these points we gave more than we received in sharp engagements. Dogras, Sikhs, Punjabis, Jats, Gurkhas, Surreys, Leicesters and the Argyll and Sutherland Highlanders gave of their best. But it was not enough, not nearly enough to halt the numerical superiority of our enemy.

The British Army under General Percival was a medley of races and religions hastily assembled and moderately equipped for total-warfare: the Japanese Army under General Yamashita was a modern homogenous military machine tuned up for its task—fully equipped, well trained in actual warfare, well trained in jungle-country operations; it was well led by ex-perienced officers and non-commissioned officers and it was inspired by a fanatical urge to win, or to die, in a national cause.

Fighting in the jungle, with all the odds against you—fighting a losing battle in the heat of the tropics—is a real test of endu-rance, whatever the race of the soldier. Flight from the enemy, day after day and night after night, produces extreme hyperæs-thesia which adds to physical strain, lowers resistance, and—in the end—destroys morale.

There is the ever present distraction of shadows in the half-light of forest maze. The silence of tall trees. The uncertainty of direction imposed on the certainty of pursuit by the relentless

enemy. The heavy rifle—the empty water-bottle—the tired feet
of a weary body, trudging through the undergrowth and the
slush. And then, with the going down of the sun, the swift
transition from imperfect vision to the impenetrable veil of
black night—the evening breeze and the jungle voices. Black
night which halts retreat only to magnify the perils of quiet
repose on mother earth.

Suddenly, out of the comparative silence, comes the nerve
shattering hiss of a sniper's rifle-bullet fired at point blank range
or from the shelter of a tree top. Panic, for a moment, and then
flight to the limit of mental and physical endurance.

For numerous reasons, blame for it all was saddled on the
shoulders of 'Malaya Command'. But the critics were merely
indulging in defensive introspection in search for an explanation, or an excuse. But it was beyond the power of 'Malaya
Command', III Corps or the A.I.F., to restore to us command
of air and sea without which we had no prospect of turning
retreat into victory. No doubt there were tactical errors for
which the local commander or 'Malaya Command' were responsible, and there were conflicting orders which resulted in
yielding ground before it was absolutely necessary. True, but
such things are not confined to the Malaya Campaign; Greece,
North Africa or Norway for that matter were not gems of
flawless leadership at the top or at the bottom.

iv. The Indian National Army

One of my jobs was to sort out Indian Army personnel from
batches of Orientals brought in as 'Japanese spies'. Lorry loads
of Indians, Malays, Chinese and Gurkhas, heavily guarded,
would be brought in to me for interrogation. In the eyes of
'Aussies' they looked alike and all coloured people in uniform
were suspect if they were found wandering in our area. As a
matter of fact this was not quite so absurd a precaution as it may
appear at first for there was good reason to suspect the loyalty of
some of the Indian troops. Many incidents, which filtered in
during the first week of the invasion, pointed to planned
desertion. And within a few hours of the unconditional
surrender of Singapore thousands of these disloyal troops were
joining the Indian National Army.

They needed no persuasion, these traitors of the 3 Indian Corps, and within a few weeks there were *15,000* volunteers in the ranks of the First I.N.A. The organization of the I.N.A., as disclosed by orders was as follows:—

Supreme Commander	General Mohan Singh	..	1/14 Punjab
2nd in Command	.. Colonel Mohd Akram	..	1/14 Punjab
G Staff	.. .. Colonel M. Z. Kaini	..	1/14 Punjab
	Colonel Arshad ..	..	5/2 Punjab
	Colonel Jaswant Singh	..	4/9 Hyderbad
A Staff	.. .. Colonel Habib-ul-Rehman		1/14 Punjab
	Colonel Man Singh	..	2/9 Jats
D.Q.M.G.	.. .. Colonel Balwant Singh	..	5/2 Punjab

(The military 'rank' was conferred on them by the Japanese).

Now for a few of the incidents. On 11th December, 1941, the 1/14 Punjabis were attacked at Changlun—N.W. Perlis—on the Thai border, by advance guard of enemy moving down from Singora.

Attack continued throughout the day. At 16.30 hours tanks went into action, on flank and rear of 1/14th. In the resulting confusion, two-hundred of the 1/14th—including Brigadier (15 Ind. Bde)—were cut off from main body but managed to rejoin it later on. Not so some others, including Captain Mohan Singh and Captain Mohd Akram, who went over to the Japanese.

From then to the fall of Singapore, two-hundred V.C.O's and I.O.R's acted under Mohan Singh and Mohd Akram as a fifth-column and propaganda unit for the Japanese Army. Led by Sub. Alla Ditta (22 Mountain Regt.) and Sub. Onkar Singh (5/14 Punjab) part of this unit were landed with the *first wave* of Japanese troops to cross from Johore Bahru to Singapore Island on 8/9th February. This unit, termed Royal Volunteers, acted as the nucleus of the I.N.A. Gestapo and was headed by Sub. Shanghara Singh (5/14 Punjab)—Sub. Mir Rehman, Jem Fateh Khan and Jem. Sadhu Singh of 1/14 Punjabs.

There were many other Indian Troops who changed their sworn allegiance during the campaign. Their deflection may have passed unobserved, at the time, and it may have exerted no influence on the campaign but I have included this short mention of it as a preface to the sorry story of the I.N.A. the propaganda rabble of the subsequent Japanese thrust through Burma to India.

v. The A.I.F. in action (Westforce)

Thirty days after the opening of the Japanese offensive we rearranged our front-line—basing our defence on North Johore. One Brigade of A.I.F.—27th—was on the West Coast and the other Brigade—22nd—on the East Coast. The 3 Indian Corps withdrew to South Johore and the new line was from Endau to Malacca: A.I.F. 27 Bde. took over the forward positions at Gemas.

On 10th January, higher command conference at Segamat decided on new composition, and distribution, of force as follows:— WESTFORCE (Major-General Gordon Bennett) comprising remnant of 9 Indian Division, part of 2 Loyals, 45 Indian Brigade (arrived Singapore 3rd January), new Indian Pioneer Battalion and the 27 A.I.F. Brigade. EASTFORCE (Lt.-General Sir Lewis Heath) composed of the badly mauled II Indian Division, 22 A.I.F. Brigade with 2/17 Dogras and Corps Troops.

Composition of Westforce, to meet dangerous threat to our left flank, was not satisfactory to General Gordon Bennett-he preferred the inclusion of his own 22 Bde., to the particularly raw 45 Indian Bde which had just arrived. Perhaps it may have been better psychologically to bring all Australian troops under their own commander but that was the G.O.C's decision based on military necessities.

On 12th January, 8 Div. Hdq. moved from Johore Bahru to Labis with Advance Hq. at Segamat. At last the A.I.F. were allowed to participate in the campaign and they were elated at the prospect of fighting Japanese: eighteen days later we were back on Singapore Island—the Malaya Campaign was over.

Plans for an ambush at Gemas—on the road north of Segamat —had been worked out. On the afternoon of 14th January between five and six hundred Japanese cyclists came down the main road—they were allowed to cross the bridge by units of the A.I.F. 2/30 Bn. The bridge was blown and most of the Japanese caught in the trap were disposed of. Next morning there was another small action which resulted in the destruction of several of the small tanks which were trying to restore the position. It was a good start but proved to have been the only bright spots in a very dismal setting.

Kuala Lumpur had been lost on 11th January—following the retirement from Port Swettenham—and Malacca followed. The

threat to Muar was developing while we were engaged in our
first encounter at Gemas. Muar was held by 45 Indian Brigade
and the Japanese were not slow to press the attack against our
left flank.

On 15th January they had pushed their attack from Malacca
to the north bank of the 600-yard wide Muar River close to the
town.

This move was a direct threat to our line of communication
from Yong Peng to Gemas. And the position became dangerous
on 16th January when the enemy crossed the river and gained
the Yong Peng-Muar Road.

The main road, Gemas-Johore Bahru, carried all our urgent
traffic and it was now jammed with transport. It was now a war
of movement on wheels and a blood-bath in the jungle. There
was too much freedom for civilians on our l-o-c and too few
military police to deal with stragglers and subversive Indians,
Chinese and Malays going up and down the road in cars or on
bicycles.

My job was concerned with field security but I had great
difficulty in maintaining—single handed—collecting stations for
suspects. I used the abandoned Yong Peng Police Station until
enemy bombers reduced it to rubble. Moving about—between
Gemas and Yong Peng—I heard a good deal about the confused fighting at Malacca, Segamat, Muar, Bakri and Batu
Pahat. The A.I.F. had its fair share of some of the hardest
fighting in the campaign and the 45 Indian Brigade were cut to
ribbons in several days of bitter fighting in appalling conditions.
Certainly there was nothing 'disgraceful' about it all. We were
defeated but not disgraced and the young Indians in the 45th
Brigade gave their lives for the cause, for which we were
fighting, without understanding very much about it.

No doubt our method of communication, between fighting
troops and Malaya Command, was defective and artillery
support not all that it might have been. Some of our casualties
could have been avoided in the confusion which followed the
Muar River engagement and flight into the jungle. But it was
not a 'war game' played over a double-whisky with lead
soldiers.

During the retreat the civilian population, Indians, Malays
and Chinese, looted right and left before joining the refugees

jamming the road to Singapore. The State Police of Johore vanished into thin air long before they were in any danger from the enemy and this put additional strain on our own military police.

As the only officer in Westforce with any knowledge of Japanese I was often called on to travel fifty miles in response to messages regarding 'arrest of spies' but these rushes never ended in the interrogation of one Japanese soldier—they were Malays or Gurkhas adrift from their units.

Infiltration and frontal attacks—at Muar and Segamat—compelled us to adjust our dispositions: superior numbers and the relentless pressure hastened retreat.

On 17th January, General Percival, accompanied by Commander of 11th Indian Division, came to Rear-Headquarters Westforce to confer with General Gordon Bennett. Discussions took place in the small bungalow I occupied at the time and before the G.O.C., arrived I talked to the A.I.F. Commander about the critical position at Muar and Segamat. General Bennett's principal regret was that his own 22nd Brigade was not at Muar but it was then too late for complicated troop movements of that kind. Already, Eastforce was in contact with the enemy in the Endau area. Timing of Japanese attacks was well synchronized and accentuated difficulty on both our flanks.

By 21st January it was clear that we could not hold Johore—a new line was fixed, Mersing: Kluang: Batu Pahat: behind which we were to withdraw to Singapore. Then, for ten days, we went on fighting; avoiding battle to escape encirclement—the campaign was a thing of the past.

On 30th January I went over the Johore Causeway with advance party to establish A.I.F. Hdq. on Hill View Estate near Bukit Timah Road Police Station. I had not loosened my pack-straps when an A.I.F. D.R., brought me an urgent message to return to Johore Bahru Hq. On arrival I was handed a satchell, taken from a dead Japanese a few hours earlier, and asked to examine contents to ascertain if enemy had knowledge of our immediate intentions.

In a few minutes I handed my report to General Bennett—it was negative. The stand-still order was cancelled, withdrawal over the causeway continued—I returned to Hill View Estate with the satchell.

The campaign was over: I met the 2 Argyll and Sutherland Highlanders fanning out over Johore Bahru foothills—they were moving in open order with bayonet fixed to cover the tail of the retreat. On the Causeway the R.E. were drilling holes in the very solid foundation—working under pressure to do what aught to have been done weeks earlier, if at all. Postponement had been due—so I was informed by a senior officer—to a desire by the responsible authority to avoid destroying the morale of the civilian population of Singapore: military precaution sacrificed to pure sentiment. The civilians knew all about the progress of the campaign—a trifle more realism might have improved their morale.

And when the Causeway was blown—31st January—the actual damage was confined to about *30 yards* of the total length of *1,250 yards* or so. In fact I interrogated the first of our own stragglers who came over the *blown Causeway* without wetting their feet.

The ration strength of the A.I.F., on 31st January, 1942 was 18,271: the total ration strength of the rest of the British Army was about 32,800—the Indian Army was just under 40,000.

CHAPTER X

SINGAPORE DEBACLE

i. *Fortress incognito*

We built an excellent Naval Base at Singapore with airfields
and local defences but it never was a fortress from a military
point of view. It was constructed when battleships were the
hallmark of naval superiority, Britain mistress of the sea and
aircraft in their teens.

In 1941 it could not have been held for long without command of the sea and the air. Times had changed. But the
British still regarded it as the 'sturdy bulwark of a far flung
Empire—the Royal oak in a tropical setting.' This lyricism was
all right for Empire Day and when it was captured by the Japanese the panegyrics gave way to lachrymatory denunciations
and demands for a scapegoat. Sentiment had been defrauded
by some one or other.

But there had been no deception—we had lost a battle, but
not the War. Of course a War is not won by avoiding combat,
to reduce casualties, but by exerting the maximum effort to
destroy the enemy—lower his morale, not encourage him by
mass surrender.

True—and the odds were against us on the mainland, and the
odds were against us on the Island. Nothing was gained by
dodging the inevitable, shrinking from a pitched battle in
Johore and then surrendering a few days later after cutting ourselves off from our water supply. But the 'fortress' drew us like a
magnet and we were trapped in a pitfall of our own contrivance.

We retreated 450 miles in 53 days and then joined a mixed
civilian population of a million who were squatting promis-
cuously—from coast to coast—in undisturbed occupation of
nearly all the so called strategic points. There were no secrets

regarding the Naval Base or the general layout of coastal batteries, fortified islands or other military arrangements—they had all been constructed by local native labour.

Except for the east coast and the Naval Base defences there existed no related system of permanent or semi-permanent forts or fortifications. There was nothing to compel an enemy to resort to siege warfare in preference to open-warfare and direct attack: there were no tank-traps, pill-boxes, barbed-wire entanglements, booby-traps, minefields, machine-gun nests, fixed or mobile searchlights, heavy or light gun emplacements arranged in an all-round connected scheme of defence for the garrison to make use of. Outside of the Naval Base defences there was little to stop an enemy—once he had landed—from fighting his way down the roads and across country to the city of Singapore. Less obstacles than were encountered during the campaign on the mainland.

Even if our troops had been fresh, and of the highest morale, the lack of any defences on the *west coast of the Island* would have depressed them. They had been badly mauled and when the Japanese made their initial attack in this sector the human barriers were soon brushed aside and the attack proceeded according to plan.

We were confronted by the modern Japanese army against which we had to stand up to and fight to a finish—or retire on the bricks and mortar of a city teeming with Asiatics who were not a bit interested in resisting the Japanese.

The system of conscription and the discipline of the Japanese army were based on absolute despotism—despotism inseparably linked with state-religion and education with a powerful sacerdotal body exercising control over people and throne and proscribing the right of the human mind to think for itself in civil or military affairs. We—in Singapore—had a multitude of commanders—numerous defence committees and all the drawbacks of Civil and Military Governors: High and Low Commissioners with a plethora of C.-in-C's., G.O.C's of three Services, to say nothing of Cabinet Representative planning on the higher level and leaving the low level of the beaches to look after itself. There was anything but real team-spirit between the Civil Government—with its emphasis on what was good and what was bad for civilian morale—and the Service Departments.

The Johore Causeway was blown on 31st January. This—in theory—severed our land connection with Johore but a much more serious matter was the capture by the enemy on 27th January of the Island's main source of water supply at Gunong Pulai in South Johore. The water was piped across the Causeway and water was as essential to the garrison as weapons and ammunition and more useful to the civilians than pep-talk on morale.

For those who may be interested in the minute details of the operations in Malaya, or on the Island, I recommend a study of General Percival's Despatch of 25th April, 1946 published in the London Gazette of 20th February, 1948. He gives a complete picture of the situation before the outbreak of the war with Japan and the day to day progress of the campaign. I do not propose to make any comment on the Despatch itself but shall continue to confine my observations to my own personal experiences.

ii. Static warfare

In the scheme of defence the A.I.F. were allotted the un-defended Western Area of the Island. Troops were disposed as follows:— *Right sector,* Causeway to Kranji River—27 Brigade. *Centre sector,* Kranji River to Berih River—22 Brigade. *Left sector,* Berih River to Jurong River—44 Indian Brigade.

44 Indian Brigade arrived on the Island on 22nd January and it was raw and untrained: the 2/19 Bn of 22 A.I.F. Brigade and the 2/29 Bn. of 27 A.I.F. Brigade were not up to A.I.F. standard.

For practical purposes we had only *four* reliable Australian Battalions for the western area. 22 Brigade had a front of 16,000 yards to defend (2/20 Bn's front was 8000, 2/18th's was 4,000 yards and 2/19th's just under 4,000 yards). And this despite the fact that 2/19 Battalion had been cut up badly at Muar and had been brought up to ration-strength by untrained men who had landed a few days earlier. It was during the very heavy fighting in the Muar area that Lt.-Col. Anderson of the 2/19th earned his V.C. An earlier V.C. was won by Lt.-Col. Cummings of 2/12 Frontier Force at Jerantut.

Not only did the A.I.F. have too few fighting men for too much frontage but they were expected to defend ground which was largely occupied by squatters. Our communication wires traversed kampongs crowded with natives and the danger, from a security point, was obvious. Lt. Col. Kappe (Div. Signals) instructed me to recce and report on the loyalty or otherwise of these natives—I did so, but the real solution lay in the total evacuation of all civilians between water's-edge and Brigade headquarters and from Brigade to Div. Headquarters. This was suggested to Malaya Command—and that was the end of the suggestion.

Freedom accorded to subersive activity may not have mattered much—under the circumstances. However, my suspicions were not based on theory. Brigadier Taylor—22 Brigade—sent for me to investigate a curious arrangement of yellow paper found near a 'fox-hole' on the hilltop over-looking his Headquarters at Ama Keng not far from Tengah Airfield.

Accompanied by the Brigade Major, and my colleague, Lt. Waite, I examined the hilltop, raided a joss-house and arrested two Chinese who—according to my reading of the evidence—had been flashing messages to Johore Bahru or signalling direction to aircraft bombing Tengah Airfield.

On the way back to Div. Hq., with the prisoners, we had just crossed the bridge over Peng Siang when two cars approached at speed. When they drew level, the occupants of the cars yelled something to the prisoners in the truck. Lt. Waite, and the escort, held on to them as the cars went off at high speed in the direction of Choa Chu Kang.

I handed the suspects to the Malay officer in charge of Bukit Timah Police Station—entering the offence in the station-log which I signed with the Brigade Major. We informed the police that we intended to continue our investigations and would return next morning for the two men. But the next morning they were gone—released by a Malay Police Officer. I reported the matter to Singapore Security Police: a European officer promised to report direct to Governor Sir Shenton Thomas regarding the very unsatisfactory conditions in the forward areas—but I never heard a single word about the affair after that.

Japanese troops were in Johore Bahru the day I was trying to solve the riddle of the yellow paper. One week later they were in occupation of Tengah Airfield. The first attacks on the Island by the Japanese were made on the Australians in the area in which I had arrested those spies, so kindly set free by Malay Police.

iii. Battle of Singapore

Our advanced Hq. was soon destroyed by Japanese artillery guided by spotters in the air and on the ground. Singapore had been placed under martial law soon after hostilities opened but the civil administration still functioned with the attendant over-lapping of authority. With the intensity of the air raids the morale, civilian and military, was now at a low ebb. Compared to my own experiences in England (1940/1) it was hardly worth shivering about. To closely packed Orientals, and bomb-shy Occidentals, it may have been a terrible ordeal: an air-raid warning was the signal to down-tools and abandon work (even at the Sime Road Hq. of Malaya Command) while they squat-ted in silly little slit trenches when there existed no more danger to them than the vibrations of their pet hooter. It was certainly no kind of preparation for raising the morale of the civilians or for raising the fighting spirit of the soldiers.

At dawn on 7th February, enemy units of the 1st Guards Div. made a surprise landing on Palau Ubin—a small island at the eastern end of Johore Straits. That was the beginning of the short Battle of Singapore. Air attacks increased. Heavy artillery began to pound us—here, there and everywhere in target practice. Fires broke out in the deserted Naval Base on which much money had been spent since 1924—now it was going up in smoke.

Many of our oil-storage tanks had been fired—clouds of dense smoke curled and whirled up from cauldrons of flaming oil and then slowly drifted westward to blot out the irradiation of an ominous sunset.

All too soon it was dark. Dark, except for the flash of gunfire and bursting shell and from the flames rising from the scorched earth. It was oppressively hot—even for Singapore—and it was strangely quiet after midnight when the bombing and shelling came to an end.

Next morning, bombers destroyed our Headquarters, inflic-ting casualties, and forcing us to move nearer the City. Soon afterwards—so exact was enemy information—22 Brigade Hq., and 44 Indian Brigade forward positions were bombed and shelled and the unit headquarters accurately straffed.

All this helped to set our nerves on edge as there was so little hitting back by our artillery and our airforce had packed up with the navy some days before. Divisional communication wires were down on the ground, cut by the bombing and shelling or snipped by fifth-columnists.

The bombardment was stepped up during the afternoon—it was abundantly clear to us in forward positions that the Western Area was being softened up prior to invasion. But there was a lull after sunset when spotting was not so easy on account of the black clouds of oily-smoke from blazing tanks which obscured our positions west of the Causeway.

It got on your nerves. It was like waiting for zero-hour to go over the top in 1916—all your past deeds flashed to your mind as your eyes were glued to the minute-hand of your wrist-watch. But it was different now. The position was reversed, all you could do was listen to the ticking of your watch and wonder 'what in hell is going to happen?'

Shortly after 20.00 hours, enemy artillery opened rapid fire so I put on my tin-hat. We were camped in the open a few hundred yards east of our latest Div. Hq. When the shelling increased in volume my companion, A.I.F. Camp Commandant, decided to walk over to Hq. for information. I took over and ordered our small group of A.I.F. camp-followers to fix bayonets and man the position we proposed to hold, while I went out on a recce.

By now the Japanese had disclosed their objective and were putting down a terrific barrage South and West of the Causeway. Our guns were silent. There was no counter-battery fire— something was wrong, somewhere. We had guns and we had shells.

I walked down the hillside and then I crawled along the flat ground for some distance, stopped and listened. Soon I could hear bursts of rifle and machine-gun fire. I set my pocket compass and decided that the firing was in 22 Brigade area: I lay flat and listened—no question about it, Japanese had landed on the Island and the A.I.F. were in action.

I returned, warned my post, and then went out again to check my information. It was now rather misty and I groped my way for a mile or so before I heard, above the barking of the kampong dogs, some shouting. I listened—it was not Malay or Chinese, it was certainly Japanese. Japanese shouting:—

'Yose-atsumeru!'—'Yose-atsumeru!': 'Tsume-yoseru—atsumeru—atsumeru!'

The dogs went on yapping— in the distance there was the flash of H.E. shells and I could hear the popping of mortars and continuous rifle and machine-gun fire. The dogs went on yapping—close at hand, in the valley below me, Japanese were calling to each other in the misty darkness: 'Draw near: draw near: gather in: get together: get together.'

'Tsume-yoseru! Yose-atsumeru! Atsumeru!'—no mistaking that for Greek. But what on earth were they doing between the 44 Indian Brigade and the A.I.F. position? I concluded that a few scouts had rushed inland and lost direction until they heard the rifle and machine-gun fire in the distance.

When I recovered my wits I returned to the hill top and met the Div. C.C.—Capt. Wiedersen. He confirmed that the 'Nips' landed about midnight and over-ran 2/18 and 2/20 Battalions: our signal lines were down and nothing had come in from 2/19 Bn.—Brigade Hq. were not then in touch with any of the Battalions: the position was obscure but it appeared that we had already fallen back in disorder in the Ama Keng area but were still holding on to Tengah airfield.

The position held by 2/18 and 2/20 Bns. was close-timbered rubber and mangrove—difficult country to hold in daylight and bad country at night. Even so it would be no picnic for attacker so they must have sprung a surprise with overwhelming force to have demoralized *three* A.I.F. Battalions. We sent off a runner to Div. Hq. to inform them of the wandering band of Japanese in our immediate vicinity. But the information may have been lost in the flood of early morning lamentations for I was asked to confirm my report about six hours later!

By 08.00 hours 9th February hundreds of bedraggled 'Aussies' were streaming down Bukit Timah Road on the way to the City. The Military Police (U.K. and A.I.F.) attempted to check them but they were in no mood for homilies from 'Red Caps'. Some paused long enough to accept a cigarette, light it, and say, 'Chum—to hell with Malaya and Singapore. Navy let us down—airforce let us down. If the 'bungs' (natives) won't fight for their bluddy country, why pick on me?'

There was more truth than discipline in the retort: we have no kodoism, no kempeitai and no bullet in the back for a straggler. But sometimes our 'dangerous thoughts' are allowed too much expression for the good of a common cause when we have our backs to the wall. We certainly had our backs to the wall —even if it was nebulous structure of distant architects and local jerry-builders. Still—even in England during war—there were 'strikes' for higher pay for making munitions or loading them aboard ships. No civilian was shot for that withdrawal of service to the State—the right to strike (official or unofficial) is part of our democracy. Those who were trotting down Bukit Timah Road that morning were on an 'unofficial strike'—not for more hard cash but for a few more years on earth. They had reached the point of asking themselves why they should die— and that is fatal in war.

We coaxed a young A.I.F. officer out of the human stream— his uniform was caked in mud, sweat lined his oil-begrimed face, he was dirty and tired, dazed and bewildered, badly shaken and mad with himself and all the world. He was a fighter, not a quitter, so we let him do the talking.

'My platoon was spread all to hell-and-gone in the rubber when they suddenly started to paste us from Johore. We knew that something was coming our way but before you could size things up boat-loads of them were ashore. What with the drifting smoke and the timber you couldn't see much until they opened out with rifle, machine-gun and mortars. Must have been thousands of them. What could we do? Ever try to scoop water with a piece of torn fishnet? It was useless—they were soon facing us, on our flanks, and working round to the back of us. We tried checking them—then we got out of it as best we could. But—*tell me* something—why was there no artillery support?'

According to Malaya Command the S.O.S. calls for artillery support remained unanswered because:—'the Very Light signals were not seen, cable communication had been severed and nothing came through on W/T., and the beach lights failed to function.'

A.I.F. Hq. acted as soon as possible by sending up 2/29 Bn. (27 Bde) to Tengah airfield to reinforce Brig. Taylor. But, soon after daylight, all that was left of 2/18 Bn. was clinging to Ama Keng village. An advance was ordered but the counter-attack was halted by enemy dive-bombers so we had to form a new line on the Choa Chu Kang-Bukit Timah Road in rear of the airfield. Soon that failed to hold and by afternoon we had retired to the River Kranji-River Jurong line fully seven miles from where the enemy had turned Brig. Taylor's right flank.

This initial disaster compelled the retirement of 44 Indian Brigade to a position based on Bukit Panjang-Bulim Road.

As we had no prepared positions to retire on the now strongly reinforced enemy could not be held. Probably the whole of the 18th Division under Lt.-General Mutaguchi and part of the 5th Division under Lt.-General Matsui were ferried over between midnight and sunset 8/9th February. Roughly then two A.I.F. Bns. had to face 10,000 Japanese in the first onslaught and while they were trying to form some kind of line in the open another 10,000 Japanese were being landed against the other two A.I.F. Bns. Four Battalions against Two Divisions and, as the young A.I.F. officer said, 'What could we do?'

A.I.F. Hq. was bombed again on 9th February so we moved back to Holland Road and then to Tanglin Barracks. By this time 27 Bde. A.I.F. had been outflanked in the Causeway-Kranji River sector, forced to retire to Bukit Timah Road and came under the command of 11 Division. Attempt was made to reform the line, counter-attack and recover ground near the Causeway but this failed. Various units of the A.I.F. were by now isolated—they had been mauled, scattered in all directions and some of them were also making for Singapore Docks.

On 10th February, General Wavell and General Percival came to our Headquarters and during the conference the building they were in was bombed. Pretty thorough fifth-column W/T communication with Japanese Headquarters. But only the staff-cars were damaged and no lives were lost. There was some plain speaking regarding the withdrawals and agreement regarding the need to counter-attack. But we had more than four Battalions (of A.I.F.) on the Island not yet *engaged* in serious operations—unfortunately there was very little fighting-spirit left. It was easier to plan counter-attacks than to execute them against the enemy.

When the 12 Indian Bde, part of a combined counter-attack,

saw a large number of enemy tanks coming down Bukit Timah
at 20.00 hours they disintegregated and uncovered the way to
Bukit Timah village.

I kept clear of Tanglin Barracks, camping in the Botanical
Gardens with Div. Commandant and a small section of A.I.F.
Hq. Lt. Waite had been replaced by Capt. Band and on 10th
February I went in to Singapore with him on duty.

The main streets, especially near the waterfront, were
jammed with mechanical transport: the Mecca of British
Troops appeared to be the precinct of the Cathedral and not in
the front line. But I was particularly concerned about the
number of 'Aussies' who had added their quota to the numerous
uniformed stragglers cluttering the highways and byways of the
City.

After a recce I reported back to Colonel Broadbent (AQMG)
who gave me instructions to round up the A.I.F. stragglers and
then escort them back to the Botanical Gardens where we had
established a collecting post. To facilitate this work, Col.
Broadbent handed over a brand-new 'battle buggy': Div.
Commandant supplied the necessary transport and we went to
town, hoping for the best.

From the point of view of military discipline it was a dis-
gusting sight for the 'Aussies' were but a small proportion of the
whole stragglers movement. The A.I.F. rendezvous was the
square near the Union Jack Club and the majority of the
stragglers were from General Base Depot or ancillary units.

When I explained my mission, to the A.I.F. military police,
they explained that the idea was all right but it would not work.

I explained 'Operation buggy-ride' to a group of men but
they went on smoking. Then I made a trip to the Cold Storage,
in Orchard Road, made some purchases and watched cases of wine
and strong liquor being thrown out of the top-storey windows
and being smashed to bits on the concrete yard—a necessary
operation in view of the heavy drinking that had been going on.

I returned to the square, distributed food and bottles of milk
and repeated my requests to the fighting-men to embus and
rejoin their chums in the front-line. Altogether we lifted in a
couple of thousand from the Square to the Gardens, fed and
re-armed them and sent them back to their units.

The same day—11th February—Lt.-General Yamashita, C-in-C Japanese Army sent us an ultimatum. He called for immediate surrender because 'the stuation was hopeless, troops were surrounded, further resistance involved unnecessary loss of life among civilian population'.

It was 11th February—'Kigensetsu'—Empire Day for Japan —Yamashita was a few days behind his time-table and anxious to announce his complete Victory to Tenno Heika so that he could worship at the ancestral shrine. Already we had been showered with leaflets most of them pointing out that the English were—as usual—leaving the fighting to Indians and Australians who were urged to co-operate with Japan—Great Japan—in the creation of a free and prosperous Greater East Asia.

However the 'English' (U.K. troops) had not left *all* the fighting to their comrades in arms. The Argyll's original strength of 850 was now a bare 200: East Surreys and Leicesters —combined in mid-December as the British Battalion—were hardly as strong as the Argyll's in bayonet-strength: the 53 British Infantry Brigade, part of 18 Div. which *commenced* landing on 13th January were ordered up-country on 14th and went into action on 16th and they had been two-months aboard ship at sea. No—the U.K. Troops fought from the first bell to the finish alone or in company with A.I.F. or Indian units.

We received instructions from Generall Wavel to bundle the enemy into the sea—to fight on and defend Singapore to the bitter end. But the admonitions, the ultimatum, the shelling and the bombing—to say nothing of the wriggling of several hundred thousand civilians, European, Chinese, Malay and Indian, did nothing to improve the military situation.

Whatever advantages there may have been inherent in concentric defence in the days of Queen Victoria they had gone in the days of King George VI, when aerobatics and aerodynamics were the monopoly of the Japanese attacking Singapore. When a disconnected *line of resistance* is loosely held by a very mixed force of Orientals and Occidentals *the will to fight in a common cause* must be there to ensure some hope of success. If it is not there then neither a Wavell or a Montgomery could do any better than a Percival fighting behind a flimsy curtain of doubt and uncertainty.

The stream of stragglers increased as the Japanese advanced. Some of the units were in formation as they entered the Tanglin area the rest were a rabble without arms.

Once I halted a formation of the Indian Army trotting down the Nizam Road. I asked the I.C.O., why he was going in the wrong direction. He replied, 'An A.I.F. Officer told us to beat it because the 'Nips' were coming over the hill.' I suggested that we were fighting 'Nips' not running a foot race with them to which he retorted, 'Quite so—but you don't remain where you are not wanted, do you?'

He called his men to attention—then they went off at a jog-trot. I was puzzled by the absurd excuse—probably based on a flash of 'Aussie' sarcasm—but the fact remains that 50 per cent. of the Indian Army which surrendered at Singapore subsequently joined the first or the second I.N.A.

The morale of the Indian Army in Malaya was tampered with long before Japanese landed in Thai. Congress leaders were in 'open rebellion' and preaching Gandhi's gospel of mass obstruction to the British war effort. Gandhi advocated in the spring of 1942 that the British should quit India, the Indian Army should be disbanded *and that Japan should be free to come to the country and arrange terms with a non-resisting people:* and those were the sentiments of many of our Indian troops in February, 1942. But I shall deal with the *splendid loyalty of the mass of the Indian Army* in a subsequent chapter.

Certainly, we had our quota of non-resisting disciples of Gandhi for by nightfall of 12th February there were too many British stragglers on the road between Raffles Hotel and the Post Office. Their share in 'bundling Japanese into the sea' consisted of residence in the string of mechanical transport lining both sides of the road. We could do nothing with them— they were genuine quitters. I suggested to Col. Broadbent that as moral persuasion had failed we should use force. But this was turned down so I recalled my transport and informed the A.I.F. Military Police. They 'chucked in their hand' then commandeered 3 armoured-cars (abandoned by a jittery unit) and returned with me to the Gardens to seek Div., permission to join the firing-line. This was refused. Two cars 'obeyed orders' the other we rigged up with extra machine-guns and more ammunition and it sneaked up the road to join the 22nd Brigade.

The 22 Bde. were holding a position astride the Bukit Timah Road and Brig. Taylor came to the Gardens to thank us for various reinforcements we had sent up. Taylor's Brigade had been pretty roughly handled but was no by means demoralized: he was in the 2nd Australian Division which relieved us on the Armentier front in 1916 and took over a network of shallow trenches. From the mud of Flanders to the village of Ama Keng —and the bits of yellow paper—quite a lot had happened since then.

iv. Slaughter of the innocents

On 13th February, General Percival visited us in the Gardens before going over to Div. Hq. Shortly afterwards I went in to Singapore on duty: the air-raid warning sounded and when we reached Orchard Road a stick of bombs fell just ahead of us.

A petrol station on our left blazed up—two cars ahead of us were punted into the air, they bounced a few times before bursting into flames. Buildings on both sides of the road went up in smoke as stick after stick was showered on us by a large formation of bombers.

Soldiers and civilians suddenly appeared staggering through clouds of debris: some got on the road, others stumbled and dropped in their tracks, others shrieked as they ran for safety.

It was a terror raid in a residential area—it served no military purpose—it was Yamashita's idea of causing 'unnecessary loss of life among the civilian population' it was kodo—the Imperial Way.

We pulled up near a building which had collapsed onto the road—it looked like a caved-in slaughter house. Blood splashed what was left of the lower rooms: chunks of human beings— men, women and children—littered the place. Everywhere bits of steaming flesh, smouldering rags, clouds of dust—and the shriek and groan of those who still survived.

I could not do enough with a small car so we dodged the many craters and went to the Cathedral where dozens of our ambulances were parked. I reported to Col. Glen White—our ADMS —and was soon back to the shambles with A.I.F. ambulances and first-aid men.

There was still no sign of the local A.R.P. when I slowed down in obedience to the signal from a frail Chinese woman who offered me her little child. She was spattered in blood and the youngster was bleeding profusely from a head wound. I cheered her up in her own language and she smiled through her tears as we helped her into the ambulance while the chaps attended to the child's wound. Then they brought over an Indian soldier. His legs were broken and his chest badly crushed by masonry: it took a little time to load up and then the A.I.F. drivers did not know where to take civilian casualties—neither did I—so we went back to the Cathedral. It was only too evident that Singapore's air-raid precaution system had already faded out under the strain.

At 14.00 hours (13th February) there was Conference of the higher command at Fort Canning. All were agreed that counter-attack was unlikely to succeed: some considered the situation hopeless—General Percival signalled a factual report to General Wavell, Supreme Commander South-West Pacific. He asked for wider authority to deal with the situation but the reply indicated that the fight should continue for as long as possible.

On 14th February, Colonel Broadbent instructed me to go to Fort Canning to obtain information regarding 44 Indian Brigade—they were out of position on A.I.F. left flank where attack was developing on a major scale. I got the information and sent it back by Capt. Band then I was handed the job of examining the satchells taken by a 2/18 A.I.F. Bn. patrol from Japanese scouts on motor-cycles who had been operating on Holland Road that morning . (All other I. Corps Japanese interpreters attached to Malaya Command had been *evacuated on night of 13/14th February*.)

I found a most instructive map in the satchell of an Artillery Lieutenant who had been shot while riding his motor-cycle. Japanese gun-positions of 12th February were clearly marked in addition to various Infantry and Artillery Headquarters. Lines of the infantry attack, from the day of landing, were indicated in blue pencil marks: Concentration areas for the Infantry were ringed in red pencil: heavy and light artillery positions for the *final assault* were ringed in blue and red circles: the various instructions had been jotted down in neat kana and kanji. The final assault was to be from Mt. Faber area to

Keppel Harbour area with a massed drive-in from Bukit Timah village towards Pasir Panjang on A.I.F. left flank.

The completed report was handed to General Percival about 16.00 hours and I continued to examine the other satchells.

I discovered another bullet-riddled map on which there was confirmatory evidence of enemy disposition on 11/12th February and precise directions concerning final assault—etc. After sending in another report to Command Intelligence in the 'battle-box' I asked for the return of the first map so that I could take it with me to explain the position to General Gordon Bennett.

Before I left Fort Canning our artillery were bombarding the enemy infantry concentrations but when I explained the matter to General Bennett and his Staff-officers, at Tanglin Barracks, I gained the impression that there was barely an academic interest in the 'final assault' or the multicoloured pencil marks.

v. Contributory causes

The position was hopeless but the C-in-C., S.W. Pacific was still determined that there should be no surrender until the limit of endurance was reached. Indeed the streets of Singapore would have made an excellent slaughter-ground. British troops, with a 'paper strength' of 90,000 would have had ample scope for inflicting heavy casualties on the enemy. 'On paper' we could have held out for many days: dirty, tired, hungry and thirsty, and for those who prefer death on the field to humiliation in a PoW-cage there was inspiration in the order to fight on.

There would have been banner head-lines in British newspapers, panegyrical references on all stations of the B.B.C., and a long roll of honour for the monuments. But the list of dead, and wounded, of the civilian population, would have been even longer—much longer with so many queer Indian, Chinese, Malay and European names on it.

Fight to the end and to hell with the consequences—that was something which General Percival was faced with. Already, during the 'evacuation of selected personnel', there had been disgraceful scenes at the docks—a panic stricken rabble fighting to get aboard ship. No—on 13th and 14th February I saw I saw enough to convince me that there could be no 'desperate fight to the finish' in cosmopolitan Singapore. There was to be no Dunkirk and there was to be no Stalingrad—no heroics, just unconditional surrender.

There had been a steady increase of terror and confusion from indiscriminate shelling and bombing. Fires were raging near the Railway Station. Refugees, pushing carts or pulling the heavily laden rickshaws streamed towards the Post Office. From the opposite direction, from the Civil Airport area, another human torrent whirled its way into the pool of misery. Near the Clifford Pier, fatigue parties were bumping cars and lorries off the bund into the sea. In the Arcade, and crouching in the passages and in the doorways, there were thousands of soldiers and civilians waiting—waiting for the end, or for something to happen, something to emancipate them from fear.

We were on an Island surrounded by the enemy—the Island was surrounded by the enemy. There was no escape. Now and again the hum of voices was quietened by the drone of approaching aircraft. A pause. Then the whistle and crash of bombs would start another movement from door to door, from alley to alley, away from the flames and the newly erected pile of bricks on the debris of the building.

And now, the crowd was at the very door of the Cathedral on the Padang—the sanctuary where the doors were never closed to those who wished to pray. The Cathedral—the hub of passive resistance—the wide open doors of the Cathedral were in sombre contrast to the grim shuttered buildings surrounding it where so many frightened souls hid themselves as they clutched their few and precious worldly belongings.

Far from this concentre of trial and tribulation black oily clouds darkened the sky. Close at hand white smoke curled lazily from the ruin of a recent fire. The overworked fire brigade struggled to quench the latest outbreak but there was no pressure in the pipes—just a spluttering trickle out of the gleaming nozzles polished as brightly as a mirror in a Shinto Shrine.

An old Chinese rickshaw-puller followed as I retraced my steps to the Padang. Each time I stopped he rushed forward, dropped the shafts, patted the filthy cushion and said 'Rickshaw—I take you—look-see everythin'.' I passed him a note and declined the invitation but walked on to the Cenotaph—the monument to those men of Singapore who gave their lives in World War I. The Cenotaph. Now the base of it was fouled by dirty rags, empty bully-beef tins, cigarette packets, butt-ends, bits of paper and unwanted kit. I read the names of old comrades—saluted and went on my way followed by the curious glances of the rickshaw-man.

vi. Unconditional Surrender

I left the gutter in the Gardens for the flagged verandah of Fort Canning guard-house on the night of 14th February. I selected the guard-house because I was interested in the Chinese who were on duty at the gate. Capt. Band was with me—he was a Civil Servant serving in the Volunteers—and as we both spoke Chinese we soon made friends with this detachment of DALFORCE.

At 09.30 hours (15th February) there was a Senior Commanders' Conference at which it was decided to capitulate. I decided to escape and went off with Lt.-Noble to complete our arrangements. On returning to Fort Canning I reported my intending departure at nightfall but was informed that no official permission to leave would be granted. I pressed the matter but it was obvious that I would be posted as a deserter if I persisted in leaving so we unloaded food, water, kit, maps and compass and resigned ourself to obeying orders.

The White Flag was taken in but the party came back with instructions from General Yamashita that General Percival himself must participate in the negotiations. Later on, General Percival, Brigadiers Torrance and Newbiggin and Major Wild from 3rd Corps went to the Ford Factory near Bukit Timah Village where they were met by Lt.-Col. Sugita, Yamashita's chief Intelligence Officer, and escorted to the main factory building.

At the Conference the rival Commanders, with their Staff-officers faced each other across a table. British representatives wore 'shorts and shirts' but the Japanese had on their stiff buttoned-up tunics and were booted and spur'd for the occasion.

General Yamashita made it clear that the terms of the capitulation were Unconditional Surrender. This was accepted by General Percival who signed the surrender instrument. Verbal instructions were given, regarding cease-fire, laying down of arms, evacuation of positions, concentration of British and of Indian Troops in specified areas and the hoisting of the KOKKI (i.e. Hinomaru, Japanese national flag) on the Cathay Building in Singapore at sunrise on 16th February as a token of surrender.

Parliamentaires completed their business. The British party returned to Fort Canning and the cease-fire was sounded at 20.30 hours—22.00 hours by Japanese time—the 'time' used when the Japanese made their 'notified' attack on Pearl Harbour.

British rule was at an end in Malaya, for the time being:— the Japanese had won the first round, 91,000 British troops— including numerous volunteers raised locally—were made Prisoners of War to learn at first hand the real meaning of Shinto and Kodo.

vii. Unauthorised escape of Major-General Gordon Bennett

A great deal of publicity has been given to General Bennett's escape from Singapore *after the unconditional surrender*.

Shortly *before* cease-fire was sounded (20.30 hours) General Bennett handed over the command of the A.I.F. in their battle-station to the next senior officer, Brig. Callaghan, informing him of his plan to escape. In order to facilitate his departure, he asked Callaghan to reply to any Japanese questioning on the subject that he had gone earlier.

General Percival was not informed until the next day and he then promoted Brig. Callaghan to a Major-General to command Australian Prisoners of War.

The judgment of Mr. Justice Ligertwood, at the conclusion of the Bennett Inquiry, on 4th January, 1946 was . . . ' General Bennett was not justified in relinquishing his command and leaving Singapore, having regard to the terms of the allied capitulation to the Japanese, but that he acted from a high sense of patriotism . . . ' To which General Bennett replied 'General Percival surrendered unconditionally and admits it; the Japanese admit it. How, then, there can be a capitulation, which is a surrender with conditions, when both sides say there was an unconditional surrender, is beyond me. However the Judge has given his decision on the assumption that there was a capitulation. I cannot understand this view. . . . '

No copy of the surrender document was given to General Percival—he never saw the original document again. Only those at the Conference knew its contents: the British relied on their memory, the Japanese on the wording of the document which brought about the surrender. General Bennett never saw it and his personal status did not differ from others who were under General Percival's command. If it was not his intention to comply with Japanese conditions, accepted by his superior officer, he could have made this clear at 09.30 hours on 15th February at the final Conference at Fort Canning or before the flag went in for the second time that day.

According to the copy of the Manual of Military Law which I had with me at Fort Canning, Chapter XIV made it clear that: 'Capitulations are agreements entered into between the *commander of armed forces* of belligerents concerning *the terms of surrender of a body of troops* . . . etc.' The Japanese terms were simple: *Mu-joken-kofuku,* and that means *unqualified submission* and not qualified submission. There were no conditions beyond what is meant by Mu-joken-kofuku.

When the white flag went in for the second time I was concerned about the safety of the Chinese unit mounting guard at Fort Canning. It was all wrong. The Japanese were pretty sure to shoot any Chinese they found in uniform—native or foreign, surrender or no surrender so I took steps to ensure prompt dispersal before cease-fire sounded. As they were shedding their uniform and donning civvies we captured a young Japanese scout in Chinese clothing. Someone blundered and popped him in the cell at the guard-house which was occupied by one of our own defaulters. In a few minutes I had to go in and stop a rough-house. I sent our man up the road to the Provost Marshall to cool off and then hastened the departure of the Chinese Coy.

They got away in good time and that saved further complications from other identification parades. Unfortunately, before the month was out, more than 5,000 loyal Straits-born Chinese had been massacred by mopping-up gangs of the Imperial Guard and the vicious Kempei-tai.

I remained in the deserted guard-house for some time talking to my Japanese prisoner. He knew about the white-flag going in but he had been kept blindfolded until locked in the cell after capture so he missed seeing the Chinese guard. But it was a bit awkward after cease-fire was sounded for me to keep him locked in the cell. However when I told him that he would be handed over as a PoW for the kempei to deal with he pleaded so hard for his life that I gathered up my kit and went up the road to Fort Canning and forgot to bolt the door of his cell.

viii. Liaison Officer

Next morning I was standing in the porch at Fort Canning when our hosts arrived—Japanese military police on English motor-cycles.

Shutting off his engine the first one yelled out:—'Koko-da!' —this is the place! Our duty M.P. shook his head and waved his hands when they dismounted and hailed him. So I decided to take over as reception committee.

Suddenly a number of cars appeared. Brakes shrieked, gears crashed, doors flew open and the M.P.'s (kempei) let out an ear splitting yell of 'Kei-rei! Kei-rei!'—'Salute! Salute!'

I thought General Yamashita, or perhaps the Minister of Education, General Araki, had arrived with copies of kodo. But the noise was for the benefit of several Staff-Officers who had come to take over Fort Canning.

There was much loud laughter and mutual congratulations on service rendered to the Empire. At last, Lt.-Colonel Sugita detached himself from the celebrations and spoke to me, in slow but distinct English. I replied in slow, distinct, Japanese.

Then I escorted them to the top floor, left wing, of Fort Canning which had been set aside for the preliminary discussions.

I indicated the accomodation and waited for the arrival of some senior officer from Malaya Command. But our Brigadiers were dying hard. They maintained an aloof rectitude and it was some time before they could bring themselves to act with their enemy and facilitate the handing -over formalities.

As the day advanced orders from Japanese were numerous and conflicting. There were many committees: each committee was an independent organ of authority and issued instructions for handing over arms and ammunition, medical supplies, hospitals, transport, military stores and equipment, fortifications and minefield and so on. Each committee issued their own permits to their opposite numbers to allow movement through the Japanese lines to permit the execution of the orders. Then there were wind-screen labels for transport, British guides for each party and zero hours for every operation.

I was handed an arm-band as one of the Committee and another arm-band as Liaison Officer and appointed official interpreter for *all* the committees. I bobbed in and out of the rooms spouting Japanese and English with more speed than accuracy I am afraid because so many people had so much to say at the same time, and they were all in such a hurry to take over.

The British did not like it at all—the Japanese thoroughly enjoyed themselves. Then I realised that to the British senior officers I was the subordinate witness of their humiliation—the bearer of bad tidings, the mouthpiece of cheeky Asiatics giving them impudent orders. But none of them could speak a word of Japanese and few of the Japanese knew English so it struck me as petty and childish to glare at me as a collaborator whenever an order ruffled their feathers.

My colleague, Major Wild, could not help because he was in a spot of bother himself. He had received instructions, at the capitulation conference, to hoist the Japanese national flag on Cathay Building at sunrise but a souvenir hunter had stolen it.

Rollicking fun but the Japanese did not like it. One of Sugita's secret-agents, a man who had been arrested a few years earlier for spying in Singapore, served his sentence and returned to Japan was back again full of bushido. He found Wild and then threatened him with death because he had 'insulted the Emperor by not hoisting his flag.' Wild attempted to explain but was taken under escort to Fort Canning—his steps accelerated by the cracking of a whip by the ex-spy. I rustled up a Nip flag from the Signal Station and prevailed on Sugita to calm the man with the whip. He agreed to drop the matter but insisted that Wild should go with him in search of a Major Morgan who had been the cause of his arrest.

Some idea of what was in store for us was made abundantly clear at Alexander Military Hospital the day before we surrendered.

During an attack on 14th February our troops retired in the direction of the Hospital. There was counter-battery fire and the Hospital was struck many times before we fell back. Enemy then made a frontal attack and rushed the Hospital: they ran amok, threw grenades, fired rifles, dashed in and out of wards shooting and bayonetting surgeons, orderlies and even patients on the operating table. They ordered the complete evacuation of the Hospital: walking-cases were marched outside and tied together in pairs; between two and three-hundred were assembled and taken to coolie-lines half a mile away. Next day they were taken out, a few at a time, and bayonetted to death: the death roll was 320.

Soon after dawn on 17th February, Japanese troops quartered at Fort Canning paraded for roll call. To the yelling of Tenko! Tenko! (Roll call!) they paraded and numbered off, then after more yells of Kashira naka, kei-rei and nao-rei—eyes front, salute, as you were—they turned to the East for the REIHAI— homage to the Tenno Heika.

Proudly they faced the 'rising sun' and chanted the Choku- yu—Imperial instructions. The air was filled with exortations of CHU-SETSU (first duty) the loyalty and fidelity of a soldier, REI-GI the code of honour and the rules of politeness, BU-YU— courage and bravery, SHIN-GI truthfulness and good faith, SHIS-SO frugality and simplicity.

I've heard it so often but it is always interesting to listen to this intoning of CHOKU-YU. The theory and practice of Choku- yu centered in the sacred name of the Tenno—the code of morals compounded of bushido, buke-hatto and all the rest of samurai law. Brutality, bred by Shinto propaganda, hallowed at sunrise and at sunset by reciting 'imperial instructions' com- piled by the professors of kodo. Kodo. —the bible of General Araki, Minister of Education—kodo the linking of Shinto and Reihai to become the fundamental basis of savagery.

Kodo, the hallowed structure of sadistic aggression—the paradox of worship (reihai) and brutality (zankoku) being one and the same thing was to be proved beyond contradiction by the majority of Allied troops who fell into the hands of the Japanese during World War II.

It was at first arranged that we should march in to the Changi area on 17th February but Sugita had agreed with General Percival's request for a 24 hour extension. General Percival instructed me to find Sugita and arrange for a conference to discuss the accommodation and water-supply difficulties arising from the order to herd 50,000 troops into an area arranged to deal with a few thousand only. Sir Shenton Thomas was to be at the conference to lodge a protest.

Sugita was late in arriving. He was curt, refused a seat and demanded to know why he had been invited to attend. General Percival explained—I interpreted. Sir Shenton protested—I interpreted. Sugita replied, 'Changi was selected by General Yamashita after full consideration of its suitability as a camp for prisoners of war who must move in today and not tomorrow.'

That was a sample of REI-GI—the code of honour and the rules of politeness. But I knew we were in for a bad time.

Japan had signed but refused to ratify the Red Cross Convention (Geneva 27th July, 1929) *dealing with Prisoners of War*. When I asked Sugita about this he replied that the only law which would apply to us was Gunji horitsu (Military Law) and not Kokusai-ho (International Law). Adding, for my benefit, that I was now under the Rules and Regulations for PoW's set out in the manual of Japanese Military Law, and would take his orders accordingly.

At first I was ordered about by Sugita and the Commander of the Kempeitai on routine work directly connected with the act of surrender. But it was soon quite clear that I was to act as an interpreter at Conferences and interrogations and it did not take long for Yamashita to clarify the status of U.K. and Australian Troops, confined at Changi. The Indian Army, on the other hand, were regarded as 'prisoners who had been set free by Japanese': they were paraded at Farrah Park, under Lt. Col. Hunt (2nd Echelon) and then taken over by Major Fujiwara. After a propaganda speech of welcome by Fujiwara (an I.O. on Yamashita's staff) the Indian Army units were 'handed over' to the arch-traitors Mohan Singh, 1/14th Punjabs, and his colleague Mohd Akram.

Mohan Singh mounted the platform and thanked Fujiwara. He was followed by an Indian civilian, Pritam Singh, who was loud in his praise for the rescuers. Then the patriots expounded their plans for the Indian National Army. There were loud cheers—from part of the audience—before they marched out to Nee Soon and Bidadari Camps.

Yamashita Law

When you read the sections in Japanese Military Law which apply to Prisoners of War you come to the conclusion that they are spoils of war to be treated as criminals and punished for 'crimes'. To be on the right side of the fence, in the event of trouble arising, from my own mis-translation or from non-compliance by Malaya Command, I set everything down in writing, sending the original to Malaya Command, second-copy to Sugita and filed a copy for my records. From 17th February to 31st December, 1942 I transmitted about 1500 Japanese orders and dealt with about 500 PoW protests and requests. No question of accuracy arose.

A few days after the surrender, Sugita sent for Major Wild who was acting as Malaya Command representative at Fort Canning.

He asked Wild to give him his impression of the Campaign—Wild declined, without consulting his superior officer, and explained to Sugita that PoW's were, by British Military and International Law, prohibited or excused from giving any information to the enemy beyond their name, rank and unit.

Sugita did not press the matter. A few minutes later, GSO I —18 Division—also refused point blank to inform Sugita when his Division commenced to land at Singapore. Then Sugita acted. He informed the kempei and the British Colonel was marched off to solitary confinement in the underground 'battlebox' across the road.

Sugita went off to Yamashita's headquarters. When he came back he dictated two orders. The first one instructed General Percival, General Heath, Commanders of A.I.F., 11 Div., 18 Div., Southern Area Troops with all Brigadiers to attend at the Chief Warden's House, Changi Jail, at 11.00 hours the following day.

When that was sent off, Sugita produced some notes from his satchell and proceeded to dictate 'a special order of the day from General Yamashita' to the effect that, 'General Percival had surrendered unconditionally, now—as PoW—he was bound to obey each and every order issued by Yamashita. Furthermore, each and every order issued by Japanese Military or Civilian Administrators was to be obeyed by all prisoners of war as if they had been issued direct to them by General Percival as

C-in-C. Also, every PoW, irrespective of rank, was to answer any question put to them, on any subject, by Japanese military or civilian personnel and to answer promptly and truthfully. Any attempt at evasion, in any shape or form, would be most severely punished.'

Sugita's exposition of Yamashita's thesis on Japanese Military Law took my breath away but I scribbled out a draft of the order and handed it over. Now, Sugita could read, write and speak English sufficiently to cross out everything which blunted the edge of the coercive weapon he was forging. He did so pretty thoroughly and advised me to translate what he said and not try and obscure the precise implications of the special order, adding that he would read the Japanese version of the 'Special Order of the Day' at the Conference the next day, I would interpret what he said and my interpretation would agree word for word with what was on the order.

At the appointed hour, Sugita read the order, I gave my interpretation of it and then handed General Percival two copies for reference and action.

General Percival pointed out that the order was contrary to International Law: Sugita replied that he was not there to discuss International Law but to transmit General Yamashita's order. General Percival insisted that International Law was the basis of relations between civilized nations and asked on what authority General Yamashita was acting? Sugita replied that he had no intention of discussing General Yamashita's authority with prisoners of war. The order meant exactly what it said, and he declined to answer any questions on its implications: every officer present must sign their name on a sheet of paper to signify that they had heard him give the order—that was all.

To complete the identification-record of the proceedings those participating in it were assembled outside the 'conference house' and photographed. The official photographer asked for a 'special photo' of Major-General Gordon Bennett but his absence from 'parade' raised no comment then or at any time after the event.

That was the start of 'Yamashita Law' but the Tokyo newspapers published the photograph with this caption:—

Q

'One of the biggest blows to the British army came when 28 of her ranking officers were trapped at Singapore. Although many of her Govermental heads had fled the doomed city, these officers were still at their posts when Japanese forces compelled General Sir Arthur Percival (centre) to sign a document of surrender on February 15.'

But 'Yamashita Law' did not originate in Singapore, or in Tokyo. It originated in the Nihon Shoki, A.D. 720, under the term 'Kamu-nagara' which may be translated 'to follow the will of *kami* without question'. Yamashita had been commanded to 'rule according to the will of kamu-nagara' and in the Japanese magazine 'FREEDOM' (published in April, 1942) I was interested to read this comment on 'Liberty':—

'To every true American, the word 'Liberty' is fraught with momentous significance. America shed her life's blood to attain her *national freedom* and Independence from British domination. Yet, what America believes in, what America fought for, she would not grant to the nations of Greater East Asia. America struggled for Independence, but would not willingly grant it to the Philippines. Today, some few thousand American prisoners are denouncing their government, for denying Liberty to others, thus plunging the nations of the East into a fearful war. Has America forgotten what Liberty means? Japan has not. *Captured prisoners, undeserving enemies by every rule of warfare, are given the best treatment, allowed every comfort and the utmost personal freedom under the circumstances.*'

Kamu-nagara, or 'Yamashita Law', was administered by all and sundry: a Japanese private soldier had the same authority as a Japanese Commander in Chief and exercised his *right* to punish in the same degree.

Changi PoW Camp

At the conclusion of the Conference I was instructed by Sugita to interpret for the kempeitai regarding the destruction —after the capitulation—of the R.D.F. (radar equipment) in Changi Jail. It transpired that a Japanese officer, concerned in the hand-over, had visited the radar room and maintained that the equipment was intact, When he visited the room a second time—some hours later—it had been destroyed. I sifted the fact from the supposition.

On the first visit the door of the radar room was locked—while the key was being searched for the Japanese officer went in and examined the pumping machinery in another room. He left before the key was found and when he returned with experts they went into the radar room and found it had been wrecked.

After some discussion with Sugita the kempei accepted my explanation and the officers concerned were released from custody, and not taken away and shot.

From the day of surrender to the end of August, 1942 we were regarded as 'captives' and not as 'Prisoners of War': the PoW administration did not take-over until August when Major-General Fukuye arrived with a large staff and numerous interpreters.

Until the arrival of Fukuye, Sugita and his Intelligence Officers controlled PoW and the civilians in Changi Jail. The link between the I.O's and the PoW's was Lt.-Okazaki the Camp Commandant. I resided outside Changi Camp, with Okazaki, until 31st December, 1942 when I was dismissed by Major-General Arimura because I had obtained money from the Red Cross representative in Singapore (Mr. Schweizer) and handed it over to Mr. Roberts (A.I.F. Red Cross agent) who was alleged to have misused it.

What happened was this. I negotiated a loan for 40,000 dollars from Mr. Schweizer on a promissory note. Ten-thousand dollars was paid over to Okazaki pending receipt of agreement to the loan from Tokyo Red Cross representative. I handed the cash to Roberts against his written acknowledgement.

On 31st December (a few days later) Major Wyett, Flt.-Lt. McAllister and Mr. Roberts—all of A.I.F.—were arrested by kempei for being involved in an escape plan. McAllister (R.A.A.F.) had previously been at Timor where he had almost escaped in a Douglas transport machine but was recaptured on the runway. His new plan included a Lockheed Hudson aircraft on a nearby landing strip. Cash was needed for the plan: Roberts, Wyett and McAllister lived together in camp.

I knew nothing about the plot neither did Lt.-Col. Semmance of Malaya Command, who was also arrested but later released.

The Australians were tried, found guilty (?) and sentenced to twenty-years imprisonment although they had not been an inch outside the wire. At a later date we received the 30,000 dollars and used it for its proper purposes—helping our sick comrades.

Rank or nature of 'crime' had no bearing on the degree of punishment meted out: one and all were treated as criminals.

The procedure adopted at first was simple. Instructions were received by Okazaki to obtain names of PoW with special knowledge, or qualifications, to answer specific questions: orders were sent to Malaya Command, Command issued instructions to Area Commanders and a list of names would be submitted from which a selection of 'suitable material' for cross-examination would be made by Yamashita's Headquarters.

Interrogations, or essay writing, went on every day after the 'unconditional surrender' until the end of 1942. Information was demanded, under Yamashita's 'Special Order of the Day', regarding almost everything connected with the British army, navy or airforce.

No one was excepted. Lieut.-Generals, Major-Generals, Brigadiers, Colonels, Majors, Captains, Lieutenants, and other ranks were called on to answer questions concerned with technical or of operational detail.

Yamashita's quiz-masters were well equipped with our military manuals, so they already knew most of the 'correct answers', so our people had to skate on thin ice to avoid adding to their stock of information regarding anything not 'in the book of words'.

Although the Japanese (at Singapore) were well informed about India by members of the I.N.A., and particularly by ex-Indian Army Officers like Capt. Gill Sing (1/18 Punjabs on Div. Staff) or Capt. Gillani (State Forces who was promoted to Lieut.-General and commanded 800 I.N.A. in Burma) they had a special Intelligence Corps working at top-speed grilling batches of Changi PoW to try and gain 'local information' about roads and railways, etc. in Ceylon and in Southeast India. At the same time (between March and July, 1942) another 'special section' of the I. Corps were doing the same job of work with regard to conditions in Northern Australia.

As Liaison Officer—working outside the PoW Camp with the Camp Commandant Okazaki—all the detail (connected with this interrogation) went through my hands. And, it seemed to me that sooner or later General Percival would have to make his stand against this intimidation and refuse to act on one of the Japanese orders sent in by Okazaki. One day (about a month after the order had been in operation) he did so and it resulted in his incarceration in Changi Jail for two days. Then, after his release on terms acceptable to Okazaki, he was placed in solitary confinement in a room near my quarters at Conference House. Day and night he was guarded by armed Sikhs until (after a couple of weeks) he had 'completed the task set for him by Colonel Sugita.'

The severity of punishment, in General Percival's case, was trifling when compared to what others suffered when their 'case' was passed on to the Singapore Kempeitai. However, in my opinion, the Japanese—for all their mental and physical activity—gained no information out of Changi PoW's which was worth a brass farthing.

On December, 4th, 1942, the Japanese Army Press Section of Imperial Headquarters (Tokyo) broadcast the contents of a manuscript said to have been written by General Percival, and —at the same time—broadcast another report attributed to Lt.-General Heath.

One day (in July, 1942) my kit was rifled. Among other items, my diary and a bottle of whisky was stolen. The thief got drunk on the whisky—the diary was sub-edited and printed as a booklet for the information of Yamashita's officers who 'congratulated' me on my summary of the campaign in Malaya.

Okazaki reprimanded the thief for stealing my whisky and drawing attention to his activities while on guard duty.

CHAPTER XI

ASIA FOR ASIATICS

i. *Japan's bid for an Empire*

Japan was well equipped for the task of creating her Empire in Greater East Asia. In 1941 she possessed the third largest Navy in the world, a battle-trained Army of three million men and a modern Airforce of 5,300 aircraft—3,200 of which were combatant type. Most of her gains were made during the first ninety days of her rash adventure. When surrender came in September, 1945 her overseas military casualties exceeded two and a half-million but she still had three million men overseas and two million men in their battle-stations on the home front. She still had 7,000 serviceable aircraft but no Navy and very little fuel oil or petrol. *

The scale of her adventure may be judged by the location of her overseas force on the day of surrender:—

Manchuria	700,000	Korea	300,000	Formosa	300,000
North China	310,000	E. China	200,000	S. China	485,000
Indo China	110,000	Malaya	95,000	Java	45,000
Celebes	55,000	Borneo	35,000	Solomons	80,000
New Guinea	42,000	Timor	70,000	Burma	63,000
		Mandated		Karafuto and	
P. Islands	45,000	Islands	100,000	Kuriles	115,000

We surrendered at Singapore with 91,000: General Itagaki surrendered 656,000 at Singapore to C-in-C. South-East Asia, Admiral Lord Louis Mountbatten. From June, 1943 to August, 1944 we put out of action 250,000 Japanese of the 8th, 17th and 18th armies in the South West Pacific.

It is four thousand miles from Tokyo to the Solomons: Japanese troops landed there on 23rd January, 1942 and were still holding out in September, 1945. We were driven out of Burma

* See Chapter XVIII and Appendix XI and XIII.

246

and forced to retire on India by the first week of May, 1942: in
November, 1944 the total strength of the British 14th Army was
750,000 men—two-thirds were Indian Army Troops—and by
August, 1945 we had liberated 85 per cent. of Burma and
counted 128,000 Japanese dead against our *total casualties of 20,000,*
in killed and missing.

We were engaged in total-war and a few figures should be
kept in mind when we enlarge on the British defeat in Malaya
and the sorry story of Singapore.

Allied resistance ceased in Borneo, Celebes, Moluccas,
Sumatra, Bali, Timor and Java on March 9th, 1942: on 6th May
U.S.A. forces in the Philippines surrendered: on 12th June, 1942
the enemy landed on Kiska and Attu, in the Aleutians. Every-
where, not only in Malaya, the Japanese Army, Navy and
Airforce overwhelmed the allies. We were *fortunate* that the
impetus spent itself before the close of 1942 and that India and
Australia escaped the claws of the despoiler.

We helped the U.S.S.R., with war materials sorely needed
by ourselves: the U.S.S.R. entered the war in the Far East *after*
Japan had been defeated. Our battle-line in Burma alone
extended for 700 miles—enemy held territory extended 2,500
miles southward from the north of Burma. The U.S.S.R. did
not move a man to help us until 9th August ,1945 *after* the atom
bomb had been dropped on Hiroshima.

No doubt there were numerous inconsistencies in the actual
conduct of the Malaya Campaign but we did contain 200,000
Japanese troops for seventy days with less than $3\frac{1}{2}$ Divisions of
fighting troops scattered over Malaya with its 1,000 miles of
coast line, and it was done without air or naval support. To
what extent this limited opposition did effect Japan's plans I do
not know. But, this is certain, had we made a stand in north
Malaya we would have been easily contained and then destroyed at leisure. This would have released enemy forces and
may have influenced an earlier attack on Australia or on India.
As it was, Japan did transport over 300,000 men for the attack
on Townsville but the first section of the armada was destroyed
in the Bismark Sea when the Japanese C-in-C., Admiral Yamamoto took his own life after 30 transports and 10 escorting
warships were sunk by allied aircraft in 72 hours.

That action saved Australia and from Australia the allied

South Pacific offensive was staged. Still it is difficult to say why the 18th British Infantry Division was sent to Singapore, when it was, for it completed its landing on 29th January, 1942 and was never used as a *Division* but was split up into units and sub-units until it lost its value as a fighting force under its commander, Major-General Beckwith-Smith. *One-third* of this gallant Division died, not in the fighting but as prisoners of war. The same remarks apply to the raw 44 Indian Army Brigade which landed on 22nd January, 1942 with 7,000 untrained I.A. troops.

To complete our role, as a delaying force, we might have done better to have staged the final battle in South Johore instead of crossing the Causeway. Our casualties would have been higher in battle and less as prisoners of war that is certain and we should have been able to hold the enemy for fifteen days at least.

To sacrifice so many troops, at the last moment, to an undefined, or confused, military objective requires an explanation which so far has not been forthcoming. If the general idea was to increase the number of a suicide-squad it certainly was a success: the *death rate* among prisoners in Japanese hands was *27 per cent* against *4 per cent* of allied prisoners of war taken by the German and Italian Armies.

Our morale—discipline and confidence—reached a low ebb because the fighting troops were not unified in their approach to a common task in attack or defence.

ii. Japan's friends

The magnitude of Japan's initial successes stimulated the morale of Japanese and impressed Indians, Chinese, Burmans, Malays, Siamese, Philippinos and others. Japanese soldiers, from C-in-C. to first-class private, were certain of ultimate success and—according to one broadcast—'When Anglo-American resistance is broken Japan will set about moulding an East which will peacefully spell Co-prosperity and Co-existence in Asia.'

As Liaison Officer I had to accompany General Yamashita, and other high-ranking naval and military officers, on their tours of inspection of Changi PoW Camp. One senior officer assured me that the Japanese Army would link hands with the German Army in India, another naval officer explained that

Australia and New Zealand were to be occupied before the end of 1942. The consensus of opinion was: England would soon capitulate, Canada and U.S.A., would make a separate peace: peace-terms, signed in London, would confirm cession of all territory captured by Axis powers. Therefore it was Japan's intention to press on with her conquests and to establish permanent garrisons, and civil administrations in all the occupied territory.

Let me give one illustration of Japanese mentality at this period of the war. One day, soon after the surrender, a Major Toyama went with Lt. Okazaki to 'inspect General Percival'. They failed to make themselves understood so I was sent for, and this is the substance of what Toyama had to say:—

Our position as PoW's was hopeless. General Percival, and all British PoW's must realise that they cannot hope to improve their status. They must accept their fate, dismiss all idea of escaping from Japanese power. PoW camps were being established everywhere, soon there would be places like Changi, in India and Australia—and in England—filled with soldiers just like 'Percival' who was always sending in complaints. You defied Dai Nippon, you surrendered and must accept the consequences, you should have died fighting like Japanese soldiers: stop complaining and reconcile yourselves to lifelong imprisonment: if you do run away from Changi you will be shot. But suppose you did escape then all you could do would be to exchange one PoW camp for another PoW camp before you were killed.

I duly interpreted Toyama's diatribe to General Percival and his senior Staff-officers. General Percival replied, 'Thanks, James. Tell Major Toyama we understand his remarks.' That was the end of the 'inspection of General Percival' but the flood of complaints went on all the same—never less than three every day.

When Japan was 'winning the war' she had many curious friends helping her quite apart from the I.N.A. There were many degrees of this fraternization—misguided, mercenary, simulated, altruistic, mischievous and dangerous. And there were various kinds of co-operation, coercive to voluntary.

There was a 'Break Away Australia from Britain' movement launched from the Palace Hotel, Shanghai, in March, 1942: the voice of the 'Australian Independence League' informed us over the radio that 'Australian Prisoners of War in Singapore, who had suffered the humiliation of British bungling, hailed the movement with enthusiasm.' This radio-caster had been well known over the Australian Radio 3 A.W., and he provided a special programme aimed at 'listeners in the homeland'. There was another broadcaster—this time a 49-year-old Briton—who told us all about Japan and aspirations on the German radio at Shanghai. He was tried, later on—and imprisoned for eight years. The others were punished in the same way after they had done their best to help the Japanese cause.

But these off-whites were swept off their feet by their many Japanese friends (?) who soon made it clear to them that, once they joined the chorus, there was no contracting-out. We had a few misguided people in the camp: one of them tried to send a cable to the Prime Minister of Australia requesting him to conclude a separate peace with Japan but I clipped his wings and sent him back to the A.I.F. where they put paid to his account.

There was another A.I.F. Major who became entangled with the meshes of 'Yamashita Law' because he was a journalist with some broadcasting experience in Australia. He allowed his enthusiasm for his profession to get the better of his judgment and before he realised his error he was in Tokyo being compelled to broadcast to Australia. Like the others, he was arrested after the surrender, tried and acquitted of mal-intent.

When this business of 'co-operating with the enemy' is closely examined by impeccable critics they should remember the sadistic nature of Japanese. Those who declined to co-operate far exceeded those who did and they paid for it, often with their lives. But most of those who composed 'Yamashita Law' have been hanged for their crimes—thousands of them—so we had better view the petty transgressors in the correct light of common sense.

iii. Dhillon's Sikhs and the I.N.A.

Humiliating and parading the 'Captives' delighted Japanese —it raised their morale and acted as a saporific to their Oriental inferiority-complex. Those who arranged the parades were always afraid of an *Incident* and warned me beforehand to notify Malaya Command of the 'extreme penalty' in store for any person involved in 'an incident'. There was never any danger to the V.I.P's but they were always preceded by armoured-cars, motor-cycle patrols and truck loads of soldiers with fixed-bayonets. And of course the movie-camera men guarded by machine-gunners.

The first 'grand parade' was staged for Yamashita, the second one was for Field-Marshal Sugiyama conducted on a tour of inspection by Yamashita himself.

At the 'introduction', Yamashita told me to tell General Percival that his troops had fought well: the fortunes of war had been against him—he was now a prisoner of war and it was his duty to obey all Japanese orders: that was all. On the second parade, Yamashita introduced me to Sugiyama and then I walked over to where General Percival was standing with his senior-officers: Yamashita asked me to name the British Officers to the Field-Marshal who politely returned their salute but made no comment.

That part of the parade was conducted in a dignified manner —no other Japanese officers were allowed to approach General Percival or his staff. When the brief inspection was over, Yamashita told me to attach myself to his senior staff-officer and accompany him on a tour of the camp. I sat alongside the driver. The other occupants of the car proceeded to discuss the failure of their efforts to proselyte the A.I.F., and to express satisfaction with the progress being made to raise the Indian National Army.

Ration strength of the I.N.A., was over 10,000 but internal difficulties were raising many problems. There was a conflict of ideas between Mohan Singh, the commander, and Rash Behari Bose, the administrator. The 1st I.N.A. broke up into groups of partisans and was 'reformed' under the leadership of Subas Chandra Bose as the 2nd I.N.A. in August, 1943—after Chandra Bose had been flown over from Germany. To stimulate the movement, which was more political than military, General Tojo came to Singapore on 18th October ,1943. He reviewed the 2nd I.N.A. and consigned it to Chandra Bose as executive head and 'Commander in Chief' with Colonel Bhonsale as Chief of Staff.

This move was followed by the 'establishment' of the Government of Azad Hind on 21st October with Chandra Bose as head

of the State. On 24th October, 1943 the AZAD HIND GOVERN-
MENT declared war on Britain and the United States of America.
The seat of Government was moved to Rangoon in December
and the first elements of the I.N.A. went to Kohima, Imphal
and Akyab battle fronts.

The first action, against British troops by the I.N.A., took
place on the Manipur frontier in February, 1944: the I.N.A.
were a drop in the bucket of slaughter which followed and they
disintegrated before the march of the 14th Army to Rangoon.

Chandra Bose left Saigon for Japan on 17th August, 1945—
his plane crashed at Taihoku, Formosa, on 18th and he died
from his injuries.

For all the military, or political, use they were the I.N.A.,
might never have existed but they were traitors nevertheless. I
have read that 'The Indian National Army was a fine body of
men whose dominating motive had been love of India's freedom.' That may be the excuse for desertion during hostilities
but there is a complete answer to that.

In *World War I*, the Indian Army numbered 1,457,000 on all
fronts. Casualties were 106,594 including 36,698 killed.

In *World War II*, the Indian Army numbered 2,500,000 on
all fronts. Casualties were 177,315 including 23,294 killed.

That is the first part of the answer. In the second place in
World War I and in *World War II every man* in the Indian Army
was a volunteer—there were no conscripts.

Decorations for bravery were numerous: 11 V.C's in the first
world war, 31 V.C's in the second world war. The maximum
number of traitors who joined the I.N.A., was 30,000 (military
and civilians) so the extent of their patriotism may be compared
with that of the loyalty of the real Indian Army. All Indians
wished to be free of British rule—that is taken for granted as a
right of self determination—but once they took the oath of
allegiance by their own religion they were bound to keep it
intact.

Those British Indians who refused to join the I.N.A., after
the surrender suffered terribly at the hands of the Japanese and
some of their vile comrades in arms. Very few of those heroes of
the Indian Army, magnificent men who were tortured or beaten
to death, were acclaimed heroic at the end of the war—very few
were praised, very few decorated or rewarded by the British

Empire posthumously or when they rejoined the base in India.

The I.N.A. failed in their crusade for freedom but it was through no fault of Subas Chandra Bose that State-Shintoism was not introduced into India. It was no fault of Congress Leaders, or of Gandhi, that the Indian Army was not disbanded and the Japanese free to come to India and arrange terms with a non-resisting people.

To arrange terms with a non-resisting people. Let me give one or two examples of the culture of the people they preferred to the British tyrant.

About two-hundred of the 2/15th Punjabs were captured by the Japanese when they took Kuching. A few joined the I.N.A. —the majority refused. Those who refused were beaten senseless, fastened to trees, exposed to the tropical sun without water and kept *alive* on 150 grammes of rice. This went on from February ,1942 to April, 1945. Then, what was left of the detachment were rounded up in Kuala Belait (Brunei. N. Borneo). The leaders of the resistance—Sub. Makhmad Anwar, Jemadars Mohd Anwar, Mohad Akram, Nazir Hussain and Lachman Singh—were placed in solitary confinement.

On 21st April, 1945, Makhmad Anwar—still refusing to obey —was taken from his cell, strung up by his feet, head swinging clear of the ground was slowly beaten to death. Slowly beaten to death! His festering wounds, caused by the brutality, were septic and maggot infected—but he refused to be a traitor.

The four other V.C.O's refused to be intimidated: they were beheaded on 3rd June, 1945. An Indian Medical Officer, Dr. Balwant Singh, helped them—his hands were chopped off because he dressed their wounds—the dresser was bayonetted on the spot—Dr. Balwant Singh was then beheaded.

Sixty Indian prisoners of war remained—twenty-five of them at death's door. On 16th June, 1945, two Japanese officers—Yamaguchi and Kamimura—arrived at Kuala Belait with two n.c.o's.

The Indians were rounded up, then tied up in batches of six: Yamaguchi proceeded to behead them one by one until he became sick: the survivors were finished off with the bayonet.

Next day the victims were dragged inside the huts and cremated. One or two avoided the round-up and fled to the jungle where they were recovered by an A.I.F. detachment some time later.

I knew those men, who were treated like that by the Japanese and I regret their passing as comrades in arms.

On 25th January, 1942, the 2/15th Punjabs were fighting a rearguard action on the Dutch position at Sanggau Ledo. A small detachment under Subadar Framurz Khan were detailed to deny the Sanggau Nullah crossing while the main body of SAFOR established themselves in new positions. Far out-numbered, the Punjabis completed their task after inflicting heavy casualties: they were ordered back but before they could move they were encircled and called on to surrender. Framurz Khan, severely wounded, ordered a bayonet charge and the small band of forty were overwhelmed, captured and disarmed. They had held off a battalion for two days.

LNk Sher Khan and three Dutch machine gunners managed to escape and hide in the undergrowth. The survivors, wounded and dying, were tied to trees. Then they were pierced with wire between the back of the ankle and the achilles tendon. Twenty-four hours later the Japanese poured petrol over them and burned them to death.

Pathans, Punjabis and Sikhs they had refused to surrender— Subadar Kartar Singh was killed, shouting 'Ya Ali' and the last words of Subadar Framurz Khan were:—

'We are dying, but dying after doing duty to God, King and Country and to die such a death is the most sacred one of all'

No—thirty-thousand deserters can not alter the heroic record of two and a half million who served in the British Indian Army: the incidents I have mentioned touch the fringe of Japanese brutality to loyal Indian troops and the full story should be read by Congress Leaders now that they have their full independence. It was not won by passive resistance but by the sacrifice of men like Kartar Singh, Framurz Khan, Makhmad Anwar and other Indians who fought with the 14th Army and destroyed the Japanese menace to their freedom.

Excuses may be made, and accepted, for the I.N.A. but not for the Sikhs who formed the infamous Changi Guard. The *volunteers* were commanded by Captain G. Singh Dhillon who held a King's Commission. Dhillon and his unit continued to wear British Army uniform and British badges of rank. They carried sidearms and rifles they had used in the Malaya Campaign but they drilled and they screamed, on and off parade, in Japanese style.

Headquarters of Dhillon's Sikhs were near the Changi Jail and they received their routine orders from Lt.-Okazaki: at first I had to interpret them and from first to last I saw how they acted for their masters. They claimed the 'right' to be saluted by British troops—not excepting General Percival. They created 'incidents' day and night: offenders were numerous for the armed renegades strutted about inside the wire and met defiance by force.

Officers or men were halted at the point of the bayonet— thrashed on the spot, compelled to 'apologise' and then made to crawl on their hands and knees before all and sundry. Refusal was punished by being manhandled by the guard to Dhillon's Hq. where the 'charge' was framed and then presented to Okazaki.

Selarang Guard Room was I.N.A. gestapo headquarters for the Changi gang of 'patriots'. On one occasion two of our men were shot dead by a Sikh patrol a *few feet* outside Culvert Gate of Southern Area. To account for the 'incident', Dhillon sent in a report that the patrol had been rushed by a number of PoW and the Sikhs had defended themselves. This was a lie. Only *one shot* had been fired near the Culvert Gate: two men were picked up, one was dead the other seriously wounded—one other man, absent from duty that night, was never recovered.

Okazaki reported the incident to his headquarters and the matter of investigation was transferred to the kempeitai: the riddle of the missing man was never solved. The wounded man recovered but he could not account for the other man who was dead—nor could anyone else in the PoW camp identify him. In the end, Major-General Keith Simmons, commanding Southern Area, was taken to Singapore and jailed for one month 'for lack of discipline in his area'.

That is a fair sample of Dhillon's methods and his 'rule' prevailed until late in 1942 when the Sikhs were relieved by the Koreans who were almost as bad but less cunning in creating the 'incidents'.

After the surrender, Dhillon was tried in India but he emerged not as a criminal but as a 'national hero'.

CHAPTER XII

JAPAN'S BRUTAL CONQUEST

i. War Crimes

By the end of September, 1943 all PoW Camps in Singapore, except Changi, had been closed. British, Australian, Indian, Dutch and Javanese Prisoners of War were sent up-country or overseas to Burma, Siam, Indo-China, Borneo, Formosa, China, Korea or Japan, or to the South Pacific Islands. They were to be brutally overworked, half-starved or beaten to death in order to bolster up Japan's all-in effort to conquer Greater East Asia.

From first to last, 87,000 allied Prisoners of War passed through Changi Camp. Due to the care and efficiency of our own medical services our *death-roll* (in 3½ years) was 850 *including* our battle-casualties. But of those who left Changi more than 30 per cent. died as a result of neglect or barbarity.

There was no lack of medical supplies or personnel when we surrendered. If Japan had observed the Geneva Conventions our total losses in 3½ years would not have exceeded 1,000 in Malaya but the Japanese commandeered our medical stores and equipments and doled out inferior drugs and chemicals in minute quantities—they stole our X-ray equipment and they treated our medical personnel as sanitary squads. Despite their efforts to kill us off we managed to treat *80,000* patients in Changi Camp Hospitals between February, 1942 and September, 1945: *10,000* minor or major operations were performed and our total losses, from all causes, was 850 dead. We had to manage without mosquito nets and to try and 'wash' linen and blankets without soap—we had more than one epidemic, we sent three complete hospital units to Siam and all the drugs and equipment the Japanese would allow us to send: we sent medical units with every draft but despite it all we lost *16,000 Officers and men in Siam alone.*

No draft left Changi without a protest being lodged in writing by Malaya Command: I interpreted at dozens of our Command protest meetings with Camp Commandants and with Generals Fukuye and Arimura. But it was not the slightest use protesting for they were merely obeying their orders.

The international military tribunal for the Far East has placed on record the nature of these orders. Sir William Webb expressed the opinion that 'the crimes of the Japanese accused were far less heinous, varied, and extensive than those of the Germans accused at Nuremberg.' That was not the majority judgment and no doubt referred to some of the 'old men' being tried for 'political murder'—Tojo, Araki and the like. But the tribunal established the fact that 'torture, murder, rape, and other cruelties of the most barbarous character were practised on such a vast scale and on such a common pattern that the *only* conclusion possible was that those atrocities were either secretly ordered or wilfully permitted by the Japanese Government or its members, or by the leaders of the armed forces.'

Nearly 50,000 prisoners of war were employed on the making of the Siam Railway—16,000 died of torture, disease or starvation. Major General Arimura, responsible for the movement orders, managed to surrender to the U.S.S.R. in Korea and up to July, 1948 all efforts to obtain his extradition have failed. General Fukuye shouted 'Banzai' just before being executed by a firing squad at Changi on 28th April, 1946: General Yamashita was executed in Manila, Field-Marshal Sugiyama committed suicide: Capt. Takakuwa, and Captain Watanabe, were executed for causing the death of 824 A.I.F. in the march-out from Sandakan.

Lt.-Colonel Satoishi with 33 of his officers and men were shot for herding 150 allied prisoners into an air-raid shelter on Palawan (P. Islands) 11th December, 1944. They were drenched with petrol before the lighted torches were thrown among them.

The American Government secured possession of Japansee orders—issued between 12th January and March, 1944—which read 'By order of the Japanese Military authorities surrendered personnel captured, with the exception of individuals needed for minute investigation, *are to be put to death on the field of battle.*'

Lt.-Colonel Sumida (Singapore Kempeitai) was shot, with

R

seven of his staff, for various brutalities, including the slaughter of several thousand loyal Chinese. General Kimura—Burma—and General Muto—Phillippines—were also shot for atrocities in Burma and for the Bataan death march of Americans. It is a long list of criminals, from private soldier to commander-in-chief, and it by no means exhausted the supply of names. By July, 1948 we had tried 940 Japanese: 290 were sentenced to death, 538 to long terms of imprisonment and 112 were acquitted. The Australians—at the same date—had tried 775 Japanese, hanged or shot 139, imprisoned 402, acquitted 234 and had another 574 still to be tried as war criminals. The American list is just as conclusive in its screening of the murderers during the war.

With regard to the major war criminals: Generals Tojo, Doihara, Itagaki, Kimura, Matsui and Muto were sentenced to death; Generals Araki, Hate, Koiso, Minami, K. Sato, Umezu —Admirals Shimada and Oka—Colonel Hashimoto, Baron Hiranuma, Hoshino, Kaya and T. Suzuki were condemmed to imprisonment for life, with Marquess K. Kido, Lord Keeper of the Privy Seal. Shigemitsu, the Foreign Minister from April, 1943 to April, 1945, got seven years and Tojo's foreign minister S. Togo received twenty years in jail.

Koki Hirota, Foreign Minister 1933-1936, received the death penalty with his soldier comrades of the kais, while Oshima—the Berlin Ambassador—and Shiratori—Rome Ambassador—received life sentences.

It must be noted that the Indian judge, Mr. Justice Pal, *did not agree* with the verdict or sentences—he recommended that all the accused be found not guilty of the charges of the indictment. But General McArthur—after the necessary delay—confirmed the sentences which had been approved elsewhere.

The part played by the Emperor received the condemnation of the President of the tribunal. In his opinion it was the Emperor who authorized war and could not be excused for doing so because his life was at stake—he was not bound to act on the advice of his ministers if he did not agree with it. The evidence proved that the Emperor accepted advice to make war against his better judgment. *

No doubt, Sir William Webb was correct. But, in my opinion,

* See Appendix X.

it made no difference if Hirohito lived or died, the gumbatsu ruled the country absolutely through the Meiji Constitution, Shinto and Kodo. One Tenno more or less made no difference to the system or the working of it. Hirohito decided to live, for, like Premier Hara, there was a great deal he could do before he indulged in Tenno hara-kiri.

The Japanese who waged war in the Far East were not the men who were in the armed services when Meiji came to the throne in 1868. The senior officers dated from 1881, the conscripts, and the junior officers, dated from 1900, the first-line troops and their unit commanders dated from 1920. Between 1920 and 1941 the intake was at the rate of 300,000 per annum making a grand total of first-line troops and reserves under the age of 40 of 6,000,000 men. It was these men, between the ages of 20 and 40 who had been thoroughly drilled in kodo and State-Shinto by Araki and his kind who—no matter where they fought—had the same killing instincts in and out of action. They had exactly the same education from five years old to twenty years old when they joined the services. For that reason there was that common pattern of atrocity which appeared to surprise the Tribunal sitting in Tokyo.

Evidence before the court proved that Japanese medical officers removed hearts and livers from healthy prisoners while they were alive. Cannibalism was authorized—allied prisoners but not Japanese might be eaten even when other food was available.

One of General Tojo's earliest orders was to the effect that commandants of PoW Camps must not be obsessed by mistaken ideas of humanitarianism.

In a report handed in after my release in September, 1945 I made these points:—

'There was an agreed policy regarding the treatment of all Officers or other ranks captured during hostilities or surrendered en masse. The policy originated in the War Office Tokyo. The basic principles of Japanese PoW administration were: extract the maximum amount of work at the minimum cost in food and medical supplies. In the end this method plunged them into an abyss of crime which engulfed the entire administration and turned Japanese into murderers pure and simple.

With regard to punishing so called 'war criminals' it seems to me that we must first of all make up our minds what it is we want to punish. All camps were run on the same lines; they did not break any of their own regulations—what they did do was to behave like beasts and not like human beings. They should be shot out of hand: if we try them we must bring evidence against individuals but it is the system which produced the criminals. How do you start punishing a system?'

ii. From Singapore to Tokyo

With the last departure for Siam—a 'working-party' of unfit men—our Changi ration strength was down to 2,500 including the patients in hospital, permanently unfit, hospital personnel and the rump of Malaya Command and Southern Area Head-quarters and the staff of the A.I.F. The camp had been reduced from 51,000 in February, 1942 to 2,500 in September, 1943. Our secret radio-set kept us in close touch with the progress of the war: Germans had capitulated at Stalingrad: saturation air-raids on Berlin: Axis forces surrendered in Tunis: Sicily invaded, Mussolini arrested, Italy out of the war: battle of Bismark Sea: South Pacific offensive—Attu recaptured. Japan's brutal conquest had been more than checked and Hitler had not defeated the U.S.S.R. by any means.

Then a cable came from Tokyo: I was ordered to Japan under escort of Captain Shiono who had just arrived at Changi with a draft of prisoners of war from Java. There was no ex-planation—and in a few hours I boarded the 10,000 tonner 'Ussuri Maru' with 500 other PoW's bound for Japan. Hardly had we piled aboard when kempei arrived and arrested four British officers—including W. Wooller the rugger international.

Then we tried to fit ourselves into the accomodation below deck. It was impossible until they agreed to our moving cargo, stowed on a hatch, and they chalked off another thirty foot alley-way. Our accomodation was now exactly 6-foot by 2-foot per man long or short, thick or thin. We were battened down in port and not allowed up on deck for about 24 hours after sailing.

Three days out from Singapore our convoy was attacked by American submarines. One 20,000 ton oil-tanker was destroyed but we evaded danger and made for Manila. During the attack we were battened-down, below deck in complete darkness. The only exit was guarded by bayonet-men. If we had been hit there would have been another 'Lisbon Maru' disaster because it was impossible for more than a few men at a time to have mounted the narrow companion-way even if permitted by the squads of armed men posted at the exit and on deck.

En route I was fortunate in receiving only three thrashings from a mad 2/Lt. whom we named 'Basher'. But we all lost an average of 10 lbs. on account of the stifling atmosphere below deck with every porthole closed in the tropics. From morning to night perspiration oozed out of every pore and every few hours we would receive instructions on some subject or other. We had one set of latrines (over the scuppers) and these were'out of bounds' after sunset unless I could persuade the armed guard that it was impossible for 500 men to regulate their bowels to order. Fifty per cent had diarrhoea: drinking water was limited to a mug or so a day and the voyage lasted a month.

I gained some information from 'friendly members' of the crew because I was the usual go-between PoW and captors and had opportunity to feel my way without being knifed. It was no longer a question of winning the war but: how can we bring the war to an end?

Japan was still sending thousands of troops and ship-loads of munitions to the South Pacific theatre of operations. In Manila, and in Takao (Formosa) the harbour and the quays were crowded with transports brimming with troops. All the ships were loaded to well below their marks but we saw all the superficial signs that the allied submarine menace was looming large in the pattern of final defeat. Traffic, in both directions, on Japan's long communication lanes was slowed down on account of a lack of full protection for convoys. Ships, heavily laden with Japan's dwindling supply of raw materials, were being sunk every day: this was slowing down the rate of production in factories and it was now almost impossible to replace material losses from any of the occupied territory except perhaps Indo China. All other routes were being marked red on the maps in Tokyo.

There were too many garrisons each with hundreds or with hundreds of thousands of troops which had to be fed and munitioned from the home base. During the first few months of the war they had command of air and sea, now they were losing it every day the war lasted. Transports were too slow and were sitting targets for submarines. A year and a half of war had brought scattered triumphs which were now valueless without the conquest of India and Australia, the main objectives of the war.

At the critical period the Japanese navy was unequal to the task of maintaining control of the sea against a hastily reformed navy of the United States of America. The initial success at Pearl Harbour had lost its place in the scheme of things to come —now, each month, the relentless pressure of a methodical mass production superior technique and amazing efficiency had turned the scales in favour of a bitter enemy. The loss of Guadalcanal and the reverse suffered at the battle of Midway Island were more than black clouds on the horizon of a setting sun. *

The crew of the 'Ussuri Maru' had made too many trips to remain under any illusions regarding the blatant propaganda fed to the masses regarding the successes of Japan's invincible Navy in the South Pacific Ocean. They were very dispirited and not at all impressed when the 'Basher' punched my nose because the black-out was not 100 per cent. perfect in broad daylight.

iii. Japan in October 1943

When we docked at Moji the Kempei came aboard. They were not interested in the other five hundred PoW's but asked Shiono why I was sitting on my baggage watched by an n.c.o.? My escort explained and produced his authority for my journey to Tokyo—but they were not satisfied. They grilled me for an hour and then I was ordered to load my kit on to a truck and drag it through the streets to a PoW Camp in Moji where they locked me in a cell.

Soon, more kempei arrived with note-books and I was examined and cross-examined regarding my history from the early days of Meiji to the perplexed days of Showa Tenno. A bowl of rice followed the interrogation but, directly the kempei went, my own guards became pally. They admired my white hair and my Japanese—so I told them tales of old Japan and they produced sake and cigarettes, extra blankets, lots of tea and rice and tucked me in for the night.

Next morning I trundled my truck to the Railway Station followed by little boys and little girls who chanted merrily:

* See Appendix XI.

'Ojii-san! Ojii-san! Horyo ojii-san!': which was quite correct—
'Grandpapa! Grandpapa! Prisoner of War Grandpapa!' and
proper but they ran away when I replied in Japanese that it was
very rude to make fun of old people—very rude, and that they
must be Chosen-jin (Koreans).

The train to Tokyo was crowded. Every seat occupied and
corridors jammed with men, women and children. But they
were quite polite and I was rammed into a corner seat and told
by Shiono on no account to move or look out of the window. An
armed n.c.o., sat with me and before we started another lot of
kempei arrived with note-books and quizzed me for twenty
minutes.

Before the war, Moji was always a 'dirty town' but now it had
deteriorated into mouldy stagnancy. Perhaps it was because
the Moji-Shimonoseki tunnel now permitted through traffic
from the mainland to Nagasaki and other places in Kyushu.
However the train started punctually: in October, 1943 the
B 29's had not yet upset timetables with high explosives. Despite
the injunctions I did look out of the window: there were quite a
number of new factories and small ship-building yards, airfields
and so on—on the way to Kobe, but nothing on a grand
scale.

At Osaka, Captain Shiono was greeted by his family: he
transferred all the loot he had brought over from Singapore—
six large cases—and then paraded his 'special captive' for their
close inspection. They were all extremely polite—one woman
handed me some sweet cakes and a packet of peanuts but the
approach of another kempei altered everything. Shiono yelled
at me to get back into the train.

The kempei examined me and when he had finished said to
my escort, 'Tell them at Kyoto if you want him taught a lesson,
I'll inform them he's on this train.' But nothing happened at
Kyoto because I was fast asleep.

At 8 a.m. we arrived at Tokyo. I was bundled into a car and
taken by Shiono to Army Headquarters some miles away. At
Hq. a Staff-Colonel interrogated me—merely asking name,
unit, rank, age, place of capture and nationality. As it checked
up with the information on the movement order he passed me
on to another room where I was interviewed by a General who
did not give his name. He said that I had been brought to Japan

to work at PoW Hq., but for the present the plan had been
dropped and I would be taken to Omori PoW Camp until they
were ready for me to start compiling a full list of all allied
prisoners of war. But that I was not to worry about my future—
nothing would happen to me at Omori.

I was then fed on fish and rice and the woman who served me
scolded me for not eating it all as it was exactly the same food
eaten by the General himself. I explained that my tummy was
very much out of order after the journey from Singapore.

Shiono came in, slipped me a packet of cigarettes, and then
in a loud voice handed me over to a Eurasian with instructions
to be careful and obey all Japanese orders.

A staff-car took us to Omori on the Tokyo-Yokohama main
road and soon after we started the Eurasian volunteered the information that I had been brought over from Malaya to act as
Liaison Officer in Japan between PoW camps and Army Hq.
and to compile a nominal roll. But I was more interested in the
environment than in his remarks as we streaked past the rest of
the mechanical traffic which spluttered along at ten to fifteen
miles an hour propelled by charcoal-burning contraptions re-
miniscent of Heath Robinson's pictorial gadgets.

Japan was short of petrol. But what struck me most, after
what I had seen in London, was the complete absence of air-
raid shelters, or A.R.P. It was October, 1943 but the authorities
in Tokyo were still confident (?) that no allied bombers would
be able to penetrate the ground and air defence of the capital.

Dolittle's solitary raid was made from an aircraft carrier and
it was dismissed as a stunt although the captured airmen were
murdered to discourage (?) the others.

There were very few men on the streets, not one woman in a
hundred wore native dress, they had discarded kimono, with
yards of material, for overalls or baggy slacks fastened at the
ankles with tape. Shops were open but very few goods were on
sale—so far as I could see when we were held up by traffic.

The general impression was one of near bankruptcy after a
dozen years of war in China and the South Pacific Ocean—it
was indeed a shabby sight for the 'heart of the nation trium-
phant in war'—it was so unlike the colourful streets of Tokyo in
pre-kodo days.

iv. Omori PoW Camp

Omori is 7½ miles due south of the Imperial Palace and 12½ miles from Yokohama. When I was a boy it was a fashionable summer resort—a place to go to, to get away from stuffy Tokyo. Now, at the age of 63 I was going there as a Prisoner of War— a melancholy reflection. The Camp was situated at the north end of reclaimed land, not far from the old No, 4 Battery close to the mouth of Meguro-gawa flowing into Tokyo Bay.

A rickety wooden bridge spanned a tidal canal separating the island from the original coast line. It was this narrow strip of water which saved us from destruction more than once during the 1945 super fire raids on Tokyo by B 29's. We crossed the bridge on foot and when we reached the sentry at the gate my Eurasian guide, and the n.c.o. escort, snarled at me in the most approved yamato-damashi style to impress the sentry of the arrival of one more captive.

I was handed over to Major Hamada, assistant Camp Commandant who signed for me with his seal of office. Then I was handed a non-escape form to sign which reminded me of the way PoW's in Changi had been herded in a modern black-hole of Calcutta and told to sign or take the consequences.

After the signing I received the usual warnings, and the usual bit by bit search of my kit but Hamada refrained from taking any souvenirs. I repacked my kit, got on my feet and stood at attention for an hour when Private Kuriyama (o.c. discipline) took over. He made another thorough search of my kit telling me in gutter-Japanese that if I did not behave he would bushido me good and proper.

The numerous kit inspections and warnings occupied two hours then I was passed fit to join my comrades in No. 2 Barracks.

Omori Camp was two months old. When I arrived it was commanded by a dug-out, Lt.-Col. Suzuki and he was succeeded by a Colonel Sakeba an old-timer thoroughly steeped in kodo— one of the genuine war criminals, one-hundred per cent sadistic.

Five wooden barracks, 100 feet by 24 feet, housed 520 prisoners of war. Each prisoner had a bed space of 4 feet by 8 feet in the double-deckers. There was an 8 feet passage down the centre of each barrack: at each end were two 10 feet by 12 feet cubicles for officers.

Barracks were fitted with glassed-in sliding windows and there was ample ventilation. The quarters were tolerable in summer but ice-houses in winter because no heating of any description was provided or permitted and the flimsy structures were erected on wind-swept ground a few inches only above high tidemark.

There were three twenty-feet long wash-racks for 520 men but most of the time in summer there was a bare trickle of water —in winter the pipes were frozen. Latrines, on the same scale, were provided: there was no arrangement for disposal of sewage and the shallow concrete lined pits were filled to overflowing and alive with millions of white maggots.

Food was vile. There was no fixed ration scale, too few rice-boilers and the mixture of rice-sweepings and kaoliang (the millet of Manchuria) topped-up with soya bean was never fully cooked. When it was 'cooked' (once a day) the mess was dumped into dirty tubs from which it was ladled into still dirtier serving-buckets: shortage of water prevented cleansing of anything from cooking utensils to a pocket handkerchief. The excess roughage, in every meal, was a constant irritant to the lining of the men's stomachs so the majority suffered from persistent diarrhoea.

Tenko!—roll-call—was at 5 a.m. in summer and 6.30 a.m. in winter: evening roll-call at any time between 6 p.m. and 10 p.m. according to the mood of the duty officer. Tenko was conducted according to Japanese rules of procedure and in Japanese. At tenko boots had to be clean, tunic buttoned-up, bedding rolled-back, kit packed or piled in rows each 12 inches wide with items in their stipulated place in the pile. No clothing was allowed to hang in the barracks even if it was dripping wet at tenko hour.

Pushing, slapping and kicking was the immediate punishment for breach of tenko regulations. I was trounced because I blinked when the duty officer was speaking to me about not standing upright, when my feet were swollen with beri beri.

Most of the PoW at Omori were from Shinagawa Camp, a few miles away. At Shinagawa there was a 'hospital' run by Captain Tokuda the vilest type of 'doctor' to put on a Japanese uniform.

Omori and Shinagawa produced a full quota of war criminals who were tried and punished after the surrender. Both places are only a few miles from the Imperial Palace but they might have been three-thousand miles away for all the difference it made to the atrocious manner in which prisoners of war were treated.

CHAPTER XIII

CONFLICT OF WAR AIMS
Resignation of Tojo

i. Propaganda and Camp news

In October, 1943, Omori camp news was obtained from the English editions of 'Japan Times' and 'Tokyo Mainichi'. There were no secret wireless-sets so the PoW had to depend entirely on Japanese versions of the progress of the war. In consequence of reading this enemy propaganda the general morale of the allied prisoners of war was extrenely low. Most of them had already suffered at the hands of the Japanese and after eighteen months of captivity were pretty depressed by the 'news'.

As the latest arrival from overseas I was able to water down the propaganda with a few encouraging facts. And in order to keep informed of what was being written in the Japanese newspapers I decided to operate an under-cover news service. It was just as well that I did so because after April, 1944 newspapers, Japanese or the foreign version, were prohibited from being circulated in the camp.

I obtained various Japanese newspapers and checked the news items in the original version. I compared the 'Mainichi' with the 'Yorodzu Chuo' to get the mild socialist and big-business reactions, and checked the 'Yomiuri' with the 'Asahi' to note the underlining of the views of moderates and militarists. Newspaper Japanese is not easy to read at a glance unless you are well up to date with the news. But it was not difficult to compare official communiques with official and unofficial propaganda and in a few months I was able to read a little 'between the lines'. Unfortunately, the only safe retreat, was the various benjo (latrines). Squinting at small characters in such evil smelling and cramped quarters was not pleasant but I survived the winter of 1943/44. By then it had not produced anything startling except that various proclamations indicated shortage of food and fuel and increasing difficulties with rail and road transport.

Slowly I detected the first signs of discontent and disillusionment and a resignation to accept a long war if Germany was defeated in the west. It became evident, from editorial comment, that the propaganda of the official spokesmen to the effect that 'Japan was consolidating her gains preparatory to further occupation of enemy territory' was inconsistent with the known facts.

As early as November, 1943 there appeared hints of discord between Army and Navy about major strategy and there appeared demands for the dispersal of Tokyo population and the establishment of realistic air-raid precautions in vulnerable areas.

From October, 1943 (when General Tojo visited Singapore) to the end of the year the communiques repeatedly 'explained' the failures of the allies to reoccupy Japanese 'front-line bases' in the South Pacific despite the fact that Japan was waging war 4,000 miles from Tokyo. It was claimed that enormous losses were being inflicted on Australians and Americans in their vain attempts to take from Japan small islands thousands of miles from the homeland.

But all this did not explain the clamour for air-raid shelters, dispersal of population or the new restrictive food regulations.

On 7th December, 1943 (second anniversary of attack on Pearl Harbour) I listened to a nation-wide broadcast by General Tojo. He said that Japan, in ninety days after bombing Pearl Harbour, had fanned out from Wake to Burma, from Gilberts to Solomons and even to the far Aleutians. War against the Allies was taken 5,000 miles away from Japan and her Navy was master of the seas from Honolulu to Ceylon. Now, on the threshold of a New Year, Japan would seek to consolidate her gains, and she would go on adding to those gains until ultimate victory was attained. Japan would win the war no matter how long it took and no matter what sacrifices had to be made.

He spoke well. There was no hesitation or faltering: he knew the truth but the spirit of kodo urged him on—encouraged by the unconquerable spirit of the people in the homeland the armed forces were determined to vanquish the enemy in 1944. But—he warned—there must be no more slackening on the home front: more and still more planes and ships were wanted and a better output of munitions to ensure success against the material superiority of the enemy.

Loss of the Gilberts, in November, 1943, was reported as a minor incident: bombing of Paramushiro (Naval base on northerly point of Kuriles) on 13th September, 1943 had been dismissed as a 'silly tip-and-run affair' made to bolster up allied morale. Even the loss of Ley (16th September) had been explained away as part 'of our plan in New Guinea to whittle down allied land, sea and air forces before we make our attack on Australia..'

Previously (when I was in Malaya) the Coral Sea and Midway battles—May and June, 1942—were claimed as 'overwhelming victories of our peerless Navy' despite the actual results of the engagements.

We kept a list of these victories over the American Navy and the printed losses exceeded the total tonnage in 1941. But it was never explained how it was replaced, so often, after being sunk so statistically each time.

Communiques were issued which detailed engagements but they hardly ever recorded Japanese naval losses or casualties. But they always referred to 'allied cowardice'.

No Japanese planes were shot down in combat—they failed to return after running out of petrol or they had crash-dived into an enemy target, generally a battleship, cruiser, destroyer or a 'large transport heavily laden with troops'.

The American navy was 'useless during night engagements'— it was badly trained and the sailors were terrified when they sighted a Japanese warship, they became confused, panic ensued and they fired blindly at each other before fleeing from destruction. On land, in the air and on the sea, one Japanese warrior 'inspired by love of country and loyalty to Tenno Heika is more than a match for ten craven enemy fighting without a cause.'

The fight to a finish on Attu and Kiska (May and June, 1943) was extolled and cited as evidence that 'the Spirit of Bushido and Yamato-damashi animated a mere handful of Japanese warriors who scorned to surrender. They fought to the end against over-whelming forces of the enemy. They died to a man. They shed their last drop of blood to prove to Americans the impossibility of inflicting final defeat on the 100 million loyal subjects of Japan.'

The main object of Japanese propaganda was to destroy the material advantages of the enemy by postulating the theory that the 'Japanese fighting spirit' completely discounted it. No matter how many aircraft, warships or soldiers were ranged against Japan she could not be defeated because the enemy lacked morale and were nothing but 'armed cowards'. To foster this thesis the communiques, and the broadcasts, stated whereas one or two Japanese destroyers had been destroyed ramming American aircraft carriers for every minor loss of that kind at least ten enemy vessels were put out of action: for every aircraft lost the enemy lost twenty in the air or on the ground. Over and over again this nonsense was blared by Tokyo radio and re-broadcast in all asiatic and foreign langauges from captured stations in occupied territory.

Despite this distortion of fact the truth began to make itself heard, at home and abroad: Japan was no longer winning the war—the official spokesman failed to explain the loss of Bougain-ville, Solomon Islands, or the naval disaster when an entire convoy—and escort—were destroyed by allied aircraft in the Bismark Sea.

This disaster ended the threat to Australia but the central theme was not the loss of men and ships but the heroic end of Admiral Yamamoto (C.-in C. Navy) who set an example to all Japan by ji-metsu (self destruction) in atonement for failure in the service of Tenno Heika. *

ii. Army and Navy disagree regarding policy. Exit Tojo

The Navy wanted to cut its losses early in 1944—to shorten the l-o-c to north of the equator and to convoy the army out of Pacific bases while there was still time and while there was enough tonnage to do so. The numerous lanes of communi-cation, radiating from Japan, could no longer be kept open with-out crippling the navy to a dangerous point. Fuel was in short supply, transportation of men and material for an attack on Australia was out of the question.

* See Appendix XI.

The decision of the Army to retain islands in the South Pacific, dominated by superior naval and air forces, could not be justified by the remote possibility of a dramatic success like the bombing of Pearl Harbour. Japan had not the yards or the raw material necessary to cope with the gigantic task of building up the naval or merchant tonnage required to support Tojo's military adventures 5,000 miles from his base of supply. The bid for an Empire in Greater East Asia had failed, the war was not lost and it was time to consider ending it in Japan's favour. *

General Tojo, and the General Staff, understood the dangers of the situation but they refused to evacuate territory without inflicting heavy casualties on the enemy. The 'Army' held the opinion (in the winter of 1943/44) that Russia would be defeated and then Germany would make a compromise-peace with the allies. In that event Japan would be left in a strong bargaining position—able to dictate terms of peace on which she would cease hostilities in the Far East.

Despite the early disagreement on major policy, men and munitions poured out of Japan. The Navy did what it could to protect convoys and units of the army were strongly re-inforced in the Phillipines, Borneo and in the South Pacific. Munition dumps were made as far south as Rabaul and every effort made to hold occupied territory to the bitter end. But things went from bad to worse in 1944. In February, Truk was attacked by an American task-force, 200 Japanese aircraft and 20 ships were lost. This was followed by attacks on Guam, Saipan, and Tinian In March, Manus (Admiralty Islands) was occupied by American troops. *

All this 'bad news' leaked out. 'Mainichi' and 'Asahi' began to criticise the 'official spokesman' for deliberately misleading the public by communique and broadcasting: the 'spokesman' was dismissed and the criticism subsided in the general interest of national unity. Then, not for the first time, there was blunt criticism of Tojo's miscalculations in the drive against India and Australia. The inspiration of naval officers could be detected in the 'conspiracy' against Tojo himself.

On 18th July, 1944, General Tojo was 'compelled' to hand in his resignation to the Tenno because the Navy declined to risk the battle-fleet to hold a chain of South Sea Islands of little

* See Appendix XI and XIII.

value to Japan. The uninformed masses, in factory and on the land, were dismayed by the dramatic exit of their hero, Tojo: Tojo who had promised certain Victory in 1944. They were even more depressed when he was succeeded by General Koiso as Prime Minister: Koiso had retired from the Army in 1938 and was appointed Governor General of Korea on 29th May, 1942.

It was the loss of Saipan, 8th July, 1944, which impelled the 'behind -the-scenes'movement to act against Tojo. The 'Jushin' —Elder Statesmen—composed of ex-premiers, co-operated with Marquis Kido (Lord Privy Seal), and Admirals Yonai, Inouye, Takagi and Okada. It was the recognised 'constitutional method' of blocking the functions of government: the naval element refused to serve in Tojo's cabinet. Admiral Shimada (Navy Minister since October, 1941) precipitated the 'crisis' by resigning office on 17th July, then Admiral Yonai refused to serve as minister-without-portfolio.

General Tojo resigned: General Koiso retired as Governor General, Korea, and formed the new cabinet on 22nd July Admiral Yonai became Vice-Premier and Navy Minister—and that ended the 'crisis'!

General Koiso was one of the pillars of the 'Imperial Rule Assistance Association', and an *active member* of the Black Dragon Society. His 'policy' was linked with that of Baron Hiranuma, and—like Hiranuma—he was an extreme 'anti-communist'. The new cabinet contained five members who had served under Hiranuma in 1939. Koiso and Tojo were not bosom friends, their personal ambitions conflicted, but they had one thing in common—they were steeped in Araki's kodo.

The next step, taken to lessen the control of policy by the army, was the formation in August of a Supreme War Direction Council made up of Premier, Foreign Minister, Army and Navy Ministers, and the Army and Navy Chiefs of Staff. The new council had direct access to the Tenno and it became the controlling authority in the country. However, to strengthen his personal position, General Koiso became a member of Imperial Headquarters with *equal status* to the Army and Navy Chiefs of Staff, and his action was sanctioned by the Tenno. *

General Koiso announced that there would be no change of

* See Appendix X.

policy—adding that Japan had 'a secret weapon which would confound the United States of America'. Perhaps he had in mind the many balloons, for bombing American towns, or the hundreds of midget submarines, or the super-battleships 'Musashi', 'Yamato' and the converted 'Shinano'. Some of the balloons crossed the Pacific Ocean and did minor damage when their gadgets exploded. But the change of cabinet had no effect on the progress of the war—and there was no attempt to conceal the bad news from the people.

The new 'policy' seemed to be to prepare the Japanese to fight on alone after 'Germany joined Italy in accepting unconditional surrender'. Inspired articles appeared all dealing with the probable attitude of the U.S.S.R. towards Japan if Germany capitulated. These articles differed in tone from those of June, 1944, after 'D. Day' when the 'opening of the second-front was *exactly* what Germany wanted in order to defeat the Allies before invading England.' But the 'Mainichi' had an excellent news-service from Sweden, Spain, Switzerland, South America, Russia and Germany so I was able to report progress-day by day.

Normandy landings were fully reported, as much space was given to Berlin versions as to those emanating from London or New York. 'Mainichi' had well informed correspondents in Geneva and in Stockholm so I had to work at full stretch in the 'benjo' to get material for the Omori 'Times'. My collaborators, chaps in the outside working parties, did a marvellous job smuggling in the forbidden newspapers. Their ingenuity matched their courage and they outwitted the censorship even when searched to the buff.

iii. 'Akirameru'

Akirameru is a word often used by Japanese to express the idea of abandoning all hope, relinquishing a plan or accepting the inevitable—resigning oneself to fate.

We had an interpreter named Ohnishi. He frequently gave me 'lectures' on culture and kodo. One day, during one of my many punishment periods (standing at attention for hours outside the camp office) he asked me if I understood the meaning of akirameru? I replied in the affirmative, adding that in my case it was no longer akirameru but 'temmei wo shiru'—taking life philosophically.

Ohnishi slapped me: 'I've told you before—the word of the Imperial Household is Law. Tenno Heika is greater than your God—there is no future for people like you.'

My crime ,on that occasion was this. We were handed copies of the 'Japan Times' and ordered to comment on an official communique which announced a 'Great Victory'. In my 'report' I pointed out that many American battleships, aircraft carriers, cruisers and destroyers had been 'sunk' without the loss of a single Japanese warship—large or small. But, the Americans landed on Guadalcanal, Santa Isabel and Bougainville and the communique did not explain the arrival of the American troops to my satisfaction.

Such comment from a 'slave' infuriated the Camp Commandant—he had me on his shinto-mat and asked me to explain the swift and complete defeat of the British in Malaya. I did so. Then he said that as I had been afraid to die for my country I had lost my status as a soldier and should bow my head in shame and not be sarcastic.

The communique was issued by the Imperial Household and was not based on the theories of a coward. I expressed regret and was told to rewrite my report in Japanese! I did that and had to stand at attention for three hours until Lt.-Col. Suzuki accepted the translation—without comment.

To provide material for propaganda Omori Camp was used as a show-place to demonstrate to young conscripts (en-route to the front) the degenerates they were fighting against. Time and again these groups would invade the camp led by guides and junior officers.

They would receive instructions regarding the habits of the captives, told to inspect them at close quarters and then to parade on the square where they were lectured by Staff-officers from the War Office. On all these occasions I was confined in one of the camp offices to prevent me from overhearing any of the 'secret instructions' being yelled at the youngsters on the square.

At other times mixed groups of newspaper men, artists, painters, authors, educationalists, members of the upper and the lower house visited us. I was confined to my cubicle but they interviewed, painted, sketched or photogtaphed many of the others to obtain 'copy' and 'local colour' for magazines newspapers and the movies.

But I did not get off scot-free. I was frequenly quizzed by Tokyo kempei and interrogated by officers from the Imperial General Staff Headquarters. For hours at a time I would be asked for my 'opinion' regarding the probability of friction between America and England, or between the Anglo-Saxons and the U.S.S.R. over the non-opening of the second-front, or if I still thought that 'Churchill' had the confidence of 'Stalin'? Did we 'trust' Russians? Did we trust Chinese? How did I think the War would end—would America make a separate peace with Japan if Germany invaded England?

It was rather silly—question and answer. But they took the trouble to make endless notes and were generous with their cigarettes. Perhaps the most interesting of my 'visitors' was Major F. Uemura from the operations section of the General Staff.

He came from Colonel Sugita (Yamashita's I.O.) who had been promoted to a job in the War Office. Uemura was interested in air-borne operations and had an English translation of a German document dealing with the subject. Sugita sent him to me to help him in his study of the German operations in Europe and the Middle East. It was an interesting document dealing with every aspect of what was to me a new method of waging war, but it was also a mass of technicalities beyond my ability to translate into Japanese military jargon. However, Uemura could read English so I got more information than I gave him on the numerous visits before he got the hang of correct heights, release speeds, glider v. ground defence, advantages of glider over other methods of troop dropping on aerodromes, etc., etc.

iv. Shinto to defeat Christianity

But the most interesting person I met during my sojourn in Omori was Professor Fujisawa. Fujisawa was an associate of Dr. Nitobe and had been connected with the working of the League of Nations, in Geneva. A brilliant scholar, widely travelled, he had mixed with the intelligentsia of America and Europe and his English was perfect. But his contact with 'western civilization' had convinced him (?) that the salvation of mankind could be only attained by its conversion to Shinto with Tenno Heika as the spiritual head and Tokyo as the centre of the universe having Japanese culture as the basis of international morality.

Fujisawa must not be confused with a babbler like Major Toyama of Changi. He came to Omori with the blessing of the War Office to lecture prisoners of war on Amaterasu, Jimmu Tenno, Shinto, Kodo and the divine Showa Tenno. Unfortunately the PoW officers who were ordered to attend his lecture in the cold bath-house were already half-starved, nearly frozen to death, bug-eaten and all too familiar with genuine Japanese culture to be interested in the mythology of the Yamato-jin.

Undismayed by his cool reception, Fujisawa changed his line of approach to the mass of unbelievers clad in rags and covered with boils and ulcers. He instructed Ohnishi to select a few beriberi intellectual captives on which to try his new gospel of salvation. I was one of those ordered to attend Fujisawa's special lectures in a nice warm room in the Camp offices.

Fujisawa regaled us with tea, cakes and cigarettes and then —having set us at ease—explained the idea behind this fraternization. He wanted volunteers, candidates for intensive instruction in Shinto, who would be taken from the camp and housed in comfortable surroundings where they would have leisure to meditate on the teaching of the thirteen sects of Shinto.

There were twenty-million practising disciples of Shinto— twenty-million could not be wrong? Surely we did not want to miss this opportunity of learning about the great way of the gods —Kamu-nagara? And, he reminded me, one of the articles of faith of Konko-kyo—which was akin to Christianity—ran:—

'If you would enter the WAY OF TRUTH, first of all drive away the clouds of doubt in your heart.'

I pointed out that Kawate Bunjiro founded Konko in 1859 and died in 1883—two years *after* I was born—whereas Christianity had existed for 1944 years and was introduced into Japan at about A.D. 1500. I preferred the revelation of Christ to that of Kawate Bunjiro or of any of the other Shinto sect founders.

Fujisawa was there to teach, not to argue. His opinion was that Japan was fighting a holy war against the materialism of western civilization: Christianity had failed and there were ethical advantages to mankind in Shinto. I agreed that there was quite a lot wrong with mankind, and the world, but doubted if the democratic nations would substitute Shinto for Christianity—for religious or administrative purposes. And I was quite sure neither the President of the United States, or King George VI of England would accept the Tenno as their spiritual father. Also, the nationalization of religion was out of fashion in the West: State-Shinto, with the Tenno venerated as divine, would not be acceptable to Christians or heathens in Europe or America. For better or for worse there could be no renunciation of Jesus Christ as the central figure in Christianity.

Fujisawa took the matter quite seriously—he wanted us as converts, so he was patient and tolerant. He agreed, it was not an easy problem to solve. It required serious study, it would take time—Rome was not built in a day. In his opinion a World Federation, based on Shinto, with Tenno the acknowledged spiritual head of a universal religion was by no means impossible. Already, Japan was the leader of Greater East Asia. Shinto, the basis of her success in arms, was spreading throughout China and India and it would reach Europe and America in time. Not in our time perhaps but in years to come when people had time and leisure to meditate on the real reason for strife and misery in the world.

We had three of these 'heart-to-heart' discussions behind closed doors. Shinto, he argued, must defeat Christianity in the end and pave the way for everlasting peace. We should welcome the opportunity to become missionaries of the true faith.

Suddenly, just as Fujisawa was about to close the third session, the door was flung open by Corporal Watanabe the n.c.o. responsible for discipline in Omori Camp. He demanded to know on whose authority Fujisawa, a civilian, was holding a meeting with prisoners of war behind a closed door?

Fujisawa was dumbfounded. He rushed out of the room to make his complaint to the Colonel: we were ordered back to barracks: that was the last we saw of Professor Fujisawa, but not of Corporal Watanabe.

v. Corporal Watanabe. 'God' in the Shinto State

Watanabe Matsuhiro, alias 'The Bird' or 'The Animal', was thoroughly impregnated with the virus of kodo the poison which had been injected into his blood-stream by the professors of shinto sadism. He was not a victim of circumstances but the personification of mythological hocus-pocus and the willing medium of Shinto propaganda. He claimed ultra-mundane perception in addition to divine authority to punish prisoners of war. He was definitely ego-centric, had no reverence for the Tenno, for he was kami in his own right—he was coequal with kempei and Tenno, the tritagonist in the Kamu-nagara puppet show.

No prisoner of war could fathom Watanabe's mentality: he was no killer with club, bayonet or sword but he superimposed a sustained mental intimidation and his persecution was planned to incite retaliation so that he could call in the guard to shed the blood of his victims. Many of my sturdy colleagues wanted to beat him to death and take the consequences but, I explained to them, that would only mean their own death and would have no effect on the fundamental principles of Japanese PoW administration.

Watanabe's first victims were men whose legs were covered with ulcers, or men who had walnut-sized boils—men with high fever, with lumbago or beri-beri—men who could hardly walk from bed to latrine. He would order them to stand upright in order to knock them down—for no reason at all. Just to show that he was 'Watanabe' responsible for discipline!

This animal was born in Kobe. I knew his family and his eldest sister was married to Lt. Okazaki who was the first Camp Commandant at Changi. He received a good education and was at a Tokyo University before being conscripted and he came to Omori in November, 1943 and remained until the end of 1944.

The fame of this savage spread to every PoW camp in Japan and he was never restrained by any one, least of all by Lt.-Colonel Suzuki or Colonel Sakeba. For a few months I was able to check him. But, as interpreter and intercessor—between madman and victim—it was written in the stars that he would end by venting his spleen on me.

Not content with individual punishment he instituted his own system of collective punishment on the slightest provocation.

And when he was tired of swinging his club or fencing-stick he would retire to his room leaving us standing for hours watched by armed sentries. But he was not alone in his madness. His brutal methods were encouraged by Cadet Fuji, the M.O., 2/Lt.

Kato, camp supervisor, and 'Dr.' Tokuda of Shinagawa Hospital.

Tokuda—'The Butcher'—never allowed a patient to remain in Hospital if there was a reason for discharging him, Fuji would never pass a man *unfit for duty* unless he was on the verge of physical collapse, Watanabe saw to it that every man, sick or well, *paraded* for work, and Kato included every man in Omori Camp as 'fit for work', in camp or in a working party.

When a draft of PoW arrived, or semi-convalescent came in from Shinagawa, they were paraded for Watanabe. He knocked them down, used judo on them, punched and slapped them to 'correct bad attitude to Corporal Watanabe.' But he did nothing on the sly—it was done in the open with the knowledge and consent of all the camp staff from Colonel to office-girl. He boasted to me that his 'authority' transcended that of Colonel Sakeba and that all he did was in agreement with Japanese Military Law: even if he did kill one of us he could not be tried or punished.

British and American medical officers who protested against Tokuda's brutality were sent to Omori to be thrashed by Watanabe—and he told them so when they arrived. Suiting his words to his actions he thrashed them directly their kit had been inspected.

One American medical officer had 'bad attitude' so he was put on 'permanent benjo fatigue' and ordered to report each evening outside the camp office window. Watanabe would then come outside, walk up to the officer, and punch him in the face. This went on, every day, for three weeks until the officer's face was black and blue and Watanabe could no longer make any impression on the pulpy flesh.

Perhaps there was epilepsy in his family to account for the electrical activity of his brain for his bad spells, when he behaved like a raving lunatic, lasted best part of a week.

The 'attack' would come on suddenly. One moment he would be talking normally then he would see red, shriek like a fiend lashing out right and left and ordering 'all officers Tenko!'

But his most astonishing characteristic was vanity and his craving to be saluted! He issued 'orders' that he was to be saluted inside and outside barracks: when he was sighted by a PoW that individual must shout, 'Kei-rei! Kei-rei!' and all others in the vicinity must stop what they were doing, stand at attention and shout—loud and clear—Kei-rei! Kei-rei! and remain at attention until he said 'Yasume! (stand at ease).

Not only that. But when they shouted 'Kei-rei!' they must bow in his direction, with the back inclined at an angle of 45 degrees, with eyes cast down in respect.

Nothing delighted him more than to rush into a full barrack and collect his quota of kei-rei's. Later on he issued further instructions: 'Corporal Watanabe's office-window, opened or closed, must be saluted by prisoners of war passing near to it or when it can be seen as they move about the camp.' The 'Bird' would take cover (outside the office) with a baseball-bat and wait to flog any person who failed to salute the window, so you had to salute shadow and substance of Watanabe.

After the raids on Tokyo commenced we had an influx of U.S. airforce personnel and these terribly undernourished officers and men were handed over to Watanabe for 'special treatment' to improve their attitude to Japan. Complaints to Suzuki or to Sakeba resulted in the intensification of the punishment for every trivial offence, and it is safe to say that more allied prisoners of war were struck by Watanabe than by any other n.c.o. in the Japanese army.

Watanabe tried very hard for more than six-months to end my life. He would have succeeded but for the fact that in December, 1944 he was promoted to Sergeant and sent to another camp. For some time I had been suffering from beri-beri, yellow jaundice and diarrhoea and was down to 95 lbs. in weight. His favourite punishment for me was to have me shout 'Kei-rei!' and bow (outside his office window) five-hundred times and then to stand at attention for a few hours. But he tired of that. He caught me standing without my fingers fully stretched and set about me like a wild-cat. When he had finished my left eardrum was broken, both eyes closed and cut, face bruised, mouth and lips cut. I was in bed for a couple of weeks, then he returned to the attack.

He caught me with a lighted cigarette in the passage between the officers' cubicles. That was a serious crime—now he *would* teach me a lesson! I followed him inside the special-prisoners' compound—he closed the gate and then marked out a small square with his fencing-stick. I stood in the square while he beat me about the face and head with his stick. He resented the way I took that punishment so he started to ram the end of the stick into my throat which was much more painful.

Still he was not satisfied—my attitude was still bad—so he dropped his stick and tried to throttle me but I twisted clear and he fell headlong into a slit-trench.

I bent down and helped him out. He dusted his clothes and I handed him his fencing-stick, resuming my stance in the little square and waited for the next part of the performance. But he walked away, told me to follow, went into his office and left me to stand outside for an hour.

Still later, he told me that the air-raids had given him some good ideas. My 'duty' was to report to Watanabe for orders— day or night—during an air-raid, or an air-raid alarm. I reported the 'alert', cancellation of 'alert', air-raid warning, cancellation of air-raid warning and cancellation of alert!

All-clear was seldom sounded until raiders had left the coast of Japan so it became a 24 hours tour of duty. The most exacting test commenced on 22nd November when northwest Tokyo was bombed for the first time. Alerts followed every few hours until 27th November when B 29's plastered the Capital and the Omori waterfront.

These daylight attacks were followed on 28/29th November by the first night attack on Tokyo. By this time I was so weak that I could hardly walk between bunk and latrine. However, on 13th December, Nagoya was bombed in a daylight raid: 18/19th there were night attacks on Omura (Kyushu) followed on 19/20th by raids on Tokyo. A lull until 22nd when the A.A.F., straffed Nagoya—an interval until 24th when Tokyo was bombed once more.

I entered Watanabe's cage and reported the all-clear—for 10 days I had no real sleep and was dazed. The 'Animal' reached for his fencing-stick and wanted to know why the fire-buckets, outside the cook-house, were empty? I stared at him. The 'Animal' roared again as I clutched at my throat, trying to speak —then I collapsed. Dr. Goad (our M.O.) and Fuji came in to the room: Fuji laughed, 'Kakke sho-shin' (beri-beri heart-failure). Watanabe laughed—'James—kakke sho-shin!'

It took me many weeks to recover but it was worth it all for Watanabe was transferred at the end of the month and the camp lost its most savage animal, Watanabe the 'god' in the Shinto State.

vi. INVASION *of the sacred soil of* JAPAN

Although newspapers carried long descriptions of the fighting on the 'second front' they kept us well informed of German 'secret weapons' which would force the British to accept surrender without the invasion of England. According to one account 'hundreds of wireless controlled planes are being sent over London. They come like a shower of shooting-stars and drop their bomb-loads to the consternation of the deluded people who are fleeing from the South Coast of England.'

However, on 15th June, 1944 we had our own 'shooting-stars' over Tokyo. We received the 'alert' which was followed by air-raid warnings but put it down to another practice. Suddenly we heard anti-aircraft fire in the direction of north Tokyo and as we watched the bursts of shells we saw, to our delight, nine large bombers speeding southward. They were travelling fast, in perfect formation, and looked like gigantic geese as they went through the light cloud.

Our expert American airforce personnel identified them as super-fortresses—B 29's—and estimated their height at 15,000 feet. We were much too elated to trouble about height, airspeed, type or altitude. They were our bombers scurrying home after bombing 'Target area No. 1: Tokyo.'—and that was the beginning of the end. They came and they went without being molested by Japanese fighter aircraft and the following day the Moji correspondent of the 'Mainichi' reported: 'A few B 29's appeared over North Kyushu. They were destroyed before any bombs were released.'

That was good news, the Moji target would be the Yawata Steel Works. Regarding the Tokyo raid the communique read: —'Several B 29's dropped bombs on Tokyo temples and schools —our fighter patrols intercepted them and they were all destroyed off the coast.'

We had many working-parties in the Tokyo area and some of the 'overseers' were civilians without the real kodo spirit. With the first appearance of B 29's the air was full of rumours— men in the working-parties brought in 'news' of a landing by American troops in Kyushu and this rumour persisted for days although it originated in the air-raid I have mentioned and was based on nothing more substantial. Still, after 15th June, the War Office issued instructions that on no account must newspapers of any kind be allowed to get into the hands of Prisoners of War.

An intensive search of the camp followed: our personal papers were taken from us (including harmless photographs and books published in Japan) and these were pawed over by Watanabe and Kato. All 'suspicious papers' were destroyed on the spot the rest were returned with the censorship stamp imprinted and the possession of any 'paper' without the stamp was a crime to receive major imprisonment.

We took avoiding action, to smuggle-in newspapers in bits and pieces, and the cross-word puzzles duly appeared with the 'correct answers' in miniature. There was no landing in Kyushu. On 6th July, Sasebo Naval Yard and Yawata Steel Works (Kyushu) were visited by more B29's: Caen (Normandy) fell to us a few days later so we were having the best of both ends of the world.

Despite the 'invincible bird-men of Japan' the U.S.A.F. continued to bomb their targets from bases like Guam and Saipan which had been captured in July. General Koiso was as helpless as General Tojo against the offensive of the super-fortresses: no amount of kodo or propaganda could alter facts now that the masses could see for themselves how easily the enemy bombed them and returned to their bases overseas.

Nothing prevented millions of Japanese from knowing that, in turn, Nagasaki, Yawata, Sasebo, Omura, Musashima, Nagoya and Tokyo had been bombed regularly from June to December, 1944. They saw the damage to aircraft works and industrial areas, and—because the whole country knew about it—the newspapers were allowed to report the 'incidents' giving approximate number of the enemy aircraft shot down and brief mentions of damage and casualities.

Invasion by air was an accomplished fact. Invasion of the sacred soil of Japan was in the offing and it began to impress itself on the thoughts of the people and the Government. More than 2,000,000 of Tokyo's inhabitants were evacuated—dispersal of the population was ordered in Kobe, Osaka and Nagoya. A.R.P. was now of more importance than reliance on the 'Kamikaze Corps' although the pilgrims flocked to the shrines, rang the bells and clapped their hands as in the days of the Mongol invasions.

In our district, thousands of houses were demolished to form fire-breaks: Omori—midway between Tokyo and Yokohama—was not a safe area. Repeated protests, regarding our safety, were made by the British and the American Governments but they were all ignored. Our camps were closed down *after* they had been destroyed by fire or bombing, and *after* we had suffered casualties. Not a single Representative of the Red Cross—Japanese or Foreign—was allowed to visit Omori until late in 1945. The policy of the Japanese Government was to extract the maximum work out of PoW's and to billet them in places most convenient to the 'war work' they were compelled to undertake. There never was an intention to protect them from danger by working away from legitimate war targets which were certain to be bombed. I was told that PoW Camps were the insurance policies taken out for the protection of the munition workers in adjacent plant, or nearby aerodromes.

The chronological stages of the defeat of Japan, by the air-force of the United States of America, is detailed in subsequent chapters.

Writing on the wall was visible in July, when Tojo resigned, and the unconditional surrender of Japan was not brought about by the dropping of two-atom-bombs. It was the result of U.S. Naval Operations: the overwhelming amphibious all-in battle tactics of task-forces followed by systematic bombing of Japan from June, 1944 to August, 1945.

During World War II, frequent reference was made by many Japanese—including Emperor Hirohito—to the 100,000,000 people who would never surrender—the 100-million patriots who would defend the sacred soil of Japan. This figure refers to the total poulation of the 'Empire' which—according to the national census of October, *1935* was as follows:—

Japan proper	69,251,265	
Korea	22,898,695	
Formosa	5,212,719	
Sakhalin	331,949	
Manchuria	1,656,763	(S. M. Ry. zone)
South Seas	102,238	
	99,453,629	
i. Residents abroad	872,807	
	100,326,436	

i. Asia	339,998	Europe	2,954	N. America	174,230
Africa	201	Oceania	153,684	S. America	201,740

Japanese residents abroad in 1949 may not be quite so patriotic or so numerous as they were in 1935 but it is not without
interest to mention that in 1935 the total *foreign residents in Japan*
was 32,641 *including* 22,741 Chinese; i.e.:—

Chinese	22,741
Americans	2,082
British	1,953
Russians	1,457
Germans	1,254
French	512
Br. Indians	395
Canadians	311
Others	1,936
	32,641

Another point to remember about the unconditional surrender is that in the total of 69,251,265 given above the proportion of men to women is about the same:—
Men 34,731,860.   Women 34,519,405.

None of the women went through the conscript system and
although they were not by any means free from kodoism they
never were sadists like the men.

CHAPTER XIV

AIR WAR AGAINST JAPAN
FIRST PHASE

i. Overall offensive (1944)

The air war, waged by U.S. Army and Navy Air Forces against the mainland of Japan, entered a definite offensive phase in November, 1944. Aircraft factories and steel-works were the first targets for formations of superfortresses (B 29's) from the operational base Guam, in the Marianas. Distance from base to targets exceeded 1,200 miles of flight over the Pacific Ocean which was not yet clear of enemy submarines or surface craft. Not more than one hundred planes were used in any one strike and bomb-load was limited to $2\frac{1}{2}$-ton at the outset. But when the ground organization was perfected on various other island bases the bomb-load reached 8-ton and number of aircraft used in one raid varied between five hundred and eight hundred-and-twenty, chiefly B 24's and B 29's.

The pattern of destruction was clearly defined in a few months: widespread bombing of industrial targets being accomplished with what transpired to be a minimum loss in planes and personnel. The cumulative effect of this destruction was to coin a new word for 'Akirameru'—'B. NIJU-KU.'—B 29! Against the power to destroy of B. NIJU-KU. the *Kami-kaze* was of no value and long before the end Japanese had abandoned all hope and resigned themselves to fate. They did not denounce Shinto, or rail against Tenno Heika, it was another instance of *shi-kata-ga-nai*—it can not be helped.

It may simplify my explanation of the *over-all offensive* of the U.S.A.F. if I zone Japan as follows:—

(a) KYUSHU—14 target areas.   (b) SHIKOKOKU—6 target areas.
(c) WEST HONSHU, from Shimonoseki to Osaka—15 target areas.
(d) CENTRAL HONSHU, north and south of Nagoya—14 target areas.
(e) NORTH HONSHU, from Tokyo to Aomori—with 20 target areas.

Japanese official reports (after the surrender) disclosed that in those sixty-nine areas no fewer than 260,000 people were killed, 412,000 injured, 2,250,000 buildings levelled to the ground and 9,000,000 people rendered homeless.

The *total* civilian casualties in England and Wales, from all air-raids was 60,854 killed and 86,159 seriously injured. Japan's casualties, mentioned above, *do not include* those caused by the use of two-atom-bombs. Those casualites were estimated at 110, 000 killed and 60,000 injured.

During November, 1944 the heaviest raid was staged by *100 B 29's* dropping *250* tons of bombs—on 1st August, 1945, *820 B 29's* unloaded *6,600* tons of explosives on five towns in North Kyushu. That was a week before the first atom-bomb was used against Hiroshima.

The July-August 1944 raids were in the nature of test strikes against zones (a), (d) and (e). These were followed on 11th and 21st November by strikes against *Omura* aircraft works in Kyushu, and on 24th against the larger *Musashino* plant, manufacturing aircraft engines and combat aircraft, in *N.W. Tokyo*. These attacks were then switched, on 27th and 28/29th, against the industrial areas of Tokyo.

In the second week of December there was a series of raids on the Mitsubishi aircraft assembly plant at *Nagoya*—13th, 17th, 22nd and night raid of 18/19th. At the same time other formations attacked *Omura* aircraft works in Kyushu, on 19th, and on 19/20th *Tokyo* was heavily attacked as a 'softener' before another raid on 24th on Musashino (Tokyo) aircraft works.

The object of all these raids was to slow down aircraft production, test air defences, and to train personnel for the pinpointing raids which were to precede the saturation raids. According to newspapers I got hold of, 'few of the raiders returned to their base . . . many shot down by ground-defence or by combat in the air . . . very little damage done except to residential areas . . . '

We saw quite enough of the fires, and the destruction, in the Yokohama-Tokyo area. From the camp we did see at least six of the B 29's brought down in flames, and saw some of the crew bail out, but from the amount of criticism in the papers, regarding inefficient A.R.P., it was evident that damage had been heavy in the Capital.

During October, 1944 there had been combined operations against Formosa, Pescadores and Ryukyu Islands. Carrier-borne aircraft of the U.S. Pacific Fleet making attacks on 9th and 17th and B 29's on 14th 16th and 17th. Japanese reports were very cautious but they made the usual claim to have inflicted heavy losses: later on the American version, claiming the destruction of 900 aircraft on the ground and in the air, and the sinking and damaging of 300 ships of all kinds, was 'denounced' as rubbish!

But there was a change in tone when Iwojima (Bonins) was shelled by U.S. warships and bombed by B 29's on 11th November. And when this was repeated, on 25th and 26th December, and Iwojima was bombed by carrier-borne aircraft and shelled by heavier units of the U.S. Pacific fleet, it was agreed that there was 'war on the home front' and that there had been attacks on Matsuwa (Kuriles) by an American task-force on 21st November.

At the end of December, General Koiso broadcast to the nation calling for greater effort to meet the 'national emergency' and reaffirming the intention of the armed forces to defend the 'sacred soil to the bitter end.' There was no promise of Victory in 1945, but General Tojo, aided by the Black Dragon and other kais, was very active in the country 'encouraging the people' and urging them to face the future with confidence because the invaders would be utterly destroyed directly they set foot ashore. His meetings were 'well attended' and—according to the reports —he was applauded and promised loyal support in the country's hour of need.

In Europe, British war casualties were 1,100,000, Bulgaria had capitulated to the U.S.S.R. and her army had reached the Polish-Czech border: British para-troopers had been 'annihilated' at Arnheim, the allied thrust into Germany had been halted but there was no indication that England was about to be invaded. Still—according to the press—there were German secret weapons and this seemed to be confirmed early in November when Mr. Churchill announced before his departure for Paris, that Germany was using the V2 rocket-bomb on London.

As I did not know the difference between a V1 and a V2—a flying-bomb and a rocket-bomb—my 'editorial comment' on that news merely confused my 'readers'.

ii. B 29's and carrier-borne aircraft. January-March 1945

Tinian and Saipan bases were available in January, 1945, but —according to the press—were not used until middle of February for attacks on Japan by super-fortresses. This may have been correct because strikes from carrier-borne aircraft began early in the new year and the heavier B 29 raids followed.

January targets were aircraft plant. The main raids were on Omura, Akashi, Nagoya and Tokyo by B 29's from Guam on 3rd, 6th, 9th, 14th, 19th, 23rd and 27th. On 4th February the factories, aircraft plant and shipbuilding yards at *Kobe* were thoroughly bombed for the first time. A week later *Nakajima* aircraft factory was bombed by 100 B 29's, and on 15th February 150 B 29's unloaded on *Nagoya:* 'Mainichi' commented that Guam, Tinian and Saipan were being used by A.A.F.

Soon after dawn, 15th February, dozens of navy-fighters and dive-bombers roared over Omori camp and we had a 'grandstand' view of overhead dog-fights and thrilling dives on the nearby aerodrome.

They were from U.S. carriers—hundreds of them—and they continued their strike the next day on the Tokyo-Yokohama aerodromes with (according to the press) a loss of 'more than 200 planes'. We did not see more than a flash of the raids and saw only a few planes crash but an American report gave their losses as 49—all types—and claimed to have destroyed 659 enemy aircraft on the ground or in the air in addition to sinking 36 vessels. These 'figures' (on both sides) seemed to us rather exaggerated after the experience we had during the Battle of Britain.

On 18/19th there was a B 29 raid on Tokyo. This night-raid was followed on 19th by daylight attack on Nakajima and Musashino aircraft plant (and industrial targets) in Tokyo area by more than 150 B 29's. Fires started during the night were plastered again and the fire-fighting services were occupied at full stretch for the remainder of the week. But the most destructive raid, to date, was on 25th February when *200 B 29's*, escorted by navy-fighters, pressed home attacks on military, air and naval installations in the Yokohama-Tokyo area.

T

March Incendiary Raids. On Tokyo: Osaka: Kobe and Nagoya

MARCH, 1945, will be a 'Red-letter Month' for many years to
come for the residents of Tokyo, Osaka, Kobe and Nagoya. It
may be called the 'Yake-tsuchi Jidai'—the Burned Earth Period
of the Showa Era when everything was reduced to ashes by
B NIJU-KU—when everything was 'yaki harete shimatsu ta';
Tokyo in flames and the Palace of Tenno Heika exposed to the
venom of the dreaded *B Niju-ku*—the flying fortresses of a relentless enemy.

B-NIJU-KU took on an additional meaning. *Niju* may be
translated, *twenty* or *double*, *ku* may be translated *nine* or *pain*,
suffering affliction, *strain* or *trouble*: the characters are different but
the pronunciation is the same. So, long before the atom-bomb
disintegrated them, their agony had been doubled by B 29's
loads of *high-explosives* and *incendiaries*. From March to July,
1945, B 29's dropped *100,000 TONS* of incendiaries on 66 towns
and cities wiping out 170 square miles of closely populated
streets, more or less legitimate 'total-war targets'.

Destruction of Tokyo (March 9/10th, 1945)

Routine targets were bombed on 3rd and 4th March by formations of 100-150 B 29's. From 5th to 9th, 'Photo Joe' came
over exactly at noon when the cook-house orderly yelled 'Come
and get it!' 'Joe' took long-distance snaps for the A.A.F. Intelligence Corps and our ex-B 24 American airmen, now prisoners
in Omori, declared that 'Joe's visits' indicated 'something big
hitting the news'. They were correct. The alert came in at 11
p.m. and soon after the alert the air-raid warnings were being
sounded all over Tokyo.

About midnight there was the drone of aircraft as the first
wave came in from the north-east. They were travelling in two
streams—from north-east to south-west and from north to
south-east.

Ground defence went into action as the first fires appeared in
Oji-ku, south of the junction of Sumida-gawa and Arakawa
waterway almost at the same time as the leading planes crossed
overhead.

Planes were flying very low. A strong wind was fanning the
fires as wave after wave came over and dropped 'baskets' of fresh
incendiaries over the industrial districts north and east of the

Imperial Palace and the factory area to the south-west, bordering Tokyo Bay. Wind direction was north to south. We were in the centre of the south-west coastal strip—between Sumidagawa and Tamagawa—and well inside the danger zone from the spreading fires.

Wave followed wave. Three hundred super-fortresses crossed the doomed City that early morning in March. They destroyed and then went on into the darkness beyond the flames, their bodies glistening as the beams of searchlights followed them until they were lost to sight in cloud. Wave followed wave. Like birds of ill omen, with widespread wings, they darted in and out of smoke and cloud to leave behind an incandescent holocaust.

Wave followed wave leaving behind men, women and children to roast in that furnace on the plains of old Musashi. The old windswept swamp of Musashi surrounded by a wilderness in A.D. 1590 when Tokugawa Iyeyasu came to the village of Yedo to rebuild his Castle.

Yedo Castle which Will Adams in 1601 helped Tokugawa Hidetada to reconstruct as the stronghold of the Shoguns—Yedo renamed Tokyo in 1868 when Meiji Tenno regenerated the nation—Tokyo was in flames.

Musashi—the wide plain of Musashi—so close to the sacred Fuji Yama, the 'soul of the earth'. Fuji the inspiration of the Shinto sect, Fuso Kyo, founded in 1870 to 'Cultivate the great truth of kamu-nagara and reach an understanding of the facts of life and death, and to cultivate the observances of the Imperial Land of Nippon and to make the sacred rites conform to the purposes of the Imperial Court of old'. And now the mountain sects could look down from their lofty shrines and ponder anew on the facts of life and death.

Look down on Tokyo the crematorium of millions of terrified souls of the earth threatened by the air-weapons of mass destruction. I thought of Fujisawa's dictum that 'Shinto must defeat Christianity' and, as I shaded my eyes from the glare from across the canal, I remembered the lines:—

> 'The wide plain of Musashi
> Has no hills at all;
> So the Moon has no shelter
> Sweeping o'er a sea of grass.'

Then I heard the tolling of bells and beating of drums in shrine and temple grounds of Omori where Shinto and Buddhist priest beckoned to the homeless victims of Araki's kodo. I stood on the bank and listened to the subdued voices of those across the narrow strip of water which divided friend and foe. It was as if mutual grief and sympathetic sadness was spreading the inspiration of the bells: there was no noise, no theological prayers, no calling to heaven for help in the hell of their surroundings. It was just the vibration of men, women and children whispering to comfort each other—that, and nothing more, could be heard.

Tokyo was burning! Tokyo was like the sounding board directing the emotions of the deluded to the ends of the Tenno's domain. Much water had passed under the Sumidagawa bridges since Tokugawa Hidetada banished Christians from Japan, and now—in the *yake-tsuchi Jidai,* western civilization was spreading the gospel of destruction and casting down the flaming torches into an ever-growing inferno. How times had changed!

In the early morning, hundreds of old men, women and young children from the Omori ward (now in flames) ferried themselves across the canal and took shelter on the seaward side of our wooden fence.

Clutching precious bundles they crouched down to avoid the heat from the raging furnace consuming their homes a few hundred yards away. We stared at them through knot-holes in the fence—they stared back at us. We smiled. There was so little between our chances of survival and theirs that we could only smile and hope for the best. Maybe they pinned their hope on the direction in which the wind was blowing for if it did change a few degrees the wooden fence which divided us would be our funeral bier.

And so we passed the time watching the buildings on the canal bank burst into flames and send showers of lighted paper, bits of cloth, fragments of scorched wood and other inflammable material across the water. It kept on swirling over in gusts of dense smoke until it began to scorch the fence and then the wooden barracks. We waited for the order to evacuate the camp but it never came because the wind held to its appointed course and died down with the coming of dawn.

Now and again we saw one of the super-fortresses stagger in flight, lose its place in the perfect formation, burst into flames, explode in the air or dive into the cauldron to become part and parcel of the inferno. Frequently we saw tiny dots float clear of a damaged plane and followed man and parachute drift to earth. More than once a suicide-plane would make its swift dive on its aerial target: a flash, momentary suspense after the impact, explosion in mid-air—then victor and vanquished crashed into fragments of metal and flesh and lost their identity in smoke and cloud.

Throughout the raid ground-defence was active and accurate —the B 29's flew in low and bombed from about 10,000 feet as against the usual 20-24,000 feet of the daylight attacks on the same targets. But, considering the volume of *flak*, we counted less planes put out of action than there should have been in view of the close formation and bombing height. Not more than fourteen came down which was a small price to pay for the destruction of from *twelve to fifteen square miles of the City*.

Japanese casualties were heavy—the first reports were truly fantastic, but the official statement (after the surrender) did confirm the rumours: *83,000 were killed, 102,000 were injured*— making a total of 185,000 casualties, for one raid!

The American official report stated that 1,667 tons of incendiary bombs had been dropped from an altitude of 7,000 feet.

This raid was the most destructive, to life and property, so far recorded in history. It exceeded that at Hiroshima, or at Nagasaki, when the atom-bomb was used.

All day (10th March) an acrid smell filled our nostrils in Omori camp. When the tide lapped our fences it cast up hundreds of charred bodies. We stared through the knot-holes at the men, women and children sprawled in the mud or jammed against the logs from the demolished timber-yards—men, women and children, the remains of human beings remained there to rot alongside others who floated in after other raids on the Capital.

It reminded me of the great earthquake in 1923, and the fires which followed it. I remembered standing in the compound of the Military Clothing Depot watching the crowds file past the great mound of ashes—the remains of thousands of people trapped inside that compound. That was in 1923 and if the raid had taken place then, instead of in March, 1945, the loss of life would have been greater, and the extent of the damage twice as great. But—in the intervening twenty-two years—Tokyo had been rebuilt.

After the earthquake there was an Imperial Rescript on Reconstruction accorded to Tokyo by Hirohito (Prince Regent) and he reassured the public as to the 'unchangeable position of Tokyo as the national capital'. Tokyo was raised from a state of ruin (one half of it had been destroyed) by the expenditure of over £100,000,000. The total area was increased to 553 square kilometers and the population was nearly 6,000,000 in 1941.

Broad well-paved streets replaced narrow thoroughfares: 250 ferro-concrete buildings replaced 200 wooden primary schools: 300—(out of 668 *wooden bridges* destroyed)—stone and reinforced concrete bridges were built and another 145 'quake and fireproof bridges' erected as fire-breaks. One hundred and eighty-five of the canals and rivers were dredged and widened : five thousand of the watercourses were deepened or drained. Water-supply, over the whole area was doubled. In 1932, one million people were supplied by hydrants; in 1941, four million people were catered for. In 'greater Tokyo' only 2,000 of the 4,500 bridges were made of wood.

To reduce the danger of fire spreading from ward to ward fireproof zones were established and only two classes of buildings were allowed: (a) reinforced concrete or brick only, (b) wooden buildings, provided designated portions were fireproof—the so-called 'fireproof zones' contained only ten per cent of category (b).

The *success* of the first large-scale incendiary raid was due to the manner in which baskets of inflammable material were planted by the successive waves of bombers. It was not a 'hit and run' affair. It was a deliberately planned low-flying attack aimed setting fire to the industrial area of the Capital. Undoubtedly at the strong wind, across the target area, spread the fire from ward to ward, and trapped the unfortunate people, despite the fire-breaks which were ineffective because of the pattern bombing. The XXI Bomber Command A.A.F. claimed that 15.8 square miles of the 'heart of Tokyo' were burned out. That was correct. Tokyo was back to the September days of 1923 and the Rescript of Hirohito—but it was only the start of the destruction of his Capital by the A.A.F.

Destruction of KOBE, OSAKA and NAGOYA

On 11th March, 1945, *300 B 29's* unloaded *2,000 tons* of high-explosives on *Nagoya*. This was followed on 13th by the first of the incendiary raids on *Osaka* when *2,000* tons of incendiaries were scattered over the industrial targets.

The damage done may be estimated by comparing it with the 9/10th March raid on Tokyo when *1,667 tons* of incendiaries were dropped on the target. On 17th March, *2,500 tons* of fire-raising material was showered on *Kobe*. In three raids, on three of the most densely populated areas engaged in the war effort, no less than 6,500 tons of H.E. and fire-bombs had been exploded.

On 18th March the battered industrial area of *Nagoya* was visited by *300 B 29's* releasing *2,000 tons* of incendiaries.

Those who were directing the destruction of Japan's potentiality to wage war were determined to leave nothing to chance.

On 19th March, *350 B 29's* scattered a mixture of dynamite and jelly-bombs on the blazing target of Nagoya to the total weight of *2,000 tons*.

In five raids the A.A.F. released 8,500 tons of explosives in the shape of 'incendiaries' and 2,000 tons of block-busting high-explosives: 10,500 tons all carried from the island bases they had captured from Japan.

To complete the programme, for the time being, *Nagoya* was the objective on 25th March when *255 B 29's* plastered the Mitsubishi aero-engine plant with 1,500 tons of H.E., and on 30th March when a *smaller* formation of *200 B 29's* dropped a mixture of H.E. and fire-bomb.

Interlocked with this specific bombing, carrier-borne U.S. Navy aircraft struck at *Kure* Naval Yard and *Kobe* shipbuilding plant on 18th March, and on *Kyushu* aerodromes on 19th March. Land-based fighters retaliated by strikes against the U.S. Task-force on 20th and 21st March, claiming numerous successes in 'a series of brilliant actions against superior forces of the enemy'.

Unfortunately, for Japan, these brilliant successes did not prevent large formations of B 29's from bombing industrial and military targets in *Kyushu* on 27th March or carrier-borne aircraft from raiding *Kyushu* air-bases on 29th and 30th March.

Three months of stepped-up action by the American Airforce had demonstrated the futility of prolonging the war. Tokyo, Osaka, Kobe and Nagoya were examples of what could be done with an unlimited supply of high-explosives and incendiaries scattered by an unlimited supply of super-bombers free to come and go as they pleased. Prolongation of the war involved the certainty of an intensification of wholesale destruction of life and property and Japan had no answer except surrender.

To resist to the bitter end?

By now it was obvious to people and to politicians alike that the U.S.A. could force the surrender of Japan without the assistance of China, U.S.S.R., or the British Empire, and that they could do it without any slackening of her contribution to the utter destruction of Germany. And, what is more, the U.S.A. alone by the exercise of her sea and air-power could bring about defeat without the necessity to land troops on the main islands.

Those who were later on to be tried as 'War Criminals' had enough intelligence to arrive at a correct estimation of the extent of their failure to establish an Empire in Greater East Asia but they lacked the courage to sue for peace and thereby save the people from further slaughter.

The exit was marked 'Unconditional Surrender'. But it was easier for them to lead their dupes through Shinto gateways and to rely on kami-kaze for another 'miracle' than it was to agree to 'Unconditional Surrender' before the enemy was established on the sacred soil of Japan. Only the Tenno could help them now and he was still casting his net in shallow waters.

There were still 2,500,000 soldiers ready and willing to fight to preserve the Shinto State in all its theanthropic glory. To them, unconditional surrender did not square with Japanese ethics—it was a foreign idea linked with western civilization and, as such, beneath the contempt of Japanese. No, it was not easy for the Tenno to lead sullen samurai, patriotic black-dragons—the protagonists of kodo—through the Torii of the Yasukuni Shrine to clap their hands before the altar of the spirits of Japanese, who had laid down their lives for the country, and proclaim their disloyalty to Amaterasu.

CHAPTER XV

FRUSTRATED EFFORTS
TO END WAR IN ASIA

i. Russia declines to intervene
Denunciation of Russo-Japanese Neutrality Pact
Resignation of General Koiso
Admiral Suzuki's Cabinet

Newspapers covered the Allied Conferences at Cairo, Teheran and Yalta. They gave greater publicity to what Stalin was reported to have said than to the 'threats, warnings and conditions for Peace laid down by Roosevelt or Churchill'. But they did not carry much information about the Yalta Conference (4-11th February, 1945) although ever since the exit of Tojo (July, 1944) there had been frequent references to the 'probable action of the U.S.S.R.' in every conceivable circumstance.

Early in January, 1945, there was a small news item: 'Cabinet has decided to send a special envoy to Moscow to consult with the Soviet Government on the general situation.' The 'Mainichi' did announce the safe arrival of the Envoy in Moscow but there was no further reference to the matter (which I saw) until the 'Imperial messenger crossed the border at Manchuli on his return to Japan'—and he arrived at Tokyo railway station on 3rd April.

There was a 'special Cabinet meeting' on 5th April and then the veil of secrecy was lifted in a most dramatic manner: Russia had denounced her Neutrality Pact with Japan.

General Koiso, and his cabinet, resigned: on 8th April, Admiral Kantaro Suzuki was appointed Premier, Foreign Minister and G.E.A. Minister. The Naval contingent of Koiso's ministry were re-appointed but there was an entirely new Army representation which seemed to indicate further divergence of views on major policy connected with prosecution of the war.

For the next few days there were rumours in the camp, based on wishful thinking, and perplexity in the columns of the press.

General Koiso's choice, as Premier, was not a good one from the point of view of Russo-Japanese relations but I do not think it had any influence with Stalin who could conclude a Pact with his bitterest enemy, Hitler, and forget that he was a 'common blood-spattered criminal'—when it suited the policy of the U.S.S.R.

Admiral Suzuki's first official act was to instruct a former Premier, K. Hirota, to interview the Russian Ambassador in Tokyo, Yakov. A. Malik to ascertain 'U.S.S.R.'s attitude towards interceding with America'. With the same object in view the new Foreign Minister, S. Togo, continued to explore the situation and Ambassador Sato, in Moscow, was instructed to make arrangements for *another* Japanese emissary to visit Stalin 'to bring about improvement in Russo-Japanese relations, and to seek the intercession of Russia to end the war'.

There is confirmation of these efforts to gain the U.S.S.R.'s support for peace negotiations in a statement attributed to Admiral Okada one of Hirohito's advisers. Okada was Prime Minister in 1936 when Admiral Saito, General Watanabe and Mr. Takahashi were killed and Admiral Suzuki seriously wounded. On 11th August, 1946, Okada declared: 'Russian officials knew *six months before Russia entered the Pacific War* of Japan's desire *to yield*. Peace could have come many months earlier *if Russia had* promptly *relayed Japanese requests*'.

ii. Yamato-damashi

Yamato-damashi—the spirit of Japan! Dr. Jiro Harada, in 'A Glimpse of Japanese Ideals' (1937) says of Yamato-damashi: 'It is the driving force in us; something in the blood which we ourselves are not always able to explain . . .' 'Crystallized, this spirit becomes the sharpest steel; scattered it falls like the petals of the cherry.'

Apart from destruction caused daily by the U.S. Airforce, conditions overseas steadily deteriorated. On 24th February, 1945, Manila was reoccupied and there was increasing pressure on the Ryukyu Islands. But the 'army' clung to the theory that the mounting casualties in the Pacific War would compel 'American public opinion' to seek 'peace suggestions' instead of paying the price for the invasion of Japan.

It was stated in the press that, 'numerous engagements with the enemy had proved that untrained American conscripts were no match for Japanese at close quarters'. To 'prove this' they never ceased to quote the story of the battles for IwoJima.

Ogasawara, better known as Iojima or Iwojima, is one of the volcano islands, in the Bonins, about five hundred miles south of Japan. It was held by about 22,000 Japanese when first attacked by U.S. warships and B 29's on 8th November, 1944, and captured on 16th March, 1945. Japanese casualties were 21,000—mostly killed—and the American losses were 4,189 killed and 15,749 wounded according to official reports.

The first landing was made by Two Divisions of U.S. Marines on 18th February,1945. Previously—25-26th December, 1944, 24th January and 30th January—it had been bombed and shelled by B 29's, carrier-borne aircraft, and ships of the U.S. Pacific Fleet.

From 15th to 18th February it was shelled by units of the U.S. 7th Fleet—including several battleships. The landing party met heavy opposition on the beaches—every foot was contested—but by the evening of 19th the southernmost airfield was occupied: four days later Mount Suribachi was taken and on 28th, Motoyama—principal town of Iwojima—fell to the Marines.

Japanese resistance stiffened but by 2nd March a 700-yard wedge was driven into their line in northern Iwojima. By now four-fifths of the island was in American hands and their killed numbered 2,200—twice the casualties suffered in the capture of Tarawa in November, 1943—but the enemy showed no sign of yielding or hoisting the white flag.

After a heavy artillery barrage on 6th March, followed by frontal attacks for five days, the garrison was split again into three small forces and destroyed by nightfall 14th March: organized resistance ceasing on 16th when Kitano Point was captured on the extreme north of the island.

Iwojima was cited as *one example* of yamato-damashi: the garrison was isolated, they died to a man.

Ten days later, U.S. Marines landed on Kerama Island 15 miles south-west of the Ryukyu Islands. This sounded the call to

Japanese to 'rise as one man in defence of the sacred soil of
Japan, inviolable by foreigners'. The response was magnificent,
but the sacrifice was in vain.

On 1st April the advance guard of U.S. Infantry and Marines
landed on the west coast of *OKINAWA,* the most important of
the Ryukyu Islands. Okinawa was blockaded by the allied fleet
and dominated by the allied airforce, but it held out for *82 days.*

Both sides flung everything they had into the contest—no
quarter was asked for or given. It was a fight to the finish between 'uninspired conscripts' and yamato-damashi. The 'conscript' won but not until *115,853 Japanese had been killed* and 7,902
of the inhabitants taken prisoner. American casualties were
85,000 (according to Japanese reports) killed and wounded in
addition to heavy losses in aircraft, aircraft-carriers, light and
heavy warships, transports and landing craft. Japanese losses
in the air were over 2,000 aircraft from April to the end of June
when the battle for Okinawa was over.

Araki's kodo, the cult of brutality, should not be confused
with yamato-damashi. The brutal fanatics, who delighted to
torture their prisoners, were of the same stock but their inspiration was not the same. As soldiers, pure and simple, they were
the 'sharpest steel' and lived and died in the true spirit of their
code. To deny that is to detract from American heroism, on
Iwojima or Okinawa, from British heroism and tenacity in the
re-taking of Burma and the long period of 'blood, sweat and
tears' during the South-West Pacific offensive of 1943-45.

U.S. Marines 'waded through blood' at Guam, Saipan,
Tinian, Leyte, Guadalcanal, Bougainville, Palau and all the
other islands they captured from Japanese. Australians fought
for every bridgehead from Santa Cruz to Borneo—and they
paid the price for each engagement.

During the first phase of the S.W. Pacific offensive the Japanese lost *160,000* out of 250,000 men in the 8th, 17th, and 18th
Armies. On Leyte they lost *32,000 killed:* Lunga *5,000,* Bougain-
ville *4,500* killed! In the fighting for Saipan the U.S. casualties
were over 10,000 but no less than *21,036* dead had been buried
by the end of July, 1944, when the Japanese had been wiped out!

When the U.S. Marines finished 'mopping up' on the Palau
Islands, in October, 1944, they had killed over *10,000 Japanese:*
the fighting for the Marshall Islands—against Roi, Wotje and in

Kwajalein—(December, 1943—April, 1944) battleships and air-craft-carriers bombed and shelled before each landing—*14,000 tons* of shells fell on Roi and Namur alone—our casualties were *286* killed against *8,122 killed and buried*.

These are but a few illustrations of the way in which the Japanese were bombed from the air, shelled from sea, battered and cut to bits. They fought bravely—it is a pity that their heroism contrasts so strangely with their atrocious behaviour to their captives. It is something in the blood 'which we ourselves are not always able to explain' as Harada puts it.

The popu'ation of Japan were told about the battles but not of the bloody details of the defeat. And, in order not to blunt the edge of yamato-damashi, the pilgrimages to Hachiman and Yasukuni Shrines were discouraged because of the vast crowds, of relatives of the forces overseas, who came to venerate the spirits of those who had died on the battlefield.

The death of President Roosevelt, on 12th April, was reported sympathetically in the press. A few hinted that it might result in lessening Allied antagonism to Japan: Admiral Suzuki, in interviews on 14th, admitted the effectiveness of Roosevelt's leadership and 'hoped for a better understanding in future between all nations'. By this time there were many advocates of peace but they were still working under cover in order to avoid being knifed by the fanatics.

There was no hint of these peace manœuvres in the press, but there is ample confirmation in 'The United States Strategic Bombing Survey' issued on 1st July, 1946. It quotes Admiral Suzuki as saying that when he assumed office (8th April, 1945): 'It was the Emperor's desire to make every effort to bring the war to a conclusion as quickly as possible, and that was my purpose.' And there is also this significant disclosure . . . ' On the one hand he had instructions from the Emperor to arrange an end to the war; on the other hand any of those opposing this policy who learned of such peace moves would be apt to attack or even assassinate him.'

There might have been a repetition of the events of 26th February, 1936, when the Tokyo Garrison mutinied, surrounded the Palace, killed Admiral Saito, Mr. Takahashi and General Watanabe, and wounded Admiral Suzuki.

Suzuki was taking no chances: 'Thus with the general staffs —Government in general—and the people—he advocated increasing war effort and determination to fight, whereas, through diplomacy and any other means available, *he had to negotiate with other countries to stop the war.*'

iii. *Peace manoeuvres. The Tenno's endeavours to end the War*

Attitude of the kodoites on the subject of ending the war was definite when Koiso resigned. They controlled an army of $2\frac{1}{2}$ million men in Japan and an army of 3 million men overseas, they were in command of all the key points, dockyards, arsenals and munition factories. The sooner an invasion took place the better—it made no difference to them where the enemy landed, they had the soldiers, airmen and munitions necessary to inflict 500,000 casualties and still remain undefeated in the hills if not on the beaches. They had enough super-men in the Kamikaze Corps to man thousands of suicide-planes: what had been accomplished at Iwojima and Okinawa would be repeated on the soil of Japan.

After a few months of the 'blood-bath' the United States of America would hesitate to add to their casualties in order to bring about 'unconditional surrender'. Then, and then only, should Japan entertain the idea of a peace settlement.

There was no answer to the B 29's. But when the enemy did land they could strike back and inflict casualties—man for man —and that would be their answer, kill and be killed.

Kill and be killed! That was the 'inspiration' of the official propaganda set forth in the newspapers, spoken on the radio and shouted from the platform up and down the country which was zoned into defensive areas each under a diehard General, on the active or the retired list, with his 'sealed orders' for dealing with the national emergency.

More than two million people had been evacuated from Tokyo—flattened by bombing and fire-raids—and, on the Tokyo-Yokohama main road, thousands of buildings untouched by bombing were razed to the ground to make strong-points with clear fields-of-fire: Kobe, Osaka and Nagoya made their preparations for fighting in the streets: the Kais were active; patriotic meetings were addressed by leading Kodoites in cities, towns and villages—Japan was ready and eager (?) to meet the invaders.

That was one side of the sacred mirror. On the other side it was quite different. The industrial plant of the Zaibatsu had been blown sky-high by the American Airforce. The accumulated assets of the 'Furoku Kyohei' (Wealthy country, strong in arms) of Meiji Tenno were vanishing into clouds of smoke and debris so the leaders of the Zaibatsu began to sneak in by the back door and join the peace clique headed by Prince Konoye and Marquis Matsudaira secure in the knowledge that the divine Tenno's edict would save them from utter destruction before it was too late.

But the dupes of the Shinto State remained ignorant of the magnitude of Japan's defeat on the sea and in the air.

The leaders knew the truth and the Navy laboured under no illusions. All that was left of the battle-fleet was five battleships, 3 carriers and 12 cruisers. But, on 7th April, 1945, they made another desperate attempt to intervene in the Battle for Okinawa only to meet with another reverse in an action 60 miles off South Kyushu. Carrier-borne aircraft from Admiral Mitscher's task-force destroyed the 72,809 ton super-battleship 'Yamato', the escorting cruisers, 'Isuzu' and 'Yahagi' and the destroyer screen.

As usual the 'official spokesman' claimed a victory but the truth leaked out through the survivors and added to the general depression caused by the continuous bombing by the A.A.F.

But to those who knew the whole truth it was a small matter compared with the decisive defeat suffered by Japan during the Battle for Leyte Gulf (23-26th October, 1944) when the 'Yamato' was damaged, her sister-ship 'Musashi' sunk with the other battleships 'Fuso' and 'Yamashiro', and the cruisers 'Mogami', 'Suzuya', 'Atago', 'Chikuma', 'Chokai', 'Maya', 'Abukuma', 'Kinu', 'Noshiro', and 'Tama' sunk with the four aircraft-carriers 'Zuikaku', 'Zuiho', 'Chitose' and 'Chiyoda' plus nine of the larger destroyers. Little or nothing of this disaster found its way into the newspapers. The Battle for Leyte Gulf had been mentioned, to account for the landing at Leyte and the subsequent capture of Manila, but the details were kept secret until after the surrender, with other particulars of the destruction of the entire Japanese Navy between 1942 and 1945.*

However, the Japanese Navy kept on fighting. Another naval and aerial counter-attack on the British and U.S. Naval units

* See Appendix XI.

blockading Okinawa was carried out during the night of 12/13th
April but the only news which was given out was, '120 of our
suicide-planes failed to return from the Okinawa battlefield
after inflicting enormous damage to the enemy fleet'.

(The Chronology of the defeat of the Japanese Navy is set out in Chapter XVIII
and in Appendix XI.)

Hirohito desired Peace—at any cost, but the Army was still
determined to fight to the bitter end'. Hirohito could have sued
for Peace and the chances are that his Edict would have been
sufficient excuse for the Navy. But, in April, 1945, the country
was at the mercy of the bayonet-men and civil war had to be
avoided. To obtain 'Peace' by inciting his subjects to kill each
other was out of the question for the Spiritual head of the Shinto
State: Japan was not Italy and 'unconditional surrender' was
demanded by the Allies.

Instead of courting civil war it was decided (?) to publicise
every item of news, from every theatre of war, outside the waters
of Japan, in order to weaken the influence of the more bellicose
leaders of the anti-peace movement. There was little or no
censorship over the press and they were not slow to give promi-
nence to the bad news for Japan.

So Hirohito bided his time. He issued Edict after Edict—
praised and rewarded thousands of his loyal subjects for their
gallantry. He called on those who were not in the armed services to visit shrine and temple, to live abstemiously according to
the traditions handed down from generation to generation. He
made his own supplications before the Imperial Shrine in the
grounds of the Palace littered with the debris of the air-raids: he
neither abdicated nor precipitated civil war. No, Hirohito was
no super-man—he was not divine. He may have been weak or
just a coward waiting for something to turn up. I do not know
the answers but I do think that his methods, under the circumstances, suited Japanese. Few men in ancient or modern history
had such a bloodless vindication of judgment when his last
Edict was issued for it was obeyed by all his subjects and im-
plemented by the machinery of a central government in full
control of seventy million people.

CHAPTER XVI

AIR WAR AGAINST JAPAN
SECOND PHASE
APRIL-JUNE 1945

i. Airfields, oil-storage and petrol plant

In rotation the main centres of Japan's aircraft industry had been pounded to pieces. Now it was the turn of the airfields, oil storage and petrol installations to receive attention.

There were heavy B 29 raids on the Tokyo-area airfields on 1st and 2nd April, followed the next day by attacks on Shizuoka, Tachikawa and Koizume in zone (d) by formations of from 200 to 400 heavy bombers. On 7th, there were simultaneous attacks by about 300 B 29's, *with fighter escort*, on Nagoya and Tokyo. While this was going on, P-47N and P-51 fighters struck against Kyushu, Kobe-Osaka and Nagoya airfields.

What interested us most at this time (in the Yokohama-Tokyo area) was the absence of kami-kaze counter-attacks on the fighters or the bombers. We put it down to shortage of petrol, or a plan to build up a strong reserve to deal with the 'invasion' but it served to reduce A.A.F. losses and enabled them to step-up their attacks from numerous new landing-strips on Bonins and Okinawa.

On 12th, 14th, and 16th the Tokyo area targets were hammered by flights of from 100 to 250 B 29's: on 19th, 20th, 21st, 23rd, 26th and 30th small formations of B 29's bombed most of the airfields in Kyushu. On 23rd there was a *150 B 29* strike against Tachikawa aerodrome.

By the last week in April, air-warfare over Japan had reached the stage when the A.A.F. had 500 B 29's and 500 other types of bombers and fighters airborne at the same time. By calculating bomb-load—for B 29's—at five-ton it was possible to arrive at an estimate of tonnage being unloaded every day. We had no means of checking figures in the newspapers but we did have many A.A.F. PoW's in Omori to 'check accuracy' of the mounting statistics and an equal number of sceptics to scoff at the figures. For my part I was content to boost the activities of the A.A.F., it was good for our morale, and I was in no danger of being proved wrong in my translations of the 'news': the 'sky was the limit' when I was puzzled by over-lapping of information contained in 'official communications' and local reporting of events and damage done.

We had excellent maps of Japan, secured for us by chaps in working parties scrounging in bombed-out buildings, so it was not difficult to plot the day's havoc in any of the sixty odd target-areas.

Oil storage and petrol installations received particular attention in May. On 3rd, 4th and 8th, Kyushu airfields were bombed by B 29's. Then, on 10th, *400 B 29's* released over *2,000 tons* of H.E., on the oil storage and petrol refining areas in Kyushu.

Next, the aerial sledge-hammer, pounded Honshu airfields to bits on 11th, striking at Nagoya on 13th when *500 B 29's* discharged an explosive cargo of *3,500 tons* into a mass of debris. Two days later twenty airfields and aerodromes on Honshu and Shikoku were attacked by waves of carrier-borne aircraft.

The 'city' of Nagoya received another visit from *500 B 29's* on 16th to churn up what was left of the industrial districts with *2,000 tons* of high-explosives of the latest type. This time the press reported 'fresh fires and considerable damage to residential and industrial districts.' The communique added the information that 'recent captives' confirm that B 29's were carrying bomb-loads of from 7 to 8 tons.

Tokyo and Nagoya were the targets on 18th, and on 22nd 'coastal targets'—shipping in Honshu and Kyushu—were hammered by B 29's and carrier-borne aircraft. There was also reports of mine-laying in Sea of Japan between Moji and Fusan, in Korea.

ii. Incendiary raid on Tokyo (23rd May, 1945)

'Photo Joe' came over again after the raid on 18th May: early on 23rd the sirens began to sound in Tokyo and Yokohama and in a few minutes the ground-defence was in action. Visibility was good and the first waves ran into a tremendous barrage of flak but the formations of from 20 to 30 B 29's—unaccompanied by fighters—pressed home their attack from the north, flying in exceedingly low for a daylight raid.

The noise from gun-fire and explosion of bombs exceeded anything we had heard before. In less than half an hour Tokyo was ablaze again: fire-fighters could do little as the successive waves dropped tons of H.E. and tons of incendiaries over a wide front.

There was little wind but the material damage was much greater than that done during the night raid of 9/10th March when 1,667 tons of incendiaries were expended on the target— now the raging furnace covered several square miles of the Capital and was still spreading when the last waves went over.

An American official report stated that *550 B 29's* dropped *750,000 incendiary-bombs* in the total load of *4,500 tons* of explosives scattered on the target that morning.

Not content with this demonstration of destructive power the A.A.F. sent over *500 B 29's with 4,000 tons of incendiaries* on the night of 25/26th May, to make sure that Tokyo was really on fire! On 28th, *450 B 29's,* escorted by P 51's and P 47's from 7th U.S.A. A.F., plastered Yokohama and Tokyo with a further *3,200 tons* of H.E.

Civilization 'measures war' by easily understood terms: *hundreds* of aircraft, thousands of tons of bombs, *hundreds of thousands of incendiaries, billions* of bullets, *millions* of men, *battleships* and *human-torpedos.* To make it readable, and not too boring, figures are explained by the enormous damage done, the great number of factories gutted, enemy 'potentiality for waging war' destroyed, and the number of casualites inflicted.

Number of casualties inflicted. Why not go into more detail for the benefit of the next generation? Why not put it bluntly: the number of men, women and children who have had their heads bashed in was greater during yesterday's attack than the number who had their stomach ripped open: the number who were trapped in buildings, crushed and roasted to death, was greater than those having arms and legs torn from their trunks: those receiving direct hits were scattered into smaller fragments than those pulverised by blast: the ratio, between the pulped and the calcinated, is as 1 is to 4: the new explosive, Mark VI, is more effective than Mark V, it strips hair, skin and flesh from bone much more neatly but we need something even better than Mark VI to increase casualties and reduce bomb-load.

On 31st May, *450 B 29's*, with a strong fighter-escort from 7th U.S.A. A.F., unleashed another *3,200 tons* of H.E. on Osaka with the usual equilibrated damage to life and property.

Perhaps it is worth recording that, despite the heavy raids in the Yokohama-Tokyo area, the Omori camp staff and the numerous Japanese in daily contact with PoW working-parties, did not alter their behaviour to us for better or for worse. We still had Colonel Sakeba but 2/Lt. Kato and Sergeant Watanabe had left the camp: 'discipline' was maintained by a Sergeant-Major Oguri and he proved to be the most humane Japanese soldier I met from 1942 to 1945 and the morale in the camp (and the discipline) went up 100 per cent.

Unfortunately our personal treatment differed—during this period—from that accorded to allied airman who bailed-out, or where shot-down, over Japan. They were treated by military and civilians with brutality equal to that accorded to army personnel by the major sadists.

iii. Combined operations

Air-war, against Japan, was aided to a maximum point of destructiveness by the combined British and American naval action against Formosa, Okinawa and the string of Islands from Kyushu to the Ryukyus. In the beginning, B 24's and B 29's, striking from bases in China, dealt with airfields, ports and installations on Formosa which straddled the South Pacific l. of c. Then, from the second week in April, allied aircraft-carriers closed in on Japan and hardly a day passed without hostile action being taken against land or sea targets by Anglo-American naval fighter-aircraft.

From March to June—1945—these task-forces staged more than fifty sorties against Formosa, Okinawa, Sakishima, Tokunoshima, Amamishima and Kikashima with concentrated attacks on the Amami and Saki group of islands.

On 4th and 5th May, battleships and cruisers of British Pacific Fleet shelled Miyakoshima, in the Sakishima group while American task-forces operated inshore against the Kuriles—from Paramushiro down-coast to Saghalien—made nine strikes from carriers and six bombardments from surface craft.

In terms of aircraft, targets and bomb-loads, the June record was impressive. Main attacks were: *Kobe* on 4th, by *500 B 29's,* —3,000 tons H.E., *Osaka,* on 6th and 8th, by *200 B 29's*—1,000 tons H.E., *Osaka and Amagasaki,* on 14th, *500 B 29's*—3,000 tons H.E, *Omuta and Kagoshima* (Kyushu) and *Hammamatsu and Yokkaichi* (Honshu) on 17th, *450 B 29's*—3,000 tons H.E.

U.S. 3rd Fleet, carrier-borne aircraft raided *Kyushu* airfields on 2nd, 3rd, 8th and 9th June. Seaplane-bases in *Tokyo area* were bombed by a small group of B 29's on 9th: *Kure and Sasebo* Naval Bases being straffed by 100 and 250 B 29's on 21st and 28th.

Aircraft and ammunition plant, in *West and Central Honshu,* were visited *seven times* between 10th and 25th, by formations of 100—200 B 29's. *Shizuoka and Toyohashi* (North Honshu) received 2,000 tons of H.E. from *400 B 29's* on 19th June. But during the month there was only one night raid, 25/26th, by a small formation of *B 29's* on *Yokkaichi:* the last raid of the month was on 29th when the Kudamatsu oil refinery was heavily damaged by B 29's.

In this manner was the stranglehold of Sea and Air Power applied—methodically and destructively. The ultimate result, long before the end of 1945, would have brought about the unconditional surrender of Japan without invasion. It would have fully demonstrated to the most extreme kodoists that they would not have an opportunity to 'get to grips' with G.I.'s on the beaches before every main city in Japan was levelled to the ground and the death roll of men, women and children too much for them to stomach.

The Russian Ambassador, and other neutral diplomats, were in touch with officials of the Imperial Household—they knew, or could have ascertained the truth and if it had been conveyed to Allied Headquarters there would have been no need to try out the atom-bomb to ascertain if it would function satisfactorily—in practice—and prove (?) to scientists what they knew about it in theory and experiment.

CHAPTER XVII

UNCONDITIONAL SURRENDER
OF GERMANY

i. Reactions in Japan

The 'peace-at-any-price' movement in Japan gained support during the period April-June, 1945. Okinawa was lost, Russia had denounced the neutrality Pact, Mussolini had been executed, Hitler cheated the hangman, Berlin was occupied by Russians, an Act of unconditional surrender of German forces had been signed at Rheims, the dream of 'India part of Japan's Empire' had been turned into a nightmare in Burma—Rangoon was retaken by the British XIV Army in which there were three Indians to every one fighter from the United Kingdom: the I.N.A. ceased to exist. And—on the home-front—the A.A.F had strangled production, and war mobilization, by destroying most of the industrial areas.

The country faced certain defeat but the Government of Japan could not muster sufficient courage to inform the commanders of the Army, in their battle-stations, that surrender should precede invasion and not take place after it.

Although the cumulative effect of air-raids curtailed our 'outside' source of information, by killing-off Korean contacts and friendly 'Nips' who sold us the newspapers, we managed to obtain at least one copy of the 'Mainichi' *every day*. During an alert our working-parties were confined to camp but—by hook or crook—we got the 'news'. We discovered ways and means of 'lifting any newspaper brought into the Camp, for the guards or the staff, after it had been read or during the temporary absence of its owner. It was necessary to 'work fast' but in ten minutes I could jot down the headlines and then decide if news in the paper did warrant a special risk to ensure its retention later in the day.

We circulated 'news flashes' and confirmed details when it was safe to do so. The near-misses, between guard-house and publication, gave us furiously to think at times and I was lucky in avoiding the consequences after being caught red-handed on two occasions.

The news from Europe was puzzling at times. For instance—the Himmler approach to the allies through Count Bernhadotte: the first intimation was that Himmler, anxious to obtain allied peace terms, had approached the Swedish Red Cross but there was a definite anti-Soviet explanation tagged to the negotiations. Himmler was after a separate peace. One report linked Hitler with Himmler, the next report gave details of 'Hitler's'orders for Himmlers arrest'. Another news item was that Hitler was to 'fight to the bitter end in Berlin' which was followed by the information that Hitler had left the 'Tiergarten airfield for his new headquarters at Berchesgarten'.

Another correspondent reported from Berlin that Hitler had issued orders to his Army to 'hold the Eastern front at all cost' and had said nothing about the Western front. Much was made of the fact that the Russian army had failed to establish bridgeheads across the Oder at Frankfort and was a spent force without ammunition!

However, in due course, it became abundantly clear that the unconditional surrender of Germany was an accomplished fact and that Hitler was dead or had escaped from Berlin.

Admiral Suzuki broadcast to the nation the Government's determination to face the serious situation which had arisen and to press on with the plans 'to meet the invasion'. This broadcast was followed by official communiques giving the complete text of *all Japanese agreements* with Germany and Italy which had lapsed through their capitulation to the enemy. Also, it was added, the act of surrender by Germany released Japan from all her obligations and she was now free to act in accordance with her own interests.

Newspapers carried long articles explaining precisely what 'unconditional surrender' meant to a defeated nation. But there was *no condemnation of Germany*—her defeat was accepted as inevitable under the circumstances. Germany's numerous conquests were detailed by military commentators as proof of her greatness as a 'fighting nation demanding her right to a place in the sun'.

Others pointed out, correctly, that Japan had gained nothing
from her wartime association with Germany, except technical
advice, and that the deflection had not altered the fact that
Japan had waged war single-handed in the Far East and
would continue to do so to the bitter end.

ii. Plans for dealing with Invasion

There were rallys and mass-meetings, conferences and demonstrations. The 'entire nation' pledged itself to follow in the steps
of the heroes of Iwo Jima and Okinawa. But a good deal of the
'shouting from the house top' may have been insincere..
very few of the 34 million females in the country wished
the war to continue, and few of the 34 million males were as
keyed up to die as the $2\frac{1}{2}$ million soldiers under orders to stop
the invaders at the point of the bayonet. But they had to encourage each other until the Tenno's Edict released them from
their suicide pacts.

B-NIJU KU's made it almost impossible for the nation to
carry on: destruction of factories, transportation and communications, made it difficult to turn out munitions even on the small
scale required by the army of $2\frac{1}{2}$ million. Losses in Naval and
Air strength could not be replaced, raw material and petrol were
below normal peace requirements, the railways were short of
rolling stock—mass production had ceased and individual effort
was no substitute. Food was short, farmers were hoarding rice,
the standard of living—never very high—was being reduced
daily, inflation was an accomplished fact, currency lost its value
as 'paper' flooded the market and barter boosted trade in the
'black-market' established in every town and village.

Our working-parties reported what was going on at the docks,
in the ship-yards, steel-works, factories and on the railway
sidings. We knew all about shortages and the paper yen and the
'value' of a shirt in the black-market from which we obtained
cigarettes, sugar, rice, canned-goods and other items included in
our PoW rackets: PoW's were adept at pillage, forage and sabo-
tage—they robbed right and left and brought in sacks of loot to
help out our 'bowl of rice'—at a price of course—and we had
many 'Sugar Barons' and 'Cigarette Merchants' to whom we
were always excessively polite. On the other hand, the 'Twis-
ters' in the engineering-shops and dockyards did their 'bit' to

spoil the jobs they were on and I am sure that many of the Yokohama built midget-submarines would never function as the makers intended.

Omori was the clothing depot for PoW camps in what was called the 'Tokyo area' so we had many opportunities for exchanging news with comrades as far north as Hokkaido and as far south as Ofuna. And then there were the leaflets dropped on us by the A.A.F. giving us 'outside information' and 'advice' for the people of Japan. A reproduction of the Japanese 'Nichi-Nichi', published by Americans in Guam was excellent, so were the Okinawa leaflets with photographs of *Japanese Prisoners of War* being cared for by U.S. Marines. Most of the articles exhorted the 'downtrodden people to rise against the militarists', and—of course, it was Crime No. 1 to be caught with a leaflet but so many fluttered to earth that it was easy to commit crimes by treading on them.

iii. The 'special' interrogation corps

Because of the destruction of plant in the Tokyo-Yokohama area the PoW Bureau decided in June, 1945 to redistribute PoW's in order to increase their productivity. There was nothing humane behind the decision: Omori Camp was to be reduced to 100 non-productive labour—'special prisoners' and invalids. The 'special prisoners' were airmen boarded-off from the other PoW's under special guards and kept alive on quarter or half-rations of rice and vegetables.

But, no sooner had one draft of a hundred left the camp than another draft arrived, in rags and tatters, from a bombed-out camp.

In addition to these prisoners of war, from near-by camps, we had 120 anti-Fascist Italians from Shangai via Manchuria and Korea camps. They remained a few weeks, then they moved to make room for *150 Japanese officers, n.c.o's and other ranks!*

This 'Special Interrogation Corps' of Japanese remained with us for six weeks. They shared our cook-house, wash-racks, bath-house and benjo and mixed with the captives in order to study their habits and language—to prepare themselves for the job of interrogating *'Prisoners of War captured during the invasion of Japan'*.

The Special I. Corps included men from each of the defence zones—from Kyushu to Hokkaido—and were grouped for intensive study under 'experts' from the War Office. The lectures were only a small part of the training: most of the day, and night was devoted to 'friendly conversation' with prisoners of war.

During an air-raid they split into groups and remained with us to study our reactions and listen to our conversation. They were not allowed to issue orders to PoW's or to interfere with them in any way—they were free to come and go as they pleased but not to give us any information regarding themselves or conditions in their part of the country.

One group was engaged on the compilation of a list of questions to be put to the 'new prisoners'—the list was divided into sections for each branch of the service; Army, Navy, Air-force and Intelligence. But they soon ran into 'dialect trouble' caused by slang and colloquialisms deliberately expanded by Cockney, Scot and Yank who assisted in the compilation of the lists.

At the end of the first month, Colonel Sakeba, assisted by 'akirameru' Ohnishi the interpreter, conducted a passing-out examination. As Omori 'British Prisoner No. 1' I was ordered to attend and answer questions put to me by the students. The standard of intelligence, of the questioners, was very low and they were much more nervous than I was during the quizzing in English.

Ohnishi told them what to ask me, speaking in Japanese, and not more than ten per cent could interpret what he said into English that I could understand so the examinations were a failure.

But what interested me most was the 'secret lectures' given by Colonel Sakeba and a Staff-officer from the War Office. I obtained my information from a Formosan anti-Jap in the special I. Corps. One lecture dealt with the subject of 'Disposing of PoW during the Invasion'. Omori was selected to illustrate the modus operandi.

> . . . After all maps and documents likely to be of use to the invader are destroyed muster PoW officers and hand over the camp to them. March out immediately but post machine-gun sections to cover the Omori bridge. When enemy troops appear the PoW will break camp and should be allowed to cross the bridge before machine-guns open fire and destroy them on the road which the enemy is attacking. If this way of disposing of them is not practicable other steps must be taken to prevent them escaping or joining incoming troops and helping them with local knowledge. . .

There was no invasion so we did not help the incoming troops with local knowledge. But, after each raid, our working-parties went over the Omori bridge to help in salvage operations. They worked alongside the natives, who searched in the gutted buildings for useful bits of property, and from first to last there was not a single incident involving civilians and prisoners of war. Truckloads of our chaps travelled over the bombed Omori-Yokohama-Tokyo area and, except for a few raised fists, no one expressed emotion one way or the other.

Depression, fatalism, all the signs of akirameru, were there—amid the desolation caused by B-Niju Ku—but there was no attempt to take it out of our hides. In the end, the Special Interrogation Corps destroyed all their documents and faded away: in the end, Colonel Sakeba was tried, convicted and sentenced to life imprisonment. In the camp, we lived and worked hard. Food was bad and scarce—fit for pigs. We slept (?) in barracks which were infested with bugs, lice, fleas and mosquitoes. But we were never depressed. We had a jazz-band and an orchestra, we staged athletic sports, we had a small 'canteen' and a library, we put on several shows, we had church service, we had a carpenters shop and a smithy, Major Frankcom ran the Post Office and we sorted and sent out of Omori more than 3½ million letters to camps all over Japan and the occupied area. Physically we were in bad shape but mentally quite sound after Watanabe's exit—we had no 'wire' but were never inclined to dig holes under the wooden fence to try and escape because we were several thousands miles from home and our friends were in the air dropping bombs and leaflets.

Some of our chaps had been in the Bataan death march, in which 10,000 Americans and Filipinos died, and for which crime General Kawane, Colonel Hirano and 13 others were duly hanged: others were picked out of the 'ditch' a few yards from the Camp or off a Pacific Island, some were from Hongkong, Singapore or Java—we were a mixed lot of races from all the services but 'pigged-it' together very well indeed.

CHAPTER XVIII

AIR WAR AGAINST JAPAN
FINAL STAGE
JULY 1945

i. *Integration of Air and Sea Power*

Destruction of 'Japan's potentiality to wage defensive warfare' was carried a stage further by even closer co-ordination of Naval and Airforce of U.S.A. with that of the British Empire. Germany was out of World War II and redeployment of striking power began before the crowds on Times Square, or Piccadilly Circus, ceased celebrating V.E. Day. There was now but one front and but one enemy to be destroyed by the prompt utilization of over-whelming resources of the democrats and their enigmatic communist ally.

Some idea of the effort made by the A.A.F., in the war against Japan, may be obtained by this comparison of bombing-tonnage which was expended in Europe and in the Pacific theatre of War

From December, 1944 to May, 1945, expenditure against Germany was 550,000 tons—in the Far East it was 200,000 tons: from 1st June to 14th August, 1945, (2½ months only) tonnage expended against Japan was 150,000 tons. Monthly average against Germany, to May 1945, was 90,000 tons—against Japan, 30,000 tons. But from 1st June, 1945 to the capitulation the A.A.F. worked up the average to 60,000 tons a month.

Number of aircraft in the air at one time never approached the western-front standard—there was nothing approaching the strike of 22nd February, 1945 by 10,000 planes against 200 targets—but it did work up to 1000, B 29's and 1,500 fighters airborne the same day. In *addition* to bombing from the air the coastal targets received attention from surface craft to the total of many thousand tons.

Daily, during July, formations of anything from 100 to 600 B 29's were over Japan. On 1st July, Kure Naval Yard and Ube (Honshu) were raided by 600 B 29's: on 2nd, Shimotsu oil refinery, on 3rd, Himeji, Tokushima, Takamatsu and Kochi (Shikoku and Honshu) were the objectives for 500 B 29's. On 6th, Kofu, Chiba, Shimizu, Shimotsu and Akashi (d) zone) were bombed by 600 B 29's dropping a load of 4,000 tons of H.E.

Tokyo area was raided on 9th by carrier-borne planes from U.S. 3rd Fleet. Attacks lasted from dawn to dusk and 1,000 odd strikes were made against airfields. The same day, Gifu, Sakai, Sendai Wakayama and Yokkaichi—zones 'c' and 'd'—were visited by bombers. Early on 10th, 'carriers' were over again in our area but in smaller numbers. The next raid was on 12th when 600 B 29's dropped 3,000 tons on Uwajima (Shikoku), Ichinomiya, Tsuruga and Kawasaki in zone 'd'.

Carrier-borne planes from U.S. 3rd Fleet went north on 14th to bomb targets in North Honshu and Hokkaido while B 29's hammered the Kofu area.

On 16th 17th and 18th there was a series of 'carrier raids' on Tokyo-Yokohama industrial-plant, airfields and harbour installations and for the first time the press admitted that British aircraft were operating against Japan. Choshu, Hitachi (N.E. of Tokyo) Fukui, Okazaki and other oil-refineries in the Osaka-Amagasaki area were raided on 16th and 19th by 600 B 29's.

According to the newspaper reports, the 'record strike' was carried out on 9th and 10th July when 2,000 aircraft, described as fighters, fighter-bombers, and super-fortresses, carried out simultaneous raids on Kyushu, Shikoku and Tokyo-Yokohama targets.

There was another 'near record' on 23rd July when 1,500 fighters, dive-bombers and torpedo-bombers from U.S. 3rd Fleet attacked Naval units in Kure naval-dockyard and shipping in Sagami Bay at the same time as 400 'Liberators' and fighters from Iwo Jima and Okinawa struck at South Kyushu airfields.

In July there were many articles in the press informing the general public how to identify Privateers, Mariners, Thunderbolts, Mitchells, Corsairs and Avengers said to be operating from the numerous task-forces or from Okinawa, Ie Jima or Iwo Jima. It was also stated, on the highest naval authority, that 14 enemy aircraft-carriers were operating in Japan's home waters.

ii. Naval operations

There had been no secrecy displayed regarding the composition of the Anglo-American Fleet operating against Japan in July, 1945.

'Mainichi' overseas correspondents supplemented information contained in official communiques. We had the names of the Commanders of British and American Pacific Fleets and the composition of the various task-forces down to the last detail—of fact or surmise. However, we were able to follow with additional interest the reported movements of the light-units in their shelling of Paramushiro, Matsuwa, Kataoka and Shimushu in the Kuriles.

But even so it came as a surprise to read one day that . . . 'Enemy *battleships* shelled the N.E. Coast of Honshu yesterday.'

Battleships shelling N.E. Honshu was news. It transpired that on 14th July, Kamaishi, 275 miles north of Tokyo, was shelled by U.S. battleships *South Dakota, Massachusetts* and *Indiana* all 35,000 ton 9-16 inch gun ships, and by the cruisers *Chicago*, and *Quincy* for over two hours. This information was followed by a brief item to the effect that, on 15th July, the 45,000 ton battleships *Iowa, Wisconsin* and *Missouri* entered Muroran Bay—South Hokkaido—and from a range of 1,000 yards shelled the town of Muroran.

We had a PoW Camp at Kamaishi, where there was a large steel works, so we did not care too much for that item of news—we had lost enough people already in the Tokyo-Yokohama area. Still—we were in the danger zone so casualties were to be expected.

A few days later, *Hitachi*—only 75 miles North of Tokyo—was shelled from a 6-mile range by units of the British Pacific Fleet, including battleship *King George V.*, escorted by light units of U.S. 3rd Fleet.

That was on 17th, and the next day it was stated that the *Iowa* had joined the battleship *King George V* and they had both shelled the coast-line for about sixty-miles. There was no report of the damage caused by the shelling and no report of any counter-action by 'Baka' death-defying kamikaze pilots or by one of the many hundred one-man submarines based on Yokohama and Kure.

While these major naval operations were proceeding, British

carrier-borne aircraft covered the action of the light-units of U.S. 3rd Fleet off the East coast of Chiba prefecture.

Taking full advantage of a dark and stormy night (18/19th) U.S. Cruisers *Topeka Atlanta, Dayton* and *Oklahoma City*, with a destroyer screen, came within three miles of shore to shell fortifications on Cape Nojima, due south of Tokyo Bay. The wind was blowing in the direction of the camp so we could hear some of the gun-fire from ship and shore batteries. This started off another of the 'Yanks have landed' rumours—not in Kyushu but in Tokyo Bay!

Continuing this battle-practice, undisturbed by any unit of what was once the third largest navy in the world with three 72,000 ton battleships, the Anglo-American battleships and destroyers proceeded along the coast to shell Shimizu, the port for the battered Nagoya, and Hammamatsu about 135 miles S.W. of Tokyo on 29th and 30th July. Other day, and night, attacks were made between 28th and 31st by destroyers of the amazing U.S. 3rd Fleet .

On night 30/31st July, part of the *battleship task-force* closed with the shore to shell Yokosuka Naval Yard, Shimizu and forts in the Yokohama and Tokyo Bay area.

While these naval operations were proceeding, official communiques were issued regarding the 'enormous successes against the enemy in the *OKINAWA BATTLE AREA!*' According to these reports the Kamikaze corps brought down 500 British and American aircraft in addition to destroying a further 400 on the ground during the period 25-31st July. The communiques stated that 'the enemy aircraft destroyed in air combat, or on the ground, during the Okinawa battles totalled 2,105.' Also— during the same period—'Kamikaze suicide-aquads sank or damaged another 10 enemy warships bringing the grand-total (for the Okinawa battles) to 408 including battleships, cruisers, aircraft-carriers, destroyers, transports, tankers, and landing-craft . . . ' The final statement gave in tabular form the type and number of vesels sunk, damaged or slightly damaged between 1st April and 31st July.

Certainly the Kamikaze suicide-squads had enough 'floating targets' to aim at for from mid-July the Anglo-American fleet consisted of 133 major units. The American Navy was represented by 8 battleships, 16 aircraft-carriers, 19 cruisers and 62 large destroyers: the British Navy by one battleship, 4 aircraft-carriers, 6 cruisers and 17 destroyers.

No doubt the combined fleet suffered heavy casualties and one report (in the New York Times of 12th August, 1945) stated that 'Baka kamikaze's' sank 20 and damaged 30 warships, with heavy loss of life. Vessels destroyed by the crash tactics of Japanese airmen included 11 destroyers, 3 escort-carriers, 2 mine-sweepers, and 2 ammunition ships: vessels damaged were 5 American and 3 British aircraft-carriers, 4 battleships, 2 escort-carriers, 3 American and 1 Australian cruiser, 11 destroyers and 1 hospital ship.

However, one thing was certain. Japan's Navy was now reduced to 'bits and pieces' and when the remnants were handed over, in September, 1945, only 52 out of 380 major warships which were engaged on active service during World War II remained afloat.

The undernoted summary of Japan's original naval strength and the wastage during hostilities should make it abundantly clear why the Anglo-American fleet was hardly molested during the latter part of July, 1945.

Type of ship	In commission 1941 to 1945	Losses 1941-5	Handed over September 1945	
Battleships	12	11	1	Nagato
Fleet-carriers	13	11	2	Hakata. Kata-Suragi
Light-carriers	7	5	2	
Heavy-cruisers	19	16	3	
Escort-carriers	5	5	0	
Light-cruisers	22	20	2	
Destroyers	162	136	26	
Submarines	140	124	16	
	380	328	52	

In addition to the 16 first-line submarines handed over there were 6 German U-boats, and—at Kure Naval base—there were 150 midget-submarines in dock on 30th August, 1945.

At the other end of the classification of submarines, Japan handed over the same day two super-submarines, 'I-400 and I-14'.

The largest of the two, 'I-400', was 396 ft. long with an actual displacement of 5,500 tons, the smaller ship, 'I-14', was

375 ft.—and about the same tonnage. Surface speed was 13 knots with fuel capacity for four months—giving a cruising range of over 30,000 miles. Both carried hydro planes with folding wings and were catapulted along a 200 ft. take-off track. Both were commissioned in December, 1944 and carried crews of 21 officers and 170 men. Both submarines had recently returned from carrying supplies to Japanese garrisons at Truk and other Pacific islands.

These super-submarines steamed across Sagami Bay under escort and tied up to the U.S. submarine *Proteus*.

With regard to Japan's merchant shipping. She began the war with about 6,000,000 tons and ended it with a bare 1,000,000 tons—about 300 vessels in all. Progressive wastage was as follows:—

	1941-42	*1943*	*1944*	*1945*
Losses:—	900,000	1,000,000	1,500,000	1,600,000 tons

According to The United States Strategic Bombing Survey—1st July, 1946—U.S. submarines sank 55 per cent and U.S. air forces 40 per cent of Japan's total loss of merchant shipping—the rest was attributed to mining during 1945.

On 12th August, 1945, U.S. Navy Department announced the U.S. losses as 51 submarines and 70 destroyers.

U.S. submarine successes included 4 of Japan's Escort aircraft carriers, 4 Fleet aircraft carriers, 13 heavy and light cruisers, and 3 battleships.

Japan's battleship fleet was not entirely modern or fully adapted to cope with modern submarines or air attack. The oldest battleships were built in 1913—*four*, 31,000 ton ships—the newest in 1940—*three*, 72,809 ton, 863 ft. long, 127 ft. beam, 35½ ft. draught, 27 knot ships mounting *nine* 18.1 in. and six 6.1 in. guns.

Battleship classification was as follows:—

Number	Tonnage	Built	Destroyed		
4	31,000	1913	*1942:2*	*1944:1*	*1945:1*
2	33,000	1915	*1944:2*		
2	34,500	1917	*1945:2*		
1	37,500	1920	*1943:1*		
*3	72,809	1940	*1944:1*	*1945:1*	

*YAMATO was commissioned December, 1941: MUSASHI in August, 1942. SHINANO was completed as aircraft carrier in November 1944 and destroyed by U.S. Submarine *Archerfish* on 28th November, 1944.

X

The progressive destruction of Japan's surface fleet, by the U.S. (and British) airforce, submarine and surface craft is as follows:—

| Type of warship | Number and year of destruction | | | | TOTALS |
	1941-42	1943	1944	1945	
BATTLESHIPS	2	1	4	4	11
FLEET CARRIERS (17,500 to 72,809 ton)	4	1	5	1	11
LIGHT CARRIERS (8,500 to 12,000 ton)	2	0	3	0	5
ESCORT CARRIERS (17,000 to 21,000 ton)	0	1	3	1	5
HEAVY CRUISERS (8,800 to 14,000 ton)	4	0	8	4	16
LIGHT CRUISERS (3,300 to 7,000 ton)	1	2	13	4	20
DESTROYERS	21	32	64	19	136
	34	37	100	33	204

Half the total of surface losses occurred during 1944.

The success of the U.S. Airforce in bombing Japan into surrender is conveyed by U.S. official statistics which may be summarised as follows: Japanese aircraft attained a peak production in June, 1944 with an output of 2,857 planes, this output was reduced to 1,003 planes in July, 1945: during the war Japan produced 32,500 aircraft of army type (excluding 3,500 combat type in service December, 1941) and 30,295 navy type (excluding 1,200 in service December,1941): TOTAL LOSSES, from all causes, was 25,500 army and 26,609 navy type.

Not only was irreplaceable plant crushed to splinters by B29's but nearly all Japan's oil and petrol installations were set alight by incendiaries some of which were of the 110-gallon tank 'napalm' (gasoline-impregnated jelly) type.

It should be emphasized that not a single item mentioned in these statistics of destruction has any connection with the use of two atom bombs, on Hiroshima and Nagasaki. It was due to the action of submarines, surface-craft and aircraft employed against Japan from 1942 to 1945 when Japan surrendered.

No doubt, in time, the atom-bomb myth will be added to the large collection of Japanese traditions, from Amaterasu to the divine Tenno of 1945, to explain away the simpler facts of a most decisive defeat and the fall of the Japanese Empire in Greater East Asia.*

* See Appendix XI and XIII.

CHAPTER XIX

THE ATOMIC BOMBS

i. Hiroshima

'With Earth's first Clay They did the Last Man's knead,
And then of the Last Harvest sow'd the Seed:
Yea, the first Morning of Creation wrote
What the Last Dawn of Reckoning shall read.
OMAR KHAYYAM.

August was ushered in by a *super-B 29-raid* on the petroleum establishments of Hachioji, Toyama, Nagaoka, Mito and Kawasaki—no fewer than *820 B 29's* released *6,600 tons* of high-explosives on the days objectives. On the night of 5/6th August another super-raid, carried out by *550 B 29's*, destroyed oil-refineries, synthetic-oil plants, storage-tanks and petrol-dumps in the same area.

Under date of 8th August this is what I scribbled on pieces of paper and circulated in Omori camp:—

Bombing raids—6/7—West Japan, 350 B 29's. Sea of Japan 70: P 51's, P 47's and 6 PB 4Y's.

Hiroshima 6th: New type of delayed-action bomb (land-mine?) detonated. Dropped from 5-6000 m. Claimed to be 'enemy's inhuman decisive revenge bomb like the V2 used on England by Germans in their last revengeful bombing.' This bomb, it is claimed, burns and scalds and it is aimed at destroying morale.

H.I.H. Prince Ri was killed in action at Hiroshima on 7 August. The new type of bomb, being dropped by B 29's, is of the parachute-suspended type: it is timed to explode in the air.

There is considerable criticism in the press of 8th, of this method of intimidation and it would appear that, unofficially, the Japanese Government—through their representative in Switzerland—has made some kind of a protest against indiscriminate bombing.

The newspaper comment is couched in terms which denote increasing anxiety for some kind of action, by the Government, to pave the way for a request for an armistice 'in the name of humanity'.

The brutality of the enemy (so the criticism reads) shows that to a Christian Nation (U.S.A.) to destroy life is counted to be righteousness, and to kill innocent citizens, to disregard humanity and the teaching of Christ, is an expression of their present faith. And (it proceeds) Japan has abundant proof of her allegations of inhumanity. 'The U.S.A. disregard of all morality is based on the consciousness of her great power—it is the extreme expression of inhumanity'.

N.B.:—Whatever the reason for this outburst it is quite a new form of desperate protest against being bombed into unconditional surrender.

There is also a growing tendency to link Soviets with China and through China with U.S.A. There is definite criticism of 'Soviet bad influence in China' and the accusation that U.S.A. and U.S.S.R. are 'deceiving China for their own ends'.

Anti-Soviet outbursts, since the closing of Potsdam Conference, and petulant criticism, is also noticable in numerous references to China, the Far Eastern War and Russia.

There may be something important behind this outcry against bombing.

The 'Gazette Lausanne' (Swiss newspaper) is quoted by 'Mainichi' to the effect that, in an editorial in issue of 6th August, the Swiss newspapers refer to 'the brutal and indiscriminate bombing of the cities and towns by the American Airforce.' It strongly advises 'the neutral Government of Switzerland to investigate the above charges and to suggest to the U.S.A. the suspension of such cruel measures of attack on a nation as indiscriminate bombing.' Then it goes on to say :'compare the indiscriminate bombing with the brutal methods of Germans in the concentration camps of Belsen, etc'.

The Swiss newspaper 'urges the U.S.A. to suspend their indiscriminate bombing and investigate this charge of irrational conduct. All the evidence (it says) from the American side confirms the 'impending wholesale bombing of Japan into subjection in line with the Potsdam Declaration and the required numbers of B 29's are available. Thus Europe is informed, in the near future, the men, women and children are to be destroyed by this type of bombing. We, who are neutrals, should not forget our rights and responsibilities and the Swiss neutral Government, faced with this problem, is in a difficult position to obtain accurate understanding of the matter, so the Red Cross, established in every country, should fullfil its duty and make an abundant investigation of the problem'.

Stimpson claims that U.S.A. has an extraordinary surplus of armed forces for the final phase of the War against Japan: U.S.A. having 2 million on Pacific front at present.

Information Bureau refers to a new American *land-mine* being used.

Pope has appealed to Truman to moderate the intensity of the wholesale bombing of Japan but Truman has replied that this cannot be agreed to.

There is increasing evidence of the destructiveness of the new land-mine: no casualties are given for Hiroshima but there is mention of its demoralizing effect on women and children.

Perhaps the Japanese Government, and their scientific advisers, were better informed than the 'Information Bureau' but the scribes (and ordinary sciolists like myself) took it for granted that a *super-land-mine* had been dropped on Hiroshima. Indeed it was not until Japanese newspapers printed reports from abroad that those outside the flattened city Hiroshima realised that it had been selected for another experiment in concentrated destructiveness.

Already more than 250,000 Japanese had been killed and buried, with a further 400,000 maimed and crippled by the bombing of 66 towns and cities. So, if the enemy was using a super-container for explosives, instead of an ordinary H.E. bomb, there was nothing but an intensification of the total-war to comment on, and it did not effect the morale of 70 million people because at least one in three had been in the target-areas for several months.

So far there had been no reports of demonstrations against the Government and no printed appeals to the Tenno to sue for Peace—it was still *shi-kata-ga-nai!*

On 7th August, B 29's bombed the Naval Arsenal at Toyama and on 8th the aircraft plant in Tokyo, targets in Fukuyama and Yawata and mine-laying in Rashin harbour (Korea) were the only items of news I recorded.

ii. Nagasaki

It was the turn of carrier-borne aircraft on 9th August: 1,200 planes, from combined fleet, operated against Koriyama, Masuda, Matsushima, Niigata, Sendai and Yabuki in North Honshu. Surface craft shelled Kamaishi steel-works.

In the report I circulated of that routine bombing of 'selected targets' I included this item of later news . . . ' Two *B 29's* dropped a land-mine on Nagasaki. *150 B 29's* bombed Kurume, in West Honshu, dropping land-mines.' That was all I knew, at the time, regarding the atom-bombing of Nagasaki.

Newspapers, which I got hold of, used the word '*ji-rai*'—

land-mine—when reporting the damage at Hiroshima *until after* the atom-bomb had destroyed Nagasaki. It was then that the word 'gen-shi'—*atom*—replaced the word ji-rai. The land-mine became '*Genshi-no-bakudan*'—atom-bomb, but I remained under the impression that numbers of 'ji-rai' (or 'genshi-no-bakudan') had been dropped by B 29's. However, after Nagasaki had been dealt with, there was no confusion of thought in the mind of Japanese reporters for they commented freely on the 'gen-shi-no-boi' (the great violence of the atom-bomb) when photographs of the Hiroshima damage were published in the newspapers.

iii. Atom-bomb casualties

After the destruction of Nagasaki, casualties for Hiroshima were announced as . . . ' 70,000 killed, 40,000 injured'. Then, on 22nd August, 1945, Tokyo Radio broadcast the information that . . . '160,000 were *killed or injured* at Hiroshima where 200,000 are homeless. 120,000 were *killed or injured* at Nagasaki'.

On 3rd September, 1945, an official report stated, '22,000 have died since the communique of 20th August making the total of known dead 53,000 at Hiroshima. It is now estimated that the final count of the dead at Hiroshima will reach 80,000'.

The 'final figures' for Hiroshima (issued in 1945) were— '78,150 killed, 69,000 injured and 13,983 missing'. This gave a total of *161,133* which agreed with the broadcast estimate on 22nd August, 1945. The statement included the information that 'Nine square miles of Hiroshima had been blasted out of recognition'.

But the casualties (at Hiroshima) continue to grow. On 29th August, 1949, it was reported from New York that the Mayor of Hiroshima (Mr. Hamai) broadcast to the American people that the 'actual total of *deaths* was between 210,000 and 240,000 which included about *30,000 troops* and *30,000 imported workers* who were not included in the official death roll in 1945 . . . '

From time to time 'revised figures' have been given for Nagasaki. The latest statement (issued by the 'Committee for the Preservation of Data of Atomic Bombing') 9th September, 1949, gives the number of killed as 73,884 and 6,796 injured or missing.*

*These figures for casualties may or may not be correct but the reader should consult the Report of the British Mission to Japan, 1946, reference Hiroshima and Nagasaki.

At the time the atom bombs were dropped the population of Hiroshima was (approximately) 320,000—including troops—and the population of Nagasaki about 260,000 of whom not more than half were in the industrial 'target' area of about *two square miles* which was also 'blasted out of recognition'.

The casualty figures, as given above, speak for themselves—grim statistics of the use of weapons of mass destruction, atomic energy applied to war. But I am tempted to make this comparison between the incendiary raid on Tokyo (9/10th March, 1945) and the blast effects of the atomic bombs at Hiroshima and Nagasaki.

At Tokyo, 15.8 miles of the city were destroyed, *83,000* men, women and children were *killed* and *102,000* others *injured* by *1,667 tons* of incendiaries dropped from a bombing altitude of 7,050 ft., by *279 B 29's*. The raid on Tokyo lasted several hours. The 'raid' on Hiroshima and Nagasaki was by one machine over the towns for a few minutes and then the killing was *instantaneous* in the target areas of two square miles or so. The 'human target' at Tokyo was a million or more whereas at Hiroshima-Nagasaki it did not exceed 600,000 men, women and children.

From a purely scientific point of view the atom bombs were a success—a hideous, revolting success. The progress of our 'civilization', on its way to its own cremation, was facilitated by a 'secret weapon' of mass destruction. The team of scientific experts responsible for its perfection, no less than the politicians, have reason to be conscious of their successful collaboration in overcoming all the difficulties which confronted them before two atom bombs were used on the Japanese.

Only two atom bombs were in existence in August, 1945, and —from first to last—they cost the United States of America no less than $2,000,000,000. But the explosive energy of the bomb was equivalent to that of 20,000 tons of T.N.T., and never before could so many human beings be obliterated, or reduced to dust, in the fraction of the speed of sound. Never before was science so exact in its calculations to produce such a compact explosive —such a remarkable coercive bludgeon. Whether it was necessary to use the atom bomb against Japan in August, 1945, is a matter of opinion.

Measured in terms of dollars and cents, per head of population killed, $2,000,000,000 for 200,000 Japanese was not expensive and it would be foolish to single out the atom bomb for condemnation because it is superior to conventional explosives used in war, and it would be even more stupid to blame the scientist because he produces what the 'world' requires for its preservation!

According to the Japanese press, President Truman broadcast to the nation at 7 p.m., 9th August, 1945. In his address he mentioned that he indicated to the Soviet delegation at Potsdam that U.S.A. had special war weapons to use against Japan, and he also stressed the importance of the U.S.A.-G.B. agreement to bring Japan to a state of unconditional surrender. To this broadcast the Japanese Government replied by protesting, through the Swiss Minister in Tokyo on 10th August, 'against the disregard of International Law by U.S.A., particularly against the brutality of the new land-mine used against Hiroshima on 6th August'. It went on to remind President Truman of his previous statement that 'U.S. bombers had as their targets industrial areas—whereas it was the residential centre of Hiroshima which had been destroyed completely on 6th August'.

iv. Why were atomic bombs used?

In June, 1945, President Truman and his advisers are said to have been in agreement not to use the atomic bomb. A policy committee, under Mr. Byrnes, it was stated, had prepared a report for President Truman and Mr. Churchill recommending that the bomb should not be used because it would not be wise for the United States of America to create a precedent for the use of such a terrible weapon.

A month later, during the Potsdam Conference, this wise decision was reversed after they had been informed of the success of the experiment carried out in the secrecy of the Mexican desert.

They also warned Japan, quite clearly, that ' . . . The alternative for Japan is complete and utter destruction . . . ' but did not specify the atomic bomb as the precise method of complete and utter destruction.

There was no need to. According to the 'rules of total-warfare' all weapons suitable for destruction are used by any power without a declaration of intention. Japan was warned. In total warfare there is no room for sentiment. The objectives are clearly defined—complete and utter destruction at the earliest possible moment after the opening of hostilities. It was mere hypocrisy for Japan to cite 'International Law' after she had ignored it for twenty years and placed herself on record as the equal of the Huns in barbarity when she had 'residential centres' in China and elsewhere at the mercy of her indiscriminate bombers.

Hiroshima and Nagasaki were *total-warfare* answers to the brutality of the Bataan death march and the 'polite bombing' of Pearl Harbour.

Mr. Winston Churchill (in the House on 16th August, 1945) stated quite clearly what Japan would have done had she been in possession of atomic bombs. Still, I shall never be convinced that it was necessary to use the atomic bomb, least of all on Nagasaki so soon after Hiroshima. Certainly not to 'prevent the sacrifice of a million American and a quarter of a million British lives in the desperate battles and massacres of an invasion of Japan'. Japan, *before the Potsdam Declaration,* had told the Soviet Union that she was ready to discuss terms of surrender with the allies.

There was almost as much secrecy observed about Japan's overtures for Peace as there was secrecy regarding the atomic bombs.

The Potsdam Three-Power Conference opened on 17th and closed on 25th July, 1945: the result of the British General Election was announced on 26th July—Mr. Attlee formed the Labour Government on 27th July and the atomic bomb was used on 6th August.

In a written reply to Mr. Horabin (Cornwall N. Ind. L.) Mr. Attlee in December, 1946, furnished this explanation:—

'No overtures for peace were made by Japan to the countries *with which she was at war* prior to her acceptance of the terms of the Potsdam Declaration, which she did not communicate to us until 10th August, 1945 15 days after the declaration had been made and four days after the dropping of the first atomic bomb.

It was known, however, that the Japanese leaders had previously been considering means of reaching a settlement more favourable to themselves tham unconditional surrender.

At Potsdam, on 28th July, Generalissimo Stalin informed President Truman and me *in strict confidence* that the Soviet Government, who had not at that time joined in the Far Eastern War, had received from the Japanese Government a proposal that they should act as mediators between the Japanese Government and the British and United States Government. According to Generalissimo Stalin, the Soviet Government interpreted this move as an attempt to obtain the collaboration of the Soviet Government in the furtherance of Japanese policy, and they had therefore returned an unhesitating negative.

The information thus furnished by Generalissimo Stalin offered no new opportunity for hastening the concluson of the war since the Japanese Government had already, by the Potsdam Declaration of 26th July, been invited in the most formal manner to surrender. . . . .'

From this it is quite clear that nothing but unconditional surrender in advance of negotiations would be accepted, as a basis for restoration of peace, no matter how many millions of British or American lives were involved in the political decision, so the atomic bombs were used.

The armed forces of Japan were too widely distributed to be incinerated in blocks of 50,000 at a time—against dispersed troops an atomic bomb is merely the intensification of concentrated air attack—it is less discriminating but more destructive and intimidating than T.N.T. packed in metal containers. The 'explosive energy of the atomic bomb was equivalent to that of 20,000 *tons* of T.N.T.' according to President Truman.

Mr. Churchill, speaking about Britain's share in atom-bomb research work, added—merely for dramatic emphasis : 'By God's mercy British and American science outpaced all German efforts'.

Deists and materialists, on the winning side in World War II, can thank their 'lucky stars' that we were not bombed into unconditional surrender by Hitler or Showa Tenno. Perhaps, Japanese first-hand experiences of atomic energy applied to war will turn her from Shinto to Christianity in order to win in the next war.

On 10th August, 1,200 carriers from combined fleet repeated the attacks of the previous day on the same targets in North Honshu.

Then on 11th and 12th hundreds of fighters and dive-bombers raided the Tokyo-area aerodromes: on 13th there was a mass demonstration over Tokyo—the record number of 1,600 strikes were made between sunrise and sunset on all the battered targets.

The end was in sight. On 14th August, 400 B 29's raided Kure and Hikari naval bases while a smaller formation struck at Osaka arsenal. In Omori we had another dawn to dusk spectacle of flight after flight of fighters and fighter-bombers machine-gunning the military targets to drive home the lessons of Hiroshima and Nagasaki.

CHAPTER XX

SOVIET INTRANSIGENCE

---

i. Potsdam Conference
The U.S.S.R. declines to intervene at Japan's request

The U.S.S.R. celebrates VJ DAY as a triumph of the Russian Army over the Japanese. But, in the final analysis, the role of the 'RED ARMY' is on the same footing as that of Italy when France was overwhelmed by Germany in June, 1940. Russia, under Stalin, like Italy under Mussolini, immobilized part of the 'enemy troops' but, in neither case were Germany or Japan short of manpower. The negative action was of no consequence to the prosecution of the war by the other axis powers.

Before the capture of the Bonins and Okinawa, by the U.S.A., the U.S.S.R. could have assisted the A.A.F. by placing at their disposal the air-bases in Kamchatka, North Saghalien or Vladivostock. They were neutral. The A.A.F. created their own air-bases and, long before the defeat of Germany, they had bombed Rashin in Korea which is only 125 miles from Vladivostok and which involved the B 29's in a round trip of 4,160 miles from Iwo Jima.

Ideologies, like oil and water, do not mix readily. But, in the extreme hour of national danger, dilutions of a 'common ideal solvent' bring about an artificial coalescence. We need not trouble about what has occured in Europe since the Potsdam Conference, but Japan's major mistake after 1939 was the approach she made to Soviet realism on the thesis that 'mutual interests in the Far East' would be served by 'common action and close co-operation'.

In April, 1941, it served the common interests of the U.S.S.R. and Japan to conclude the Neutrality Pact: *only two months later* it was more than convenient to abide by the pact because the U.S.S.R. was retreating before Hitler's storm-troops. But in

March, 1945, when General Koiso's special pleaders were in Moscow, trying to persuade her friends (?) to obtain terms of surrender from the Allies, Stalin denounced the inconvenient pact.

Japan was acting on her interpretation of Soviet Imperialism which is essentially the same as that of Tsarist Russia. But the practical ethics of Stalin demanded an indispensable element in 'Pacts'—w:th Germany or Japan—and, in 1945, it was sure that Japan could not survive World War II as a Power to be reckoned with in Asia. It is true that there was no Stalin in Tsarist Russia when the Russo-Japanese Treaty of 30th July, 1907, was concluded with the secret clauses giving Japan a free hand in Korea and regulating Russian and Japanese spheres of influence in Manchuria, and Stalin had nothing to do with the Russo-Japanese Treaty of June, 1916 (which followed Japan's 21 demands on China in 1915) with more secret clauses which bound Japan and Russia in a *military alliance* to fight any third power attempting to establish domination over *China*. But 1916, or 1941, was not 1945 and Stalin had already secured another *secret treaty* which re-established Russia in Manchuria at the expense of China.

Japanese envoys were working in the dark in July, 1945: the Soviet Ambassador Malik, in Tokyo, was too ill to discuss politics so the Japanese Ambassador Sato, in Moscow, was instructed to see the Vice-Commissar for Foreign Affairs and place before him the Japanese Government's urgent request for their services in placing before the allies *overtures for peace*, not for the furtherance of *Japanese policy*.

According to my notes, based on 'Mainichi' reports, Sato saw the 'Head of the Soviet Foreign Affairs Bureau on July 14th, Mr. Molotov on 15th and Mr. Stalin on 16th before he left by plane for the Potsdam Conference which is to be held on 17th July'.

This urgent attempt to obtain allied terms, through the U.S.S.R., took place *ten days before* the Potsdam Declaration, and it is referred to in the Japanese Government's broadcast of 10th August, 1945, in these words:—' . . . the Japanese Government several weeks ago asked the Soviet Government, with which neutral relations then prevailed, to render its good services *in restoring peace* with the enemy Powers. Unfortunately these efforts in the interests of *Peace* having failed . . . . etc. etc.'

The Potsdam Declaration was signed by President Truman and Mr. Churchill and approved (by radio) by General Chiang Kai Shek, and there was nothing in it to indicate that Japan had approached the U.S.S.R. In fact it was not until two days later—28th July—that President Truman and Mr. Attlee were informed *in strict confidence* about a Japanese proposal.

The opening paragraph, of the Declaration, states that the *three powers* 'having conferred and agree that Japan should be given an opportunity to end the war'—the concluding paragraph reads . . . 'We call upon the Government of Japan to proclaim now the unconditional surrender of all the Japanese armed forces and to provide adequate assurances of their good faith in such action. The alternative for Japan is complete and utter destruction . . . .'

ii. Soviet intervention in the War
YALTA *secret agreement concerning the entry of the Soviet Union into the War against Japan*

When the Koiso Government were sounding the U.S.S.R. regarding her attitude towards the War in Greater Asia they were in ignorance of the terms of the YALTA AGREEMENT signed at Livadia on 11th February, 1945. General Koiso resigned on 6th April when Russia denounced the Neutrality Pact with Japan.

The text of the secret Yalta Agreement is as follows:—

> The leaders of the three Great Powers, the Soviet Union, the United States of America and Great Britain, have agreed that in two or three months after Germany has surrendered and the war in Europe has terminated the Soviet Union shall enter the war against Japan on the side of the allies on condition that:
>
> 1. The status quo in Outer Mongolia (The Mongolian People's Republic) shall be preserved.
> 2. The former rights of Russia violated by the treacherous attack of Japan in 1904 shall be restored—namely—(a) the southern part of Sakhalin as well as all the islands adjacent to it shall be returned to the Soviet Union; (b) the commercial port of Dairen shall be internationalized, the pre-eminent interests of the Soviet Union in this port being safeguarded and the lease of Port Arthur as a Naval Base of the U.S.S.R. restored; (c) the Chinese Eastern Railway and the South Manchurian Railroad which provides an outlet to Dairen shall be jointly operated by the

establishment of a joint Soviet-Chinese Company, it being understood that the pre-eminent interests of the Soviet Union shall be
safeguarded and that China shall retain full sovereignty in Manchuria.

3. The Kurile Islands shall be handed over to the Soviet Union.

It is understood that the agreement concerning Outer Mongolia
and the ports and railroads referred to above require concurrence
of Generalissimo Chiang-kai-shek. The President will take
measures in order to obtain this concurrence on advice from
Marshal Stalin.

The Heads of the three Great Powers have agreed that these
claims of the Soviet Union shall be unquestionably fulfilled after
Japan has been defeated.

For its part the Soviet Union expresses its readiness to conclude with the National Government of China a pact of friendship
and alliance between the U.S.S.R. and China in order to render
assistance to China with its armed forces for the purpose of
liberating China from Japanese yoke.

J. V. STALIN. FRANKLIN D. ROOSEVELT. WINSTON S. CHURCHILL.

The 'former rights of Russia' in China are to be restored on
condition that the U.S.S.R. enters the war against Japan: the
spoils of imperialism, lost as a result of the defeat in the Russo-
Japanese War, are to be handed back to the heirs of Tsardom as
the price to be paid by the upholders of democracy, to the expon-
ents of communism for their co-operation in the common cause.

During World War I, Japan was bribed to co-operate by the
gift of Pacific Islands north of the equator. These islands became
the front-line bases for Japan's bid for the conquest of Australia
in 1942. Before the outbreak of World War II, these Pacific
Islands were referred to by Japanese militarists as her 'life-line'
and were fortified accordingly.

President Roosevelt may or may not have been led astray by
Mr. Stalin but I venture to suggest that the Yalta bribes were
inconsistent with the Atlantic Charter (14th August, 1941) and the
United Nations' Declaration of 1st January, 1942, which was signed
by China, the United States and the United Kingdom. In the
Atlantic Charter we have 'certain common principles'—I quote
the first two : 'First, their countries seek no aggrandisement,
territorial or other. Second, they desire to see no territorial changes
that do not accord with the freely expressed wishes of the peoples
concerned.' These common principles were agreed to by the
U.S.S.R. when they signed the United Nations' Declaration,
and—what is more to the point—they form part of the Anglo-

Russian Treaty of Alliance signed on 26th May, 1942, for part of Article 5 reads . . . 'They will take into account the interests of the United Nations in these objects and they will act in accordance with the two principles of *not seeking territorial aggrandisement for themselves* and of *non-interference in the internal* affairs of other States.'

Port Arthur as a *Soviet Naval Base* was certainly not in accord with the freely expressed wishes of the peoples (Chinese) concerned. And with regard to the 'violation' of the former rights of Russia (in Manchuria) by the treacherous attack of Japan in 1904 this is as valid as the establishment of those former rights in 1896 when Japan (by *force majeure*) returned to China the territory which had been ceded to her in 1895. Russia marched in when Japan marched out—that is all. Then, after her defeat in the Russo-Japanese War, the 'former rights of Russia in Manchuria' were transferred back to Japan with China's consent.

The U.S.S.R. *claim* to Sakhalin and the Kuriles is based on these simple facts: in 1800 the Japanese were settled in the Kuriles and in Sakhalin: the Russo-Japanese Treaty (1855) which was negotiated by Admiral Putiatin fixed the boundary, in the Kuriles, between Iturup and Urup islands but the Russo-Japanese Treaty of 1875 gave the whole of Sakhalin to Russia and the Kurile Islands to Japan. However, after Russia's defeat in 1904-5, she ceded to Japan the southern half of Sakhalin in lieu of an indemnity. From 1905 to 1945, Russia accepted the position and by virtue of the Yalta bribe recovered the territory without risking an encounter with Japan.*

The Kuriles were used by Japan, during *World War II,* as advanced bases for her army, navy and airforce. The largest island, Etorofu, was the assembly point for the attack on Pearl Harbour. And now, in 1949, the U.S.S.R. has reconditioned all the old fortifications, rebuilt 16 airfields, and has made Paramushiro a fighter and bomber base, with dive-bombers based on Matsuwa (the former Japanese submarine and Navy headquarters) and coastal and anti-aircraft defences sited conveniently along the 700-mile cluster of islands. Why?

According to the White Paper, issued 5th August, 1949, by the State Department, covering United States relations with China

* See Appendix IX.

—1944 to 1949—the decisions taken at Yalta were considered to be justified and advantageous but for reasons of military security it was considered 'too dangerous for the United States to consult with the Nationalists on the Yalta agreement'. This may mean that President Roosevelt did not take 'measures in order to obtain (China's) concurrence on advice from Marshal Stalin' before he died on 12th April, 1945? Another point of interest is that Senator Vandenberg is reported as saying : 'The two principal mistakes of the United States were first, the price paid at Teheran and Yalta, at China's expense, for Russia's belated and unnecessary entry into the Japanese war; and, secondly, the well-intentioned, but impracticable, insistence upon a Nationalist-Communist coalition.'

China was not consulted when the Yalta secret agreement was signed at Livadia on 11th February, 1945, but (according to the White Paper mentioned above) the Soviet Union in 1944 gave an assurance to Major-General Hurley (U.S.A.) that they had no intention of recognizing any Government in China except the Kuomintang headed by Chiang Kai-shek. However (according to my information) it was not until July, 1945, that Chiang Kai-shek's envoy was called to Moscow to discuss the Yalta secret agreement with the U.S.S.R. and the first of these Soviet-Chinese discussions were interrupted when Marshal Stalin and Mr. Molotov left Moscow for the Potsdam Conference, on 16th July.

It was not until 6th August, 1945, that Mr. T. V. Soong and Mr. Wang Shih-chieh (Kuomintang representatives) arrived in Moscow to discuss the Yalta Agreement and they were not received by Marshal Stalin until 14th August, when the U.S.S.R were 'at war with Japan', to sign the relative Sino-Russian agreement.

iii. U.S.S.R. declares war on Japan

To revert to the Potsdam Conference. Marshal Stalin and Mr. Molotov remained in Berlin after the departure of President Truman, Mr. Churchill and Mr. Attlee. Suddenly, on 6th August, the Soviet leaders left by air for Moscow. Directly they arrived they attended an extraordinary meeting of the Soviet Supreme Council to discuss 'Far Eastern Problems and to arrive at an important decision regarding the Potsdam Declaration'. At least that was what the 'Mainichi's Moscow Correspondent' reported.

According to my notes: 'Mr. Molotov sent for Ambassador Sato on Thursday (9th) and informed him that because of an understanding with U.S.A. and Great Britain the U.S.S.R. demanded that Japan should capitulate and unless she did so Russia would attack. This ultimatum was conveyed to the Japanese Government but they have not yet replied to it. Without waiting for a reply, Russian troops made a sudden attack on Japanese troops in various parts of Manchuria. It appears—from numerous news items—that Molotov attached no time limit to his ultimatum but the substance of it is in line with the Potsdam Declaration of 26th July: Japan to withdraw all her troops from occupied areas and from Manchuria, Korea and Formosa and to confine herself to Japan proper. The Japanese Government had not sent any reply up to noon on 12th, but —according to another report—on 10th August at 11 a.m., Maisky (?) Chief of the Soviet Far Eastern Bureau called on Sato and handed him the formal declaration of war on Japan. Sato was placed under detention in his Moscow quarters. So far there is no mention of a Japanese reply to Soviet demand of 9th August.'

We had expected news of that kind for some time and had made certain of obtaining Tokyo newspapers. What with leaflets, bombing, shelling and atom bombs there was more 'news' than I could cope with. However, the Information Bureau stated on 10th that . . . 'Action of Soviets and use by Americans of land-mines has brought about an exceedingly difficult situation. On 9th, Soviet armed forces increased on border-line in Sakhalin and on border N.E. Korea. Russian troops crossed Korean-Soviet border and were engaged by Japanese defence units. Formations of up to 80 Soviet planes have been engaged and driven off. On 9th some Soviet troops crossed into South Sakhalin but were driven back. Soviet declaration of war coincided with aggressive action in various theatres of war . . . '

CONDITIONS attached to the YALTA AGREEMENT made it necessary for the U.S.S.R. to enter the war against Japan *in two or three months* after Germany surrendered which was on 7th May, 1945. By declaring war on 9th August, 1945, it would seem that the U.S.S.R. did qualify for restoration of her rights in China and elsewhere. Perhaps the news regarding the dropping of the atomic bomb on Hiroshima on 6th August was the deciding factor? In any case it was imperative for the U.S.S.R. to act before British or American troops landed in Sakhalin, Kuriles or South Manchuria. Perhaps the reluctance to transmit Japan's repeated requests for intervention was based on a desire to *prolong hostilities* until U.S.S.R. entered the war against Japan? Russia was not at war with Japan until 10th August, 1945, and her Ambassador in Tokyo (to say nothing of the negotiations in Moscow) was being pressed to take action favourable to Japan six months earlier. But action was swift when it was obvious that Japan was about to accept the terms of the Potsdam Declaration.

Mr. Byrnes, the former United States Secretary of State, in his book *'Speaking Frankly'* discloses that it was President Roosevelt's military advisers who persuaded him to pay Russia's price for entering the war against Japan. The terms of the 'secret agreement' made at the Yalta Conference were not made public until *after* Moscow radio on 27th January, 1946, announced that the United States and Britain had conceded possession of the Kuriles to the U.S.S.R. Mr. Byrnes had left the Yalta Conference before the Agreement was concluded and knew nothing about it until after the Japanese surrender.

The full text of the Agreement was published in *The Times* on 12th February, 1946, and in other newspapers, but there have been modifications of its terms, since it was signed on 11th February, 1945, as they applied to China. Port Arthur is to be a joint naval base, Chinese authority in the free port of Dairen was clarified, the Railroads are to be operated as a joint proposition under a single administration, under Chinese sovereignty, as a commercial enterprise. And—no doubt—General Mao-tse tung, the communist leader of China in 1949, will safeguard Soviet interests in Manchuria.

The Soviet High Command had the satisfaction of announcing 'great victories over the Japanese' and by 20th August they had accepted the surrender of 513,000 men including 81 generals. One order contained the following *'order of the day'* addressed to Marshal Vassilievsky, C.-in-C. Soviet forces in the Far East, from Marshal Stalin:—

'To-night at 10 p.m. our capital, in the name of the motherland, will salute our gallant Transbaikal and Far Eastern Forces and the Pacific Fleet, and also the Mongolian army under Marshal Choy-pao-san, who have liberated Manchuria, South Sakhalin, and part of the Kurile archipelago, with 24 artillery salvos from 324 guns. May the Red Army and Fleet live and prosper.'

The U.S.S.R. declared *war* on Japan at 11 a.m. on 10th August: Japan's acceptance of the Potsdam Declaration was broadcast, and cabled to the United States of America, at 07.00 hours on 10th August. In other words Russia *declared war after Japan* had *accepted unconditional surrender* so the terms of the Yalta Agreement may or may not be complied with.

Admiral Suzuki, on 28th July, broadcast to the nation that the terms in the Potsdam Declaration were unworthy of official comment and would be *ignored* by the Government. He mentioned that aircraft production was above expectation and he was quite satisfied to leave questions of defence to the military authorities.

But a fortnight later the Potsdam Declaration figured largely in the affairs of the nation.

According to my notes: 'August 11th—no news yet about special cabinet meetings. Soviet declaration of war, 10th, coming so soon after demands of 9th to cease resistance, has taken the entire nation by surprise—they seem dazed by this addition to the day and night bombing. It is too soon to say that no action will be taken to try and obtain peace instead of obliteration, and it would appear that the Emperor may be forced to save the people from destruction. No doubt the extreme militarists will resist but the bulk of the army (in Japan) would obey the Emperor, leaving the problem of the action of overseas commands a matter of conjecture . . . '

'12th August—this appeared in an editorial . . . "The centre of the nation is the heart of the Emperor. And for Japanese there is one person to whom the people turn. The decisions and the orders of the Emperor will be obeyed with respect and he will be served by all the nation with loyalty. The duty of the people is to accomplish his will in the utmost difficult position now faced by his 100 million subjects who will combine to have unity of action. In one's heart there is a means of escape which of its own accord will suggest itself. The Soviets have declared war on us and we shall meet this new challenge to our national qualities, and we shall pray as we defend the Constitution and keep it intact . . . "

'General Anami, War Minister, has issued a *special order of the day* in which he enjoins all officers and men to face the terrible situation they are in with all their courage and loyalty. He concludes: "In our hearts there is a means of escape which of its own accord will suggest itself." This is another way of saying— "Death in preference to ignominous surrender." Anami stresses the point that the Emperor's orders must be obeyed and that the "centre of the nation is the heart of the Emperor".'

General Anami was one of the first to commit hara-kiri after the Emperor's broadcast to the nation on 14th August, 1945.

CHAPTER XXI

JAPAN'S UNCONDITIONAL SURRENDER

---

i. *Showa Tenno's problem*

The Tenno agreed to surrender unconditionally to save his subjects from annihilation. But in order to avert civil war it was necessary that his Edict should be obeyed and that his 'divine authority' should remain unimpaired. It was a nation not an army which was involved in his decision: the armed forces, at home and overseas, had not yet realized the inevitableness of defeat. Two million men were at their battle stations in Japan waiting for the enemy to land, three million men were overseas —in Manchuria, China, Burma, Malaya, Borneo, Philippines, Indonesia and South Pacific Islands.

As Supreme Commander of the armed forces the Tenno could not ignore their fighting spirit, he could not sacrifice their honour to save civilians. His soldiers were in no danger from the atom bomb and would fight on as they fought at Iwo Jima and Okinawa.

To obtain consent to unconditional surrender from that scattered army, and to give adequate assurances of their good faith in such action, was no easy matter even for the Tenno of the Shinto State. And if it was to be accomplished it had to be done through the undisputed and unimpaired prerogatives of the Tenno upon whose person obedience and loyalty was centered and upon which the Shinto State had been created.

On 9th August, 1945, millions of leaflets were showered on the main islands of Japan. This is how they read:—

'We are in possession of the most destructive weapon ever designed by man. A single one of our atomic bombs equals the explosive power carried by 2,000 of our Super-Fortresses. This is an awful

342

fact for you to ponder. We have just begun to use this weapon. Before using this bomb again to destroy every resource which your military have to prolong this useless war we ask that you now petition your Emperor to end this war. Take steps now, or we shall employ this bomb promptly and forcefully. . . . . '

Mass slaughter in Hiroshima and Nagasaki by atomic bombs, to say nothing of the terror and destruction caused by B 29's, had created adequate conditions in one hundred widely separated places without the need to contemplate more destruction before sending in petitions to the Tenno. Already the total tonnage, dropped by the A.A.F. on Japanese targets, had reached 250,000 tons of H.E. and 100,000 tons of incendiaries including the latest type weighing 800 lb. which sets fire to an area of 300 ft. by 100 ft. on impact! Fire-bombs had improved since the days of 'Molotov's baskets'.

Some reports gave the total number *killed* in all bombing raids as nearer 500,000 than 250,000: we had 35 major raids in Tokyo-Yokohama area by a total of over 6,500 *B 29's* and 3,500 of the carrier-borne aircraft from November, 1944, to middle of August, 1945, and they had released 40,000 tons of H.E. and 6,000 tons of fire-bombs and machine-gun bullets.

The Tenno could have shirked his task, abdicated in favour of his young son or resorted to the traditional seppuku before the Shrine of his ancestors, but this would not have solved the immediate problem—it would have postponed the solution—that is all.

ii. Qualified 'unconditional surrender'
Preserving Tenno's prerogatives as a Sovereign ruler

On 9th August, immediately after receiving Molotov's ultimatum, the Supreme War Direction Council met in Tokyo. They were in conference all day but arrived at no decision which could be conveyed to the Tenno. Admiral's Suzuki and Yonai, with Foreign Minister Togo, were for accepting the Potsdam Declaration, but General's Anami and Umezu, with Admiral Toyoda, were against any *unconditional* acceptance. The full cabinet met the same afternoon but only to announce that three were for unconditional, three for conditional and three for modified acceptance.

Admiral Suzuki requested an Imperial Conference and this convened at midnight.

At this conference the decision was taken, on the recommen-
dation of the Tenno, to bring the war to an end. In the early
hours of 10th August the Tenno received twenty-one of his advisers, including his brothers Princes Chichibu and Takamatsu,
Prince Konoye, General Tojo, Baron Hiranuma, Admiral
Suzuki and his full Cabinet. The Potsdam ultimatum was
accepted on the understanding that it did not prejudice the
prerogatives of the Tenno. It was decided not to make the final
decision known to the public pending a reply from the United
Nations.

It was not a question of asking for the recognition by the
United Nations of the 'divinity of the Tenno' but of their acceptance of his 'constitutional rights' under the system of *Sai-sei-itchi*
or 'religious practices of the nation and the government administration indistinguishably and inseparably united and completely identified in one entire whole' as Professor Genchi Kato
puts it. Tenno as spiritual head of the Shinto State and C.-in-C.
of the armed forces.

The Japanese acceptance was cabled to the United States at
07.00 hours on 10th August through the Swiss Government.
Then, Tokyo Radio repeated the message, at dictation speed,
at 12.53 and 18.00 hours as follows:—

'The Japanese Government today addressed the following communication to the Swiss and Swedish Governments for transmission
to the United States, Britain, China and the Soviet Union:—

In obedience to the gracious command of His Majesty the
Emperor, who, ever anxious to enhance the cause of world peace,
desires earnestly to bring about an early termination of hostilities
with the view to saving mankind from the calamities to be imposed
upon them by the further continuance of the war, the Japanese
Government *several weeks ago* asked the *Soviet Government,* with which
neutral relations then prevailed, to render its good offices in
restoring peace with the enemy Powers.

Unfortunately these efforts in the interest of peace having failed,
the Japanese Government, in conformity with the august wish of
His Majesty to restore general peace and desiring to put an end to
the untold sufferings entailed by the war as quickly as possible
have decided upon the following:—

The Japanese Government is ready to accept the terms enume-
rated in the joint declaration issued at Potsdam on 26th July by
the heads of the Governments of the United States, Great Britain
and China and lately subscribed to by the Soviet Government
with the understanding that the declaration does not comprise any

demand which prejudices the prerogatives of His Majesty as a sovereign ruler.

The Japanese Government sincerely hope that this understanding is warranted and keenly desire that an explicit indication to that effect will be speedily forthcoming. . . . '

iii. The disillusioned Japanese

The population of Tokyo knew what was afoot: Foreign Minister Togo had called on the Soviet Ambassador—they had heard about the foreign language broadcast—everyone was talking of Peace!—of Hiroshima and the latest news from Nagasaki, the atom bomb—and the warning leaflets littering the streets.

The air over Tokyo was quiet that day. There had been no local air-raid warning—no B-Niju-Ku or other enemy aircraft rushing across the sky. Men, women and children stopped work in blitzed buildings and flocked to the centre of the City to join the crowd prostrating themselves before the sublime Palace of the Tenno.

Many of them had lost everything they had possessed in the great fires which had raged so furiously for days across the 'wide plain of Musashi' and reduced the City to rubble even as the pride of the Japanese Navy, the battleship 'Musashi', had been destroyed in Leyte Gulf the year before. All was lost but they did not blame God—they reproved themselves that they—the people—had failed the Tenno.

In Omori camp the prison guards chanted the choku-yu just as other Japanese soldiers had chanted it after Singapore had been captured from the British. There was no trace of bitterness—voices were loud and clear as they turned to the East to bow to the Palace and renew their faith in their Tenno.

Reply from the United Nations came on Sunday—12th August—it acknowledged receipt of Japan's communication, stated that it had been considered by the allied Governments who had decided to reply—as follows:—

'With regard to the Japanese Government's message accepting the terms of the Potsdam Declaration but containing the statement 'with the understanding that the said declaration does not comprise any demand which prejudices the prerogatives of His Majesty as Sovereign Ruler' our position is as follows:

From the moment of surrender the authority of the Emperor and the Japanese Government to rule the State shall be subject to the Supreme Commander of the allied Powers who will take such steps as he deems proper to effectuate the surrender terms. The Emperor will be required to authorize and ensure the signature of the Government of Japan and Japanese Imperial General Head-quarters of the surrender terms necessary to carry out the pro-visions of the Potsdam Declaration, and shall issue his commands to all the Japanese military, naval and air authorities and to all forces under their control wherever located to cease operations and surrender their arms, and to issue such other orders as the Supreme Commander may require to give effect to the surrender terms. Immediately upon the surrender the Japanese Government shall transport prisoners of war and civilian internees to places of safety as directed, where they can quickly be placed aboard allied transports.

The ultimate form of Government of Japan shall, in accordance with the Potsdam Declaration, be established by the freely ex-pressed will of the Japanese people. The allied Powers will remain in Japan until the purposes set forth in the Potsdam Declaration are achieved. The Allies now await the Japanese Government's reply.'

Crowds continued to gather in the vicinity of the Imperial Palace on the 13th. The press contained no information of the progress of the peace overtures—the air-raid warnings heralded the approach of enemy aircraft. All day long the fighters and the fighter-bombers machine-gunned and bombed their targets in our area. What was happening?

Far into the night the Cabinet debated the implications of the Potsdam Declaration and its effect on the legal position of the Tenno. In the end, thirteen ministers accepted the United Nation's conditions and three declined. Admiral Toyoda, Navy Chief of Staff, maintaining that the Allied reply avoided an answer to the main point, which was 'The Tenno is divine and could not accept orders from an earthly being'.

Admiral Suzuki, faced with opposition from General Anami, General Umezu (Chief of the General Staff) and Admiral Toyoda (Chief of Naval General Staff) who refused to sign the acceptance document, appealed to the Tenno who convened an Imperial Conference for 10.00 hours 14th August. It was at this conference that the Tenno, after hearing the opinions of the thirteen ministers, ordered the Cabinet to draft an Imperial Rescript which he would broadcast to the nation at noon. At the same time, Japan's acceptance was to be dispatched to the United Nations.

During the final Conference, the A.A.F. were bombing Kure, Hikari Naval Base and Hiroshima with *400 B 29's* while formations of 'Thunderbolts' and 'Lightnings' were plastering Osaka Military Arsenal. And, at intervals, other aircraft dropped millions of leaflets explaining to the Japanese the nature of the Allied reply to Japan's surrender offer.

From time to time, Tokyo Radio warned the people of Japan to stand-by for a vital announcement affecting the future of the 100 million subjects of the Tenno. Then came the special announcement that the Tenno would speak to his people at noon that day. But this did not interfere with the bombing programme of the A.A.F. From dawn the fighters and the fighter-bombers were in action in the Tokyo-Yokohama area 'shooting-up' the targets: even when the Omori camp-staff and guards were parading in front of the main office for the Tenno's broadcast we were watching a formation dive-bomb the adjacent aerodrome.

iv. *Tenno speaks to the heimin*

Precisely at noon, 14th August, 1945, the recorded voice of Tenno Heika was broadcast over Tokyo radio. The kodoites and the people of the soil listened in silence:

'To our good and loyal subjects: After pondering deeply on the general trend of the world and the actual conditions obtaining in our Empire today, we have decided to effect a settlement of the present situation by resorting to an extraordinary measure. We have ordered our Government to communicate to the Governments of the United States, Britain, China and the Soviet Union that our Empire accepts the provisions of their joint declaration. 'To strive for the common prosperity and happiness of all nations as well as for the security and well-being of our subjects is the solemn obligation which has been handed down by our Imperial Ancestors and which lies close to our hearts. Indeed we declared war on America and Britain out of our sincere desire to ensure Japan's self-preservation and the stabilization of East Asia, it being far from our thoughts either to infringe upon the sovereignty of other nations or to embark on territorial aggrandisement. But now the war has lasted for nearly four years. In spite of the best that has been done by everyone, the gallant fighting of the military and naval forces, the diligence and assiduity of our servants of the State, and the devoted service of our 100,000,000 people, the war situation has developed not necessarily to Japan's advantage, while the general trends of the world have all turned against her interests.

'The enemy, moreover, has begun to employ a new and most cruel bomb, the power of which to do damage is indeed incalculable, taking toll of many innocent lives. Should we continue to fight, it would only result in the ultimate collapse and obliteration of the Japanese nation and lead to the total extinction of human civilization. Such being the case, how are we to save millions of our subjects, or ourselves atone before the hallowed spirits of our Imperial ancestors?

'This is the reason we have ordered the acceptance of the provisions of the joint declaration of the Powers. We cannot but express the deepest sense of regret to our allied nations of East Asia, who have consistently co-operated with the Empire towards the emancipation of East Asia.

'The thought of those officers and men, as well as others who have fallen on the field of battle, of those who have died at their posts of duty or those who have met with untimely death, and those bereaved families, pains our heart night and day.

'The welfare of the wounded and war sufferers and of those who have lost homes and livelihood are objects of our profound solicitude. The hardships and sufferings to which our nation is to be subjected hereafter will certainly be great.

'We are keenly aware of the innermost feelings of all our subjects. However, it is according to the dictate of time and fate that we have resolved to pave the way for a peace for all generations to come by enduring the unavoidable, and suffering what is insufferable. Having been able to save and maintain the structure of the Imperial state, we are always with you, our good and loyal subjects, relying upon your sincerity and integrity.

'Beware most strictly lest any outbursts of emotion, which may engender needless complications, or any fraternal contention and strife, which may cause confusion, lead you astray and cause you to lose the confidence of the world. Let the entire nation continue as one family from generation to generation, ever firm in its faith in the imperishableness of its divine land and mindful of its heavy burden of responsibilities and the long road before it. Devote your united strength to construction for the future. Cultivate ways of rectitude, further nobility of spirit, and work with resolution, so that you may enhance the inate glory of the Imperial State and keep pace with the progress of the world. . . . '

Then there was silence—except for the rush of aircraft over the camp. Those who had been listening to the voice of the Tenno remained at attention for a few moments. Then Colonel Sakeba left his place in the parade and the next senior officer yelled 'Kei-rei' and those present saluted as if Sakeba was the Emperor in person.

The recording of the Tenno's message was kept in the Palace after it had been made. Some fanatics attempted to seize it before it was taken to the Tokyo broadcasting station. One report stated that Lt.-General Mori, Commandant of the Imperial Guard, was killed because he had allowed the recording to be taken to the radio station, and then the conspirators, led by a son-in-law of General Tojo, rushed there but were too late to stop the broadcast. However, directly the Tenno ceased speaking, Admiral Suzuki resigned with the rest of his Cabinet but received the Imperial Command to remain in office pending new appointments. General Anami, War Minister, lost no time in ending his own life.

The broadcast was full of excuses and explanations for years of aggression in China, and in Greater East Asia '*to ensure* Japan's *self-preservation* and the *stabilization of East Asia*, it being far from our thoughts either *to infringe upon the sovereignty* of other nations or to embark on *territorial aggrandisement*'.

The chief credit for bringing about the unconditional surrender of Japan goes to the XXI Bomber Command of the A.A.F., to the U.S. Marines, the combined navies and the 'Aussies' who helped the Marines to capture the island bases in the South Pacific.

CHAPTER XXII

THE END OF AGGRESSION

---

i. Japan's new Supreme Commander

The Omori camp staff, and the guards, accepted the unconditional surrender calmy. There was only one incident on the night of the Tenno's broadcast. A number of n.c.o's, and some of the camp staff, got drunk on sake and beer. They held a 'conference' and decided to use their swords on the A.A.F. 'special prisoners' still under guard in the special barracks.

Bubbling with yamato-damashi they advanced on the unarmed captives. Fortunately, one of the sentries gave the alarm and held them off at the point of the bayonet. As 'go-between' I attended, saw what was happening, gave the alert and had all the lights turned out in our barracks, went in to the 'special barrack' to warn them and then returned in time to see three of the guard holding the mob in check. Just then, when things were a bit tricky, 'Gentleman Jim' (Lt. Morigishi) appeared and took over.

One burly Sergeant-Major retired, bleeding profusely from a slash in the neck, a few others were manhandled and then bundled into a spare barrack-room. One by one, Morigishi called them out and disarmed them and received a nasty gash across the palms of his hands from one drunken fanatic. However, it all ended in a few cuts and a little blood-letting.

Next morning, after tenko, a Lieutenant from the Imperial Guard arrived. He came and apologised to me for the incident, emphasising that the culprits were 'camp staff' and not regular soldiers, and that in future an officer, and not an n.c.o., would be in command of the Omori camp guard. But, beyond Morigishi's action, none of the people who ran amok were punished.

The next few days, during the Manila negotiations, it was impossible to obtain a definition of our status under the terms of the cease-fire. Colonel Sakeba declined to discuss the matter and the camp staff continued to act as if they had never stood in silence listening to the Tenno's broadcast. On the other hand there were six-hundred prisoners of war in Omori camp and they had been informed by me of the exact position day by day —some wanted to take charge of the camp but I was against that as quite unnecessary.

I realised that it was one thing for the Tenno to accept unconditional surrender—by referring to it as 'acceptance of the joint declaration of the Powers'—and quite a different matter to convey the full implication of it to every unit commander of Japanese forces 'wherever located'. That would take a few days even with wireless communication, and we were not that well fed (or stocked with food) to take over the camp and feed ourselves on still shorter rations of rice and water.

On 15th August, President Truman brought matters to a head —he addressed this message to the Japanese Government:—

'You are to proceed as follows:—

(1) Direct the prompt cessation of hostilities by Japanese forces, informing the Supreme Commander of the Allied Forces of the effective date and hour of such cessation.

(2) Send emissaries at once to the Supreme Commander with information of the disposition of Japanese forces and commanders and with full powers to make any arrangements directed by the Supreme Commander to enable him and his accompanying forces to arrive at the place designated by him to receive formal surrender.

(3) For the purpose of receiving such surrender and of carrying it into effect, General Douglas MacArthur has been designated Supreme Commander for the Allied Powers, and he will notify the Japanese Government of a time, place and other details of the formal surrender . . . . '

The same day, General MacArthur instructed the Japanese Government to 'cease hostilities immediately . . . send a representative to American Headquarters Manila to receive instructions for carrying out the surrender terms: for the flight to Manila the code word would be 'Bataan': the party to travel in a Japanese plane to Ie Island (N. of Okinawa): exact date and hour of departure from southern tip of Kyushu, route and altitude of flight and estimated time of arrival to be broadcast six hours in advance: acknowledgement by radio of the Japanese broadcast required prior to take-off of the aeroplane: from Ie the Japanese party will be transported to Manila in an American aeroplane.'

There was some delay. The Japanese envoy, accompanied by fifteen others, arrived at Ie Shima on the morning of 19th. and then emplaned in a C-54-transport for the six-hour flight direct to Manila. Principal envoy was General Takashima, vice-chief of I.J.G.S., and after arrival at Manila the credentials of the party were examined by Lt.-General Sutherland, General Mac Arthur's Chief of Staff, before they went into conference.

During a four hour session the Japanese were given their general and specific orders and left Manila the following morning (20th) arriving back, in Tokyo, on 21st August with twenty-five pages of instructions covering the initial occupation of the Tokyo-Yokohama area. General MacArthur did not meet any of the Japanese delegation.

ii. Intermission

On 15th August, Admiral Suzuki's resignation had been accepted. The following day, Prince Higashi Kuni, cousin of the Tenno, member of the Supreme War Council and chief of the Home Defence forces, became Prime Minister. The Tenno's eldest daughter was married to the Prince's son so the appointment was in keeping with the divine traditions.

Prince Higashi Kuni commanded the Second Army in China from 1938 to 1940. He held the rank of General at the age of fifty-two and was alleged to be in opposition to General Tojo's South Pacific adventure as early as 1942.

On 16th August, Higashi Kuni, as Prime Minister and Minister of War, broadcast instructions to the nation, and particularly to the Army, to observe the Imperial Rescript to lay down arms, because 'The decision has been taken to cease fire and return to Peace.'

However, on 18th the air-raid warning sounded and within a few minutes we were watching a dog-fight between two 'Liberators' and some Japanese fighters! Two fighters crashed in flames and one of the 'Liberators' was damaged. Shortly afterwards two A.A.F. bombers went over the camp at high speed—making for the Yokohama area followed by anti-aircraft fire from ground defences.

We were puzzled—what was happening? In order to calm the nervous, and stop the rumour-mongers, I explained that the existence of an armistice was no reason for relaxation of vigilance in the service of protection, or of the readiness of troops for action, or for exhibiting positions to the enemy which could not be detected during combat. There had been no news of any envoy leaving Japan—up to the 18th—and there was still no news of the signing of a partial or a general armistice so—I presumed—it was another case of 'Photo Joe' taking snaps.

That was accepted as reasonable. But my stock fell very flat the next morning when the anti-aircraft batteries opened-up again.

I managed to get hold of a 'Yomiuri Hochi' of 20th and 'Mainichi' of 22nd August. The 'Yomiuri Hochi' published more 'cease fire orders', explained the Potsdam Declaration, said that Mr. Grew (former Ambassador) had been appointed 'Nippon kanri by President Truman' (Japan Administrator) on 18th August, that De Gaulle had arrived in Washington and the Chinese delegates had reached Manila, also—which *was news* to us—according to Lisbon 'British Naval units had landed in Japan to rescue the Prisoners of War'.

On the back of the single-sheet, of the 'Yomiuri Hochi', was the reproduction of the latest photographs of the atom bomb damage in Hiroshima. Close to it was an illustration of two Japanese ancient warriors—clad in armour, carrying pikes as they dashed into battle in accordance with 'Episode No. 242' in a serial connected with the 'good old days of the Samurai'.

The 'Mainichi' gave full details of the mission to Manila and, under date of 05.00 hours 22nd August, Imperial Headquarters announced the arrangements for the landing:—

'The first group of the allied occupation forces are scheduled to arrive in succession, beginning on 26th August in the Tokyo area. In order to avoid conflicts, it has been decided that the landings will be made according to the following arrangements:
'The first group of landing forces to occupy the mainland around metropolitan Tokyo, Chiba, Kanagawa, Yamanashi, and Shizuoka prefectures, beginning on Sunday. Starting on Saturday air operations will begin over the mainland.
Airborne troops will begin to arrive at Etsugi airfield as an initial landing force from Sunday. On the same day the allied fleet will enter Sagami Bay, while part of its forces, comprising light surface craft, will enter Tokyo Bay.

Other occupation forces will land from the air and the sea at Atsugi and Yokosuka sectors from Tuesday.

Japanese armed forces in the territory within a line linking the east bank of the Kanagawa, Chiba City, the estuary of the Tamagawa, Fuchu, Hachioji, Otsuki to the southern end of Izu will be made to evacuate the area as speedily as possible. Peace maintenance forces within this area will be reinforced by detailing armed police and naval peace preservation corps in addition to the ordinary police.

Government offices and public institutions within the area will function as usual and the general public are also required to go about their business calmly as usual. Special notices will be given as the occasion demands regarding measures which may be required to prevent confusion. Contact between the allied forces and the Japanese authorities will be made through a channel especially established for that purpose.

There will be no direct contact between the general public and the allied landing forces.'

I had just finished translating the 'Mainichi' when Colonel Sakeba sent for the three senior PoW officers (Dutch, American and British) to convey to them some important news.

Akirameru-Ohnishi acted as interpreter. When he had finished handing out the cigarettes, Sakeba said, 'I have just returned from Army Headquarters. They authorize me to say that an armistice has been arranged. If there is no hitch in the negotiations the war will be terminated soon. You may be released to return to your homes in a few weeks, but at the moment there is no alteration in your position as prisoners of war. If you have any recommendations to make do so now.'

As we were supposed to know nothing about the exact state of affairs we pretended to be surprised and overjoyed, smiled and thanked Colonel Sakeba. However, I made three requests: no more discrimination against American airmen; equalization of rations and the immediate release from civil jail of Private Rae, of The Royal Scots, sentenced in September, 1944 to two years hard labour for defending himself against attack by a civilian overseer.

Ohnishi hesitated before misinterpreting my requests so I repeated them in Japanese. Sakeba replied that he would look into the matter—later. I pressed my points and he agreed to equalization of rations, there and then, and would telephone to PoW headquarters about the other matters.

Private Rae was released on 24th August and we dealt with the other matters ourselves.

iii. Freedom. 29th August 1945

We had typhoon-weather on Friday 24th August. Our wooden-walls were flattened. Tokyo radio announced that the first landings, of the occupying forces, had been advanced from 26th to 28th owing to the weather conditions, and that General MacArthur would land at Atsugi aerodrome on 31st.

Camp guards had been reinforced, sentry posted at both ends of Omori bridge: Tokyo-Yokohama road was crammed with people moving out of the occupation zones. Inside the camp the 'Special Interrogation Corps' were setting fire to their many lists of questions to be put to the invaders.

On 26th the A.A.F. sent over more bombers. This time, instead of atom bombs, incendiaries and high-explosives they dropped oil-drums packed tight with clothing, medical supplies, sweets, emergency rations and *American* cigarettes. Plane after plane came in low, skimming the roof-tops, in 'Operation Oil-drum', and there was some *indiscriminate bombing* which destroyed bits of our barracks so we signalled 'Go slow—or go home.'

Some of the fighter aircraft, from the carriers, dropped packets of chewing-gum and cigarettes dangling from parachutes made from their pocket-handkerchiefs—others dropped the latest edition of the 'Yorktown News'—'Special Air-mail to Prisoners-of-War-Camps. Western Budget.' So we were kept busy picking up all the good things from the A.A.F., instead of dodging their pellets.

On the third day of 'Operation Oil-drum', Wednesday 29th August, I had just walked out of No.2 Barracks when a 'hedge-hopper' came whizzing over the bath-house. There was a roar and a crash as a gift from Uncle Sam made a direct-hit on the ledge of my bunk window. It shattered the glass, smashed the table, whizzed through the sliding-door and exploded in the passage between the bunks scattering tins of meat in all directions.

Had that 'packet' arrived a few minutes earlier it would have bashed my head, showered Parker with broken glass and hit Darby and Crossman full in the middle: Parker had been 'bagged' at Hongkong in December, 1941, Lt.-Commander

Crossman, D.S.O., and Lt. Darby (ex *H.M.S. Indefatigable*) had been fished out of the sea on 9th August, 1945.

Soon afterwards I was reading the 'Yorktown News' of 28th August, 1945: 'A Berlin woman who wants a hair-do must take to the beauty-shop her own hot water or a brick of pressed coal. Gas is so scarce that beauty shops are not permitted to keep a flame burning all day' when someone popped his head into the shattered bunk and said, 'You're wanted out in front, sir! I think its them Red Cross blokes again.'

Red Cross representatives had been in the previous day and I had called the attention of Mr. Junot (Geneva Delegate from the International Red Cross) to the condition of Private Rae's emaciated condition—and his maimed feet—so I took with me a 2,500 word statement, signed by Rae, for his information. But, before I reached the front office, I heard shouts of 'It's the bluddy Yanks with tommy-guns! We're free—we're free!'

I was introduced to Lt. Donald Perry of U.S. Cruiser *San Juan* and then to Commodore Roger Simpson, of the special task-force. We stared at each other. Then Simpson said, 'Now, listen, Major. First we take patients out of Shinagawa Hospital. Then evacuate your stretcher cases. After that we will clear this camp. Let's go and select your embarkation points.'

We walked over to the bank of the canal. By then some of the G.I's had rigged up their gadgets and were talking to the base-unit, *San Juan*, where the assault-boats were standing-by waiting for instructions. Then Lt. Perry spoke to the U.S. Hospital Ships *Benevolence* and *Marygold*: 'Operation rescue in force: processing station set up on beach at Omori PoW Camp: be ready for your mercy work.'

We had 120 sick and stretcher-cases (one-fifth of ration strength) but we soon had them on the canal bank ready for the assault-boats. But it was late in the afternoon before the Higgins' boats nosed in and dropped their fore-end. Then we took off the 'sacred soil of Japan' those frail men who had suffered so much from their filthy Japanese jailers.

When the embarkation was complete, the American senior PoW officer told me that Colonel Sakeba had sent for him and raised objections regarding the 'unauthorized action' of the G.I.'s—he had received no instructions from the War Office; and that I was to report to his office.

Tide was going out. It was getting dark. We had a few
G.I's with tommy guns and Sakeba had a lot of Japanese troops
—the next boats were not due in for some hours, on account of
tide.

I talked it over with Lt. Perry. We decided to ignore the
angry Colonel, and his protests, but to arrange to meet any real
trouble which might crop up.

But Sakeba was dying-hard. He came to the parade-ground,
with a Staff-colonel from the War Office, and told the American
senior PoW officer to instruct our men to return to barracks—he
sent for me. Sakeba repeated the instructions to me. But I
pointed out that Commander of special task-force was in charge
of the operations. The W.O. Staff-officer then complained that
no notification of the evacuation of prisoners of war in the Tokyo
area had reached the War Office who were responsible for our
safety. It was dark, no further movement should be made until
it was daylight.

I declined to alter the movement order. Sakeba was angry,
but his companion said, 'What is the strength of the landing-
party?' I replied, 'Sufficient to comply with Commodore
Simpson's orders.' That made him smile: 'There will be no
interference with Commodore Simpson's orders. We are responsible to General MacArthur for your safety. There are
thousands of civilians just across the canal. Some of them may
be foolish enough to cause trouble for you. There may be loss of
life. Do you accept that responsibility?'

I was tired and fed up with Japanese so I replied, 'I accept
full responsibility for obeying Commodore Simpson's orders, I
don't intend leaving Omori until all personnel have been taken
off, but that in no way releases the War Office from protecting
us here and at Shinagawa.'

That ended the matter—they went off clanking their swords.
But by now it was pitch dark. Boats were having some trouble
owing to low tide in the narrow unlightened channel which led
into the canal and then to our small beach. We started a series
of bonfires and at last two boats nosed in but they were for
Shinagawa Hospital.

There was some confusion about Shingawa. The line was
down and we could not get through to them so the two boats
chugged off in that direction. This made me think hard about

the many thousands of excited civilians on the Yokohama-Tokyo road—I remembered what occurred at Alexander Hospital, Singapore, on 14th February, 1942, so decided that it was time I went myself to see what was happening at Shinagawa.

Before Sakeba could stop me I was sitting in a Yokosuka Naval Base car bound for Shinagawa. The driver had brought in Red Cross representatives who had probably forgotten all about him so he raised no objection when I explained my objective.

An armed sentry challenged us at the camp entrance, another stopped us at the bridge and the third one stopped us on the other side of the bridge. We were allowed to proceed and in a few minutes the headlights of the car were pointed in the direction of Tokyo. We zig-zagged slowly to avoid craters and debris from the gutted factories and dwelling houses on either side of the road.

Nothing stirred on the dark highway to the capital of Japan. No one challenged us. We drove on into the murk without meeting one human being on the road. Suddenly the headlights picked up a dog chasing a cat into the ruins of a dealer in udon (macaroni)—we laughed. I suggested that we pulled up and lit a couple of fags.

The driver thanked me profusely when I gave him a packet of 'Lucky Strike' cigarettes. We smoked and talked for a minute or so—then on again, busy with our own thoughts until we turned off the main road and came to a sentry post close to the Megurogawa bridge. We were told that the car could go on no further, as the bridge was dangerous, but the sentry would take me to the guard commander.

There was a plank-walk on the bridge. I was escorted over by another sentry and picked my way to the entrance to the Hospital, in complete darkness. Telephone and electric-light wires had been destroyed by the 'Operation Oil-drum' bombers but, by the aid of my torch I located the O.C. party. He reported that there had been no trouble at all—the last stretcher-cases were leaving. While we were talking the despicable Dr. Tokuda was pretending to help with one of the stretchers: I told the O.C. some of his history and he replied, 'Don't worry pal—we've got him taped, he'll be for the hot-seat along with lots more of the cute bastards.'

It was exactly 00.04 hours on 30th August when the infamous Shingagawa Hospital was evacuated and I retraced my steps to the Megurogawa Bridge, and Omori.

iv. Finis

By the time I returned all American PoW's had been taken out of Omori camp—the British contingent and the G.I's remained to be dealt with. No boats were due in so I retired to my rather battered bunk for an easy. Hardly had I settled down to a quiet smoke with Parker when a sentry wandered in—just to say, sayonara.

I was glad to see him. He was the chap who held off the drunks at the point of his bayonet and threatened to shoot if anyone moved in the direction of the special barracks. We had lots of 'good eats' but he was not interested in food, or smokes, he wanted a few words with me. He was very serious. 'In a few minutes you will be gone. I'll never see you again. All this will be like a dream—but I shall not forget.'

Parker moved out. I told the chap that we all appreciated what he had done that night. He cut me short: 'I did not come to talk about that—I did my duty to Tenno Heika, do not speak about that. I come to ask for a souvenir—something of yours, something to remind me of you, and this camp.'

Luckily, in my holdall, I had an old Northumberland Fusilier great-coat button—my souvenir of World War I. I got it out and handed it to him with an explanation of the motto 'Quo Fata Vocant' (where destiny calls) and the crest of St. George killing the Dragon.

He was pleased. Asked a few more questions about my kami (St. George) and shuku-mei (fate preordained from a former life) wrapped up his kata-mi (souvenir) in a Red Cross handkerchief I gave him, picked up his rifle, stood up and saluted: 'Sayonara—o-daiji-ni'—turned and walked away.

Curious people: 'Sayonara-o-daiji-ni'—if it must be so, take good care of yourself.

I made a final tour of the camp with the O.C. landing-party, to round up the stragglers who had been sleeping-off the effects of home-brew, then he recalled the G.I's and we mustered on the canal bank. All-clear was reported. Clutching my souvenir, of World War II—the nominal-roll of prisoners of war in the Tokyo and North Honshu area—I clambered aboard the Higgins assault boat a free man at 04.00 hours 30th August, 1945.

In the distance, searchlights were flitting from cloud to cloud or sweeping along the battle-scarred waterfront of Tokyo—as we went down channel and left behind the dying embers of our signal fires. It had been a long day—and a long night. Dawn was breaking as we came to the lee of the U.S. Hospital Ship *Benevolence,* in Tokyo Bay: it was good to breathe sea-air, as free men, after three and a half years ashore in the custody of Japanese who believed in the unification of the ordinary functions of government with the veneration of the divine Imperial ancestors and practiced all the tricks of the devil under the name of bushido and sai-sei itchi.

APPENDICES

APPENDIX I

Emperors of Japan from B.C. 660 to 29

			Length of reign		
1	Jimmu	660	79	years	Died 581 at age of 127
2	Suizei	581	33	,,	
3	Annei	548	37	,,	
4	Itoku	510	35	,,	
5	Kosho	475	83	,,	
6	Koan	392	102	,,	
7	Korei	290	76	,,	
8	Kogen	214	56	,,	
9	Kaika	158	61	,,	
10	Sujin	97	68	,,	
11	Suinin	29	99	,,	

At the age of 45, Jimmu Tenno—accompanied by his tribe and his brother Itsuse—crossed over from the island of Kyushu to Yamato on Honshu. The invaders were engaged for eight years in fighting against the tribes lèd by Prince Nagasune in Kibi. It was during this fighting that Itsuse was killed. Jimmu married Princess Isuzuyori, of IZUMO, and settled down to rule in his 'Palace' at Kashiwabara in Unebi. Jimmu's title, at first, was Mikoto—a lord, a prince—and his rule was confined to the family clan and the other 'great clans'. This rule—or government—was called MATSURI-GOTO: *matsuri* means the veneration of the Imperial Ancestors, and the word *goto* means administration.

The Chinese characters, for the Japanese word matsuri-goto, are *sai-sei*. To this combination of *Saisei* was added another character— *itchi*—compound to make the phrase SAISEI-ITCHI or the combination of *Church and State-Government*.

The 'Sacred Mirror of Amaterasu' was enshrined in the Tenno's 'Palace' as the uji-gami (clan deity) of the Tenno's clan until the reign of SUJIN (97 B.C.) when it was taken to the village of Kasanui to be enshrined as the deity of the Imperial family, then—in 29 B.C.— during the reign of Suinin Tenno the Sun Goddess became the centre of the national faith. This, in a way, was the start of Jinja (Shrine) Shinto—when the 'sacred mirror' was enshrined in the KO-DAI-JINGU on the banks of the Isuzu River in ISE, by Suinin's daughter Yamato-hime-no-mikoto.

The Imperial Clans, at this period, were referred to as YAMATO and those outside their control were spoken of as IZUMO CLANS.

One of Jimmu Tenno's many titles was : Hatsukuni-shirasu-Sumera-Mikoto—'Supreme Majesty who laid the foundations of the Empire'; a title which was also held by Sujin Tenno.

APPENDIX II

Emperors of Japan from A.D. 71 to 593

12	Keiko	71	18	Hanzei	406	24	Ninken	488	29	Kimmei	539
13	Seimu	131	19	Inkyo	412	25	Muretsu	499	30	Bidatsu	572
14	Chuai	192	20	Anko	454	26	Keitai	507	31	Yomei	585
15	Ojin	270	21	Yuryaku	457	27	Ankan	534	32	Sujun	588
16	Nintoku	313	22	Seinei	480	28	Senka	536	33	Suiko	593
17	Richu	400	23	Kenso	485					(Empress)	

Keiko is credited with eighty children. His son, Yamato-Takeru-no-mikoto, helped him to subdue the Kumaso tribes, and he used the 'Sacred Sword' on this expedition. After his death this 'Sacred Sword' was enshrined at Atsuta Jingu by his consort Miyasu-hime-no-mikoto: the 'Sacred Jewel' was enshrined in the Imperial Palace.

Seimu appointed clan chieftains (O-omi and O-muraji) as court officials to assist in the administration of the country and in this way extended his authority beyond the 'Capital'. *Chuai*—son of Yamato-Takeru-no-mikoto—was killed in action against the Kumaso tribes. Chuai's third wife, a Korean, became famous as the Empress Jingo who—as Regent—was responsible for the expedition to Korea. Her son, *Ojin,* fostered overseas trade with China and Korea and established the 'amabe'—marine department.

During the reign of *Nintoku,* Buddhist priests came over to Japan from Korea—about 372. *Yuryaku* had a brutal nature and, among other crimes, he is credited with the murder of *Kenso's* father.

After *Keitai* came to the throne, 507, three Clans—SOGA, MONO-NOBE and NAKATOMI—began to exert their influence in the country.

Soga Umako's daughter was married to the Emperor Kimmei and this widened the Soga influence at Court. In 552, during Kimmei's reign, some Buddhist priests came over from China. Among them was the Chinese priest 'Shiba Tachito' and he was allowed to build a temple in Yamato and instal in it a Buddha. But, Kimmei was not in favour of Buddhism and rejected Buddha images sent to him from Korea which were, however, welcomed by the Soga clan.

Bidatsu, and Moriya of the Mononobe clan were opposed to the spread of Buddhism and they caused all the images to be thrown into the Yodo-gawa at Osaka.

Soga Umako placed *Yomei* and *Sujun* on the 'throne', but—in 592 —he had *Sujun* poisoned and replaced him by *Bidatsu's* consort who reigned as *Suiko* with Prince Shotoku as REGENT until 628.

APPENDIX III

Emperors and Empresses of Japan from A.D. 629 to 770

34	Jomei	629		42	Mommu	697	
35	Kogyoku	642	Empress	43	Gemmyo	708	Empress
36	Kotoku	645		44	Gensho	715	Empress
37	Saimei	655	Empress	45	Shomu	724	
38	Tenchi	662		46	Koken	749	Empress
39	Kobun	672		47	Junnin	759	
40	Temmu	673		48	Shotoku	765	Empress
41	Jito	690	Empress	49	Konin	770	

Soga Umako died in 626 and the next Tenno—*Jomei*—was put on the throne by Soga Emishi. *Jomei* abdicated in 641. Soga Emishi by-passed the Shotoku line and selected, as the next 'divine ruler', the great-grand-daughter of *Bidatsu, Kogyoku,* and when she abdicated in 644, Soga Emishi selected Kogyoku's younger brother, Prince Karu, as *Kotoku Tenno.*

Previously, Soga Emishi, had selected Prince Yamashiro—son of Jomei—to succeed him but this was not approved of by Soga Iruka who attacked Yamashiro with the result that Yamashiro and twenty-three of his family committed hara kiri. This event roused the clan of Nakatomi Kamatari to action and they helped other clans to destroy Soga Iruka and this brought about the abdication of Kogyoku.

Nakatomi Kamatari and Prince Naka—son of Kogyoku—combined forces and made others join in their attacks on the Soga clans and this resulted in the destruction of many of the Soga clan leaders —including Naka's father-in-law Soga Kurayamada. Prince Naka refused the throne and continued, with the help of Nakatomi Kamatari, to clean up the administration of the country. They set up three ministries—Saidaijin (left), Udaijin (right) and Naidaijin for the Interior which was taken over by Nakatomi Kamatari.

When *Kotoku* died—654—Prince Naka still refused the 'honour' of Jinno, as he had not yet completed his numerous reforms, so the ex-Empress Kogyoku returned to the throne as *Saimei.* However, in 662, Prince Naka was enthroned as Tenchi Tenno.

Nakatomi changed his name to FUJIWARA KAMATARI and from then the Fujiwaras replaced the other rival clans to become the ruling faction in the country.

(N.B. Further details, covering the period 629–770, are to be found in the first part of Chapter II.)

APPENDIX IV

The FUJIWARAS and the EMPERORS of JAPAN from 782 to 889

50	Kwammu	782	54	Nimmyo	834	57	Yozei	877
51	Heijo	806	55	Montoku	851	58	Koko	885
52	Saga	810	56	Seiwa	859	59	Uda	889
53	Junna	824						

Kwammu instructed Fujiwara Tanetsugi to arrange for the transfer of the 'Capital' and the 'administration' from Nara to a new site—away from the growing influence of the Buddhist priests.

In 784 the Court was moved to Nagaoka, in Yamashiro, about thirty miles from Nara and then to Uda—several miles further to the East.

Heijo, Saga and *Junna* (three sons of Kwammu) succeeded after Kwammu. Heijo soon retired, to become a monk. His son, Prince Takaoka, went to India, so Saga came to the throne for a few years when he abdicated in favour of Junna.

JUNNA was the last of the Tenno to exercise any ruling power—his successors, from 833 to 1194 lived in seclusion and confirmed the decrees of the various Fujiwaras.

Montoku appointed Fujiwara Yoshifusa, 'Minister of the Right' (851). Fujiwara Yosifusa married a daughter of *Saga Tenno* and their daughter, Aki, married *Montoku Tenno*. The son of Fujiwara Yoshifusa's daughter came to the throne as *Seiwa Tenno* in 859 and in 866 Fujiwara Yoshifusa became SESSHO—Regent: the office of Sessho was previously confined to Princes of the Imperial Family. So, Yoshifusa became Regent, father-in-law of *Montoku Tenno* and grandfather of *Seiwa Tenno*.

SEIWA TENNO decreed that the Sessho, and the Chancellor, should govern the country and he would hear their reports. He then created the office of KWAMPAKU—that is, REGENT for adult sovereign.

The Sessho-Kwampaku took precedence over all Japanese except the Tenno, and the Fujiwaras continued in this office until 1868.

Yozei was a homicidal maniac so he was removed from the throne by Fujiwara Mototsune: *Koko* reigned for three years and was replaced by his son *Uda*.

Fujiwaras were mothers, or wives, of *Yozei, Koko* and *Uda*.

Other Fujiwaras, who were Sessho-Kwampaku in this period, were Tanetsugi, Yukinari, Tsunigawa and Fuyutsugu.

APPENDIX V

SAMURAI RULE

HOGEN *and* HEIJI WARS: *1156 to 1160*

Rebellion of TAIRA MASAKADO: Two of the great samurai clans were the TAIRA and the MINAMOTO—in western and eastern Japan. TAIRA were descendants of KAMMU TENNO (782) and MINAMOTO of SEIWA TENNO (859).

The most belligerent of these warrior families, at this period, was the SEIWA GENJI of Settsu, Yamato and Mino, but most of the samurai were interested in the Imperial succession, and spoiling for a fight.

In 898 the Emperor Daigo decided to dispense with the services of a Fujiwara Regent and this precipitated a minor civil war in which the Court were defeated by the combined forces of FUJIWARA HIDESATO and TAIRA SADAMORI. The trouble originated after the death of DAIGO, 930, when TAIRA MASAKADO was planning to move the Imperial Court to his domain in Kanto—the eight provinces of Sagami Bay, Tokyo.

As a result of this fighting the samurai controlled the country: the MINAMOTOS made Tsurugaoka, KAMAKURA, their headquarters and the FUJIWARAS lost most of their influence with the Imperial Court, but for some years there was fighting against the ABE Clan in Mutsu —in the north of Japan by the Minamoto generals Yoriyoshi and Yoshii.

Emperors			*Emperors*			*Emperors*		
60	Daigo	898	65	Kazan	985	70	Go Reizei	1047
61	Shujaku	931	66	Ichijo	987	71	Go Sanjo	1069
62	Murakami	947	67	Sanjo	1012	72	Shirakawa	1073
63	Reizei	968	68	Go Ichijo	1017	73	Horikawa	1087
64	Enyu	970	69	Go Shujaku	1037	74	Toba	1108

The rule of the REGENTS was nominal from reign of SHUJAKU to reign of MURAKAMI, but the FUJIWARAS continued to supply wives for the Tenno until Go REIZEI in 1047: for instance Fujiwara Michinaga's three sons-in-laws were all Emperors.

Ten Emperors—Shujaku to Go Reizei—ruled during a period of 116 years.

The mother of Go REIZEI was not Fujiwara.

Go Sanjo and his son Shirakawa started the system of IN—retired Sovereign—and they administered separately of the Regent while a son, or a grandson, sat on the throne. The retired Tenno became a monk but maintained a court.

HOGEN WAR

After the death of TOBA TENNO (1123) there was more internal friction over the succession. However, Sutoku was selected in 1124 and he was followed by Konoe in 1142.

Emperors		Emperors		Emperors	
75 Sutoku	1124	76 Konoe	1142	77 Go Shirakawa	1156

TAIRA KIYOMORI and MINAMOTO YOSHITOMO had been in favour of KONOE whereas TAIRA TADAMATSU and MINAMOTO TAMEYOSHI backed SUTOKU. So, when Konoe died (1155) his faction placed Go SHIRAKAWA on the throne, and this became the reason for more civil war. During this HOGEN WAR the Sutoku followers were defeated and Taira Tadamatsu and Minamoto Tameyoshi were put to death. TAIRA KIYOMORI became the de facto ruler of the country.

TAIRA KIYOMORI's eldest sister was married to GO SHIRAKAWA and his daughter was married to Shirakawa's son.

HEIJI WAR

Emperors		Emperors		Emperors	
78 Nijo	1159	80 Takakura	1169	81 Antoku	1180
79 Rokujo	1166				

Nijo succeeded Go Shirakawa who abdicated in 1159. The MINAMOTOS attacked the retired Tenno and Court and killed Fujiwara Shinzei but the final outcome of the struggle was to leave TAIRA KIYOMORI in full control of affairs. Nijo was followed by Rokujo but he was soon deposed in favour of Go Shirakawa's son TAKAKURA who had married Taira's daughter Toku. Taira Kiyomori—now in full control of the Tenno and Imperial Court—planned to move his capital to Fukuhara, Kobe, in 1180 when Antoku succeeded Takakura.

However, in August, 1180, after destroying part of Nara, Kiyomori was compelled to return to Kyoto with the Court, Tenno and retired Tenno—and he died there in 1181.

The Heiji War was followed by more tribal fighting. The eldest son of MINAMOTO YOSHITOMO, YORITOMO, clashed with the TAIRA clan of HOJO TOKIMASA. The Hojo (Taira) army was forming-up at Ichi-no-tani, near Kobe, when Yoritomo's generals attacked and defeated them at Ikuta and Suma in 1184.

TAIRA (or Heike) troops fled to Shikoku and reformed. In 1185 they boarded their fleet and sailed to Shimonoseki followed by MINAMOTO (or Genji) fleet. The fleets met at Dan-no-ura (Shimonoseki) in 1185 and Heike were destroyed.

ANTOKU TENNO had thrown in his lot with TAIRA and surrendered at Dan-no-ura to Yoritomo's brother Yoshitsune. However, Yoshitsune was banished to Mutsu by his brother who became the real ruler of Japan as MINAMOTO YORITOMO in 1185.

KAMAKURA

YORITOMO made his headquarters at Kamakura but he decided to station his father-in-law, HOJO Tokimasa, in Kyoto. Yoritomo was given the title of Bakufu, General of the Imperial Guards, and his headquarters was known by the name of BAKUFU. In 1192 he received the status of Sei-i-tai-Shogun (SHOGUN) and for the following 700 years Japan was ruled by Shoguns.

Emperors			Shoguns			Regents	
82	Go Toba	1186	Minamoto	Yoritomo	1192		
83	Tsuchimikado	1199	,,	Yoriie	1199	Hojo Tokimasa	1199
84	Juntoku	1211	,,	Sanetomo	1203	,, Yoshitoki	1205
85	Chukyo	1221	Fujiwara	Yoritsune	1220	,, Yasutoki	1225
86	Go Horikawa	1222					
87	Shijo	1233	Fujiwara	Yoritsugu	1244	,, Tsunetoki	1242
88	Go Saga	1243	Imperial			,, Tokiyori	1246
89	Fukakusa	1247	Prince	Munetaka	1251	,, Nagatoki	1256
90	Kameyama	1260	,,	Koreyasu	1266	,, Tokimune	1270
91	Go Uda	1275				,, Sadatoki	1284
92	Fushimi	1288					
93	Go Fushimi	1299	,,	Hisakira	1289	,, Morotoki	1300
94	Go Nijo	1302					
95	Hanazono	1308	,,	Morikuni	1308		
96	Go Daigo	1319–1338				,, Takatoki	1315

Minamoto Yoritomo died in 1199 but his system of BAKUFU rule lasted for 140 years to the end of Go Daigo's reign. The TENNO was a titular ruler only and the administration was SHOGUN: REGENT and COUNCIL. Minamoto Yoriie became a monk before he was assassinated.

The REGENT HOJO Yoshitoki killed off most of the Yoritomo leaders and, in 1219, when Sanetomo was visiting the Tsurugaoka Hachiman Shrine (Kamakura) at night he was waylaid and beheaded. Sanetomo's death was followed by the removal of Yoriie's son who was decapitated by Hojo Yoshitoki. With the death of Kugyo (son of Yoriie) the house of MINAMOTO YORITOMO was brought to an end.

Go Toba (then a retired Tenno, or HO-O) turned to the Buddhist priests for help in restoring the dignity of the throne in 1221. He declared that the KAMAKURA REGIME was illegal and the samurai supporting it were traitors. The HOJO REGENT, Yoshitoki, took strong action against the 'loyalists': *Go Toba* was banished to Oki, *Juntoku* to Sado and *Tsuchimikado* to Tosa. Go Toba's manors were taken over by Hojo and Minamoto clans and this was the real start of the feudal system of Daimyo and Shomyo.

HOJO TOKIYORI—1246:1255—decreed that all future REGENTS were to be chosen from the FUJIWARA houses of Ichijo, Nijo, Kujo, Konoe and Takatsukasa and not, as previously, from Kujo and Konoe only. Also, Fujiwaras continued to supply Empresses and consorts for the Shoguns.

The power of the HoJo began to decline after the REGENCY of TOKIMUNE (1823) because of the corrupt life followed by them in Kyoto.

But it was not until Go DAIGO came to the throne (1319) that the Imperial Court attempted to assert itself again. The Regent—Takatoki—had been unsuccessful in subduing revolts in the northern parts of the country and Go Daigo took the opportunity to set up his own son as Crown Prince in defiance of the Regent's ruling that the throne should be held alternately by Go-Fukakusa's line and that of Kameyamas. This revolt against authority was quelled and Go Daigo was exiled to Oki to join Go Toba and the others. However, some of the followers of Go Daigo continued the insurrection. The Regent's party ordered the ASHIKAKA general, Takauji, to destroy them but the Ashikaga clans joined the Imperialists and captured Kyoto. At the same time, a MINAMOTO (family of Yoshiie) clan came down from the north and made a surprise attack on KAMAKURA which they stormed and destroyed. As a result of the subsequent fighting the HoJo army was slaughtered.

HoJo TAKATOKI with his family and 800 retainers fled to the Toshoji Temple where they all committed hara kiri in 1333 and this ended the rule of the HoJo family and with it the end of Kamakura as the military capital of Japan.

ASHIKAGA SHOGUNS: *1338 to 1568*

Ashikaga Takuji was appointed SHOGUN and proceeded to recover KAMAKURA for the HoJo Tokiyuki. Civil war resulted with Ashikagas against the Imperial Family. A battle was fought at Minatogawa, near Kobe where the Imperialists were defeated and Takuji returned in power in Kyoto. Go DAIGO surrendered and was imprisoned but escaped after two months and fled to YOSHINO where he set up a rival Court when KOMYO was placed on the throne in 1338, by Takuji.

Go Daigo ruled (?) without a Regent and made his eldest son, Prince Morinaga, SHOGUN. For fifty-five years there were two sets of Emperors in the Northern and Southern Courts.

In Kyoto (Northern Court) Takuji as SHOGUN maintained KOMYO as TENNO from 1338 to 1349, and in YOSHINO, Go-Murakami was TENNO from 1339 to 1368.

Northern Court: Kyoto				*Southern Court: Yoshino*		
Komyo	1338	(Kogon 1332)	97	Go Murakami	1339	
Suko	1350		98	Chokei	1369	
Go Kogon	1352		99	Go Kameyama	1374	abdicated for
Go Enyu	1372		100	Go Komatsu	1393	
Go Komatsu	1384–1392					
			101	Shoko	1413	

Takuji made his headquarters in Kyoto and it was called MURO-MACHI.

MUROMACHI ERA *1393–1569*

WARS of ONIN and BUMEI 1467–91 caused by succession friction and during fighting Kyoto was wrecked, Tenno fled to Shogun's palace.

ONIN wars resulted in the destruction of many of the older houses of the nobility. There was no central government and the Throne was set aside as of no importance and from 1465—Go Tsuchi Mikado —to 1528—Go Nara—the Imperial Family were reduced to penury. The SHINSHU sect became prominent at this period. From 1491 to 1568 it was a continual struggle for power between the new race of feudal lords. Kamakura was replaced by Odawara as a Samurai Headquarters and there was another Samurai headquarters, Lord Ouchi at YAMAGUCHI on the Inland Sea.

In MINO, SAITO DOSA ruled, and near SAITO, ODA Nobuhide ruled in place of his former master Lord SHIBA. ODA was from the TAIRA Shigemori clan who were masters of all OWARI, Oda a minor clan. Nobuhide's son was the famous ODA NOBUNAGA. Near to ODA was the MATSUDAIRAS in the west.

Other leaders were TAKEDA Shingen of Kai and UESUGI Kenshi of Echigo who had replaced his master Lord UESUGI. Further north was the SATAKE of Hitachi and DATE and SHIMAZU in Kyushu.

At this period the professional warriors were called BUSHI and the farmer-class warriors GOSHI. In 1560, IMAGAGAWA Yoshimoto of SURUGA marched on Kyoto.

Emperors and Ashikaga Shoguns—1338–1568

	Emperors		Ashikaga Shoguns		
97	Go Murakami	1339	Takuji	1338	
98	Chokei	1369	Yoshiakaki	1358	
99	Go Kameyama	1374	Yoshimitsu	1367	
100	Go Komatsu	1393	Yoshimochi	1395	
101	Shoko	1413	Yoshikazu	1423	
102	Go Hanazono	1429	Yoshinori	1428	murdered
			Yoshikatsu	1441	
103	Go Tsuchi Mikado	1465	Yoshimasa	1443	
			Yoshihisa	1474	
			Yoshitane	1490	
104	Go Kashiwabara	1501	Yoshizumi	1493	
			Yoshitsane	1508	
105	Go Nara	1528	Yoshiharu	1521	
106	Ogimachi	1558	Yoshiteru	1545	murdered
			Yoshihide	1565	
			Yoshiaki	1568	

Restoration of Sai-sei-itchi

106	Ogimachi	1558–1586	Oda Nobunaga 1569–1582		*Vice-Shogun*
107	Go Yozei	1587–1612	Toyotomi Hideyoshi: *Regent*	1582–1598	
			Toyotomi Hideyori: "	1598–1615	

When Imagagawa Yoshimoto of Suruga marched in the direction
of Kyoto, 1560, he was accompanied by Matsudaira Motoyasu but
they were met by the forces of Oda Nobunaga and defeated at Okehazama. Oda recalled Ogimachi Tenno to Kyoto and restored
something of the lost prestige of the Tenno and his Court. Matsudaira, and his forces, then attached himself to the new ruler—Oda
Nobunaga—who set up Ashikaga Yoshiaki as SHOGUN. In 1569,
Matsudaira Motoyasu changed his name to TOKUGAWA the surname
of his ancestor MINAMOTO YOSHISUE. Matsudaira kept the surname
of TOKUGAWA for the main house and for his heirs.

ODA NOBUNAGA found it convenient to depose the SHOGUN, Ashikaga Yoshiaki and this resulted in fighting against the Buddhist
priests and he destroyed many of their temples. Oda was joined in
his many expeditions by Hashiba Hideyoshi, a peasant soldier, who
—at a later date—changed his name to TOYOTOMI HIDEYOSHI. Oda
was a good but brutal administrator and, in the end, was murdered
by one of his followers—Akechi Mitsuhide—who became dictator.

Akechi Mitsuhide was attacked and soon disposed of by Hashiba
Hideyoshi who was made KWAMPAKU by Ogimachi Tenno in 1585
and—as TOYOTOMI HIDEYOSHI—re-established the rule of sai-sei-
itchi, and like ODA who had repaired the 'Palace' and rebuilt the
KO-DAI-JINGU of ISE tried to restore SHINTO as kamu-nagara.

APPENDIX VI

Tokugawa Shogunate: *1600–1868*

Toyotomi Hideyoshi was opposed by the Hojo clan (Odawara) and the Date clan (Sendai)—the Hojo party were attacked and defeated by Tokugawa and their fief was handed over to him as a reward. Tokugawa made his headquarters in the eight provinces of Kanto. Hideyoshi, in addition to restoring law and order, embarked on the conquest of Korea and China. These expeditions were not a great success and, about 1596, a Chinese envoy arrived with 'edicts and robes' and Hideyoshi was made 'Emperor of Japan' under the suzerainty of China. This did not suit Hideyoshi who wanted to be made a Ming Emperor in his own right so he broke off relations with China in 1597 and sent another force to conquer Korea. Hideyoshi (at first) had no children so he adopted sons of Oda and Tokugawa but appointed an adopted nephew, Hidetsugu, as heir with the title of Kwampaku. Then, Hideyoshi had a son—Hideyori—so he ordered Hidetsugu to commit hara kiri. When this order had been obeyed he made Hideyori his heir and, at the age of three, Kwampaku. The next step was the appointment of a supreme court of elders (Tairo) composed of Tokugawa, Maeda and Churo to look after the infant Regent. Hideyoshi died in 1598, the Tairo recalled the Japanese army from Korea and Maeda was made Hideyori's guardian.

Tokugawa had made his headquarters at Yedo in a small castle on the wide flat plain of Musashi. Fighting broke out between Tokugawa and Uesugi, Ishida and Mori. At the village of Sekigahara—west of Kyoto—a final battle was fought on 21st October, 1600 which was won by Tokugawa's army. Tokugawa—now Tokugawa Iyeyasu—was made Shogun by Go-Yozei Tenno in 1603. By his conquest over his rivals he gained control over $4\frac{1}{2}$ million koku of rice and passed on another 1 million koku to Maeda.

In 1603, Toyotomi Hideyori—the Regent—was married to the grand-daughter of Tokugawa Iyeyasu. In March, 1614, Tokugawa forces marched against the Regent Hideyori in Osaka Castle. Fighting went on until the summer of 1615 when the Castle was stormed, Hideyori, his mother, and his son of eight, were desposed of thus bringing to an end the house of Toyotomi. All the Hideyoshi Shrines were destroyed and—by edict of the Tenno—Hideyoshi was removed from the rank of a deity.

Hidetada—son of Iyeyasu—was appointed Shogun in 1605 (on the retirement of Iyeyasu) and in 1620, Hidetada's daughter, Kazuko, was married to Go-Mizu-no-o Tenno. Under the Tokugawas there were three classes of Daimyo: 'Shimban' (related houses), 'Fudai' (the hereditary vassal clans) and 'Tozama' (outside feudatories—the Lords who were not 'Fudai') and by 1613 no less than 190 new Daimyo had been created to build up the Tokugawa Shogunate. Every Shogun—no matter his mental capacity—was *ipso facto* the Dictator of Japan from day of appointment.

APPENDIX VII

Emperors under the Tokugawa Shogunate—1600–1868

	Emperors			Tokugawa Shoguns	
107	Go Yozei	1587		Iyeyasu	1603
108	Go Mizu-no-o	1612		Hidetada	1605
109	Myosho	1630	Empress	Iyemitsu	1623
110	Go-Komyo	1644		Iyetsuna	1651
111	Go-Saiin	1655		Tsunayoshi	1681
112	Reigen	1663			
113	Higashiyama	1688			
114	Naka-no-Mikado	1710		Iyenobu	1709
				Iyetsugu	1713
				Yoshimune	1717
115	Sakuramachi	1736			
116	Momozono	1748		Iyeshige	1745
117	Go-Sakuramachi	1764	Empress	Iyeharu	1763
118	Go-Momozono	1772			
119	Kokaku	1780		Iyenari	1787
120	Ninko	1817			
121	Komei	1847		Iyeyoshi	1837
				Iyesada	1853
				Iyemochi	1858
122	Meiji	1868		Yoshinobu	1866

Go-mizu-no-o abdicated in favour of his daughter, by the sister of Tokugawa Iyemitsu, *Myosho* who, at the age of seven, was the first female sovereign for 860 years. When Iyemitsu died many of his vassals, including councillors Hotta and Abe, committed JUNSHI. This mass suicide was prohibited by the Tokugawa adviser, Tadakiyo, as contrary to Japanese ethics.

With the death of Tokugawa Iyetsugu (1716) the main line of the Tokugawas came to an end and the next heirs were selected from the branch houses of Kii, Owari or Mito: Yoshimune was from the house of Kii and he ruled with an iron hand for thirty years—Iyeshige, who followed, was feeble in mind and weak in his administration. He found it necessary to express his objection to the interest taken by *Momozono Tenno* in SHINTO and his divine rights. But this did not check the revival in Shinto. The next SHOGUN, Iyeharu, took stronger measures and among those loyalists who were put to death was Yamagata Daini.

During the rule of Shogun Iyenari, when Matsudaira Sadanobu was REGENT, Kyoto was destroyed by fire and had to be rebuilt.

With the enthronement of *Kokaku* (1780) the loyalists—those opposed to the Tokugawas—indulged in propaganda regarding the restoration of 'Imperial Divine Rights'. One of the leaders of the movement, Takayama, started the custom of bowing to the Imperial Palace in Kyoto and he was forced to commit hara kiri. But, Iyenari continued to maintain his feudal regime for fifty-years before leaving the task to his successor Iyeyoshi in 1837.

On 8th July, 1853, during the reign of KOMEI TENNO, Perry made his first visit to Japan. The following year, bowing to the display of force, the Shogunate concluded the Shimoda Treaty.

And, in 1858 the Townsend Harris Treaty was concluded but Komei Tenno (on the advice of the loyalists) refused to sign it so the Tokugawa Shogunate signed in his place which was contrary to their powers of administration which were limited (?) to internal affairs.

Komei Tenno's sister was married to the new Shogun Iyemochi and he conferred with the Tenno—regarding a repudiation of the Treaty and a drive against the foreigners. This anti-foreign party was backed by the CHOSHU house of Mori but—at this period—the SATSUMA Clans took up a neutral position. CHOSHU clans then pressed the Tenno and—in 1864—they made an attack on the Tokugawa Shogunate forces but were defeated by the Tokugawas who were assisted by Matsudaira Katamori (Lord of Aizu) and some of the SATSUMA clansmen.

In 1865, Saigo Takamori and Okubo Toshimichi of SATSUMA joined forces with Kido Takayoshi of CHOSHU and began preparations to depose the Tokugawas and restore full power to Komei Tenno.

However, in 1866, Iyemochi was succeeded by Yoshinobu and in 1867 Komei Tenno died. He was succeeded by MEIJI TENNO—a boy of fifteen—and on 19th November, 1867, Shogun Yoshinonu agreed to hand back all administrative power to the Tenno.

In 1869, Yedo—renamed TOKYO—was proclaimed as the IMPERIAL CAPITAL: the Court and the Tenno took up residence and the new 'Imperial System' was established. This consisted of: an Imperial Prince as head of the Government with Ministers of the 'Right' and the 'Left' with eighteen CLAN LEADERS from the SATSUMA—CHOSHU—TOSA and HIZEN Clans. The leaders of the 'Government' were: Sanjo Sanetomi, Iwakura Tomomi, Saigo Takamori, and Okubo Takamori of the SATSUMA CLANS. Kido Takayoshi, ITO Hirobumi, and Inouye Kaoru of the CHOSHU CLANS. OKUMA Shigenobu —HIZEN—and Itagake of TOSA.

SAIGO agitated for an expedition to Korea but he was opposed by OKUBO. This dispute started the Satsuma Rebellion of 1877 which was put down by Prince Arisugawa's new army of conscripts and the disgraced SAIGO committed hara kiri at Kagoshima, the Satsuma Clan Capital. But, OKUBO was assassinated in 1878.

The first 'Prime Minister' (before the Constitution) was Prince Sanjo Sanetomo of the SATSUMA CLAN.

APPENDIX VIII

PREMIERS *under* MEIJI, TAISHO *and* SHOWA

MEIJI *1868–1912*

Marquis Ito	1885
Count **Kuroda**	1888
General Prince Yamagata	1889
Prince Matsukata	1890
Marquis Ito	1893
Prince Matsukata	1896
Marquis Ito	1898
Marquis Okuma	1898
Prince Yamagata	1899
Marquis Ito	1900
General Prince Katsura	1901
Prince Saionji	1906
Prince Katsura	1908
Prince Saionji	1911
Prince Katsura	1912

TAISHO *1912–1926*

Admiral Count Yamamoto	1913
Count Okuma	1914
General Count Terauchi	1916
Mr. Hara	1918
Viscount Takahashi	1921
Admiral T. Kato	1922
Admiral Count Yamamoto	1923
Viscount Kiyoura	1923
Baron Wakatsuki	1926

Okuma, Takahashi and Hara were assassinated.
December, 1923 attempt on the life of the Crown Prince caused Yamamoto's resignation.

SHOWA TENNO: *1926–1945*

General Baron Tanaka	1927	
Mr. Hamaguchi	1929	Assassinated
Baron Wakatsuki	1931	
Mr. Inukai	1931	Assassinated
Admiral Viscount Saito	1932	Assassinated
Admiral Baron Okada	1934	
Mr. Koki Hirota	1936	
General Hayashi	1937	
Prince Konoye	1937	
Mr. Hiranuma	1939	
Prince Konoye	1939	
Admiral Yonai	1940	
General Tojo	1941	
General Koiso	1944	
Admiral Suzuki	1945	April
Prince Higashi-Kuni	1945	August

APPENDIX IX

Chronology of China, Russia and Japan from 1837–1937

1837–
1839   Opium trade disputes with the British.
1839   War between England and China—cession of Victoria Island:
        Hong-Kong.
1842   Treaty of Nanking—establishment of exterritoriality.
1851   Treaty of Aigun between Russia and China.
1857   British capture Canton: second China War.
1858   Allies capture Taku: Treaty of Tientsin.
        Territory north of Amur River ceded to Russia by China.
1860   Allies capture Peking. China ceded to Russia the maritime
        province of Manchuria with 600 miles of coastline including
        Vladivostok.
        Taiping rebellion: 1850:1865—crushed by Li Hung-chang
        and General Gordon. Mohammedan rising in Yunnan.
        1856–1873: Chinese-Turkestan risings. 1864–1877.
1858   Japanese-American Treaty of Amity and Commerce—treaty
        ports and establishment of exterritoriality.
1867—December: Restoration of Meiji Tenno.
1867   French annex part of Cochin China.
1871   Sino-Japanese Treaty of Tientsin. 1874 Japanese expedition
        to Formosa. 1876 Japanese treaty with Korea. 1881 China
        recognised Japanese sovereignty over Ryukyus.
1884   Franco-Chinese War—France occupies Annam.
1894   Sino-Japanese War. 1895 Japan occupies Formosa.
1895   Russo-Chinese Military Alliance: Chinese Eastern Railway—
        Manchuli to Vladivostock—agreement: Russian occupation
        of Port Arthur, Dairen and Manchuria.
1897   Germany establishes herself in Shantung with possession of
        Tsingtau.
1898   British obtain recognition of special rights in the Yangtze area
        and lease of Wei-hai-wei as naval base.
1899   Anti-foreign movements in north and central China.
1900   Boxer Rebellion: Allies occupy Taku. 1901 relief of Peking—
        Boxer indemnity £67,500,000 shared by allies.
1902   Anglo-Japanese Alliance.
1904–
1905   Russo-Japanese War: Japan re-occupies Manchuria and takes
        over the Russo-Chinese agreements: second Anglo-Japanese
        Alliance—for ten years.
        Reform movements started by Sun Yat-sen in 1898 failed but,
        in 1907 the Empress of China agrees to reforms—she (Empress
        -Dowager) and the puppet Emperor die in 1908.

1909   Provincial Assemblies, and in 1910 National Assemblies were established in China.

1910   Korea annexed by Japan.

1911   Anglo-Japanese Alliance renewed for ten years.
Wuchang revolt against Peking government: Chinese Republic proclaimed: Sun Yat-sen 'President': Yuan Shi-kai compromises with Sun over the future of the Dynasty.

1912—February: Chinese Emperor abdicates: Sun resigns in favour of Yuan Shi-kai.

1912—July: Death of Mutsuhito—Meiji Tenno: Yoshihito enthroned as Taisho Tenno.
Population of Japan increased, from 1868 to 1912, from 32 million to 50 million. Density of population (Japan proper) was increased from 225 per square mile, in 1868, to 350 per square mile in 1912.

1913   National Assembly of China meets in Peking: Yuan Shi-kai consolidates his military position and negotiates foreign 'Reconstruction Loan' without the consent of 'Parliament': Kuomintang (Sun's party) revolts: Yuan dissolves 'Parliament'.
Military dictatorship, financed by Yuan Shi-kai, replaces the Manchu rule: Canton Government established by Sun: from now on China is ravaged by rival Tuchuns and their bandits.

1914—January: Chinese Parliament dissolved and Yuan Shi-kai becomes Dictator.

1914—August: Outbreak of World War I. Tsingtau captured from Germany by Japanese troops.

1915—May: Japan presents 'Twenty-one Demands'.

1916—June: Death of Yuan Shi-kai: Li Yuan-hung becomes the new President.

1917—June: Li resigns: Feng Kuo-Chang is President by the consent of the Tuchans: China enters the World War.
(In June, 1916, Russia and Japan concluded a military alliance to fight any third power attempting to establish dominion over China.)

1918   End of World War I. Hsu Shi-chang replaces Feng as 'President': Sun establishes 'Southern Government' at Canton.

1919—July 25th: Soviet Government renounces all privileges extorted from China by the former Tsarist Government.

1921—May: CHINESE COMMUNIST PARTY formally constituted.

1922   Hsu resigns 'Presidency' in favour of Li Yuan-hung: second Congress of Chinese Communist Party—decides to co-operate with Sun Yat-sen: Soviet Government sends mission to China, headed by Mr. Joffe.

1923—January, 26th: Joffe-Sun joint declaration of mutual support and sympathy to the cause of national unification and independence of China: Soviet military and civilian advisers sent to Canton to undertake, under the control of Sun, the modification of the internal organization of the Kuomintang and the Cantonese Army: Li Yuang Hung disposes of the 'Presidency' to Tsao Kung.

1924—March: First National Congress of the Kuomintang: the admission of Chinese Communists to the party on condition that there is no preparation of the proletarian revolution: this co-operation continued to 1927: in May, 1924 the Soviet Government recognized by China and this followed the abolition, by U.S.S.R. of their exterritorial rights in China.

1923—September: Earthquake in Tokyo-Yokohama area: in December attempt on life of Crown Prince of Japan who had acted as REGENT for Taisho Tenno since 1921.

1925 Death of Sun Yat-sen.

1926 Chiang Kai-shek assumed leadership of Kuomingtang: end of 1926, Chinese Communist Party suggested to Chiang to nationalize all landed property except those belonging to workmen, peasant or soldiers; reorganization of the Kuomintang: elimination of all military leaders hostile to communism.

1926 Death of Taisho Tenno and enthronement of Hirohito as Showa Tenno.

1927 Chinese Nationalist Government established at Wu-han: under Communist inspiration the provinces of Hunan and Hupei adopted Soviet methods of government as a prelude to a Communist Revolution: April, 1927, Chiang established his government at Nanking and ordered a purge of communists from army and civil service: the Central Executive of the Kuomintang excluded Communists from the party and ordered the Soviet advisers to leave China: Communism had gained strength in Kiangsi and Fukien in addition to Hunan and Hupei.

1928 Chang Tso-lin—ruler of Manchuria—was 'advised' by the Japanese Government to retire from his exploits in Peking and return to Mukden: he left Peking 3rd June, 1928, for Mukden —an explosion wrecked his train as it was approaching Mukden and he was killed: he was succeeded—as ruler of Manchuria under the Japanese—by his son Chang Hsueh-liang: he was advised not to co-operate with the Kuomintang or operate outside Manchuria but he defied the Japanese and was made C.-in-C. North-eastern Frontier Army under the Kuomintang.

1929—May: Chinese (Manchuria) attacked Soviet consulates and employees on Chinese Eastern Railway: in November the Soviet government retaliated with a military force sufficient to defeat the Chinese and, in December, the status quo was restored.

1929—July: Japanese government re-adopted a policy of 'goodwill and neighbourliness' instead of the positive policy of the militarists under General Tanaka: from 1928 the relations between

Chang Hsueh-liang and the Japanese militarists in Manchuria deteriorated rapidly and were at a critical stage in 1930.

1931—April: Conference of 'Peoples Foreign Policy Association, was held at Mukden, attended by delegates from various parts of Manchuria—main subject, liquidating the Japanese position in Manchuria.

June: Captain Nakamura, travelling in disguise in Mongolia, was captured by Chinese and killed with a Japanese n.c.o., Suigi, a white-Russian and a Mongolian.

1931— September, 18th: Japanese Army goes into action after an explosion had damaged a small section of track on the South Manchuria Railway near Mukden.

1930–
1931   There was a depression—with considerable unemployment— in Japan. This surplus of labour was absorbed by expansion in armaments and it suited the policy of the militarists.

Gold standard was abandoned by Japan in December, 1931 and this led to a rapid increase in exports despite adverse trading conditions in China.

Total expenditure on the ARMY was 31 per cent of tne total Revenue in 1931.

1931   Mukden occupied by Japanese troops: Kirin and Tsitsihar occupied: Chang Hsueh-liang banished from Manchuria: League of Nations create a Commission of Inquiry under Lord Lytton.

1932   Japanese troops occupy Chinchow: Sino-Japanese hostilities at Shanghai: Independence of Manchuria is proclaimed—Pu Yi (ex-Emperor of China) becomes the Chief Executive: Japanese capture Shanghai: Japan recognizes Manchukuo as an independent State.

(General ARAKI, Minister for War 1931-1934–founded KODO)

1932—May 13th: Hirohito orders withdrawal of Shanghai expedition: 15th May, Inukai—Premier—killed by cadets and young officers.

1933   Japanese army shells Shanhaikwan and operates outside Manchuria: Japanese troops occupy Chengteh, capital of Jehol—Eastern Inner Mongolia: Japan withdraws from the League of Nations: U.S.S.R. offers to sell C.E. Railway to Japan: Tientsin and Peking occupied by Japanese troops: U.S.A. recognises the U.S.S.R.

1934   Pu Yi crowned as Emperor of the Empire of Manchutikuo: Japan's 1934–1935 budget Yen 2,112,000,000 of which the Army's share was Y 937,000,000: Japan's population—in Japan proper—exceeded 65 million, density estimated at 455 per square mile.

1935   Young officer group active—Major-General Nagata is killed by Lt.-Col. Aizawa.

1936—February 26th: Tokyo Garrison mutiny: Finance Minister

Takahashi had opposed War expenditure—with other members of the Japanese Cabinet—he was killed as well as Admiral Saito and General Watanabe.
November 25th: Germany and Japan sign the Anti-Comintern Pact.

1937—July 7th: Japanese troops conducting night operations at LUKOUCHIAO, a few miles south-west of Peking, were fired on by Chinese troops at 11-40 p.m. It was this incident which brought about the 'North China Emergency' which was the prelude to the Sino-Japanese War of 1937–1945.

It was estimated that the cost of defeating China—1937–1938 —would be Yen 2,600,000,000: the first Sino-Japanese war cost Yen 200 million, Russo-Japanese War another Yen 2,000 million, the Siberia Expedition (against Russia) cost Yen 700 million. To the Japanese military economists—and the zaibatsu—the provision of Yen 2,600 million, in 1937, for the subjugation of China was a mere bagatelle and they explained the financial backing for aggression by publishing tables. According to one expert, Yutaka Noda, director of the Noda Economic Research Bureau: 'Japan's national earnings in 1936 are probably Yen 20,000 million per annum. It is apparent that, in any future war if it is carried out on the scale not exceeding that of the World War, Japan can spend annually Yen 13,200 million for four years at least.'

In this connection the undernoted explanation is given:

Comparitive Wartime Economic Conditions

	1904–1905 Russian War	(In Yen 1,000) 1936
Specie reserve	116,962	1,425,000
Bank deposits	751,428	13,968,000
Paid-up corporate capital	887,606	16,726,667
Value of foreign trade	606,638	5,725,873
Revenue and expenditure	509,817	4,617,091

(Production is 8 times greater than in 1904).

1937—November, Shanghai captured by Japanese: Italy joins the Anti-Comintern Pact: Chinese capital transferred from Nanking to Chungking: Nanking captured by Japanese 13th December.

1938 to 1945

1938—October: Japanese capture Canton. Japanese government proclaim 'New Order' in East Asia.

1939—October: Chinese defeat Japanese troops at Changsha.

1940—July–October: Burma Road closed by British. Japanese invade Indo-China. Japan joined Axis Pact.

1941—April 13th: Russo-Japanese neutrality pact signed. July: Japanese agreement with Vichy France for the occupation of Indo-China. Mr. Churchill pledged British aid to U.S.A. if she is attacked by Japan: Chinese forced out of Ichang.
December 7th: Japanese aircraft attacked Pearl Harbour, Manilla, Shanghai, Malaya, Siam and Hong-kong.

1942   Kinghwa, Chekiang Province, captured by Japanese: Fukien Province invaded.

1943—January: The Chinese puppet government of Nanking declares war on U.S.A. and Great Britain. May 20th: The U.S.A. and Great Britain ratify treaties with China renouncing exterritorial rights. November: Cairo Conference (Roosevelt, Chiang Kai-shek, Churchill) declaration—Japan to be stripped of all her conquests in the Pacific—all the territory stolen from China to be restored—independence of Korea secured. Changteh captured by Japanese in December

1944—May: Chinese troops drive towards northern Burma and attack across Salween River, Yunnan. Japanese attack in Honan and Hupeh provinces, Changsha captured by Japanese. August: Chinese offensive—Ichang area. December: Japanese retire from Kweichow.

1945—February 11th: YALTA CONFERENCE—secret pact with U.S.S.R. regarding Manchuria, Outer Mongolia, Sakhalin and the Kurile Islands as conditions for U.S.S.R. participation in war against Japan. March: Lashio (Burma) captured by Chinese. April 5th: U.S.S.R. denounces Russo-Japanese neutrality pact. May: Chinese counter-attack West Hunan. July 26th: Potsdam ultimatum to Japan. August 6th: atom bomb Hiroshima. August 9th: atom bomb on Nagasaki. August 10th: Japan's offer to surrender broadcast from Tokyo at *07.00* hours, U.S.S.R. declares war on Japan at *11.00* hours on August 10th. August 14th: Japan accepts allied terms—unconditional surrender.

Japan's population of 80 million confined to the main islands of Japan—density of 575 to the square mile.

August 1st, 1947 the actual population was 78,220,840—increase of 5,851,698 since 1945. Under the allied repatriation scheme (excluding U.S.S.R.) 4,451,261 Japanese had been returned to Japan by 1st August, 1947.

1946—September 11th: Japanese in Tokyo petitioned the Supreme Commander, the Soviet Embassy and Prime Minister Yoshida asking for the return to Japan of Japanese detained by the U.S.S.R. The following day, General Derevyanko (Soviet member of the Allied Council for Japan) refused to discuss the return to Japan of Japanese civilians and prisoners of war in Russian hands. It was admitted that there were 800,000 Japanese soldiers held by the Russians. General Derevyanko claimed that the Japanese inhabitants of the Kuriles and

Saghalin enjoyed living conditions unknown in Japan and had equal rights with Soviet citizens, and that the Japanese were now eligible for Soviet citizenship.

From 10th August, 1945 (after Japan's offer to surrender had been broadcast) to 28th August, 513,000 Japanese prisoners, including 81 generals, had surrendered in Manchuria to the Russian command.

APPENDIX X

Wartime Imperial General Headquarters

The regulations governing the Wartime Imperial General Headquarters were promulgated by Imperial Decree No. 293 of December 28th, 1903. These regulations were cancelled on 17th November, 1937, and the following regulations substituted:

MILITARY REGULATIONS No. 1 (Imperial Headquarters Laws):

Article 1. The Emperor may establish an office for the Supreme Command of the army and navy in time of war or emergency, when this is necessary.

Article 2. The Chief of the General Staff and the Chief of the Naval General Staff shall head their respective staff officers in attending a war council called by the Sovereign, advising the Sovereign on operations and effecting the co-ordination of the army and navy so as to attain the ultimate purpose of the operations.

Article 3. The organization and service of the Imperial General Headquarters shall be separately regulated.

APPENDIX XI

Chronology of the defeat of the Japanese Navy

(a)   Japan declared war on the assumption that Germany would defeat Russia and the British Empire, and that the United States would be forced by circumstances to negotiate for peace on Axis terms.

The main objectives were India, Australia and New Zealand: by the end of December, 1941, Japan's successes included Pearl Harbour—4,000 miles from Tokyo—Wake and the Gilbert Islands—2,000 to 3,000 miles away and, in January, 1942 the front was extended to Solomon Islands and New Guinea. At the end of February, 1942, Timor, Java, Borneo, Sumatra, Malaya, Siam and Burma had been fully occupied—the Aleutians provided small bases in June.

(b)   Japan's Navy had its first check during the Battle of the Coral Sea—4–8th May, 1942. Several destroyers were lost in addition to the aircraft-carrier SHOHO of 12,000 tons.

(c)   The first heavy defeat took place during the Battle of Midway —3–6th June, 1942. Actual losses, suffered by Japan were:— Cruiser MIKUMA (13,000 tons): Aircraft-carriers AKAGI (36,000 ton)—KAGA (35,000 ton)—HIRYU and SORYU both 17,500 ton class and several destroyers. (4 cruisers and 3 battleships were reported as damaged). The U.S. fleet lost the A.C. YORKTOWN.

(d)   On August 23–25th, Battle of the Eastern Solomons, the aircraft-carrier RYUJO (8,500 ton) was lost. On October, 11–12th, Battle of Cape Esperance—while making for Guadalcanal—a convoy suffered heavily: 5 destroyers and the cruiser FURUTAKA (8,800) were lost. On October 26th, Battle of Santa Cruz Island, the cruiser YURA (5,700 ton) was destroyed.

(e)   The second heavy defeat was during the Battle of Guadalcanal—November 6–15th. The 31,000 ton battleships, HIYEI and KIRISHIMA, and the cruiser KINUGASA (8,800) were the major losses.

LOSSES for the year were: 2 battleships, 6 carriers, 5 cruisers and 21 large destroyers. (Cruiser KAKO was sunk by submarine on 10th August).

(f)   Under pressure of allied air attacks, Japan's heavier ships were withdrawn early in 1943. Transports were convoyed by destroyers (1900 ton class).

(g)   According to Vice-Admiral Takata (Yokohama, 9th September, 1945) the worst shock of the war came during the Battle of Bismark Sea, 1–3rd March, 1943. A convoy of about 40 ships, including 10 destroyers, was repeatedly attacked by allied aircraft for seventy-two hours. Not one ship escaped. When the disaster was reported to Admiral Yamamoto—C.-in-C.—he decided to see for himself what had happened to the convoy—then he crash-dived the recce plane in to the flotsam. The loss of life was probably in the region of 40–45,000 for the forty transports and warships destroyed, and put an end to the invasion of Australia.

(h)   With the withdrawal of the Navy, losses for the rest of 1943 were not heavy: 8th June, battleship MUTSU (37,500 ton), 10th June, aircraft-carrier HIYO (28,000 ton), cruisers JINTSU and SENDAI (5,900 ton) 13th July and 2nd November, and the escort-carrier CHUYO (20,000) on 4th December. The super-battleship YAMATO was damaged by submarine *Skate* on 25th December, and the seaplane tender NISSHIN (9,000) was sunk on 22nd July.

(i)   U.S. submarines were active early in 1944. The cruisers AGANO (7,000 ton)—16th February—KUMA (11th January) and NAKA (17th February) of 5,700 ton class, TATSUTA (13th March) and YUBARI (27th April) of 3,500 ton class, NAGARA (5,700 ton) 7th August and NATORI (5,700 ton) 18th August, and OHI (5,700) 19th July, were all disposed of by U.S. submarines. And, during the Battle of Phillipine Sea (between Luzon and Saipan) 19–20th June, the aircraft-carriers SHOKAKU (30,000) and TAIHO (31,000) shared the same fate, as well as the escort-carrier OTAKA (20,000 ton) on 18th August, and the escort-carrier UNYO (20,000) on 6th September.

(j)   The third, and decisive defeat, was the *Battle for Leyte Gulf*, 23–26th October, 1944. Actual losses were as follows:—

Battleships: FUSO (33,000 ton), YAMASHIRO (33,000 ton) and MUSASHI (72,809) and the YAMATO (72,809) damaged.

Cruisers: MOGAMI and SUZUYA (13,000 ton) ATAGO, CHIKUMA, CHOKAI and MAYA (12,200 ton), ABU KUMA, KINU, NOSHIRO and TAMA (5,700 ton)

Aircraft-carriers: ZUIKAKU (30,000 ton) ZUIHO (12,000 ton) CHITOSE and CHIYODA (11,000 ton).

Destroyers: Nine.

Japan's navy was now reduced to:—

Battleships	6
Carriers	5
Escort Carriers	2
Cruisers	15

(k)   After the Battle for Leyte Gulf, to the end of 1944, the losses
from submarine and air action were:—
Battleship KONGO (31,000 ton) 21st November. Battleship
SHINANO (72,809) converted to aircraft-carrier, 28th November.
Cruisers: NACHI (12,700 ton) 5th November. KISO (5,700) 13th
November. KUMANO (14,000 ton) 25th November. *Carrier:*
UNRYU (18,500 ton) 19th December. *Escort-carrier:* JINYO
(21,000 ton) 17th November.

(l)   From 1st January to 31st July 1945, the destruction of the
balance of the Japanese fleet proceeded as follows:—
Battleships: YAMATO (72,809 ton) 7th April. HYUGA (34,500)
              24th July. HARUNA (31,000) and ISE (34,500) on
              28th July. NAGATO (37,500) damaged 28th July?
Cruisers: ISUZU and YAHAGI (5,700) both on 7th April.
              HAGURO (12,700) 16th May. ASHIGARA (12,700)
              8th June. AOBA and OYODO (8,500) both on 28th
              July. TENRYU (3,300) 24th July. TONE (12,000)
              24th July.
Carriers: AMAGI (18,500) 24th July. Escort-carrier KAIYO
              (17,000) 24th July. (HAKATA and KATASURAGI both
              damaged in the Yokosuka dockyard).

The old battleship ASAHI (11,440 ton) used as a repair ship
was destroyed 25th May, 1942, and the AKASHI (9,000) was sunk
30th March, 1942.
The old cruisers: AZUMA (8,640 ton) and KASUGA (7,080) were
both destroyed on 18th July, 1945. IWATE (9,180) and IZUMO
(9,180) on 28th July, 1945.
Seaplane tenders: MIZUHO (9,000) was sunk on 2nd May,
1942: the AKITSUSHIMA (9,000) on 24th September, 1944 and
JINJI (5,100) on 10th October, 1944.

This summary of destruction does not take into account the sinking
of Japan's large auxiliary fleet—gunboats, mine-sweepers, coast-
defence craft, small destroyers, armed merchant-vessels, etc., etc.,
or the large and small submarines.

Japan was defeated before the atom bomb was used: Admiral
Halsey, U.S. Navy, is reported to have described the atom-bombing
of Hiroshima and Nagasaki as '*an unnecessary experiment*'.
In 1946 there were two atom-bomb experiments at BIKINI—a coral
atoll in the Marshall Islands. These experiments are said to have
cost £25,000,000 and the target ships included 4 U.S. battleships,
2 carriers and 2 cruisers: 1 German cuiser and the Japanese battleship NAGATO and the cruiser SAKAWA.
The first experiment—1st July, 1946—was the dropping from a
height of six miles and the explosion at 1,500 ft. over the target

battleship NEVADA. Five ships were sunk—the SAKAWA, U.S. *destroyers* LAMSON and ANDERSON, and *attack transports* GILLIAM and CARLISLE.

Vice-Admiral Blandy, U.S. Navy, is reported to have stated that there was no reason to believe that the days of the aircraft-carrier and destroyer were over. He had seen ships in worse shape *after attacks by Japanese suicide bombers.* The *scientists* pointed out that *only one bomb* had been exploded over the targets!

The second experiment—25th July, 1946—was based on the explosion of an atom-bomb as a depth-charge. This press-button atom-bomb detonation produced better results: battleship ARKANSAS (26,100) turned turtle, carrier SARATOGA had her triple-skinned hull ripped open and sank within seven hours—other ships, including the Japanese battleship NAGATO, were beached to avert sinking: other minor craft (transports and destroyers) some distance from SARATOGA were scarcely damaged.

This stage-managed, pin-pointed, series of experiments provided ample material for scientists and naval experts to work on in preparation for World War III. No doubt the required number of atom-bombs—quite a few thousand I should say—will be ready. But the best targets will be on land not on the sea: New York would be target No.1—the largest city in U.S.A. which has at present the largest stock-pile of atom bombs: London as target No.2—and so on. Unless of course the democrats decided to experiment on the communists—and struck the first blow.

The three largest warships afloat during World War II were sunk by torpedo from submarine or destroyer, or by aircraft—the Japanese super-battleships MUSASHI, YAMATO and SHINANO: and their only remaining battleship, NAGATO almost survived the two Bikini atom-bomb tests, in 1946. Carrier borne, and land-based U.S. and British aircraft, had no difficulty during July, 1945 in sinking 3 *battleships, 4 cruisers, 4 old cruisers, 1 carrier* and *1 escort carrier,* with ordinary H.E. bombs. And, during the war, submarines and aircraft destroyed 5,000,000 tons of Japan's merchant shipping in a little over 3½ years.

APPENDIX XII

Christianity in Japan: 1542–1640

In the third century B.C., the Indian King Asoka confronted by the struggle between two hostile religions—Brahmanism and Buddhism—decided that both should be equally privileged and honoured in his dominions. His edicts, of religious tolerance, were based on the teaching of Buddha. 'Even as the ocean has everywhere but one taste, that of salt, so my doctrine has everywhere but one essence, that of deliverance.' And it may be mentioned, for what it is worth, that when the Portuguese arrived at Tanegashima, 35 miles from Osumi in Kyushu, in 1542, the Daimyo Shimazu of Satsuma (Kagoshima) accepted Christianity as a superior form of Buddhism.

But the Portuguese who came in 1542 supplied firearms to the Daimyo of Kyushu, and they were the traders of the new religion so it was left to the Society of Jesus, the Jesuits, to introduce Roman Catholicism to the Japanese. Ten years after the arrival of the traders, (on 16th September, 1552) Otomo Hachiro, Lord of Yamaguchi, presented to the missionaries the Daido (Great Way) Temple in Yamaguchi 'that they may found and erect a monastery and house in order to develop the law of Buddha.' Trade, and the new 'Buddhism', prospered in Kyushu and spread to the main island of Japan.

The de facto ruler of Japan (1560–1582) was Oda Nobunaga and when he had disposed of his opponents he 'recalled to the throne' the exiled Ogimachi Tenno and established him in Kyoto. Ogimachi's reign covered the period 1558–1586 and he was in favour of religious tolerance but Oda Nobunaga was hostile to Buddhism because it cut across his powers of dictatorship. He invited some of the foreign Christian priests to visit Kyoto and explain their religion, trade, and ambitions. They accepted the invitation and arrived in 1568.

Nobunaga decided to use the new religion in his campaign against the Buddhist priests. He gave instructions for the building of a temple in Kyoto to be named, after the era of Ogimachi Tenno, Eiroku.

This enraged the Buddhists of Mount Hiye (outside Kyoto) because to name a temple in that way was throwing contempt upon the royal throne of the whole Empire. They petitioned the Tenno, pointing out to the Tenno that the Enryaku-ji (on the flank of Mount Hiye) which was built by Dengyo Daishi—founder of the Tendai sect—in 805 was the only permitted exception: Enryaku was the era of Kwammu Tenno: 782–805. Their objection, from a national point of view, was well founded—Dengyo Daishi and Kobo Daishi broke away from the Nara tradition and expounded new interpretations of the Niwokyo, Konkomyo-kyo and Hokeyo scriptures and disseminated a new 'understanding of Japanese nationalism', and the object of their new

389

faith was not in the 'interpretation of the scriptures as the words of Buddha, but in the fact that to believe in them meant the welfare and prosperity of the *state centered in the Tenno*.'

Ojimachi Tenno requested Nobunaga to change the name of the new temple. He agreed to do so—part of his 'policy' was the unification of the country under the 'divine traditions'—and the first Christian church in Kyoto was named Namban-ji. And it may be added that Nobunaga destroyed the Enryaku-ji monastery on Mount Hiye and slaughtered the monks as part of his policy—destroying the power of Buddhism in Japan.

After a few years, Nobunaga began to regret his policy of building up the new sect—of Christianity. Many of his Daimyo supporters had embraced Christianity, of their own volition or on account of the lead given to them by Nobunaga, and when they heard that he proposed to expel the Christians from Namban-ji they advised him against it. But this did not prevent men like Araki, Governor of Settsu, or Takayama (known as Don Justo Takayama when he was banished to Manila by Tokugawa Iyeyasu) from rising in rebellion and it was only through the intervention of his generals, Sakuma, Kunaikujo and Otezan that the 'rebels' reaffirmed their allegiance to Nobunaga and saved Namban-ji from the fate of Enryaku-ji.

Nobunaga was killed by Akechi Mitsuhide on 2nd June, 1582 and the new dictator was Hideyoshi who was far from sharing Nobunaga's views on Christianity or its value as a weapon against Buddhism. Early in the year 1587, Hideyoshi completed the conquest of Kyushu by defeating the Daimyo Shimazu of Satsuma at Kagoshima. At that time the number of Christians in Kyushu was estimated to exceed 125,000, and in July 1587, Hideyoshi issued his edict—all foreign missionaries to leave Japan within twenty days and only the *foreign merchants* to remain. Twenty-six of Hideyoshi's principal officers had become Christians and they helped their religious brethren to escape from Kyoto before Namban-ji was razed to the ground in 1588. Four of the Padres were arrested, put aboard a Dutch ship and sent back to Holland. All those who would not recant were executed, and the Christian sect in Kyoto was completely destroyed, but this did not stop the spread of the religion in Kyushu.

Early in the year 1597 the Spanish galleon, *San Felipe*, went ashore at Tosa in Shikoku. Twenty-three Franciscan and three Jesuit priests were 'taken prisoner' and subsequently paraded through the streets of Kyoto, Osaka and Sakai. Then they were taken to Nagasaki and on 5th February, 1597 were crucified—to bring home to the Christians in Kyushu the error of their ways. Churches were destroyed and the Kyushu Daimyo were forbidden to become Christians. Hideyoshi died in 1598 and he was succeeded by Tokugawa Iyeyasu who was appointed Shogun by Go-yozei Tenno in 1603.

At first, Tokugawa Iyeyasu encouraged the foreign traders but was suspicious of the missionaries and their activity in Kyushu. In 1614, Tokugawa forces attacked Osaka Castle, the stronghold of Hideyoshi's son, Hideyori the Regent, and at the same time ordered all missionaries to leave Japan. In 1615, Osaka Castle was captured— Hideyori and his mother, and his son of eight, were destroyed and this brought to an end the house of Toyotomi. The Hideyoshi shrines were destroyed and, by the edict of the Tenno, his name was removed from the ranks of the deities.

In 1616, by order of Tokugawa Hidetada, fifteen of the foreign priests in Kyushu were put to death, and foreign trade restricted to Nagasaki and Hirado. By 1624 the persecution of Japanese and Foreign Christians was in full swing, and in one revolt (?) in 1630 'the Christians were killed to a man'. The Portuguese sent an embassy to protest against the persecution (1635) but the four envoys and fifty-seven members of the crew were taken off the ship and beheaded.

The Shimabara Rebellion: 1637–1638

In addition to the Princes of Kyushu, who sent an embassy to the Pope in 1591, other missions left Japan. In 1614, the Daimyo of Sendai sent an envoy to the Pope, and in 1615, Tokugawa Iyeyasu sent a Tokugawa official to Europe. He returned to Japan in 1622 and it was his report which convinced (?) the Tokugawas that it was not to their advantage to permit the spread of Christianity, and it may have been the Dutch and English traders, who came to Japan between 1609 and 1613, that spread the impression that 'Roman Catholics' were the spearhead of foreign aggression.

Shimabara (Minami Takagi-gun, Hizen, Nagasaki-ken) and the nearby island of Amakusa were early strongholds of Christianity and when the Hideyoshi persecutions started the Kyoto Christians fled to these districts. In 1637 there were probably sixty or seventy thousand Japanese Christians in this area who were determined not to recant. Samurai, farmer and peasant they preferred death to apostacy, and their decision to revolt against the local authority came about in a simple manner.

On 25th October, 1637 a retainer of the Matsukura Daimyo, of the Castle of Takaji, who was Governor of the villages in Shimabara, went to Fukaiemura to investigate rumours about a new disciple of Jesus Christ, a Japanese youth named Shiro Tokisada, who was to lead Christians in their struggle against the Shogunate, and in the house of Sashiki Sajiemon he saw a picture of the Christian God which he tore down and threw into the fire. For this sacrilegious act he was beaten to death by the villagers.

When the report of this murder reached Takaji Castle, four hundred armed retainers were sent to punish the villagers but when they made their attack the next morning they were met and defeated by a thousand Christians and compelled to retire in confusion. The 'rebels' pushed on to the town, outside the castle, looted it and then made an attempt to enter the castle but were forced to retire after losing more than two hundred of their number.

The Christians on Amakusa island now joined the conspirators besieging Takaji Castle and they were reinforced by others from Kamitsura, Oyano, Chizuka, Soshojima and Yanaginoseto bringing up the total to over thirteen thousand. Messengers were sent to Nagasaki and (according to native accounts) the war cry was 'Cut off the heads of all those who will not yield to the Christians, set fire to their houses, and offer these victims as a sacrifice to the God of War.'

On 18th November, the Christian 'army' attacked Tomioka Castle but were beaten off with heavy losses and on 23rd compelled to fall back to Karatsu in Shimabara. By this time the Shogunate had taken steps to deal with the revolt and various detachments, supplied by non-Christian Daimyo in Kyushu were marching on Shimabara so the Christian 'army' decided to reconstruct the old castle of Hara, at Shimabara, and use it as their stronghold against the Shogunate.

The Massacre of Hara Castle: 28th February, 1638

By 10th December, 1637, twenty thousand armed Christians and seventeen thousand women and children were within the defences of Hara Castle. On 20th December they were attacked by eighteen thousand Shogunate troops who were unable to get to grips with the defenders and ceased operations after suffering several hundred casualties. The next attempt to reduce the Castle was made on 30th December, but this was a failure, resulting in the loss of 2,500 more men, so the commander withdrew his force to await reinforcements.

On 4th January, 1638, Hosakawa Higo-no-kami arrived with twenty-six thousand men—Kuroda of Nagaoka, Shimadzu of Satsuma, Terazawa of Hyogo, Kuroda of Fukuoka and Matsudaira of Idzu followed with their contingents and by the end of January the total number had risen to one hundred and twenty-five thousand. The Castle was surrounded, more than fifty junks guarded the sea coast and even the Dutch Commercial Resident at Hirado had to send two Dutch ships, guns and ammunition: only one was supplied (the de Ryp of 20 guns) and it remained on the station for two weeks.

The militant Christians knew that their days were numbered so they took the initiative on 21st February by daring night attack on part of the investing army. The 'enemy' were taken by surprise, more than five hundred were killed, in hand-to-hand encounters, but the desperate enterprise merely postponed for a few days the certainty of ultimate defeat.

Matsudaira Idzu-no-kami, commander of the Shogunate army, abandoned his plan to starve the 'rebels' into surrender. Orders were passed for a general attack at noon on 27th February. This was a success: the outer defences were captured and the position consolidated during the night. At dawn, the entire force under the command of Matsudaira entered the body of the castle and got to grips with the defenders. The odds were against the Christians: thirty-seven thousand were killed . . . , 'the place was filled with dead bodies, in heaps, and the blood flowed in red streams . . . ' . . . all but one-hundred and five of the 'rebels' died for their faith in Hara Castle on 28th February, 1638: the army of the Shogun lost twelve hundred killed and seven thousand wounded.

All the Christians were beheaded. Thousands of heads, in sacks, were taken to Nagasaki to be exhibited and then buried under a mound. Three thousand and thirty three of the 'heads' were taken to Amakusa and buried at Tomioka. There is a monument, 'The Tomb of Bones', at Hara Castle, another monument on Tateyama Hill at Nagasaki, and a third monument was erected at Tomioka on 25th July, 1648, to remind the Christians of the Massacre of Hara Castle.

After the massacre, in 1639, the Portuguese were deported to Macao and from that date until 1873 Christianity was forbidden in Japan under pain of death. And, after the massacre, the persecution was intensified—neither men, women or children were spared. Most of the Japanese Christians, who escaped the slaughter, recanted and it was not until 1863 that Roman Catholic priests returned to Nagasaki where they erected the Church of the Twenty-Six Martyrs. By the year 1868 there were more than five thousand converts in Takahama, Shimabara, Amakusa and Hirado and this brought about a renewal of the persecution because Christianity was not in accordance with Japanese law relating to foreign religions. Protests were made by the Treaty Consuls, particularly regarding the arrest, and exile from Kyushu, of 4,100 Christians who were handed over in batches to 34 selected Daimyo for detention and treatment. The Japanese Government made its attitude clear to the Treaty Powers in the 'Proclamation Issued Against Christianity 1868', but a few years later (1873) they altered their attitude and religious freedom was established in the country.

In 1636, there were about 200,000 Japanese Christians: in 1935, according to official figures, there were only 287,299 with 1,872 churches. In 1949, out of a population of 82,000,000 there were not more than 375,000 Japanese Christians so it would seem that in spite of the efforts of the missionaries, the expenditure of 10 million American dollars and the distribution of 4 million Bibles, the present day Japanese is in no hurry to abandon Shinto or Buddhism.

APPENDIX XIII

RISE AND FALL OF THE JAPANESE EMPIRE: 1868–1945

i. 'To The British People'—from The Shiunso

The Shiunso, a Japanese Patriotic Society led by Mr. Tetsuma Hashimoto, was one of the Japanese Foreign Office propaganda units engaged in educating the public in the affairs of Empire. In October and November, 1937, at the height of the 'China incident', the Shiunso was busy with advice to the British people regarding their faults, and criminal actions, and it may help 'to see ourselves as others see us' if I quote some of the Shiunso's statements before giving the details of Japan's expansion overseas from 1868 to 1945.

A long statement, issued in November, 1937, begins like this:—

'... The areas England has gained by invasion in the past one century and a half are as follows:

1	In Asia	1,972,305	square miles
2	„ Europe	26,712	„ „
3	„ Africa	3,234,485	„ „
4	„ America	4,010,188	„ „
5	„ Oceania	3,187,822	„ „

When to the above-mentioned territories the total area of 973,770 square miles of mandated territories obtained as a result of the World War, and the area of England, reaching 93,988 square miles, are added, the territory of the *British Empire* reaches a total of 13,499,270 square miles . . . more than *91 times* that of *Japan proper*. The population of England which controls the above-mentioned vast area is only a little more than 47 million, certainly far smaller than that of *Japan proper* which is about 70 million. . . .'

And then, according to the Shiunso, 'when England obtained Australia she carried out massacres of the natives . . . and then sent her prisoners and criminals to Australia, making it an open prison of England, and when she obtained New Zealand, natives were massacred and the population reduced to less than 40,000. While the island has an area of more than 100,000 square miles.

After occupying Africa and the South Seas, instead of killing the natives they gained huge profits by selling them as slaves.

We ask the British people to open a world map. In Asia, in Australia, in Africa, in America and in Europe there are territories painted the same colour as England.

How did those territories become British Possessions? They have never become British territories 'peacefully by discussions', a term used by *The Times*, London, in attacking Japan in connection with the present China incident.

Are the British people not ashamed of, in their democratic principles and in the name of Christ, the procedure by which India, Africa, Australia, and other territories are occupied?

For occupying those territories the ancestors of the present British people killed many innocent and defenceless people, and it is still remembered that in extreme cases, innocent inhabitants were herded together by hunting dogs and then mercilessly killed as though they were game animals.

The British people criticized the Italian expedition to Ethiopia, Italy pointed out the British history of merciless invasion, and said that Italy was only following the example of England, but was doing only one-tenth of what was done by British people.

A close examination of the history of conflicts of nations in the twentieth century will reveal that various nations had fallen prey to the cunning policies based on the avarice of England and thus there were caused conflicts between countries which should not fight, or those which had no need of fighting. It is indeed a regrettable condition. Particularly, France, the Netherlands, China, the Soviet Union, and other countries in the near future—the United States at some distant future—will commit crimes at the instigation of England and feel really sorry.

Thus as far as the British tyranny and inhumanity as viewed from Japan's standpoint are explained she has no right nor ground whatever to call other countries invaders. The first nation to be judged by God and men is Great Britain herself.

What is the greatest suffering of Germans? Why is Italy so irritated? What caused Italy to start the Ethiopian question? *What does Japan need most for existence?* All are because Great Britain monopolizes vast natural resources.

When this attitude of Great Britain is compared with the diplomacy of the Soviet Union, it is seen that the U.S.S.R. is showing her true wolfish self, and thus all are cautious in dealing with her, but Great Britain is clothing her wolfish self in sheeps' fur, and is satisfying her avarice by cheating. Thus the crime of Great Britain is several times greater than that of the Soviet Union. . . . '

ii. *Population and Living Space*

With regard to Japan's population, and the need for Colonies this is what the Shiunso had to say: (1937)

'In his book 'Danger Spots in World Population,' Dr. W. S. Thompson, American authority on population problems, says that the pressure of population increase in Japan will become greater year after year, and finally the Japanese will take a hint of *dying in battles* instead of dying of hunger, and Americans would not hesitate to praise the choice made by the Japanese, because Americans despise the surrender to fate. Thus he urges the English to reflect in regard to the distribution of surplus natural resources, but England, blinded by her own avarice, is making her own argument and says that to possess a greater population than the country is able to support is an unpardonable crime. Again they say that the best advice the British can give to Asiatics is that they should adjust properly their own population. They hint that the population problem of Japan should be settled by birth-control.'

It is intersting to note that in *1949*, Dr. Thompson recommended birth control as the only effective way of relieving the pressure of population. The Prime Minister, Mr. Yoshida, favoured birth control and so did Dr. E. A. Ackerman of the University of Chicago after a survey of Japan's natural resources.

The Japanese population rise has been as follows:

Year:	1868 *Estimated*	1903	1920	1925	1935	1940	1947	1949	1950	1970
			Census					*Estimated*		
Millions:	32	45	56	60	69	73	78	82	84	105

(Figures are for Japan proper, 142,270 square miles).
(Present (1949) excess of births over deaths is about 1,500,000 per annum)

Alteration of population during Meiji, Taisho and Showa eras is as follows:

MEIJI	*1868–1912*	*TAISHO*	*1912–1926*	*SHOWA*	*1926–1949*
	32 to 50 million		50 to 60 million		60 to 82 million

iii. Territorial Expansion

In the year 1850, the 'Japanese Empire' of 142,270 square miles or so, and about thirty million people, was of no importance to the rest of the world. However, by the end of 1942, this 'Empire' covered about 3,285,000 square miles and the 'subjects' numbered about 350,000,000 asiatics from Mongolia to New Guinea. That was the full extent of the territorial expansion and it compared not unfavourably with the 13,499,270 square miles of the much older British Empire which the Japanese set out to emulate.

Fortunately, because of the military power of the United States of America, Japan failed to reach her main objectives, Australia and India. Had she done so, and if Germany had defeated the U.S.S.R., the 'Japanese Empire' would have included 1,800,000 square miles of India and 2,977,600 square miles of Australia, in addition to the 104, 850 square miles of New Zealand.

The clash between the United States of America and Japan was as inevitable as the attempt by Japan to conquer the entire Indian Ocean and South Pacific area of the British Empire, and it may be opportune to quote the words of the historian, E. S. Creasy as set down in his 'Fifteen Decisive Battles', on this subject. Writing in 1851, regarding the victory of the Americans over Burgoyne at Saratoga, A.D. 1777, he makes the following comment:

'The importance of the power of the United States being then firmly planted along the Pacific applies not only to the New World, but to the Old. Opposite to San Francisco, on the coast of that ocean, lie the wealthy but decrepit empires of China and Japan. Numerous groups of islets stud the larger part of the intervening sea, and form convenient stepping-stones for the progress of commerce or ambition. The intercourse of traffic between these ancient Asiatic monarchies and the young Anglo-American republic must be rapid and extensive. Any attempt of the Chinese or Japanese rulers to check it will only accelerate an armed collision. The American will either buy or force his way. Between such populations as that of China and Japan on the one side, and that of the United States on the other—the former haughty, formal and insolent; the latter bold, intrusive, and unscrupulous—causes of quarrel cannot be doubted. America will scarcely imitate the forbearance shown by England at the end of our late war with the Celestial Empire; and the conquests of China and Japan, by the fleets and armies of the United States, are events which many now living are likely to witness. . . . '

Those words were written in 1851, two years before Commodore Perry entered Uraga Bay and fourteen years after the *s.s. Morrison* attempted to open up trade with Japan. But the clash between the United States of America and Japan, from 1941 to 1945, brought about the fall of the 'Japanese Empire' only to restore to the Soviet Union her dominant position in China and the Far East. Territorial expansion, British, American, Russian or Japanese is one and the same thing—imperialists, empire builders or communists have one thing in common, the master-race ruling others for their own benefit. All the slaughter in the South Pacific war zone, and in Japan, has resulted in the substitution of the U.S.S.R. for Japan and the spread of red-communism in China and South East Asia, and the disintegration of the British Empire in the Indian Ocean and South Pacific area—slowly, but surely.

iv. The Rise of the Japanese Empire

Expansion was in three stages, roughly as follows:

			Approximate area	
1	Japan proper (Honshu, Hokkaido, Kyushu and Shikoku)		140,000 square miles	
	1875–1876	Kuriles and Luchus	3,000	,,
	1895	Formosa and Pescadores	13,600	,,
	1905	Saghalien (southern half)	10,000	,,
		Kwantung and S.M. Railway zone Manchuria	1,500	,,
	1910	Korea	71,000	,,
	1918	Mandates (Pacific islands)	1,000	,,
			240,100	,,
2	1918 to 1937	Manchuria and North China	545,500	,,
		Fengtien	74,000 square miles	
		Kirin	102,000 ,,	
		Heilungkiang	170,000 ,,	
		Jehol	52,000 ,,	
		Hsingan and Tungsheng	147,500 ,,	
3	1937 to 1945		2,497,000	,,
		China (roughly Peking to Canton—500 by 1500 miles)	750,000 square miles	
		Indo-China	260,000 ,,	
		Siam	200,000 ,,	
		Burma	230,000 ,,	
		Malaya	53,000 ,,	
		Java	48,000 ,,	
		Borneo (Br. & N.E.I.)	280,000 ,,	
		New Guinea	330,000 ,,	
		Sumatra	160,000 ,,	
		Celebes	72,000 ,,	
		Philippines	114,000 ,,	

* Approximately 3,282,600 square miles

* Excluding various South Pacific and Indian Ocean islands.

Japan's conquests, from Hong Kong to the Solomon Islands, gave her control of nine-tenths of the world's supply of rubber, two-thirds of tin, almost unlimited supplies of crude petroleum, tungsten, tea, sugar, rice, phosphates and quinine—to cite only a few of the 'spoils of war' as the Army solution of the population problem—the method which had been adopted in Manchuria and North China. But in addition to the 'control' of raw materials, necessary for her planned economy, Japan by 'adding' $2\frac{1}{2}$ million square miles to her 'Empire' had enlarged her sphere of influence in South East Asia, and 'Under the aegis of Japan down-trodden East Asiatic nations have over-thrown the yoke of British imperialism. The victorious Japanese army has been welcomed by the native population wherever it has gone. For Dai Nippon's creation of a Greater East Asia has set alight a flame which cannot be extinguished. For centuries the East has suffered humiliation and oppression. Today, with Japanese leadership it is united, making East Asia a better place to live in. And so today, Dai Nippon holds the dominant position in the Far East.' The Japanese who wrote that, in 1942, did not reckon with the power of the United States of America, or with the survival of the British Empire in Greater East Asia.

v. The Fall of the Japanese Empire

In an 'Estimate of Japanese National strength at the outbreak of the Greater East Asia War as of December, 1941.' prepared for the Imperial Japanese General Staff, the following occurs:—

' . . . In a greatly changing world situation, the policy adopted by the Japanese Empire is to attain a position of self-sufficiency based upon national strength which it can maintain independently.
    In determining the over-all policy of war or peace, it is always necessary to make a proper estimate of the Nation's strength. However, because of extreme difficulty in obtaining complete data and because of the many complicated and unpredictable factors in the changing material resources situation, an estimate of the actual strength of the Empire is not a simple matter. Thus, it is dangerous practice to translate national strength into mathematical terms and use them without hesitation as the criteria in deciding on war or peace. . . . '

Japan's conquests, in Korea, Formosa, Manchuria and China to the end of 1940 had added many 'square miles of territory' but the 'Scarce items preventing complete self-sufficiency.' were Rice, Fuel, Essential war materials and Transport capacity. During 1941 and 1942, and part of 1943, the 'scarce items'—rice, fuel, iron ore, nickel, crude rubber, tin, copper, lead, cobalt, manganese, and so on, were obtained in sufficient quantities from Indo-China, Siam, Burma, Borneo, N.E.I., Malaya and the Philippines to meet the military requirements, and production capacity,.
    But, during 1943, the political and military situation changed—Japan had lost the war. China refused to capitulate, Germany had

not defeated Russia and had not invaded England—the United States of America had made no overtures for a separate peace with the Axis Powers, on the contrary their Army, Navy and Airforce had gained the initiative in the South Pacific Ocean and was making a terrific counter-attack on Japan's 'Empire in South East Asia', on her Navy and on her 'Transport capacity'.

The creation of the modern Japanese Empire occupied about fifty years—from the Sino-Japanese War of 1894 to 1943—the destruction of it was brought about in the short space of two years by the concentrated efforts of the United States, and British, Army, Navy and Airforce. It was not due to the explosion of atom bombs on Hiroshima and Nagasaki but to the unqualified defeat of Japan's Navy and Airforce, and the destruction of her merchant marine.

In a Survey of National Resources, June, 1945, the Japanese Government were informed that the increasing air raids were disrupting land and sea communications and essential war production: the food situation had deteriorated: it was almost impossible to continue to meet the requirements of total war: morale is high but there is no faith in the present regime—criticism of the government and the military are increasing: compared with requirements there was a surplus of manpower: available shipping space had been reduced to a total of 1,000,000 tons: Japan, Manchuria and China will have to rely on their own sources for fuel oil: Steel, the production of which was vital had been reduced to a mere 250,000 tons from January to June, and it was impossible to maintain the production of aircraft—on account of the air raids and the lack of raw material and fuel.

Japan's defeat in World War II, and the 'Fall of the Japanese Empire' may be attributed to the 'dangerous practice of translating national strength into mathematical terms and using them without hesitation as the criteria in deciding on war or peace'. Hitler made the same mistakes as Tojo, and the Japanese militarists, and in Hitler's case, 'The Battle of Britain'—which began over land on 10th August, 1940—upset his mathematics but it did not prevent Japan from making the same miscalculation on 7th December, 1941. Germany lost the war, when she lost 'The Battle of Britain' and the 'Battle of Japan' was won by the American Airforce in August, 1945: there is a connection between the two air battles and they may be listed with the other 'Decisive Battles of the World' if we care to investigate the chain of causes and effects and speculate on what probably would have happened if either of those battles had come to a different termination in World War II—war is not an exact science and history is 'more than a series of necessary phenomena, which follow inevitably one upon the other'.

vi. A Peace Treaty with Japan

According to General MacArthur, Japan might become either 'a powerful bulwark for peace, or a dangerous springboard for war' and according to Dr. Jessup (American Ambassador-at-large) and other authorities on Japan 'The Japanese people have progressed to a point where they deserve a peace treaty which will give them responsibility for managing their own affairs, with certain necessary safeguards.' And it is this 'Peace or War' problem which (so it seems) has to be solved before a Peace Treaty can be concluded with Japan.

In the Declaration of Cairo (December, 1943) the Governments of Britain, China and the United States reaffirmed the policy of 'Unconditional surrender' and stated that: 'It is their purpose that Japan shall be stripped of all the islands in the Pacific which she has seized or occupied since the beginning of the first world war in 1914, and that all the territories that Japan has stolen from the Chinese, such as Manchuria, Formosa, and the Pescadores, shall be restored to the Republic of China . . . Japan will also be expelled from all other territories which she has taken by violence and greed, and in due course Korea shall become free and independent. . . . ' All that, and more, has been accomplished: the Emperor has been stripped of his 'divinity'—sovereignty is vested in the people—Japan has 'renounced' war for all time and forsaken 'permanently' the right to establish armed forces: there is a new Constitution, drafted by Americans. But, the most important item—in the Peace Treaty—from the American point of view—is how to maintain military control over Japan in order to have a 'springboard' from which to dive from the 'cold war' into the 'hot war' with the U.S.S.R. and her communist partner China, when and if it materializes within the next five years.

It is not in the interest of the U.S.S.R. to conclude Peace Treaties with Germany or Japan—except on their own terms, the acceptance of Moscow controlled 'Communism' and subordinate position in the Russian Empire. Britain, and the United States, gain nothing by their present 'delaying tactics' but an inferior status in the Far East and have earned the amusement of the U.S.S.R. the contempt of China and the indifference of Japan. All the prestige which existed in 1945—all that followed on the victory over the Japanese Empire —has been lost by 'jumping like a cat on hot bricks' at the crack of Stalin's whip. Perhaps, if we had fewer conferences, less talk and more action, based on simple facts, the drafting of a Peace Treaty with Japan could be accomplished in a few weeks. In any case the wording of a Treaty 'and the necessary safeguards' will not decide the case for or against war with the Russian Empire in Europe and in Asia.

INDEX

WAR IN THE FAR EAST, THE (Japan and World War II)

GEORGE ALLEN & UNWIN LTD
LONDON: 40 MUSEUM STREET, W.C.1
CAPE TOWN: 58–60 LONG STREET
SYDNEY, N.S.W.: 55 YORK STREET
TORONTO: 91 WELLINGTON STREET WEST
CALCUTTA: 17 CENTRAL AVE., P.O. DHARAMTALA
BOMBAY: 15 GRAHAM ROAD, BALLARD ESTATE
WELLINGTON, N.Z.: 8 KINGS CRESCENT, LOWER HUTT

A SHORT ECONOMIC HISTORY OF MODERN JAPAN

by G. C. Allen

Demy 8vo   Third Impression   12s. 6d. net

'Much the best introduction to this fascinating but difficult subject.'—MANCHESTER GUARDIAN

'Likely to remain for some time the best introduction to the subject in the English language . . . should be carefully read by all who are concerned with present policy and administration in Japan and with its future development.'—THE ECONOMIC JOURNAL

'An important book . . . a fair and thoroughly documented survey.'—CONTEMPORARY REVIEW

IMPERIAL JAPAN

by A. Morgan Young

Demy 8vo   12s. 6d. net

As editor of the *Japan Chronicle*, the only British newspaper in Japan, with twenty-four years' close touch with all happenings, Mr. Young had exceptional opportunities of becoming acquainted with the details of the story of an advance in power and dominion.

JAPAN : RECOLLECTIONS AND IMPRESSIONS

by Grace James

Demy 8vo   12s. 6d net

This book gives a vivid picture of life in Tokyo as seen through the eyes of an English family during part of the Meiji era (1885-95), and also impressions of Japan revisited in 1934.

Old beliefs and ceremonies are described and their survival in the passionately fostered national spirit of Japan is scrutinized.

KOREA TODAY
by George M. McCune

Cr. 8vo   25s. net

Here is the first comprehensive study of Korea since its libera-
tion and division. Written by an outstanding American
authority with long personal knowledge of the country, it
provides an analysis of the American and Russian military
occupations, the efforts of the United Nations to deal with the
problem of unification of the country, the political and
economic policies followed in the northern and southern
regimes, and an appraisal of the U.S. programme of economic
and military aid to South Korea. A useful appendix of documents, tables and bibliography, together with a note on
Korean demography, is included.

THE STAKES OF DEMOCRACY
IN SOUTH-EAST ASIA
by H. J. van Mook

Demy 8vo   15s. net

Will national independence bring to the peoples of South-
East Asia liberty and democracy? Or will it mean corrupt
government, factional strife and insolvency? Or will it mean
eventual absorption by totalitarian communism?

In this book the author analyses these questions, using the
case history of Indonesia since 1940, in which he played a
leading role, to illustrate his points. He gives an outline of the
history of South-East Asia, its domination by the West and its
convulsion by war and nationalism.

DRAGON FANGS
by Claire and William Band

Demy 8vo   18s. net

'A record of discovery, a diary of unexpected, even undesired,
experiences (in the New China), honestly written'.—NEW
STATESMAN

GEORGE ALLEN & UNWIN LTD.